The Resurgence of East Asia

East Asian expansion since the 1960s stands out as a global power shift with few historical precedents. *The Resurgence of East Asia* examines the rise of the region as one of the world's economic power centers from three temporal perspectives: 500 years, 150 years and 50 years, each denoting an epoch in regional and world history and providing a vantage point against which to assess contemporary developments.

The three perspectives each have something valuable to offer to the understanding of the present rise of East Asia and the modern world system, and their combination offers a contrast to the national and global studies that have recently dominated the literatures of development and globalization. In offering a comprehensive understanding of the present East Asian dynamic in light of the region's historical heritage, the authors present several alternative hypotheses about the ongoing East Asian renaissance, whose plausibility remains to be assessed in the light of unfolding evidence.

This collection is a valuable resource for students of Asian and world history, international politics, comparative and historical sociology and Asian studies.

Giovanni Arrighi is Professor of Sociology at Johns Hopkins University, Baltimore, Maryland. His latest books are *The Long Twentieth Century: Money, Power and the Origins of Our Times* (1994) and *Chaos and Governance in the Modern World System* (1999, with Beverly J. Silver).

Takeshi Hamashita is Professor of History at the Institute for Southeast Asian Studies, Kyoto University and the Institute of Oriental Culture, Tokyo University. He is co-author of the six-volume Japanese work, *Maritime Asia* (2001) and numerous works on the political economy of East Asia.

Mark Selden is Professor of Sociology at Binghamton University and Professorial Associate, East Asia Program, Cornell University, New York. His recent books include, *Chinese Society: Change, Conflict and Resistance* (with Elizabeth J. Perry) and *Islands of Discontent: Okinawan Responses to Japanese and American Power* (with Laura Hein).

Asia's Transformations

Edited by Mark Selden, Binghamton University and
Cornell University, USA

The books in this series explore the political, social, economic and cultural consequences of Asia's transformations in the twentieth and twenty-first centuries.
The series emphasizes the tumultuous interplay of local, national, regional and
global forces as Asia bids to become the hub of the world economy. While focusing on the contemporary, it also looks back to analyze the antecedents of Asia's
contested rise.

This series comprises several strands:

Asia's Transformations aims to address the needs of students and teachers, and the
titles will be published in hardback and paperback. Titles include:

Ethnicity in Asia
Edited by Colin Mackerras

Chinese Society, 2nd edition
Change, conflict and resistance
Edited by Elizabeth J. Perry and Mark Selden

The Resurgence of East Asia
500, 150 and 50 year perspectives
Edited by Giovanni Arrighi, Takeshi Hamashita and Mark Selden

The Making of Modern Korea
Adrian Buzo

Korean Society
Civil society, democracy and the state
Edited by Charles K Armstrong

Remaking the Chinese State
Strategies, society and security
Edited by Chien-min Chao and Bruce J. Dickson

Mao's Children in the New China
Voices from the Red Guard generation
Yarong Jiang and David Ashley

Chinese Society
Change, conflict and resistance
Edited by Elizabeth J. Perry and Mark Selden

Opium, Empire and the Global Political Economy
Carl A. Trocki

Japan's Comfort Women
Sexual slavery and prostitution during World War II and the US occupation
Yuki Tanaka

Hong Kong's History
State and society under colonial rule
Edited by Tak-Wing Ngo

Debating Human Rights
Critical essays from the United States and Asia
Edited by Peter Van Ness

Asia's Great Cities: each volume aims to capture the heartbeat of the contemporary city from multiple perspectives emblematic of the authors own deep familiarity with the distinctive faces of the city, its history, society, culture, politics and economics, and its evolving position in national, regional and global frameworks. While most volumes emphasize urban developments since the Second World War, some pay close attention to the legacy of the longue durée in shaping the contemporary. Thematic and comparative volumes address such themes as urbanization, economic and financial linkages, architecture and space, wealth and power, gendered relationships, planning and anarchy, and ethnographies in national and regional perspectives. Titles include:

Hong Kong
Global city
Stephen Chiu and Tai-Lok Lui

Shanghai
Global city
Jeff Wasserstrom

Singapore
Carl A. Trocki

Beijing in the Modern World
David Strand and Madeline Yue Dong

Bangkok
Place, practice and representation
Marc Askew

Asia.com is a series which focuses on the ways in which new information and communication technologies are influencing politics, society and culture in Asia. Titles include:

Asia.com
Asia encounters the Internet
Edited by K. C. Ho, Randolph Kluver and Kenneth C.C. Yang

Japanese Cybercultures
Edited by Mark McLelland and Nanette Gottlieb

RoutledgeCurzon Studies in Asia's Transformations is a forum for innovative new research intended for a high-level specialist readership, and the titles will be available in hardback only. Titles include:

1. Chinese Media, Global Contexts
Edited by Chin-Chuan Lee

2. Imperialism in South East Asia
"A fleeting, passing phase"
Nicholas Tarling

3. Internationalizing the Pacific
The United States, Japan and the Institute of Pacific Relations in war and peace, 1919–1945
Tomoko Akami

4. Koreans in Japan
Critical voices from the margin
Edited by Sonia Ryang

5. The American Occupation of Japan and Okinawa*
Literature and memory
Michael Molasky

*Now available in paperback

Critical Asian Scholarship is a series intended to showcase the most important individual contributions to scholarship in Asian Studies. Each of the volumes presents a leading Asian scholar addressing themes that are central to his or her most significant and lasting contribution to Asian studies. The series is committed to the rich variety of research and writing on Asia, and is not restricted to any particular discipline, theoretical approach or geographical expertise.

China's Past, China's Future
Energy, food, environment
Vaclav Smil

China Unbound
Evolving perspectives on the Chinese past
Paul A. Cohen

Women and the Family in Chinese History
Patricia Buckley Ebrey

Southeast Asia
A testament
George McT. Kahin

The Resurgence of East Asia

500, 150 and 50 year perspectives

Edited by Giovanni Arrighi,
Takeshi Hamashita and
Mark Selden

 Routledge
Taylor & Francis Group
LONDON AND NEW YORK

First published 2003 by Routledge
2 Park Square, Milton Park, Abingdon, Oxon, OX14 4RN

Simultaneously published in the USA and Canada
by Routledge
270 Madison Ave, New York NY 10016

Routledge is an imprint of the Taylor & Francis Group

Transferred to Digital Printing 2006

Typeset in Baskerville by Wearset Ltd, Boldon, Tyne and Wear

British Library Cataloguing in Publication Data
A catalogue record for this book is available from the British
Library

Library of Congress Cataloging in Publication Data
The resurgence of East Asia : 500, 150 and 50 year perspectives /
edited by Giovanni Arrighi, Takeshi Hamashita, and Mark Selden.
    p. cm. – (Asia's transformations)
Includes bibliographical references and index
1. East Asia–Economic conditions. 2. East Asia–Commerce.
3. East Asia–Economic integration. I. Arrighi, Giovanni.
II. Hamashita, Takeshi, 1943– III. Selden, Mark. IV. Series.
    HC460.5 .R475 2003
    330.95'03–dc21

                                                    2002153863

ISBN 0-415-31636-7 (hbk)
ISBN 0-415-31637-5 (pbk)

Contents

Figures

Tables

Notes on contributors

Giovanni Arrighi is Professor of Sociology at Johns Hopkins University, Baltimore, Maryland. His latest books are *The Long Twentieth Century: Money, Power and the Origins of Our Times* (1994) and *Chaos and Governance in the Modern World System* (1999, with Beverly J. Silver).

Wei-An Chang is Professor of Sociology at National Tsing Hua University in Taiwan. His books include *Economy and Society: A Social-Cultural Analysis of Taiwan, Hong Kong, and Mainland China*, with Chu Yin-wah; *Taiwan's Industrial Organization, Structure, and Competitive Strength; Culture and Economy: Weberian Sociological Research*; and *Classical Sociological Thought* (all in Chinese).

Takeshi Hamashita is Professor of History at the Institute for Southeast Asian Studies, Kyoto University and the Institute of Oriental Culture, Tokyo University. He is co-author of the six-volume Japanese work, *Maritime Asia* (2001) and numerous works on the political economy of East Asia.

Gary G. Hamilton is Professor of Sociology and the Jackson School of International Studies at the University of Washington. His recent books include *Cosmopolitan Capitalists: Hong Kong and the Chinese Diaspora at the end of the 20th Century*, *The Economic Organization of East Asian Capitalism*, with Marco Orrù and Nicole Biggart, and *Asian Business Networks*.

Po-keung Hui teaches Cultural Studies at Lingnan University, Hong Kong. He is the author of *What Capitalism is Not* (2002, in Chinese), and co-editor of the Cultural and Social Studies Translation Series (1996–2002, six volumes, in Chinese).

Ho-fung Hung is a PhD candidate in Sociology at Johns Hopkins University. The author of numerous articles in Chinese and English, his dissertation explores the dynamics of early modernity and contentious politics in Qing China. His "Orientalism and Social Theory: China, Europe, and the Comparison of Civilizations from the Jesuits to Weber" was published in *Sociological Theory*.

Peter J. Katzenstein is the Walter S. Carpenter Jr. Professor of International Studies at Cornell University, New York. He has written widely on issues of political economy and national security in both Europe and Asia. His recent work on regionalism in world politics includes *Network Power: Japan and Asia* (1997) and *Tamed Power: Germany in Europe* (1997).

Peter C. Perdue is T. T. and Wei Fong Chao Professor of Asian Civilizations and Professor of History at the Massachusetts Institute of Technology. He teaches courses on Chinese history and civilization, Chinese social and economic history, and the Silk Road. He is the author of *Exhausting the Earth: State and Peasant in Hunan, 1500–1850 A.D.*, and the forthcoming *China Marches West: The Qing Conquest of Central Eurasia, 1600–1800.*

Kenneth Pomeranz is Professor of History at University of California, Irvine. He has written *The Great Divergence. China, Europe and the Making of the Modern World Economy* and co-authored (with Steven Topik) *The World that Trade Created.*

Mark Selden is Professor of Sociology at Binghamton University and Professional Associate, East Asia Program, Cornell University, New York. His recent books include, *Chinese Society: Change, Conflict and Resistance* (with Elizabeth J. Perry) and *Islands of Discontent: Okinawan Responses to Japanese and American Power* (with Laura Hein).

Kaoru Sugihara is Professor of Economic History at Osaka University. His Japanese books include *Patterns and Development of Intra-Asian Trade* (1996) and *The Rise of the Asia-Pacific Economy* (2003). He is currently working on the role of East Asia in global history.

Acknowledgments

This volume, seven years in the making, is the product of collaboration involving researchers in the United States, Japan, Hong Kong and China. We acknowledge with thanks the support for our work from the American Council of Learned Societies and the Social Science Research Council which made possible the convening of workshops at the Fernand Braudel Center of Binghamton University, the Chinese University of Hong Kong, and the Institute for Global Studies in Culture, Power and History at Johns Hopkins University. In the course of these workshops we have benefited from the critical insights and suggestions of numerous scholars including Mitchell Bernard, Thomas Berger, Francesca Bray, Christopher Chase-Dunn, Stephen Chiu, Bruce Cumings, Ramon Grosfoguel, David Harvey, Ali Khan, Paul Kramer, Stuart W. Leslie, Weihsun Mao, Aihwa Ong, William Rowe, Sonia Ryang, Keith Schoppa, Takashi Shiraishi, Beverly Silver, Alvin So, Robert Wade, Immanuel Wallerstein, Wang Hui, R. Bin Wong, Suk-Ying Wong, and Wang Zhengyi. We gratefully acknowledge the superb administrative and technical support provided by Donna DeVoist of the Fernand Braudel Center and Dr. Felicity Northcott of the Institute for Global Studies in Culture, Power and History at Johns Hopkins University.

Introduction

The rise of East Asia in regional and world historical perspective

Giovanni Arrighi, Takeshi Hamashita and Mark Selden

Two events of world historical significance have marked the closing decades of the twentieth century: the demise of the USSR as one of the world's two military superpowers and the rise of the East Asian region as one of the world's economic power centers. Of these two events, the demise of the USSR has been most readily perceivable, and indeed has attracted most attention, not only because of the dramatic character of the political denouement, but also because it fits well into common understandings of the rise and fall of empires. The rise of East Asia, in contrast, remains a disputed fact overshadowed not just by the demise of the USSR but even more by the subsequent economic resurgence of the United States at a time of persistent economic recession in Japan and the 1997 economic crisis in the region at large. Moreover, in contrast to Soviet disintegration, the rise of East Asia is a process that has no single dramatic punctuation and does not fit comfortably into historical understandings that pivot on national states.

As we shall see in the book's concluding chapter, by some indicators the East Asian rise does appear to have slowed down in the 1990s, especially in Japan. Nevertheless, thus far the slowdown has been accompanied by unabated expansion elsewhere in the region, notably in China, producing a situation with potential to transform both regional and global dynamics. Taking the region and the period as a whole, the East Asian expansion since the 1960s stands out as a global shift of economic power with few precedents in world history. No shift of such proportions can occur without pauses and temporary setbacks, as witnessed by the US-centered Great Depression of the 1930s during the early twentieth-century global shift from Western Europe to North America (Arrighi and Silver *et al.* 1999: 95–6, 274–5). But pauses and setbacks should not prevent us from seeing the underlying trend.

The aim of this book is to assess the origins of this shift in light of a large-scale, long-term dynamic that has seldom been invoked in the mushrooming literature on the phenomenon. Our basic premise is that the exceptional economic dynamism of the East Asian region in the closing decades of the twentieth century should be viewed as the joint product of a single process operating at the world-regional level rather than as the sum of separate processes operating primarily at the national level. In this we concur with Bruce Cumings' (1987: 46) assessment that a country-by-country approach is misleading because it "misses, through a fallacy of dis-aggregation, the fundamental unity and integrity of the regional effort in this century." Focusing on the economic achievements of the last half-century by Japan and its former colonies South Korea and Taiwan, Cumings (ibid.: 47) finds that "an understanding of the Northeast Asian political economy can only emerge from an approach that posits the systemic interaction of each country with the others, and of the region with the world at large." Like Cumings, we put the systemic interaction among the region's countries and between the region and the world at large at the center of our analysis. We go further, however, in both temporal and spatial terms. By extending the discussion of contemporary developmental issues to a long-term historical perspective, and by exploring a broad spatial conception of the East Asian region, we can offer a new under-standing of the region's dynamic across time and space.

The three temporalities of the East Asian dynamic

As Gilbert Rozman has noted:

> East Asia is a great region of the past, having been in the forefront of world development for at least two thousand years, until the sixteenth, seventeenth, or even the eighteenth century, after which it suffered a relatively brief but deeply felt eclipse. Projecting recent patterns of achievement by countries in the region and by transplanted persons whose families have moved abroad, most observers now agree that East Asia promises to be a great region of the future.
>
> (1991: 6)

As this passage implies, three distinct time frames or temporalities define the relationship of East Asia to the world at large. There is, first of all, the "short run" of recent patterns of achievement by countries and territories in the region and by the region overall. The relevant time frame for the analysis of these patterns is the half-century that encompasses the defeat of Japan in the Second World War, the establishment of a Communist regime in China, anti-colonial revolutions throughout the region leading to the dismantling of colonial empires, the division of East Asia and the world into two antagonistic blocs dominated respectively by the United States and the Soviet Union, and finally, the overcoming of deep divisions as a result both of economic interaction and political and strategic shifts, making possible the emergence of a new regionalism. These events thoroughly reorganized the region in its internal and external relations, creating important preconditions for its subsequent economic ascent. But the events themselves and the ways in which the region was reorganized can only be understood in the light of the trends and events of a second temporality.

This second temporality is the "long" century that separates us from the "relatively brief but deeply felt eclipse" of the prestige and power of the region in the mid-nineteenth century in the wake of the decline of the Qing and Tokugawa regimes in China and Japan, the defeat of China in the Opium Wars, the subsequent collapse of the Chinese empire, and the colonization of large parts of East Asia. The events that most decisively shaped the region in this "long" century began with the relative decline of East Asia in military and economic terms, the advance of Western power in the region in the form of colonial regimes in its peripheries and the sharp decline in the power of its core states (China and Japan), giving rise to the Meiji Restoration of 1868, Japan's industrialization and subjugation of substantial parts of East Asia, successive Chinese revolutions from the 1860s through 1911 to 1949 and beyond, the recurrent invasions and wars that set Japan against China throughout the first half of the twentieth century, and Japanese efforts to displace China as the regional hegemon, to reorganize the region with itself at the center, and to drive the Western colonial powers from the region. Once again, however, the events that shaped East Asia in this period can best be understood as the outcome of processes encompassed by an even longer temporality.

This longer temporality invites and enables us to seek connections between the present rise of East Asia and the region's earlier position "in the forefront of world development," as Rozman put it in the passage quoted above. Substantial literatures pivoting on concepts of incorporation, colonialism, modernization and "response to the West" tend to imply a more or less complete displacement of the East Asian historical heritage of this earlier period. We disagree and see instead processes of hybridization and cross-fertilization accompanying the emergence of Western economic and military power as significant forces in the region from the sixteenth to the eighteenth centuries, and continuing in new ways throughout and subsequent to the era of imperialism and revolution in East Asia. In these processes, elements of the East Asian historical heritage would repeatedly reassert themselves to shape interactions within the region and between the region and the world at large right up to the present.

In short, we propose an analysis of the East Asian regional political economy along three distinct temporal dimensions, embedded within one another in Russian doll fashion. The long perspective is defined by the historical heritage of a period spanning the sixteenth to eighteenth centuries in which East Asia remained in the forefront of world development in the spheres of state-making and national economy-making, while inter-actions and hybridization between the European and East Asian regions intensified. The intermediate perspective begins with the eclipse of East Asian wealth and power in the face of the nineteenth- and twentieth-century challenge of Western imperialism. Even before the end of this period we nonetheless note signs of resurgent power in East Asia, most notably in the formation of the Japanese empire, but also in revolutionary processes in China and elsewhere that would subsequently bear fruit. Finally, the shortest perspective is defined by the region's economic renaissance following its reorganization during and after the Cold War era. The collective claim of this book is that each of these perspectives has something valuable to offer toward the understanding of the present rise of East Asia and the modern world system and that their combination offers fresh light on the future of regional and global processes.

East Asia as a world region

The notion of a distinctive and dynamic East Asian historical heritage is at the foundation of our entire investigation. It underlies both what we understand by East Asia as a world region and the different temporal per-spectives we deploy in the analysis of the regional dynamic. And yet, the identification of a regional historical heritage is a task fraught with difficulties:

> The concept of heritage – even more so for a region than for a country – poses difficulties of interpretation. It threatens to be vague and all-encompassing. Any overview must somehow chart a course through multisided, multidisciplinary, multicountry, and multiperiod demands of scholars with an interest in heritage.
>
> (Rozman 1991: 22)

Rozman sought a way out of these difficulties by focusing on the Confucian intellectual tradition – a tradition that has developed over two and a half millennia. Useful as it is in highlighting some common and distinguishing features of developments in East Asia, this focus ignores the irrelevance of Confucianism to the historical trajectory of much of the region that we examine (from large areas of Southeast Asia, including Indonesia, Malaysia, Thailand, Myanmar and the Philippines, to Mongolia, Tibet and Manchuria in Inner Asia), the great differences in the nature and degree of penetration of Confucianism even in the societies on which it did make an impact, and the question of the relevance of Confucianism to contemporary dynamics in much of the region. Moreover, such a focus tends to obscure the systemic character of the social, economic and political interactions in a region shaped by the topographies of seas, land, rivers and mountains, and by the interplay of political and economic exchanges, linking predominantly agrarian and pastoral cultures, as well as maritime and continental regions, that over time have given rise to a distinctive multifaceted East Asian world-regional formation.

Like the contributors to another volume on East Asia (Katzenstein and Shiraishi 1997), the contributors to this volume tend to agree with Karl Deutsch's conceptualization of world regions as groups of contiguous countries markedly interdependent over a wide range of dimensions that vary in space and evolve over time. As Peter Katzenstein notes, this view "supports an approach that reflects change not stasis and thus uncovers the constructed character of essentialist arguments, yet avoids portraying the world as a totally fluid agglomeration of continuously shifting, relationally defined identities" (1997: 11–12). Thus understood, the concept of "world region" includes, but has a broader meaning than, Fernand Braudel's and Immanuel Wallerstein's notion of "world-economy" – an expression which they hyphenate to underscore that it "only concerns a fragment of the world, an economically autonomous section of the planet able to provide most of its own needs, a section to which its internal links and exchanges give a certain organic unity" (Braudel 1984: 22).

We speak of East Asia as a world region rather than a world-economy both to eliminate a major source of confusion about the spatial scope of the entity in question and to downplay the economistic aspects of Braudel's definition. Thus, while we use the term "world" to convey the idea that we are talking about a (relatively) autonomous and organic entity encompassing a multiplicity of interrelated material cultures and polities, we use the term "region" to convey less ambiguously than a hyphen the idea that we are talking about a "section of the globe." At the same time, we drop the term "economy" to signal our understanding that the autonomy and organic unity of the entity in question rest also on political and cultural rather than exclusively economic foundations.

Indeed, in setting the boundaries of the East Asian region we rely as much on the nature and extent of inter-state relations as we do on the nature and extent of cross-border economic transactions. More specifically, the boundaries of our East Asian region – which include Northeast,[1] Inner and Southeast Asia – are defined primarily by the indigenous, China-centered inter-state system that was in place long before European governmental and business organizations became significant players in the region (Figure I.1). The idea of an inter-state system was originally developed to describe the European system that was eventually institutionalized at Westphalia in 1648. Wallerstein (1974a; 1974b) made this inter-state system one of the two main constituents of his "modern world system" or "capitalist world-economy" – the other constituent being the axial division of labor that encompasses the system's separate political jurisdictions. More recently, Japanese scholars specializing in the

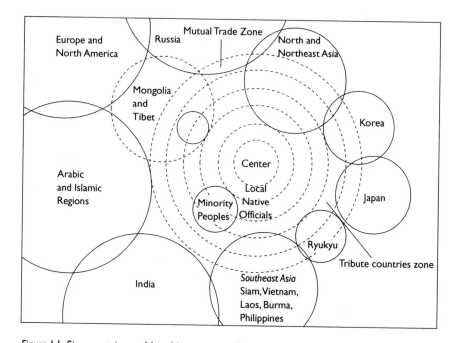

Figure I.1 Sino-centric world and inter-regional relations in Asia

Source: Adapted from Takeshi Hamashita, *Network Power. Japan and Asia* (Ithaca: Cornell University Press, 1997), p. 122.

reconstruction of the structures and mode of operation of the China-centered tribute-trade system have highlighted the existence in East Asia of an inter-state system different from but comparable with the European (see Ikeda 1996, for an overview of the contribution; see also Hamashita, Chapter 1, this volume). Peter Perdue (1996, and Chapter 2, this volume) has suggested that at least until the nineteenth century the East Asian inter-state system with China at its core may have gravitated more toward Central Asia than toward Southeast Asia, as this reconstruction implies (see also Fitzpatrick 1992, for a similar interpretation). But this alternative interpretation strengthens rather than weakens the assessment of the comparability of the East Asian and European inter-state systems.

The existence of an East Asian inter-state system simplifies considerably the task of setting the spatial boundaries of the East Asian world region, as well as the transformations undergone by the region over the periods encompassed by our investigation. Bounding world regions always presents problems. Most of them arise from the two different meanings that have been attributed to the term region. The definition we have adopted, focusing on interdependencies and interactions among contiguous territories/locations, is not the only, nor indeed the most widely used definition of world region. Just as widely used is a definition that focuses on commonalities that provide contiguous territories with a distinct identity, cultural or otherwise (Harvey 2001: 225; Lewis and Wigen 1997: Chapter 6).

Strong interdependencies and dense transactions can of course exist among culturally homogeneous territories. Indeed, some measure of shared values is generally a condition for the strengthening of interdependencies and the proliferation of transactions, an argument frequently applied, for example, to contemporary Europe. And this in turn may well make the parties involved more homogenous culturally or otherwise. If this is the case, there is no contradiction between the two definitions of region and either one can be used in bounding regions empirically. At the same time, however, interdependencies also require some diversity, and may in turn promote development along divergent paths through specialization and differentiation, as in the historic relations between agrarian China and pastoral-nomadic Inner Asia. When this is the case, the two definitions of region yield different results and the empirical identification of a particular region requires that we privilege one definition over the other.

The nature of the problem can be illustrated with reference to the contradictory world-regional location of Southeast Asia. Most discussions of Southeast Asia have focused on the issue of whether it constitutes a world region in its own right on the basis of the commonality criterion. On the one hand, Southeast Asia has been denied world region status on account of the derivative and heterogeneous nature of its religious, literary, political and economic heritage. Thus, "by comparison with Europe or even South Asia," Victor Lieberman finds the category Southeast Asia "artificial and residual" (1993: 476). "Wherever one looks," write Martin Lewis and Karen Wigen in summing up the evidence, "differences seem to be more prominent than similarities" (1997: 175). On the other hand, the status of Southeast Asia as a world region has been affirmed on the basis of commonalities derived from the recent experience of European and Japanese colonialism or from pre-colonial legacies – a perspective sometimes reified by the existence of Southeast Asian studies as a field of scholarly inquiry. Particularly persuasive is Anthony Reid's contention that, in spite of multiple external influences and internal differences, a common cultural substratum provides the region with a distinctive identity – an identity characterized, among other things, by the importance of commercial and financial relations in cementing the social order and the comparatively high status of women (1988; 1993).

Whatever the empirical validity of these contrasting views, we depart from both by defining world regions on the basis of interdependencies and interactions rather than commonalities. From this standpoint, from the sixteenth century Southeast Asia was first and foremost the crossroads of inter-regional trade linking Northeast and Inner Asia to South Asia and to Europe, both via the Cape and the Americas. This meant that the volume and variety of the maritime traffic passing through the region were extraordinary by contemporary standards – wholly comparable, in Archibald Lewis' words "to that of the Mediterranean or the northern and Atlantic coast of Europe" (quoted in Braudel 1984: 486–7). It also meant, however, that the strongest interdependencies linked Southeast Asian territories, not to one another, but to the territories of nearby (South Asia, and Northeast Asia) or faraway (Europe and the Americas) regions. By our definition, therefore, Southeast Asia does not qualify as a world region but constitutes instead a sub-region of a larger social-spatial grouping.

In situating Southeast Asia in a larger regional grouping, we face the additional problem of assessing the comparative importance of intra-regional and inter-regional interdependencies. Privileging the latter would lead us to adopt what André Gunder Frank (1998: xv, xxv) has called a "globological perspective." From this perspective, as early as the thirteenth century a single global economy encompassing the whole of Afro-Eurasia (and after 1500 the Americas as well), not only actually existed, but decisively influenced the dynamics of all its regional components (see, among others, Abu-Lughod 1989).

From this perspective, there is no room for world-economies (in Braudel's sense) or world regions (in our sense) but only for geographical groupings such as Southeast Asia of no analytical significance except as loci of *global* interactions. In rejecting this perspective, we are not denying the far-reaching and wide impacts of global trade before and especially after 1571 – the year of the founding of the crucial entrepôt of Manila that Dennis Flynn and Arturo Giraldez (1995: 201) take as the beginning of truly global trade. Rather, we claim that at least through the early nineteenth century Northeast, Inner and Southeast Asia jointly constituted a single world region in the sense that interactions within and between these sub-regions were more important in shaping developmental processes and outcomes than their interactions with other regions of the global economy.

We base our claim on two main considerations. One concerns migration and private trade. For throughout early modern and modern times Southeast Asia has been the primary destination of substantial flows of Chinese emigration. These flows, in turn, gave rise to dense and extensive networks of private trade, remittances and communications, both legal and illegal, that encompassed maritime East Asia. The second consideration concerns the China-centered tributary-trade networks. These networks encompassed not just Northeast and Inner Asia but Southeast Asia as well. In certain periods and in certain subregions, the formal political economy of tributary trade prevailed over the informal economy of private trade. Often, however, the opposite was true. Either way, some combination of tributary and private trade linked the territories of North-east, Inner and Southeast Asia in a dense web of exchanges and transac-tions, both economic and political, that makes it appropriate to speak of a single East Asian world region encompassing all these subregions (see Arrighi *et al.*, Chapter 7, this volume; Hamashita, Chapter 1, this volume; Perdue, Chapter 2, this volume).

In sum, our conceptualization of East Asia as a world region focuses pri-marily on interactions among governmental and business organizations. Many of these organizations, particularly those operating out of Southeast Asia, interacted on a regular basis also with extra-regional organizations. We nonetheless maintain that intra-regional links and exchanges provided East Asia with a certain organic political-economic unity distinct from the global system of interactions in which it was embedded. Two con-sequences follow from this conceptualization, one concerning variation over time and one concerning variation over space.

Our sensitivity to temporal factors supports an approach attentive to changes in the constitution of East Asia as world region, and indeed in the extent to which it constitutes a world region at all. The longer (500-year) temporality is meant to capture the consolidation of an East Asian world region in the context of increasing interaction among world regions, East Asia included. The intermediate (150-year) temporality highlights a moment of overwhelming influence of inter-regional interactions. Although we take issue with the contention typical of world-systems analy-sis that this overwhelming influence resulted in a complete decomposition of the East Asian region within the structures of the European-centered modern world system, we recognize that for most of this period a tend-ency toward the "de-regionalization" of East Asia was at work, in spite of Japan's attempt in the first half of the twentieth century to create an East Asian region centered on itself. Finally, the shorter (50-year) temporality focuses on a period in which this tendency was reversed and a process of "re-regionalization" set in, in spite of, and perhaps in part precisely because of, an unprecedented degree of integration of East Asia within the structures of the global political economy.

As the volume's concluding chapter underscores, re-regionalization does not involve a return to earlier forms of regional interdependence and interaction. Rather, it involves the emergence of forms of regional integration that originate as much from the legacy of the indigenous tribute-trade system and other earlier forms of intra-East Asian inter-action, as from the legacy of the clash/encounter with the European-centered modern world system. In any event, the East Asian world region will be conceived as a continually changing reality, recurrently in the process of being made and unmade.

Our conceptualization of the East Asian region, focusing on interde-pendencies rather than commonalities, supports an approach that reflects not just change over time but also diversity over space. As we have seen in arguing for the inclusion of Southeast and Inner Asia in the East Asian world region, we do not presume that the units whose interdependencies make East Asia a world region all fit a particular model of organization and institutional behavior. On the contrary, we conceive of the East Asian world region as being characterized by at least as much internal diversity of material cultures, economies and polities as Braudel's Mediterranean world-economy.

This diversity is not just hard to describe. It also complicates considerably the analysis of world regions as evolving totalities. As we shall see in the next section, the contributors to this volume have resorted to different strategies of methodological simplification in order to obviate these difficulties. For all their differences in research design, the chapters of the book nonetheless complement one another in reconstructing the East Asian regional dynamic in its geographical and historical complexity. National diversity and intra-national and regional conflicts and competition are integral aspects of this complexity. We do not deny, therefore, the usefulness of national studies, particularly those sensitive to the interplay of regional and global forces. We simply claim that the East Asian regional dynamic is something more than and different from the sum of the separate national dynamics. In numerous ways, this regional dynamic has constrained, driven and shaped the development of the region's economies, polities and societies over a long historical time.

The East Asian dynamic in world historical perspective

As David Harvey (2001: 117) has stated:

> There are many windows from which to view the same world ... The view from China looking outwards or from the lower classes looking up is very different from that from the Pentagon or Wall Street. But each view can be represented in a common frame of discourse, subject to evaluation as to internal integrity and credibility.

While sharing the common frame of discourse highlighted above, the chapters of this book observe the evolving structure and dynamic of the East Asian region from different "windows," each characterized by a particular angle of vision and substantive focus.

The first two chapters describe the inner structure of the region as a whole but with a somewhat different substantive focus. Focusing on the dense and extensive trading networks that forged the coastal areas of maritime East Asia into a diverse but well-integrated economic-commercial realm, Hamashita in Chapter 1 shows that, even at the height of their colonial power, European states colluded to reinforce elements of the historical East Asian tributary system. Focusing on China's political-military interaction with Inner Asia, Perdue in Chapter 2 recognizes the importance of commercial exchanges but sees security as the overriding problem that made military rather than commercial and productive power the decisive force in inter-state relations. As previously noted, we do not regard these contrasting views as contradicting one another. Rather, we see them as complementing one another in jointly defining our understanding of the historic East Asian regional system. Moreover, the view from different parts of the region, for example, a maritime versus an overland perspective, may produce distinctive understandings of the dynamics that produce regional complementarity or hierarchy.

The book's three central chapters adopt a narrower angle of vision and focus on specific but particularly significant aspects of the East Asian dynamic in comparison with the Western dynamic. Sugihara in Chapter 3 focuses on the development of techniques/technologies of production at the level of national economies. Hamilton and Chang in Chapter 4 focus on the structure of business organizations operating within national societies. And Pomeranz in Chapter 5 focuses on the gender division of labor within and between households in core regions of the East Asian and European regional economies. As we shall see below, these different foci and perspectives complement one another in defining our understanding of the trajectory of social and economic development in East Asia.

Finally, the book's two concluding chapters, like the first two, analyze the East Asian region as a whole. They do so, however, from a comparative perspective. Katzenstein in Chapter 6 compares the East Asian and European technological orders by focusing on the role that Japan and Germany have played in their formation and transformation. Arrighi, Hui, Hung and Selden, in Chapter 7, in contrast, focus on the role of capitalism and inter-state relations in promoting, first, a global shift of political-economic power from East Asia to Europe and North America, and then, the beginning in recent times of a seeming reversal of that shift.

The common premises of the book concerning the constituent elements of the East Asian world region are jointly laid out in the first two chapters. Taking aim at the land-based and state-centric perspectives that, in spite of multiple challenges, are still dominant in Asian studies scholarship, Hamashita examines the ways in which the seas, their coastal areas, and port cities provide defining features of East Asia. Seas and other waterways have long served in effect as "highways," port cities as strategic nodes that facilitate tributary, trade, migration and other interchanges that define the regional constellation. Carrying his analysis through the late nineteenth century, Hamashita offers an Asia-centered analysis of regional forces that continues well into the era of imperialism, with the extension and hybridization of many earlier principles of political and commercial intercourse into the colonial era.

Perdue argues that many of the features that Hamashita explains in terms of maritime waterways and their coastal areas and port cities apply equally to land borders which he sees not as lines dividing autonomous states but as zones of intensive interaction. Trade and tribute missions are important aspects of this interaction. In times of instability, however, these are also major war zones. Indeed, he notes the importance of extending the analysis of Asian regionalism to the realm of military conflict. While China and Inner Asia developed important trading relationships, he holds that Chinese statesmen were above all preoccupied with Inner Asia because of their fears of attack from the steppes, or their own expansive activities seeking to press outward their borders into the steppe.

The other five chapters all adopt an explicitly comparative perspective. Each highlights an important aspect of a common story about divergence, convergence and hybridization within East Asia and between the East Asian and European/Western regional systems. This common story can be summed up in three main propositions.

First, the great nineteenth-century divergence in the political and eco-nomic fortunes of East Asia and Europe was at least in part based on earlier, less visible divergences in the developmental trajectories of the two world regions. Thus, focusing on the different trajectories of national economic development in the two systems, growing in part out of demo-graphic differences involving the more densely populated regions of the East Asian core, particularly China and Japan, Sugihara sees the East Asian trajectory culminating in a labor-intensive "industrious revolution" and the European/North American trajectory culminating in a capital- and natural-resource-intensive "industrial revolution." Focusing on family structure and gender roles, Pomeranz highlights a divergence between an East Asian tendency toward a sharpening of the gender division of labor and a European tendency toward a sharpening of the geographical divi-sion of labor. Focusing on the different structures of the East Asian and European inter-state systems, Arrighi *et al.* detect a divergence in the six-teenth through the eighteenth centuries between a European tendency toward the formation of overseas empires and intense inter-state competi-tion for mobile capital on the one hand, and an East Asian tendency toward national economy-making and little overt inter-state competition for mobile capital, on the other. Focusing on differences in the organ-ization of commercial and industrial activities, Hamilton and Chang also see a divergence between a Chinese and a European/Western pattern occurring since Song times.

Second, the predominance of a particular tendency within each of the two regional systems did not involve a lack of differentiation among the components of each system. On the contrary, in some respects, differences within East Asia are seen to have been as important as differences between world regions. Thus, Perdue highlights differences between pastoral-nomadic logics prevailing in Inner Asia and the agrarian foundations of much of rural China. Pomeranz underscores significant differences between a Japanese and a Chinese pattern of gendered labor due to the lesser spatial mobility of female labor in China. Hamilton and Chang see the emergence in late Qing China of "buyer-driven commodity chains" linking a highly decentralized, rural-based production system to a system of mass distribution controlled by merchant groups organized flexibly on the basis of occupational specialization and region of origin, as differentiating the Chinese path of development not just from the European but from the Japanese path as well. Peter Katzenstein compares German and Japanese approaches to technology, not because they are emblematic of common patterns throughout their regions, but because these patterns differentiate them both from one another and from other technological regimes within their respective regions.

Finally, the deepening inter-penetration of the two regional systems within a single global system since the nineteenth century has not entailed uni-directional convergence of the East Asian pattern of social, economic and political interaction toward the European/Western pattern as many analysts, particularly those working within a modernization paradigm, have presupposed. On the contrary, the chapters that explicitly address the issue see as much divergence as convergence both between and within regions. To the extent that they see convergence, they do not see it erasing differences. Rather, they see it as being strongly conditioned by path dependence. More important, they see convergence proceeding as much toward East Asian as toward European/Western patterns.

Thus, Arrighi *et al.* see the US regime established in East Asia after the Second World War as unwittingly reviving certain key features of the historic East Asian tribute-trade system, such as a regime of "gifts" and trade between the imperial and vassal states that was very favorable to the vassal states. Similarly, Hamilton and Chang see the US "big buyers" that operate today in East Asia through flexible production networks as replicating certain organizational features characteristic of the "big buyers" of Late Imperial China. Pomeranz, for his part, finds that, in spite of points of convergence, the European, the Japanese and especially the Chinese patterns of gendered division of labor have continued to evolve along distinct paths, each with its own implications for economic development and women's emancipation.

Sugihara goes further than any of the other contributors to the volume in upholding the view that the present re-emergence of East Asia as workshop of the world can be traced to processes of path dependence and hybridization. In his view, the incorporation of Western technological advances within East Asian institutional frameworks – first pioneered by

Japan and now taking root in a growing number of East Asian countries – is not just the main secret of East Asian economic success. It is also the most promising route toward a more egalitarian and ecologically sustainable global economic expansion.

This view contrasts sharply with that advanced in Katzenstein's chapter. Katzenstein compares the role of Japanese governmental and business agencies in shaping the post-Second World War technological order in East Asia with the role of German agencies in Europe. In some respects his analysis complements and supplements that of the other chapters (including Sugihara's) by richly documenting the limits of East–West convergence even at a time of unprecedented (and increasing) global political–economic integration. As in the other chapters, in Katzenstein's too, history and geography continue to matter in conditioning and shaping local responses to the establishment of the US world order.

In other respects, however, Katzenstein's analysis departs from that of other chapters, especially Sugihara's. While noting similarities between the Chinese and Japanese approaches to the problems of technology, like Hamilton and Chang, Katzenstein emphasizes differences rather than similarities between Chinese and Japanese business networks. More fundamentally, unlike Sugihara, he does not see the developmental path opened up by Japan as leading toward greater equality among nations regionally and globally. Rather, he sees the rapid improvement of Japan's technological profile as being based on and reproducing an East Asian division of labor more hierarchical than the Western European. Katzenstein does not rule out the possibility that in coming decades regional leadership in key industries could pass from Japanese to East Asian firms of another nationality – particularly to firms located in the "China Circle." But he sees no reason to anticipate that this change of leadership would undermine the relatively hierarchical character of the regional division of labor.

Arrighi et al. concur in part with this assessment. Using a different set of data than Sugihara, they reach the same conclusion as he does that over the past half-century the East Asian economic advance has made a major contribution to the reduction of inter-regional income inequality, particularly by narrowing the gap between East Asia, on the one hand, and Europe and North America, on the other. But their data also show that, as Katzenstein argues, income inequality among East Asian states has increased through the 1980s and remains among the highest in the world. As they conclude, it is not at all clear at this point in time which of the two tendencies will eventually prevail.

In sum, the chapters of this volume start from the common premise that the present East Asian dynamic can only be understood in light of the region's historical heritage and reach important common conclusions concerning the nature of that heritage and its consequences played out in diverse temporal and spatial rhythms. Since the chapters have observed the same reality from different "windows," and since their authors examine the landscape using different lenses, they do not always reach the same conclusions. For the most part, these different conclusions are compatible with one another, reflecting the multiple lineages of the ongoing regional economic renaissance. On some important issues like those discussed above, they constitute alternative hypotheses about the ongoing East Asian economic renaissance whose plausibility remains to be assessed in the light of the unfolding evidence. They nonetheless remain united in the conviction that the historical parameters of the East Asian region, and not simply the nations and localities that constitute it, have shaped and continue to shape both regional outcomes and the nature of interactions linking East Asia and the global political economy. This means, further, that understandings of globalization processes that fail to engage factors of regionality, whether in the sixteenth century, the nineteenth century or in the early twenty-first century, are likely to miss critical dynamic elements.

Note

1 We use the term Northeast Asia to include China, Japan and Korea, preserving the term East Asia for the larger region that is the object of this study.

References

Abu-Lughod, Janet. 1989. *Before European Hegemony: The World System A.D. 1250–1350*. New York: Oxford University Press.

Arrighi, Giovanni and Beverly J. Silver *et al.* 1999. *Chaos and Governance in the Modern World System*. Minneapolis, MN: University of Minnesota Press.

Braudel, Fernand. 1984. *Civilization and Capitalism, 15th–18th Century*, vol. III: *The Perspective of the World*. New York: Harper & Row.

Cumings, Bruce. 1987. "The Origins and Development of the Northeast Asian Political Economy: Industrial Sectors, Product Cycles, and Political Consequences," in F.C. Deyo (ed.), *The Political Economy of New Asian Industrialism*. Ithaca, NY: Cornell University Press, pp. 44–83.

Fitzpatrick, John. 1992. "The Middle Kingdom, the Middle Sea, and the Geographical Pivot of History," *Review* XV, 3: 477–522.

Flynn, Dennis O. and Arturo Giraldez. 1995. "Born with 'Silver Spoon': The Origin of World Trade in 1571," *Journal of World History* VI, 2: 201–11.

Frank, André Gunder. 1998. *ReOrient: Global Economy in the Asian Age*. Berkeley, CA: University of California Press.

Harvey, David. 2001. *Spaces of Capital*. New York: Routledge.

Ikeda, Sato. 1996. "The History of the Capitalist World-System vs. The History of East-Southeast Asia," *Review* XIX, 1: 49–76.

Katzenstein, Peter. 1997. "Introduction: Asian Regionalism in Comparative Perspectives," in P. Katzenstein and T. Shiraishi (eds), *Network Power: Japan and Asia*. Ithaca, NY: Cornell University Press.

Katzenstein, Peter and Shiraishi, Takashi (eds) 1997. *Network Power: Japan in Asia*. Ithaca, NY: Cornell University Press.

Lewis, Martin W. and Karen E. Wigen. 1997. *The Myth of Continents: A Critique of Metageography*. Berkeley, CA: University of California Press.

Lieberman, Victor. 1993. "Local Integration and Eurasian Analogies: Structuring Southeast Asian History, *c.*1350–*c.*1830," *Modern Asian Studies*, 27: 475–572.

Perdue, Peter C. 1996. "Military Mobilization in Seventeenth- and Eighteenth-Century China, Russia, and Mongolia," *Modern Asian Studies* XXX (4): 757–93.

Reid, Anthony. 1988. *Southeast Asia in the Age of Commerce 1450–1680*. vol. I, *The Lands Below the Winds*. New Haven, CT: Yale University Press.

Reid, Anthony (ed.) 1993. *Southeast Asia in the Modern Era: Trade, Power and Belief*. Ithaca, NY: Cornell University Press.

Rozman, Gilbert. 1991. *The East Asian Region: Confucian Heritage and its Modern Adaptation*. Princeton, NJ: Princeton University Press.

Wallerstein, Immanuel. 1974a. *The Modern World-System*, vol. I: *Capitalist Agriculture and the Origins of the European World-Economy in the Sixteenth Century*. New York: Academic Press.

Wallerstein, Immanuel. 1974b. "The Rise and Future Demise of the World Capitalist System: Concepts for Comparative Analysis," *Comparative Studies in Society and History* XVI, 4, 387–415.

Chapter 1

Tribute and treaties

Maritime Asia and treaty port networks in the era of negotiation, 1800–1900

Takeshi Hamashita

States and the seas

Countries functioning as territorial states have long distinguished themselves from others by establishing boundaries, extending their territory even out to sea. The result has often been inter-state disputes such as clashes over 200-mile sea zones and conflicting claims to islands, as in the case of the Spratly Island issue with potentially large oil revenues at stake.[1]

The state has long claimed sovereignty, and in the days when all things were thought to belong ultimately to the state, negotiations and conflicts focused on exclusive possession of territory defined by formal boundaries.

The meaning of the seas cannot be fully appreciated as long as they are seen as opposed to the land and as long as one's focus is on the land. The seas, in fact, form and set the conditions of the land. The seas and the land should be understood not as being separated by the coasts, but as part of a larger whole in which the land is part of the seas (and vice versa). The sea forms, in short, a road, a basis for communication and network flows, not a barrier.

Looking at Asia from the viewpoint of the seas brings into focus the features that identify it as a maritime region *par excellence*. The seas along the eastern coast of the Eurasian continent form a gentle S curve extending from north to south (Figure 1.1). The chain formed by the seas that outline the continent, its peninsulas and adjacent islands, can be seen as shaping the premises of Asia's geopolitical space. The "maritime areas" thus formed in and around Asian lands are smaller than an ocean and less closely associated with the land than are bays or inlets.

Let us follow the "Asian seas" from north to south. The Sea of Okhotsk shapes Kamchatka and Siberian Russia. Further south, it merges into the Sea of Japan; then comes the Bohai and the Yellow Sea. These, with the East China Sea, embrace the Korean Peninsula, the Japanese archipelago, and the islands of Okinawa. The chain of seas then divides in two. On the east is the Sulu Sea leading to the Banda, Arafura, Coral, and Tasman Seas. On the west is the Java Sea that stretches west and connects with the

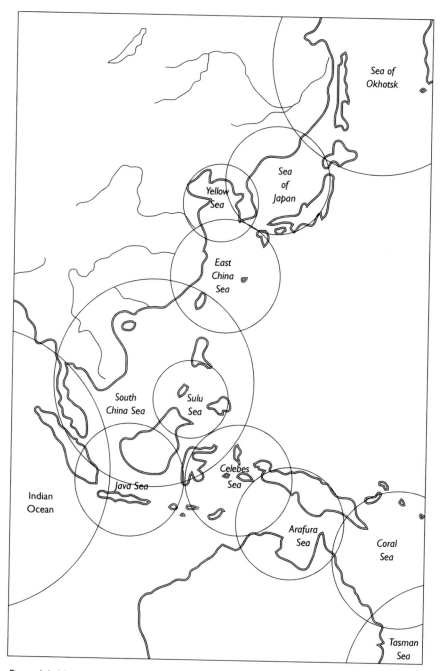

Figure 1.1 Maritime zones of Asia

Source: Takeshi Hamashita, *China-Centered World Order in Modern Times* (Tokyo: University of Tokyo Press, 1990). Used by permission of the publisher.

Strait of Malacca and thence to the Bay of Bengal. From the intersections of these seas, trade networks formed, pivoting on places like Nagasaki, Shanghai, Hong Kong, Malacca, and Singapore.

Asian studies in China, Japan and the West has, from its inception, revolved around the history of land-based states. However, to grasp the totality, particularly the regional integrity, it is necessary to study Asia in terms of the interfaces and exchanges that take place within and among maritime zones and that cross state boundaries.

The emergence of maritime zones

If the areas presently called East Asia and Southeast Asia are understood to be the maritime realm shaped and defined by the East China Sea and the South China Sea, the historical land–sea system of the region can be understood logically. The maritime world that functions here is not merely one of seas. Rather, it is composed of three elements. One is the coastal area where land and sea intersect. In the seventeenth century, the Kangxi emperor issued an order forcing the South China coastal population to move inland in an attempt to separate them from the influence of the powerful anti-Qing leader Zheng Cheng-gong (Koxinga) whose maritime empire extended from Fujian and Guangdong to Taiwan. This demonstrates the pivotal role of coastal areas in the maritime world.

Another important element is the sea-rim zone comprised of coastal areas. Along this rim are trading ports and cities that comprise the key nodes of the maritime area. These ports are not so much outlets to the sea for inland areas as points that connect one maritime zone to another. Historically, the merchants of Ningbo, located on the Chinese coast, for example, amassed wealth predominantly through coastal and maritime trade rather than from continental trade. Ningbo merchants played a particularly important role in trade with Nagasaki. Other maritime links that flourished in the eighteenth and nineteenth centuries included Pusan–Nagasaki–Fukuoka trade linking Japan and Korea, the Ryukyu–Kagoshima route between the Ryukyus and Southwest Japan, Fuzhou–Keelung linking Southeast China and Taiwan, and Aceh–Malacca–Guangzhou linking the Dutch East Indies, Malaya, and Southeast China. Notably, the maritime concept has reappeared today in the concepts of the Japan Sea-rim and Yellow Sea-rim trade zones.

The third element of the maritime world is the port cities that link maritime regions through long-distance trade. Among cities of this type which flourished in the nineteenth century are Naha, Guangzhou, Macao, and Hong Kong. Okinawa's Naha, for example, had long-established trade links with Fuzhou while Guangzhou's links were with Nagasaki and Southeast Asia. Port cities linking the South China Sea and Indian Ocean included Malacca, and later Singapore and Aceh in Indonesia. In contrast to the land, the maritime world encompassed coastal trade, cross-sea trade, and chain-of-seas connections, for example, those linking the South China and East China seas. The result was an open, multi-cultural realm that was diverse and well integrated.

To understand the operational principles of the maritime world, it is necessary to examine the interplay of political, economic, and cultural factors that unfolded there.

The major historical principle that loosely unified the maritime world of East Asia was encapsulated in the tribute-trade relations, which functioned from the Tang through Qing dynasties, from the seventh century to 1911. This China-centered order nevertheless permitted Korea, Japan, and Vietnam to assert themselves as "centers" vis-à-vis smaller neighboring states under their sway. The region was sustained by a hierarchical order defined by the Confucian conception of a "rule of virtue." Like any hegemonic order, it was backed by military force, but when the system functioned well, principles of reciprocity involving politics and economics permitted long periods of peaceful interaction.

In the China-centered order, tributary states sent periodic tribute missions to the Chinese capital, and each time rulers of tributary states changed, China dispatched an envoy to officially recognize the new ruler. In unsettled times, Chinese forces sometimes intervened to prop up or enshrine a ruler. Tribute relations were not only political but involved economic and trade relations as well. In exchange for the gifts carried to the Chinese court, tribute bearers received silk textiles and other goods from the emperor. Specially licensed traders accompanying the envoy engaged in commercial transactions at designated places in the capital. In addition, more than ten times as many merchants as these special traders exchanged commodities with local merchants at the country's borders and at designated ports. In short, lucrative trade was the lubricant for the tributary system defining regional political, economic, and cultural intercourse. The sea routes and major ports of call of the tribute missions sent by Ryukyu to China, for example, were clearly established. Navigational charts were devised based on seasonal winds and on the points and lines established by surveying the coasts and observing the movements of the stars.

Not only overseas Chinese merchants based in East and Southeast Asia but Indian, Muslim, and European merchants participated in this tribute trade, linking land and maritime zones.[2]

A maritime zone, therefore, was also a tribute and trade zone. Moreover, such zones broadly defined flows of human migration. In Tokugawa Japan stories about castaways were often told to inspire fear, discouraging people from attempting to leave the land. In fact, however, when castaways were discovered, they were to be taken along the tribute route back to their home country at that country's expense. Along the coast of

Kyushu, private Chinese ships often took advantage of this rule, intentionally drifting up along the coast, and engaging in a brisk illegal trade before officials arrived to do their duty.[3]

Tribute trade and Ryukyu networks

To see what a trade zone was like, let us look at the Ryukyus.[4] The Ryukyu Kingdom regularly sent missions to Southeast Asia to obtain the pepper and sappanwood it could not produce locally, and presented these to China as part of its tribute trade. The first volumes of the *Lidai Baoan* (*Rekidai Hoan* or *Precious Records of the Ryukyu Kings*), a collection of official Chinese tributary-trade records, states that during the Ming period (1368–1644), the Ryukyus engaged in commercial transactions with Southeast Asia, including Siam, Palembang, Java, Malacca, Sumatra, Annam, and Patani.[5] It can be assumed that Japan, Korea, and China were among the trade partners in addition to these Southeast Asian countries. The Ryukyus, in short, was part of an extensive trade network. Stated differently, this far-flung Ryukyu network pivoted on but was by no means limited to the Ryukyu tribute trade with China.

The trade network had two distinctive features. One was that trade with Siam and other Southeast Asian countries was vigorous between the early fifteenth century and the mid-sixteenth century.[6] The other was that, as far as we know from the *Lidai Baoan*, Ryukyuan trade with Southeast Asia declined while trade with Korea and Japan increased.

This phenomenon prompts us to ask two questions concerning the Ryukyus: what happened to the trade with Southeast Asia after the mid-sixteenth century? And what was the nature of the trade with Manila and Luzon in the context of Ryukyu trade with Southeast Asia?

In examining these questions, we note that the Ryukyus were involved in two trade routes between the South China and Southeast Asia. One route ran along the island chains on the eastern side of the South China Sea from Luzon to Sulu and the other stretched along the coast of the continent on the western side of the South China Sea from Siam to Malacca (Figure 1.2).

The eastern route started from Quanzhou (or Fuzhou) in Southeast coastal China, and spanned the region between the Ryukyus, Taiwan, and Sulu. This route not only carried the trade with Southeast Asian tributary states but also, from the sixteenth and seventeen centuries onward, the trade with Spain centered at Manila – exchanging silk for silver – and with the Dutch East India Company centered on Taiwan. At the same time, the route ran farther north from Fuzhou where soybean and soybean meal arrived from North China in exchange for rice, sugar, porcelain, and silk. The western route, starting from Guangzhou, linked various parts of Southeast Asia following the coast to major Southeast Asian tributary

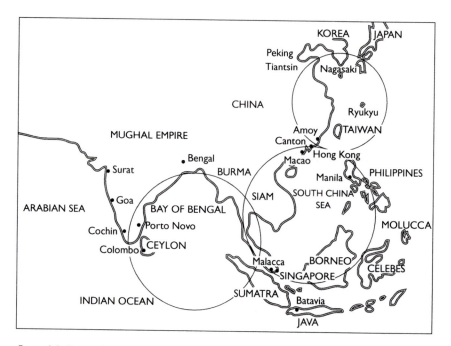

Figure 1.2 East and West maritime routes

Source: Takeshi Hamashita (1989: 249).

states, including Siam, Malacca, and Sumatra. Rice, marine products, and spices were major items imported to Guangdong from Southeast Asia and then traveled inland to Guangxi, Hunan, and other parts of South and Central China. China's exports to Southeast Asia were predominantly rice and sugar.

In 1666, ninety-six years after the records of official trade with Southeast Asia stopped appearing in 1570, the Ryukyu King Sho Shitsu asked that pepper, which was not produced locally, be excluded from the list of tribute goods. The Chinese court approved. This suggests that over the preceding century, using non-official trade channels, Ryukyu was able to obtain pepper from Southeast Asia for inclusion in its tributary shipments to China. Behind this development lay the increase in China's rice trade with Siam, bringing more merchants from the Chinese coast to Southeast Asia. Ryukyuan traders were able to obtain pepper and sappanwood either by joining Chinese merchants trading in Southeast Asia or by direct purchase from them.[7]

Even after being invaded by the Satsuma domain of Tokugawa Japan in the early seventeenth century, the Ryukyu Kingdom continued to dispatch tribute envoys to Qing China. At the same time, it sent envoys to

Tokugawa shoguns in Edo (present-day Tokyo). Ryukyu relations with Korea also continued.

After the Ryukyu Kingdom was abolished and the Ryukyus became a Japanese prefecture in 1879, Naha, which had been an important trading port linking the Ryukyus with East and Southeast Asia, lost these linkages and a new treaty port system emerged through treaties with western countries. Ryukyu trade was thereafter routed exclusively through Japan, and Japanese merchants controlled much of it. Hong Kong and Singapore played important roles in the emerging treaty port system that would redirect trade routes throughout Asia and between Asia, Europe and the Americas.[8]

The era of negotiation in the tributary-trade zone

From the 1830s to the 1890s the nations and regions of East Asia entered a period that can be called the era of negotiation, one characterized by multilateral and multifaceted intra-regional negotiations. The origins of the historical issues that the era poses can best be grasped not from the conventional perspective of Asia's "forced" opening from the "impact of the West," but rather from a perspective that focuses on internal changes in the East Asian region.

Changes in the historical international order of East Asia began with adjustments in the tribute relationships centered on the authority of the Qing emperor. Tributary states and trading nations (*hushi guo*) on the periphery of the Qing empire, based on their newfound economic strength, no longer strove to maintain as close a relationship with the Qing as before, and in each of them internal conflicts erupted between reformist and conservative factions. A variety of negotiations ensued between the Qing and its tributary and former tributary states.

By the early nineteenth century, the Qing's ability to maintain control over peripheral and minority regions on China's borders was severely weakened. Criticism and resistance by ethnic groups mounted against the rule by aboriginal officials (*tusi/tuguan*) and against the Office of Border Affairs (*Lifan yuan*) charged with managing "barbarian areas" (*fanbu*). With the weakening of state control, economic activity in the coastal trading regions picked up, and various economic and political forces on the periphery began to advance claims.

Forces hostile to the weakened Qing took advantage of the changing East Asian regional tributary order and of American and European efforts to conclude treaty relations with East Asian countries. This created at least the appearance of nations, these being the entities required for the establishment of treaty ports and the conclusion of treaties, thereby extending European diplomatic norms and treaty negotiations into Asia. As we will note, however, significant elements of the former tribute-trade order remained.

The changes in any one of (1) internal relationships within the East Asian region; (2) relationships within the Qing sphere of influence; or (3) relations between East Asia and Europe and the Americas, would have been sufficient to delineate an historical era. Focussing on the simultaneous appearance of changes in all three as one complex, and viewing the sixty-year period from the 1830s to the 1890s as the era of negotiation, allows a fuller understanding of the conceptual underpinning of the East Asian regional order, one manifested through the process of negotiation.

The most direct expression of the special characteristic of this era was the increased dynamism of relations within the East Asian region, centered on the ties between treaty ports. One interpretation has referred to this special characteristic as the coexistence of tribute and treaty relations. This approach, predicated as it is on a view of the tribute relationship as the conceptual basis of the East Asian international order centered on China and the treaty relationship as the principle underpinning international relations in Western Europe, naturally considers this period as one of transition in East Asia from the tributary order of the old era to the treaty order of the new. The tribute system, however, was essentially an expression of the Chinese world order (*huayi*), an historically evolved hierarchy of "civilized" and "barbarian" peoples, which defined region-wide geopolitical relations. Intellectuals in the nations and regions of East Asia shared the ideal of hierarchy extending outward from a Middle Kingdom (*Zhonghua*), but also from Japan and Vietnam in defining relations with their weaker neighbors, and this could hardly disappear easily or quickly. The concept of the treaty relationship, on the other hand, was derived from Western European international relations, and although international relations based on the concept of national sovereignty – sovereign, territorially defined nation-states – required the creation of these conditions in non-European societies, in the period under review, the result was a mere correspondence of forms. The internal and external relations of East Asia were by no means immediately governed by the new treaty relations.

In the situation that actually developed out of the interaction between these two concepts and the clash of two historical systems, this chapter will show not only that tribute and treaty relationships were not mutually incompatible, but that in East Asia the tribute concept tended to subsume the treaties. The concepts of East and West did not spatially overwrite one another, but rather it can be said that the tribute concept, that is the concept of a hierarchical order, remained primary, with the treaty relationship subordinated to it.

In 1839, the Daoguang emperor issued an historic edict trying to change Qing tributary-trade relations with Annam, Ryukyu, and Siam. He ordered them to reduce the frequency of tributary missions to the Qing court from a range of once each year to once in three years respectively to just once in four years in each case. This policy change was prompted in part by a Qing fiscal crisis requiring reduction in expenses associated with tributary missions. It was also associated with Qing efforts to strengthen control over tax revenues derived from coastal trade by bringing the trade under central control by various measures including redirecting it from distant ports where local officials corruptly siphoned off revenues that the center sought. This change of policy can also be called a change from tributary trade to mercantilism initiated by the Qing state.

When the Ryukyu Kingdom vigorously protested this reduction in the frequency of tributary missions, the Daoguang emperor agreed to restore annual trade missions from the Ryukyus to Fuzhou. Nor was the Qing able to implement the new trade and financial policy designed to control emerging economic strength in south China and the South China Sea area, the regions dominated by Chinese, western, Taiwanese, and Southeast Asian Chinese merchants that was beyond the control of Beijing. While all of these had previously participated in the tributary trade, all now sought to extricate themselves from the tributary relationship, seeking more lucrative private trade throughout the South China Sea and the East China Sea independent of state missions. The result was booming trade between China and Southeast Asia in the mid to late nineteenth century, trade largely beyond the control of the capital.[9]

The expansion of relations between the treaty ports

The conditions under which competition between a regional international order based on the historically hierarchical politics of East Asia, on the one hand, and the mutually contractual treaty diplomacy newly begun with Europe and the United States, on the other, were most visible in the treaty ports. The interplay of the two orders propelled the expansion of inter-treaty port ties.

A broad survey of the treaty port era in East Asia from the 1834 termination of the English East India Company's exclusive right to trade with China through the Sino-Japanese war of 1894–5 yields the following historical themes.

Treaty relations, whether between European and Asian nations or within the Asian region itself, were concluded as binational relationships. Taken as a whole, however, they bound the treaty ports together in a multilateral relationship. Although pacts like the Sino-British Treaty of Nanjing concluded in 1842 and the 1844 Sino-French Treaty of Whampoa were each concluded between two nations, through their extension into the Treaty of Kanagawa and the United States–Korea Treaty of Amity and Commerce, mutual access among the treaty ports became possible. A critical issue in the Asian treaty ties of Europe and the United States concerned intra-Asian relations among the treaty ports. Chinese merchants and Western trading firms struggled to secure a place in Asian trade networks, constructing bases in the treaty ports and linking them.

This trend of establishing a presence in the treaty ports was not the result solely of European pressures. Treaties of commerce and treaties of friendship began to be concluded within Asia as well. These included the 1876 Treaty of Kangwha between Japan and Korea, the 1882 Regulations for Maritime and Overland Trade Between Chinese and Korean Subjects (*Zhongguo Qiaoxian shangmin shuilu maoyi zhangcheng*) and the 1885 Tianjin Treaty between China and Japan. These commercial treaties concluded between Asian nations dismantled the framework of managed trade of the previous tribute-trade era, and the merchants of the coastal trading ports began to join in the inter-treaty port trade in great numbers, thereby strengthening previous private trade networks.

Of course, treaty relations concluded within Asia were modeled on the treaties with the West in an era of Western predominance. They differed, however, in their intention and in the process of their implementation. Sometimes the maintenance of suzerain–vassal relations was openly expressed; at other times the pretense of the geopolitical relationship enshrined in the historical tribute tie was maintained while in practice trade goals were pursued. During treaty negotiations, each side employed American and European legal and diplomatic advisors and conducted negotiations based on their proposals. The situation resulting from these internal and external relations made the substance of this era of negotiation even more broadly multilateral. The 1882 Regulations for Maritime and Overland Trade Between Chinese and Korean Subjects, discussed below, illustrate the special character of the region and the era. A close examination of this treaty reveals how the suzerain–vassal relationship was maintained through a period of tumultuous change.

After the opening of the five ports (Canton, Amoy, Fuzhou, Ningbo, and Shanghai) by the 1842 Treaty of Nanking, local Qing officials supervised customs. When the Shanghai county seat was occupied in the 1853 Small Sword Society uprising, however, the Shanghai Circuit Intendant was forced to flee. The American, British, and French consuls thereupon offered jointly to collect customs duties in his place in an attempt to strengthen their control over European and American merchants trading with areas under the control of the Taiping rebels. The Qing government later expanded this method of customs collection to the other treaty ports as a means to assure revenues. A foreign inspectorate of customs was established in each port with an Inspector-General of Customs in Peking. The inspectors had the same standing as the Chinese Superintendent of Customs (*Haiguan jiandu*), but in practice the foreign customs inspectors controlled operations. The Chinese maritime customs system, including the role of foreign maritime customs inspectors, in the treaty ports from the 1850s gave an institutional "guarantee" to inter-treaty port relations.

The maritime customs system, initially begun to strengthen the central finances of the Qing as well as to consolidate relations between the European powers and the Qing, naturally affected China's vassal states. The maritime customs system was applied to Korea, and in the 1880s Paul Georg von Mollendorff of the Tianjin maritime customs was dispatched as Korean maritime customs inspector. A debate sprang up at that point concerning the problem of the duties to be paid by ships entering Korean ports that had previously docked in Chinese treaty ports. The question was whether foreign ships that had paid the 5 percent *ad valorem* import tax stipulated in the Sino-British tariff agreement for vessels stopping in any Chinese treaty port should pay only the 2.5 percent Qing domestic transport tax (*zikou banshui*) or be regarded as carrying foreign goods and therefore pay an additional 5 percent import tax when they entered Korean treaty ports. Behind this lay a difference in perceptions concerning whether Korea was a Chinese vassal state or an independent nation.

Elsewhere, the tributary system was under attack as a result of changing inter-state relations with Japan strengthening its grip on the Ryukyus, with Vietnam succumbing to French colonial rule and Burma to British rule. Nevertheless, in each of these cases, treaties negotiated with China granted Chinese merchants special tax relief in trade with these tributary areas. This constituted recognition by Japan, France, and Britain of the continued salience of certain Chinese tributary prerogatives. The tribute system did not simply yield to the treaty system.

As can be seen in the tax collection problem of Korean maritime customs, the treaty ports confronted the historical tribute or vassal relationship of the Chinese world order in East Asia. Viewed from another angle, the application of the logic of the historical East Asian world order became an issue in the operation, perception, and position of the treaty ports even though they had been formally opened through treaties with Western powers. This suggests that the historical background of the treaty ports themselves must be taken into consideration. The treaty ports were of course neither newly constructed nor recently opened as ports; the five southeast China ports, in fact all the treaty ports, had histories dating far back as trading ports, and in China's North–South coastal trade and South China–Southeast Asia trade they had long been sites of tribute-trade activities. Merchant guilds functioned in all of them, each had a historically developed trading region, and commercial networks had long formed around them. After acquiring the right for their nationals to reside in the treaty ports, European and American merchants competed for commercial concessions in long-developed commercial networks.[10]

The issue, always apparent in American and European treaty negotiations with the Qing, of how to handle treaty ties between the Qing and its vassal states, framed relations among the treaty ports. When Western countries entered into treaty negotiations with nations or regions within the Qing sphere or under its influence, they treated the suzerain Qing as one concerned party in the negotiations. In short, ostensibly bilateral treaty relations could only be concluded by taking the Qing and the entire tributary relationship into consideration. Thus the tribute relationship, which formed the background to the relationship expressed in the treaty, was directly and indirectly incorporated within it.[11]

Vassal states and treaties: the negotiation of the 1882 Regulations for Maritime and Overland Trade Between China and Korea

From tribute to trade: change and continuity in the tributary relationship

Trade regulations between the Qing and Korea were concluded on October 4, 1882 under the Superintendent of Trade for the North (*Beiyang dachen*) and Governor-General of Zhili (*Zhili zongdu*) Li Hongzhang. From the Qing, Zhou Fu, the Customs Daotai of Tianjin and Li Hongzhang's private secretary, and the Expectant Intendant (*Houxuan dao*) Ma Jianzhong were appointed as representatives. On the Korean side, the Envoy to China, Cho Yong-ha, the Assistant Envoy Kim Hong-jip, and Secretary O Yun-jung were appointed.[12]

Li Hongzhang recorded the most important points of the negotiations and the contents of the regulations: (1) Ma Jianzhong was first sent to Korea where he investigated actual conditions through discussions with the Korean side; (2) Li supervised Zhou Fu and Ma Jianzhong in consulting the precedents (*zhanggu*) informing the relevant Chinese statutes, and carefully examining international law; (3) the regulations differed from those defining relations between two nations as they were to regulate traffic with a vassal state; and (4) article eight of the regulations stated that Li Hongzhang and the Korean king shall in future make determinations through consultation. Although criticised by some Chinese for intentionally altering the old system in the pursuit of profit, the regulations preserved the suzerain–vassal hierarchy.[13]

The regulations sought to assure "equal" trade, based on the premise that Korea was a Chinese vassal state. In drafting the regulations, the negotiators were deeply conscious of Sino-Japanese relations in connection with the Korea issue. Li Hongzhang notes, for example, that O Yun-jung, the chief Korean negotiator in preparing the regulations, feared that the Japanese would use the regulations as a pretext to increase demands on Korea. Examination of the contents and special characteristics of the treaty's preface and eight articles clarifies these issues.

The Preface confirmed the fact that Korea had long had titles conferred as a vassal state and that there was no change in that determination. Given that, and in light of the fact that the prohibition on sea trade (*Haijin lun*) had earlier been abandoned and trade by land and sea was being conducted with foreign nations, the merchants of the two countries were to conduct trade with each other, sharing the profits equally, while existing rules for frontier trade would be modified as circumstances required. These regulations for maritime and overland trade resulted from China's intent to treat its vassal state generously; the benefits they conferred were "understood to apply to the relations between China and Korea only." In this way, the Preface, while emphasizing the goal of increasing China's trading profits from the transformation in tribute trade with Korea and in the frontier trade in the northern part of Korea, simultaneously reaffirmed the suzerain–vassal relationship.[14]

The first Article established that nationals of each country would be supervised by trade commissioners dispatched from their own country and that each country would bear the cost of maintaining its own agents while they resided in the other nation. In short, China's Superintendent of Trade for the North (Li Hongzhang) would appoint trade commissioners to those treaty ports already opened by Korea; those trade commissioners were equal in standing to the Korean officials that were their counterparts; the Korean king would likewise dispatch a high official to reside in Tianjin and representatives to reside in each of the treaty ports; they too were equal in standing to the local Chinese authorities. What is of particular interest here is the enactment of a provision for "treaty port diplomacy," that is, China and Korea each dispatched commissioners to each other's treaty ports just as the European nations and the United States appointed consuls to the treaty ports. Furthermore, the determination that each nation was to bear the cost of maintaining its own officials was a significant change since the expenses of the tributary missions had all previously been covered by China. The posting of commissioners of equal rank, however, was in keeping with the historical ranking order. In short, there was both continuity and change in the tributary relationship between China and Korea.

The second Article dealt with consular jurisdiction in conflict resolution. Thus, in the case of an incident involving Chinese merchants in a Korean treaty port, if one Chinese merchant brought charges against another, then the Chinese trade commissioner would adjudicate. For incidents concerning property, if the accuser was Korean and the accused Chinese, then the Chinese side would arrest and try the accused. If convicted, the criminal would be turned over to the Korean authorities. In the reverse case, the Korean side would arrest and try the accused and turn the convicted criminal over to the Chinese. However, in Chinese treaty ports, if a Korean was involved in an incident, whether accuser or accused, the Chinese still adjudicated. This determination of the consular jurisdiction of the trade commissioners of both nations was extremely one-sided, and the consular jurisdiction of the Korean trade commissioner was essentially not recognized in Chinese treaty ports. The third Article determined customs payments and allowed the free passage of fishermen in the coastal areas of both countries. It stipulated that:

> Ships grounded on either coast under stress of weather shall be allowed to anchor at whatever place this occurs, to buy provisions and have the necessary repairs done; but while the local authorities shall take charge, all relevant expenses shall be borne by the owners of the ship.

Ships entering ports that had not yet been opened would have both cargo and vessel confiscated. Fishermen living in P'yongyang and Hwanghae provinces in Korea, and in Shandong and Fengdian provinces in China, however, were permitted to take on provisions and water in those areas. Comparing this regulation with tribute trade, we note a shift from the practices under the latter of (1) tax exemption: and (2) China paying the costs of returning grounded or damaged ships to their home country. The new regulations required that customs duties be levied and that the costs of ship repair be borne by the ship's owner. This regulation reveals how heavy a burden tribute trade was for the Chinese state. The opening up, moreover, of trade along the Yellow Sea and Bohai coasts, which had been strictly limited during the era of tribute trade, was a big change.

The fourth Article consisted of tax regulations applied to goods transported between China and Korea and another regulation governing transactions in the interior of the two nations. It stipulated that it was permissible to lease land and buildings in the treaty ports; when Chinese goods were transported from one treaty port to another a sum equal to half of the export duty paid on them was to be collected as an import tax; Korean and Chinese merchants were allowed to set up shops and engage in commerce only in Peking and in Yanghawajin and Seoul, respectively, while trade in other parts of the interior required special permission from the trade commissioners. Korean merchants were required for the first time to pay the Chinese *lijin*, domestic transport tax. The arrangements for the domestic transport tax and for transit passes established between China and the countries of Europe and North America were adopted without change in the Chinese–Korean regulations. The formal designation of Peking and Seoul as "open cities" (*kai shizhang*) preceded the opening of these cities to Europe and the United States. Customs agreements previously entered into with Europe and the United States were selectively adopted here.

The fifth Article aimed at converting the frontier trade to tariff trade.

Because frontier trade was carried on at various remote places like Uiju, Hoeryong, and Kyongwon, there had been "numerous difficulties arising from the authority exercised by local officials." As a result, Ch'aengmun and Uiju on the Yalu River and Hunchun and Hoeryong on the Tumen River were designated as open trading locations, customs were set up in these newly opened markets, and a 5 percent *ad valorem* tax was collected on all goods except red ginseng (*hongshen*). Article five constituted a change in trade on the frontier and in seaports, where the scale of commerce had been largest under the earlier tribute-trade regime. The reference here to "difficulties" with local officials was an attack on the diversion of trade revenues into local finances. The 5 percent tariff was the center's attempt to establish control over tax revenues on the frontier.

The sixth Article forbade the merchants of both countries from dealing in opium (importing or domestic production) or arms, permitted the import to China of Korean red ginseng with a 15 percent *ad valorem* tax, and established a permit system for the export of red ginseng from China (both Korea and North China exported red ginseng). This article clearly identified problems in the actual conditions of trade as the Qing sought to tighten its control over revenues. Article seven attempted to strengthen ties with Korea. The trade which was formerly limited to the overland route via Ch'aeng-mun, was now extended to the sea (Figure 1.3).

The regulations provided that the Superintendent of Trade for the North dispatch a merchant vessel of the China Merchant's Steamship Navigation Company, a government-sponsored enterprise, with troops on board to provide security for each location. It stipulated further that while the Chinese state provided security, the Korean state bear a portion of the costs. This clause had powerful military overtones in providing not only security with respect to China–Korea trade but also strengthening Korea's domestic defenses with an eye to Japan–Korea conflict (Figure 1.4). Article eight stipulated that revision of the regulations was to be handled through consultation between the Superintendent of Trade for the North on the Chinese side and the Korean king.

The eight articles led to great changes in the form of trade. This can be summarized as a Chinese attempt to make the existing tribute trade consistent with the forms of treaty port trade. The primary Chinese goals were: (1) reforming the one-sided financial burden that tribute trade placed on China; (2) redirecting to central finances, that is customs finances, the tribute-trade revenues that were in practice absorbed by local officials; (3) confirming the trend of expansion in the activities of coastal fishermen and in the so-called frontier trade. The regulations further affirmed the general framework of the suzerain–vassal relationship and maintained the historical relationship of rank between the two countries through the inclusion of the equal relationship between the Superintendent of Trade for the North and the Korean king, the equal relationship

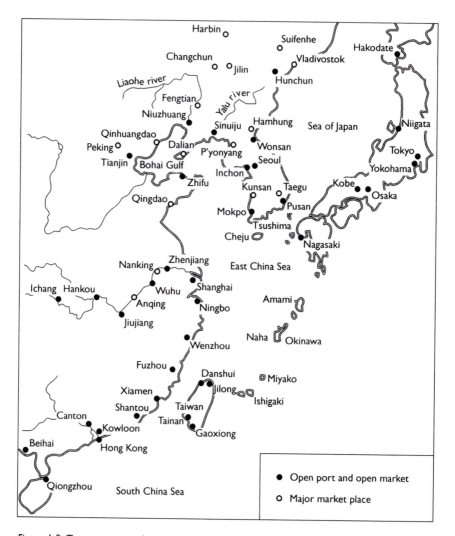

Figure 1.3 Treaty ports and opened cities in East Asia in the 1880s

Source: Takeshi Hamashita, "Tribute and Treaties: East Asian Treaty Ports Network in the Era of Negotiation, 1834–94," *European Journal of East Asian Studies* (Brill, Leiden, Boston, Koln, 2001), Volume 1.1: 62.

between the trade commissioners, and other provisions. But where China had formerly borne the costs of tributary trade, it now sought (successfully) to impose an equal share of costs on Korea.

The introduction of the 1882 regulations had two consequences. The first was criticism by the Korean king and the Korean side concerning the

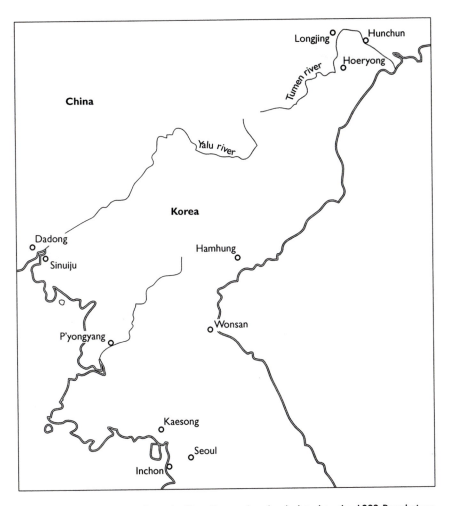

Figure 1.4 Trading points along the Sino-Korean border (related to the 1882 Regulations for Maritime and Overland Trade Between Chinese and Korean Subjects)

Source: Takeshi Hamashita (2001: 68).

shift of the financial burden previously borne by the Qing. The second was further expansion of the border trade by merchants of both countries, which had begun to flourish, invigorating trade throughout the entire region.

These regulations were implemented at a time of great tension on the Korean peninsula, with Chinese troops entering Korea to counter the growing Japanese influence.

Korean criticisms of the Qing

The Korean side, which had long profited from tribute trade, took three types of actions when it became clear that the Qing policy of cutting back financial support meant that those profits would be reduced.

1 Attempts to maintain the former profits of the tribute trade by exploiting the gap between the regulations and the Chinese side's treatment of Korea as a vassal state and its attempt to maintain the tribute order.
2 Pointing out that, while the gist of the regulations was equality and fairness, in practice the regulations violated that spirit, the Chinese side's advocacy of reciprocity in the regulations notwithstanding.
3 Advancing the theory of the Japanese threat, specifically noting that the trade regulations gave the Japanese an excellent pretext to intervene in Korea, and pressuring the Qing to reconsider implementation of the regulations.[15]

These approaches reveal the Korean side adroitly combining tribute, treaties, and East Asian international relations to defend its historical interests.

The trade regulations had the immediate effect of subjecting the Korean tribute missions to Chinese taxation. About two months after the conclusion of the regulations, when Korea attempted to present tribute in Peking, a 4 percent *ad valorem* tax was collected from them at the border gate (*bianmen*) of Fenghuangcheng. Duties were also collected at the Chongwen gate, which opened to Shanhaiguan and Peking. This was unprecedented in the more than two hundred years of the Qing dynasty. Yet from another angle, it also represented a reaffirmation of the special tributary relationship since Korea was asked to pay only 4 percent whereas all others were subjected to a 5 percent tax. In addition, the practice of borrowing funds from Chinese merchants was also forbidden. The head of the tribute mission strongly expressed the hope that tribute trade would be made free of duty, as it had been before.[16]

Li Hongzhang's response to the first Korean criticism was that since tribute was an issue for the Ministry of Rites (*Li Bu*) and new taxes an issue for the Ministry of Revenue (*Hu Bu*), the regulations were a matter that should be referred for investigation to the *Zongli Yamen* (Office for the Management of the Business of Foreign Countries). He thus dealt with this critique simply as a difference between jurisdictional organizations. Li then reviewed the prohibitions and prohibited goods under tribute trade. The Ministry of Rites had forbidden tribute emissaries from trading at the Imperial Despatch Office (*Huitongguan*) and from dealing in a number of items including weapons and gunpowder. It had also forbidden foreign merchants who were returning home from taking people, lumber for ship-building, iron nails, sesame, or grain with them. The private purchase of raw silk and silk products were also proscribed. However, in the case of a request from the Korean king, such prohibited items as copper, iron, horses and mules, bows, and raw silk had all been approved for export. There was also a precedent from 1793 proscribing the purchase of copper cash. Since most of these restrictions had been lifted with the opening of treaty port trade, Li concluded that the economic benefits enjoyed by the Korean side were far from negligible.

Concerning the second criticism, that the terms were unfair to Korea, O Yun-jung argued that:

> Examining the texts of international law, an article of mutual equality is to be found in every one. Although we have enjoyed your country's favor, the conditions offered other countries differ from those given Korea. Although you say it is unavoidable in the tributary order, this is different from the ceremony of "Serving the Great" (sadae)

and requested the removal of the "unequal" clauses. Customs Daotai Zhou Fu argued against this that:

> In the concept of sadae there is of necessity a place for the small and for the great. This is no empty ceremony; it depends on a real obliga-tion. Therefore, the fact that in international law different terms are used for the commercial traffic of vassal nations is irrelevant to this case.[17]

Zhou Fu, in response, also rejected the claim of inequality in Article two, asserting the need to distinguish between great and small. The Chinese view was that the regulations exemplified the sadae relationship.

On the third point of the Japanese threat, O Yun-jung pointed out that while liberalizing passage of fishing vessels along the coast was a good thing, it would provoke the Japanese, who had been demanding whaling access to the East China Sea. Furthermore, he warned that the open cities stipulated in the fourth Article would lead to Japanese demands that Taegu and Hamhung be opened. He therefore requested that this Article and Articles three and four not be revealed to foreign nations.

Zhou Fu dismissed this argument completely. As for Qing differen-tiating regulations with Korea from those with other countries, the Korean side had been taken in by arguments foisted on them by other nations. Japanese officials, he believed, mocked Korea as positioned some-where between half and total dependence. Concerning Article three, Zhou pointed out that the Japanese were not the only ones taking advantage of the situation, and greater attention should be paid to smugglers. On Article four, he stated that if cities were opened to trade, not only Japanese merchants but also Chinese merchants would go into the interior, thus stimulating the development of Korean commerce. These counter-arguments were natural extensions of the principles underlying the Qing foreign policy that had replaced managed tribute with mutual trade.

The expansion of northern commerce

Implementation of the Trade Regulations produced a change in functioning of the tribute-trade system on China's northern border with Korea. There efforts were made to reform managed border trade and implement commerce, to replace the existing border trade with tariff-based trade. Li Hongzhang, in a memorial to the throne of February 18, 1883, presented a four-article proposal to reorganize the border trading cities of Jilin province and Korea that made the provisions for open cities in Article three of the regulations even more concrete.[18]

> Article One. In the past, during the first month of the year the merchants of Jilin Province traveled to Hoeryong to trade, and once every two years they would go from Hoeryong to Kyongwon. Since Kyongwon and Hunchun are only sixty *li* apart, however, it is more convenient to conduct trade at these two locations. The trading route should therefore be divided in two: one route shall go from Heishidao on the border of Dunhua County to Hoeryong in Korea; the other from Hunchun to Kyongwon District. It is anticipated that the merchants of the Jilin provincial capital, of Ningguta, and of Hunchun will reap twice the profits as a result of this.

This regulation can be considered an administrative measure to improve market conditions. In other words, it can be regarded as a policy response to the need to increase the profitability of the northern trade.

> Article Two. Customs should be established at Hunchun and on the border of Dunhua County. In the past, border trade was transacted only when the Yalu River froze over. Furthermore, in the past there were no ferries on the Tumen River. From now on, however, trade will be transacted throughout the year, so ferry landings and buildings should be constructed on both banks and inspection boats sent from the Jilin side.

This regulation was aimed at providing the port and customs facilities that would become necessary as a result of trade. Investment would be undertaken to strengthen the so-called border trade.

Article Three. Tariff regulations should be determined and goods categorized and taxed accordingly. The main goods going from Jilin to Korea are horses, hides, and cloth, and while the first two have hitherto been taxed according to Jilin tariff regulations, because cotton cloth is exchanged for imported goods, it has not been heavily taxed. Now, because of the switch to trade, everything other than the first two items should be taxed according to our tariff schedule and customs receipts issued. The tariff rates shall be 5 percent *ad valorem*, except for ginseng at 15 percent.

The third clause established tariff rates and attempted to apply the 5 percent *ad valorem* tax that was the basis of Chinese customs to Korean trade.

Article Four. Commissioners will be dispatched from Jilin to the two locations of Hoeryong and Kyongwon in Korea to supervise the Jilin merchants. Local Korean officials are not qualified to supervise these matters, so officials from the Jilin side should be posted. Food and fuel costs should not be treated as public expenditures, as the Japanese consul does, but rather should be paid for out of the budget items for the envoys despatched to each customs post, so as not to place a burden on Korean officials or merchants. Consideration should be given to the possibility of dispatching Korean commissioners to the two county seats of Dunhua and Hunchun.

Reciprocity and mutuality are stronger here than in the regulations. Li's injunction to dispatch Chinese supervisors because "local Korean officials are not qualified to supervise" offers an ironic footnote to the issues of international customs administration and extraterritoriality in China.

Taken as a whole, Li Hongzhang's proposals sought to expand trade and secure through tariffs a source of revenue for China's central finances. About a week later, however, the military governor of Shenyang (Shenjing jiangju) and others criticized this proposal in a memorial to the throne. Emphasizing border security, they urged that entry and exit be restricted to the Fenghuang border gate, as it had been up to that time. This reflected their wariness concerning the human traffic across the frontier that would expand as a result of trade. They also noted the necessity of following precedent, vividly displaying the frontier-defense mindset of regional officials.[19]

The Twenty-four Rules for Traffic on the Frontier between Liaodong and Korea, concluded in March 1883 by Chen Benzhi, Circuit Intendant of the East (*Dongbian daotai*) for the Qing and O Yun-jung on the Korean side, established a free-trade area in Zhonggang near Uiju. Although the establishment of customs and implementation of duties followed the above Trade Regulations, at the same time the rules clearly stipulated that tributary missions would not be taxed, tribute would continue, and unrestricted passage on the tribute road by merchants was prohibited. The result was that tariff trade and tribute trade existed side by side.[20] The opening of the north of the Korean peninsula led to the formation of a region of mutual interchange and negotiation stretching from Japan in the south to Siberia in the north.[21]

The expansion of Chinese maritime customs to Korea

Korean merchants and Qing merchants

The drive to extend the Chinese customs system to Korea can be regarded as one institutional basis for regarding the period from the middle through the latter half of the nineteenth century as an era of negotiation, one shaped, moreover, by the multilateral trade between treaty ports. This movement, through the management of Korean maritime customs from Peking, was a gamble on the increased customs revenue anticipated from expanded trade. China simultaneously strove to maintain influence over Korea through maritime customs. The treaty ports and open cities in Korea constituted a bid to share in profits by not only using the cities of the North opened through Chinese initiative, but also to make active use of the treaty ports of Korea previously opened through Japanese initiative.

The management of trade through the treaty ports and open cities advanced on two fronts. The first was the termination of the special concessions granted to Korean merchants operating under the old tribute trade; the second was an attempt to secure customs revenue from Chinese merchants in Korean treaty ports by controlling their activities. Viewed from a different angle, we witness the advance in Korea and throughout East Asia of Chinese merchants into the trading activity of the treaty ports and open cities after their establishment in East Asia.[22]

Looking first at the termination of the special concessions for domestic trade for foreign merchants under tribute trade, a report from May 19, 1883 by the Gansu provincial Circuit Intendant Gong Jinjie, indicates that one Mun Ch'o-un, a Korean merchant, had been actively purchasing ginseng and other Chinese medicines in Gansu. The report stated that the fact that he engaged in trade even though there were no trading ports or open cities in Gansu violated the trade regulations of the two nations.[23] The movements of this same merchant were persistently tracked, and about half a year later the Governor-General of Sichuan, Ding Bozhen, reported that he was buying ginseng and Chinese medicine in Gansu without a permit.[24] Korean merchants used the special concession for "free trade" in the interior under the tribute trade to engage in a lively trade, despite the tracking of Chinese officials seeking to reform old practices through enforcement of the trade regulations. The principal products that Korean merchants dealt with were ginseng, raw silk, and silk cloth, and we can infer that these goods were primarily intended to meet Japanese demand.[25]

Chinese merchants rapidly entered Korean treaty ports. This was particularly notable in the ports opened through Japanese "initiative." On the eleventh of February 1884, a year and a half after the conclusion of the Trade Regulations of September 1882, the Superintendent of Trade for the North, Li Hongzhang, quoted the report of Chen Shutang, a trade commissioner who had been dispatched to Korea. The report omits Pusan and Wonsan, but it does list, according to region of origin, Chinese merchants and employees in Seoul, Mapo, and Inchon.

1 Chinese merchants based in Seoul
  Zhejiang Group: six offices (Tongyuxian, Tianfeng, Gongji, Chaokang, Gongping, Xiechangmou); total of eighteen staff.
  Shandong Group: thirteen offices (Zhonghuaxing, Hexingshun, Huiji, Heyang, Hengtaixing, Gongheshun, Renfengzhan, Fuxiangsheng, Yongyuanshun, Fuyuhao, Dexingcheng, Gongshengho, Fuxing Zhonghua); total of forty-one staff.
  Chinese employees: Department of Machinery (Kigiguk), one Tianjin Chinese; Mollendorff official residence, four Ningbo Chinese; American legation, two Cantonese; Ch'ao p'an-so-chai, two Shandong Chinese; Tangzho, seven Jiangxi Chinese and one Shanghai Chinese; total of seventeen staff.

2 Chinese merchants based in Mapo
  Shandong Yuchang, seven Chinese; Shandong Dexiang, five Chinese; Jardine, Matheson & Co. (two Cantonese, three Zhejiang Chinese); Xiehuan shunchuan (one ship with six Shandong merchants); total of twenty-three staff.

3 Chinese merchants based in Inchon
  Guangdong Group: three offices (Zhizhonghe, Yian, Guangshenglong); total of seventeen staff; Yonglong shunchuan one ship (six staff).
  Shandong Group: Two offices (Yonglong shunchuan, Gonghuzhan); total of thirteen staff.
  Zhejiang Group: two offices (Daihe shun, Gongzhi); total of eighteen staff.
  Chinese employees: Maritime Customs – two Zhejiang Chinese, one Jiangxi Chinese, one Guangdong Chinese; Customs Inspectorate – two Zhejiang Chinese, two Jiangsu Chinese; Ha-pai-lo affiliates – one Zhejiang Chinese; total of nine staff.

4 Other
   Translators: Wu Zhongxian, Mollendorff; Zhou Zhangling, Inchon
   Customs; Tang Shaoyii, Pusan Customs; all Cantonese.
   Secretaries: Tang Zhaoxian, Mollendorff, from Jiangxi.
   Counselors: Wang Mingchang, from Anhui.

In short, after the opening of the Korean ports, merchants from coastal
provinces like Shandong, Jiangsu, Zhejiang, Guangdong, and Guangxi
moved immediately into Korean treaty ports. Their activities surpassed
those of the Japanese merchants they competed with. The Japanese, as
can be seen in the report of February 1895 from the acting Consul-
General at Pusan, Kato Masuo, addressed to Foreign Minister Mutsu
Munemitsu, displayed a strong sense of crisis that 'their' Korean ports had
been taken over by aggressive Chinese merchants.[26] Thereafter the population of Chinese merchants in Korea increased rapidly from 162 in 1883
to 2,182 in 1893, 3,661 in 1906, and 11,818 in 1910. There were few
women, only one-tenth to one-thirtieth of the male population, and the
immigration pattern was one of migrant workers.

The era of negotiation premised on trade among treaty ports above all
resulted in the expansion of Chinese merchants into treaty ports throughout East Asia. Chinese merchants from the coastal provinces, freed from
the trade control of the Qing center with the disintegration of state power
in the first half of the nineteenth century, linked together via trade the
regions of coastal China, Japan, Korea, and beyond. This Chinese mercantile capital was a source of anxiety for Japanese, Korean and Hong Kong,
as well as European, merchants, all of whom found the competition from
Chinese merchants to be fierce. The Qing state was also concerned about
the dynamic thrust of coastal Chinese capital throughout Asia. It was precisely in order to manage and control their activities, and assure the flow
of tax revenues to the Chinese state, that the extension of Chinese maritime customs to Korea became an issue.

The conflict over Korea–China relations and the Korean maritime customs – independent nation or vassal state?

Trade among the treaty ports was by no means limited to the Chinese
ports, but spread to treaty ports throughout East Asia with the expansion
of treaty relationships. While trade among the treaty ports was sustained,
on the one hand, by Chinese merchants who advanced into Korea, Japan,
and elsewhere, Qing China's attempt to apply the maritime customs
system of its own treaty ports to Korea and also to install foreign maritime
customs officers led to the dissemination of the customs system of trade
among treaty ports throughout Asia.

On October 3, 1883, Robert Hart, Inspector-General of the Imperial

Maritime Customs in Peking, reported on the current condition of arms exports.[27] The movement of arms was strictly monitored, with the transfer of arms to Korea via Shanghai of particular concern to Hart. Earlier that year four cannons and fifty-four cannon balls were delivered by an English ship from Hong Kong to Shanghai, where Jardine, Matheson & Co. filed a customs report and transferred them to Korea the same day, again via a British ship. Because these arms were brought into Korea via Shanghai, Hart, who was concerned about arms sales, "discovered" a customs problem.

Although Korea was recognized as a tributary state of China, the treatment of customs would differ depending on whether Korea was regarded as a foreign nation or in the same fashion as each of China's other provinces. If Korea were classified as one of China's provinces, when foreign goods are trans-shipped, then a receipt of payment of import duties or a customs waiver should be obtained and a bill of lading issued. However, if Korea were classified as a foreign state, then, according to the treaty, it would be sufficient to issue a receipt for the goods and not necessary to have a bill of lading. Since the determination of Korea's position was of great importance concerning China's relations with the outside world, this matter could not be settled by the Inspector-General alone.[28]

In this way, it could be said that Hart sought, through the concrete issue of maritime customs procedures, a solution to the practical problem of the recognition of Korea as an historical vassal state of China and an approach to the determination of the nature and scope of the relationship. The handling of customs opened questions pertaining to the role of trade in East Asian tribute relations. Li Hongzhang made the following response to Hart's question:

> Foreign goods on which import duties have been paid at Chinese customs and that are then trans-shipped to Korea, whether by Chinese or foreign merchants, shall be treated as delivered to a foreign state and import duties shall be paid according to the customs regulations of Korea. Exported Chinese goods, after payment of export taxes, can be disposed of freely, even though duties for foreign merchants and Chinese or Korean merchants differ. The tax on ships (levied by tonnage) will be paid by ships entering Chinese ports and paid again after entering Korean ports. The Chinese customs regulations and the Regulations for Maritime and Overland Trade Between Chinese and Korean Subjects will be enforced in parallel ... China's favorable treatment of its tributary kingdoms differs from the European and American treatment of their dependent territories as provinces, a point that will be examined in more detail in the future.[29]

In response to Hart's attempt to situate the vassal state issue within diplomatic relations, one can probably say that Li Hongzhang, while asserting that Korea was autonomous in both foreign relations and domestic administration, distinguished it both from European and American colonies and provinces, thus leaving room for negotiation concerning Korea's special status. Hart met Li in 1889 and again touched on the vassal state question, stating that if Korea was not a vassal state of China, then the debate as to whether it was or was not should itself be stopped. He went on to say that if it were a vassal state, on every available occasion foreign nations should be informed to that effect. Moreover, Korea as well should be made to acknowledge this.[30] To Hart's view of vassal states as colonies, Li Hongzhang withheld response, but to his claim that if it was a dependency, then corresponding customs procedures were necessary, Li replied clearly that Korea was a foreign nation, autonomous in domestic administration and foreign relations. Although their perspectives on vassal states and dependencies differed, neither attempted to take the other to task on the issue. This was an expression of the special characteristic – negotiating among different principles of sovereignty – of the era of negotiation.

In fact, the open cities and treaty ports established in the Regulations for Maritime and Overland Trade Between Chinese and Korean Subjects were exempt from maritime customs. The position of this frontier trade activity is comprehensible neither on the basis of the treaty principle, based on relationships between states, nor the tribute principle, based on the suzerain–vassal relationship. Rather it suggests the possibility of a third concept that could be called a "regional principle" (*chiiki genri*), one that sought to encompass core–periphery trading activities by both parties. The development of maritime customs, moreover, functioned as a means to subsume a broad region, so that here as well a process of negotiation based on a regional principle can be discerned

Foreign advisors and the loan issue

In the era in which negotiations concerning treaty relations were initiated with Europe, the United States, and Japan, the employment of Westerners as advisors was indispensable. In Korea, around 1882, when the negotiation of the Regulations for Maritime and Overland Trade Between Chinese and Korean Subjects with the Qing began, a debate ensued over the employment of Westerners. In particular, Cho Yong-ha warned the Korean king that if Westerners were not employed in handling negotiations, Korea might lose its autonomy. Li Hongzhang, in response, strongly recommended the former German consul in Tianjin, Mollendorff, as genial, loyal, and expert in Chinese as a result of five years of experience in China's maritime customs. He also recommended that the Koreans employ three Chinese advisors: Ma Jianzhong, who had previously conducted negotiations with Korea, his older brother, Ma Jianchang, and Li Shuchang.

In December 1882, Mollendorff was engaged as a diplomatic advisor and as Inspector-General of Customs for Korea, and foreign advisors were introduced into Korea. In 1883, a customs agreement was signed with Japan, and treaties were also negotiated and signed with England and Germany. In July 1885, Mollendorff resigned, and Owen N. Denny, former American consul in Tianjin, replaced him as diplomatic advisor, while Henry F. Merrill took the post of customs inspector. While Mollendorff mediated between Korea and the Qing, with the emergence of the Japanese problem, the situation frequently became intractable. As a result, the duties of customs inspector and diplomatic advisor were subsequently split into two posts. In the interim, however, the Qing attempted to exert diplomatic influence in Korea through a former customs inspector who was appointed and dispatched from China, exploiting his position as diplomatic advisor. In effect, the Qing tried to incorporate the principle of the suzerain–vassal relationship into the maritime customs system and to maintain it through the relationship among treaty ports.

Institutional reform on the Korean side also adapted to this situation, and in 1882 a new Office of State Affairs (*T'ongni kimu amun*) was set up for diplomatic negotiation. Moreover, the Department of Relations with China (*Sadaesa*) and Department of Neighborly Relations (*Kyorinsa*), which had handled relations with the Qing and Japan respectively, were merged and a Foreign Office (*T'ongni kyosop t'ongsang amun*) was established with responsibility for multilateral negotiations. This process also was a response to the organizational changes that followed the opening of the five Chinese ports.

The conditions on the occasion when Merrill took up his post as Maritime Customs Inspector in Korea, were as follows:

1 The king of Korea had been informed that Merrill would be appointed by the Superintendent of Trade for the North, that is, by China, with the title Inspector-General of Customs for Korea, and that he was to take charge of all particulars of customs revenue.

2 After Merrill took office, maritime customs in Korea were to be conducted on the same principles as the Chinese maritime customs. Merrill was to receive instructions exclusively from the Superintendent of Trade for the North and the Korean Resident-General (*Chaoxian zongshu*), and he was to be subordinate to no other party.

3 After taking up his post, Merrill was to devote himself exclusively to maritime customs duties, but if the Korean government requested that he perform other duties, he would do so to the best of his ability. However, he was not to neglect his customs duties.[31]

4 Merrill, as Inspector-General of Customs for Korea, was to be well compensated.

5   The Inspector-General of Customs could at any time return to his duties in the Chinese maritime customs, and the Superintendent of Trade for the North could at any time recall him. Here Qing China, through the appointment and dispatch of the maritime customs inspector, established a position of strength with respect both to the Inspector-General and the China–Korea relationship. This can be regarded as an attempt to maintain Chinese suzerainty.[32]

To support the diplomatic negotiations of Korea, the Qing planned to make a loan to Korea. This was a pre-emptive move designed to counter any Japanese loan. The use of Korean maritime customs revenues as security for the loan clearly went beyond the loan form used by various foreign nations in Qing China and Korea.[33]

The Korean maritime customs regulations and tax code

In July 1883, Takezoe Shin'inchiro and Min Yong-mok of Japan and Korea signed trade regulations. This signing took place nearly seven years after the 1876 Treaty of Kanghwa, during which time no maritime customs had been established and no duties collected.

The customs regulations regarding Korean export duties were extremely simple: all exports were taxed at 5 percent *ad valorem*. Duty-free items were currency, gold, and silver, and it was forbidden to export red ginseng. Products were divided into eleven categories: medicines and spices; dyes and pigments; metals and tools; fats; textiles; writing implements and paper; food, beverages, and tobacco; general merchandise; ships; currency, gold, and silver; and contraband (fake medicine and so forth). Import taxes started at 5 percent *ad valorem* and rose to 8, 10, 15, 20, 30, and even 35 percent. Import duties were established for specific Japanese products, such as silk and paper at 8 percent. A protectionist character on the Korean side, although slight, is discernible. The absence of duties on silver and gold was an application of Chinese maritime customs provisions.[34]

Among the thirty-nine articles that make up the customs regulations, the main difference from Chinese maritime customs regulations concerned Korean inland customs and the fact that no tax was collected on transfers among treaty ports. The regulations basically conformed to the Chinese maritime customs, and no inland customs were stipulated. Although previous research has examined the bilateral relationship by focusing on the Japanese advance into Korea (see Table 1.1), it is also possible to view this process as Japan striving to gain a share of the advantages that Korea already provided to China, or that were constructed on the basis of a Chinese–Korean relationship that retained important elements of suzerainty.[35] The era of negotiation in the second half of the

Table 1.1 China's trade with Korea, 1883–1910

Year	Imports	Exports
1883	2,608	2,314
1886	29,643	102,093
1889	120,440	200,096
1892	132,425	464,984
1895	55,741	638,063
1898	952,307	1,086,748
1901	513,516	1,178,608
1904	879,320	1,390,695
1907	1,494,204	2,169,560
1910	2,382,113	2,629,433

Source: Yang Chaochuan and Sun Yumei (1991: 146–7).

Note
Units: maritime customs taels.

nineteenth century, and the oppositional relationship between Europe and Asia, can also be regarded as one shaped by the negotiation of internal, multilateral Asian relationships.

Conclusion: treaties between Korea and the United States, France, England, Russia, and Japan

Up to now "Western impact," "opening" of Asia, and "modernity" have been used more or less synonymously in the literature. Moreover, all have essentially been understood as products of the Western impact on Asia, a challenge–response framework pioneered half a century ago by John Fairbank and Teng Ssu-yu in their classic *China's Response to the West*. In this view, China and Asia are invariably placed in the position not of an actor or initiator but of an object acted upon, and the West is considered to have provided the impulses that transformed Asian tradition. In this view, the treaties concluded with the Western nations become the point of departure for Asia's modernity. What has been attempted above, however, could perhaps be called an effort to rethink the indigenous sources of Asian modernization in the context both of the historic tribute framework and of interaction with the West. Among the East Asian and Southeast Asian relationships that formed around relations with China, the second half of the nineteenth century in Okinawa and Korea poses extremely important historical issues concerning the question of how to interpret the totality of these relationships. The expansion of Korea's trade with China and the growth of Russian influence in North and Northeast China and Korea,[36] Japan's encroachment from the South, the approach of the United States from the East, the Chinese maritime customs and the approach of England, France, and Germany from the West – all turned not just on bilateral relationships with Korea but on complex, multilateral relationships, some of them of long historical vintage, encompassing the entire East Asia region. This is what allows this period in East Asia to be called the era of negotiation.

Korea, under the opposition between the domestic currents of *sadae* and civilization (*kaehwa*), took as its fundamental negotiating stance a position between "equality" in relations with Europe and "semi-autonomy" in its relations with the Qing. In response, the countries of Europe tried to build relationships with Korea, while at the same time deeply involving themselves in negotiations between China and Korea. The United States negotiated the draft of its treaty with Korea with the Chinese Superintendent for Trade with the North, Li Hongzhang, and in the treaty of 1882 the US president even sent a letter to the king of Korea expressing the opinion that as China and Korea had a suzerain–vassal relationship that historically took precedence over treaty relationships, there would be no conflict with the new treaty.[37] England, as well, can be considered not to have diverged significantly from a policy of deepening trade relations with Korea in line with, and taking advantage of, the expansion of the maritime customs system to Korea. The European countries and the United States premised many of their actions, so to speak, on the existence of East Asian international relations with the historical Qing tributary relationships of East Asia at the center.

Japan's negotiating approach with China and Korea differed significantly from that which it took toward other, particularly Western, nations. In a word, rather than negotiation, borrowing a page from the Western colonial powers in their colonizing thrust into large parts of East Asia, Japan opted for open confrontation with both the Qing and Korea in an effort to break the pattern of Chinese suzerainty over Korea in order to bring Korea within the Japanese sphere. In the years 1872 to 1874 Japan severed its historical relationship premised on ties to Korea through Tsushima Island and pressed for Korean "independence" from the Qing, beginning with the 1876 Treaty of Kanghwa and continuing through the 1895 Treaty of Shimonoseki. The pattern of negotiation visible in this process was not predicated on historical East Asian international relations as encapsulated in the tributary-trade system that defined relations throughout the maritime region. From one perspective, Japan was even more aggressive in pursuit of bilateral treaty relations than were America or Europe. From the early Meiji times on, Japan precipitated sharp clashes in peripheral regions of the Qing Empire, including the Liuqiu (Ryukyu) Islands, Taiwan, and Korea. For example, the 1876 Kangwha Treaty left unresolved a problem that had occurred twice (in 1869 and 1875) when Korea refused to recognize the new Meiji government because of conflicts with earlier protocol: specifically, it rejected Japanese attempts to terminate diplomatic relations mediated through Tsushima. Viewed from the perspective of "negotiation," it can be said that Japan clearly tried to renegotiate the tributary relationship. Having failed in this, it abandoned negotiation altogether.

The first Article of the Treaty of Kanghwa stated that "Chosen (Korea) being an independent state enjoys the same sovereign rights as does Japan" (*Kyu kankoku joyaku isan gekan*). This constituted an attempt to separate Korea from its suzerain–vassal relation with the Qing on the basis of the principle of equality between nations. At the same time, however, when Japan tried to approach the Qing to secure the special privileges won through the European and American treaties and extended to others through most-favored-nation clauses, the contradictions between the two became clear. When the Qing sharply pointed this out, Japan not only ceased to participate in bilateral negotiations with China, but also faced the problem of choosing between the West and Asia.[38]

The result of the combination of Japan's impetuous negotiating strategy and successive military actions was the destabilization of East Asia. A serious re-examination is necessary of how Japan's pursuit of Westernization in state formation led it to violate core principles of the international order in East Asia. For example, following the collapse of Japanese treaty negotiations with the Qing over the Liuqiu (Ryukyu) Islands in the years 1886 to 1888, Japan abandoned negotiation in favor of "direct action." The Sino-Japanese War of 1894–5 marked the end of the era of negotiation in East Asia and became a landmark in Japan's military advance over the next half century.

Although the Chinese world-order conception and the nation-state conception originally differed, in the second half of the nineteenth century, through the intersection between *Zhonghua*, the conception of China as a cultural center, and *Zhongguo* or China as a modern state, Asian nationalism came to take on new forms. Historically, Asian nationalism can be seen as springing from the criticism directed toward Chinese imperial prerogative encapsulated in the tributary-trade system by various countries that shared the concept of suzerainty associated with *Zhonghua*.

By the end of the Qing, many countries on the periphery sought to reduce the grip if not break free entirely of Chinese suzerainty by actively incorporating the West. At that point treaty negotiations took on great importance. For the Qing, facing superior Western power at a time of internal decline, treaty relations always remained subordinated to historic principles of the Chinese world order associated with suzerainty and the tribute-trade order.

Notes

1 R.D. Hill, Norman G. Owen and E.V. Roberts (eds), *Fishing in Troubled Waters: Proceedings of an Academic Conference on Territorial Claims in the South China Sea*, Centre of Asian Studies, Hong Kong: University of Hong Kong Press, 1991; Dalchoong Kim, Choon-ho Park, Seo-Hang Lee and Jin-Hyun Paik (eds), *UN Convention on the Law of the Sea and East Asia*, Seoul: Institute of East and West Studies, Yonsei University, 1996; Frederic Lasserre, *Le Dragon et la mer*, Montreal: Harmattan, 1996; Mark J. Valencia, Jon M. Van Dyke, and Noel A. Ludwig, *Sharing the Resources of the South China Sea*, Honolulu: University of Hawai'i Press, 1997; Eric Denece, *Geostratégie de la Mer de chine méridionale*, Paris: L'Harmattan, 1999; Lee Lai To, *China and the South China Sea Dialogue*, London: Praeger, 1999; Hans J. Buchholz, *Law of the Sea Zones in the Pacific Ocean*, Singapore: ISEAS, 1987.

2 Takeshi Hamashita, "The Intra-regional System in East Asia in Modern Times," in Peter J. Katzenstein and Takashi Shiraishi (eds), *Network Power: Japan and Asia*, Ithaca, NY: Cornell University Press, 1997: C.R. Boxer, *Dutch Merchants and Mariners in Asia, 1602–1795*, London: Variorum Reprints, 1988: Dianne Lewis, *Jan Compagnie in the Straits of Malacca, 1641–1795*, Athens, OH: Ohio University Press, 1995.

3 David E. Sopher, *The Sea Nomads: A Study of the Maritime Boat People of Southeast Asia*, National Museum, 1977; James Francis Warren, *The Sulu Zone 1768–1898*, Singapore: Singapore University Press, 1981; Ng Chin-Keong, *Trade and Society: The Amoy Network on the China Coast 1683–1735*, Singapore: Singapore University Press, 1983; Dian H. Murray, *Pirates of the South China Coast 1790–1810*, Stanford, CA: Stanford University Press, 1987; Jacques Dars "La marine Chinoise du X siècle au XIV siècle," *Economica*, 1992; Jennifer Wayne Cushman, *Fields from the Sea: Chinese Junk Trade with Siam during the Late Eighteenth and Early Nineteenth Centuries*, Studies on Southeast Asia, Ithaca, NY: Cornell University Press, 1993; Tony Wells, *Shipwrecks and Sunken Treasure in Southeast Asia*, Singapore: Times Editions, 1995; Yoneo Ishii (ed.), *The Junk Trade from Southeast Asia: Translation from the Tosen Fusetsu-gaki, 1674–1723*, Singapore: Institute of Southeast Asian Studies, 1998.

4 Atsushi Kobata and Mitsugu Matsuda, *Ryukyuan Relations with Korea and South Sea Countries: An Annotated Translation of Documents in the Rekidai Hoan*, Kyoto: Kawakita Printing Co., 1969; Gregory Smits, *Visions of Ryukyu: Identity and Ideology in Early Modern Thought and Politics*, Honolulu: University of Hawai'i Press, 1999.

5 *Lidai Baoan*, Taipei: Guoli Taiwan daxue, fifteen volumes, 1972.

6 Sarasin Viraphol, *Tribute and Profit: Sino-Siamese Trade, 1652–1853*, Cambridge, MA, 1977.

7 David Bulbeck, Anthony Reid, Lay Cheng Tan, and Yiqi Wu (eds), *Southeast Asian Exports since the 14th Century: Cloves, Pepper, Coffee, and Sugar*, Singapore: ISEAS, 1998.

8 Banno Masataka, *Kindai Chugoku seiji gaiko shi*, Tokyo: Tokyo daigaku shuppankai, 1973.

9 Here we find the real historical context of the so-called "Opium War," which has hitherto been viewed as a clash between West and East. Within the framework put forward here, it should be seen as a clash between North and South China with the stakes centered on the expanding rice trade between Southeast Asia and South China, a trade in which western merchants also were deeply involved. See *Lidai Baoan*, second series, vol. 170; James M. Polachek, *The Inner Opium War*, Cambridge, MA: Harvard University Press, 1992.

10 Furuta Kazuko's "Shanhai nettowaku no naka no Kobe," in *Nenpo kindai Nihon kenkyu* 14, Yamakawa shuppan, 1992, discusses East Asia in the mid-nineteenth century, as does Kose Hajime's "Jukyu seiki matsu Chugoku kaikojo kan ryutsu no kozo," in *Shakai keizai shingaku* vol. 54, no. 5 (1989).

11 Hamashita Takeshi, *Chugoku kindai keizai shi kenkyu*, Kyuko shoin, 1989.

12 Ma Jianzhong, one of the negotiators dispatched by the Qing, while on the one hand insisting that Korea was a vassal state, actively sought the conclusion of treaties with foreign nations, taking the position that treaties "harmed neither affairs of state nor the conditions of the people." Ma Jianzhong, *Shinkezhi zhixing*, vol. 4.

13 Li Hongzhang, "Yi Qiaoxian tongshang zhangcheng," in *Yi shuhan gao*, vol. 13.

14 Kyu Kanmatsu joyaku isan gekan, *Kokkai toshokan rippo chosa kyoku*, 1965.

15 Li Hongzhang, "Qiaoxian shijiang Yu Yungzhong jielue," in *Yi shuhan gao*, vol. 13.

16 Zhongyang yanjiuyuan jindaishi yanjiuso (ed.), *Qingji Zhong-Ri-Han guanxi shiliao*, Taibei, 1972, pp. 1052–3.

17 Li Hongzhang, "Yi Chaoxian tongshang zhangcheng," in *Yi shuhan gao*, vol. 13.

18 *Qingji Zhong-Ri-Han guanxi shiliao*, pp. 1114–17.

19 Ibid., pp. 1118–19.

20 Kyu Kanmatsu joyaku isan gekan, *Kokkai toshokan rippo chosa kyoku*, 1965.

21 In 1884, Russia concluded a Treaty of Friendship and Commerce, trade regulations, and a tariff agreement with Korea, thus opening up direct negotiations between the two nations. Furthermore, in 1888 the Regulations for the Frontier Trade on the River Tumen were concluded, and Kyonghung near the border was made an open city. Also, in 1896, military training officers were employed by Korea.

22 Kagotani Naoto, "Ajia kara no 'shogeki' to Nihon no kindai," in *Nihon shi kenkyu*, vol. 344 (1991).

23 *Qingji Zhong-Ri-Han guanxi shiliao*, p. 1150.

24 Ibid., p. 1224.

25 Tashiro Kazui, *Kindai Nit-Cho tsuko boeki shi no kenkyu*, Sobunsha, 1981.

26 *Hisho ruisan kanko kai, Hisho ruisan Chosen kosho shiryo gekan, 1936*; Yang Chao-ch'iao ch'u-pan kung-szu, 1991.

27 *Qingji Zhong-Ri-Han guanxi shiliao*, pp. 1204–5.

28 Ibid., pp. 1213–15.

29 Reflecting these circumstances, the Korean maritime customs returns in the decennial report of the Chinese maritime customs include material for the three ports of Inchon, Pusan, and Wonsan from 1884 as an appendix; see *China, Imperial Maritime Customs, Decennial Report 1882–1891*, Shanghai, 1893.

30 Li Hongzhang, *Yi shuhan gao*, vol. 19.

31 See Ko Pyong-ik, "Choson haegwan kwa Ch'ongguk haegwan kwa ui kwan'gye" (*Tonga munhwa* number 4) and Pu Chong'ae, "Choson heagwan ui ch'ongsol kyongwi" (*Han'guk saron*, vol. 1, 1973).

32 Li Hongzhang, *Yi shuhan gao*, vol. 19.

33 Ibid.

34 "Chaoxian haiguan zhangcheng ji shuize," in *Qingji Zhong-Ri-Han guanxi shiliao*, pp. 1270–87.

35 Table 1.1 shows the expansion of Sino-Korean trade from 1883 through 1910. In Sino-Korean trade there was a fundamental export surplus from China. Comparing China and Japan in Korean trade, while Japan dominated exports, China accounted for 20–45 percent of imports; Yang Zhaochuan and Sun Yumei, *Chaoxian huaqiao shi*, Zhongguo huaqiao chuban gongsi 1991, pp. 140–1.

36 Concerning Russia, see Forestry Bureau, Agriculture and Commerce Ministry, Kankoku shi (1906) and Sasaki Yo, trans. and ed., *Jukyu seiki matsu ni okeru Roshia to Chugoku*, Tokyo: Gaikokugo daigaku Ajia-Afurika gengo bunka kenkyujo, 1993.

37 Okudaira Takehiko, *Chosen kaikoku kosho shimatsu*. Toko shoin, 1969; Yi Pu, "Shufeldt 1880 nyon ui Cho-Mi kyosop." On the occasion of the signing in May 1882 of the United States–Korea Treaty of Amity and Commerce the letter addressed to the king of Korea by the president of the United States makes clear that Korea was a vassal nation of China and states that the United States would not interfere with the relationship with China. This appears to imply a restrictive treatment of the Korean–American treaty. *Kyu kanmatsu joyaku isan gekan, Kokkai toshokan rippo chosa kyoku,* 1965.

38 Kasuya Ken'ichi, "Kindaiteki gaiko taisei no soshutsu – Chosen no baai o chushin ni," in Arano Yasunori, Ishii Masatoshi, and Murai Shosuke (eds), *Ajia no naka no Nihon shi II: Gaiko to senso,* Tokyo: Daigaku shuppankai, 1992.

Chapter 2

A frontier view of Chineseness

Peter C. Perdue

In this chapter, I offer a frontier perspective on East Asian development. By "frontier perspective," I mean a focus on political, cultural, and economic interactions on the edges of the major states of the East Asian region, where they border each other, and where they abut on other regions of the globe. I have argued that East Asian frontiers, like regions or states, have common features that deserve comparative analysis (Perdue, forthcoming b). This view resolves some of the paradoxes of nationalist historiography, and complements the regionalist perspectives in this volume.

The other writers in this volume focus almost exclusively on China's maritime frontiers, but their perspective needs to be complemented by a discussion of the continental frontiers like the northwest. Often what they deem special characteristics of China's maritime region are common to all her frontier regions. Nomads on the "grassland sea" and caravan traders on the Silk Route could play the same role as maritime traders and pirates. The frontier encouraged people with remarkably diverse religions, languages, and customs to live together, as each found their own particular economic niche.

A frontier perspective complements an analysis based primarily on the impact of foreign trade, by stressing the equal importance of military and geopolitical considerations. At least up until the end of the eighteenth century, imperial China's policies and institutions generally put more emphasis on security and commerce in the northwest than in the south and southeast. The Han and Tang dynasties directed most of their commercial and military resources toward Central Asia. Even the officials of the Southern Song (1127–1279 CE), who developed southern coastal and overseas trade most extensively, still had to put most of the state's budget into warding off threats of invasion from the north. The great nineteenth-century shift in China's global position meant not only a change in power and trade balances, but a large geographical reorientation of imperial attention to the south and the coastal regions. The Qing officials faced something like the Southern Song situation while still maintaining a large continental empire: they profited from southern coastal trade, but had to maintain defenses on their expanded land frontiers. Strategic decisions changed trade flows, just as commercial opportunities influenced military and diplomatic relations. Regional perspectives on China should include attention to the connections between military and commercial interests on both frontiers. Giovanni Arrighi has argued that inter-state competition (military and economic), combined with the concentration of capitalist power, propelled the expansion of the capitalist world-economy over the globe (Arrighi 1994: 13; Arrighi et al., this volume). China's empire did not conquer the globe, but it also combined military and commercial power effectively to expand its territory in the eighteenth century. On China's frontiers, where the nexus of coercion and capital is particularly clear, we can find useful information about the processes that distinguish China's imperial experience from that of the West.

Nationalism and its discontents

Viewing China from the frontier helps to highlight problems with the nationalist historiography of China still predominant among many Chinese and international scholars. Where nationalists distinguish China sharply from the rest of the world, we look for similarities and interactions with other societies; where nationalists stress fixed cultural essences, we find productive hybrids and constructed traditions; where nationalists insist on China's one-sided victimization, we find complex relationships including both oppression and collaboration.

The nationalist approach stresses China's differences from the rest of the world: its vast size and population, and its long continuous recorded history, epitomized in the Chinese phrase dida, renduo, lishichang (large country, many people, long history). It focuses on how the sharp conflict between Western colonialism and a victimized China produced increasingly radical responses in the twentieth century. Ultimately, in this account, the Communist Party put into practice the anti-traditionalism of the May 4th movement, discarding the backward imperial past and totalistically embracing scientific modernity and revolutionary politics.

Many scholars are now well aware of the deficiences of this conventional view. By drawing a sharp line between "tradition" and "modernity," and between China and other nations, it artificially fixes the essence of complex cultural ensembles. A great deal of research has demonstrated the intellectual, social, and cultural continuity between the Qing and twentieth-century China, and many Qing features have re-emerged in reform China of the 1980s and 1990s. Recognition of China's active participation in the contemporary world casts doubt on the utter uniqueness of her civilization. Yet until very recently, much of our interpretation of Qing history was still dominated by concepts of a distinctive, continuous

Chinese civilization, relatively unaffected by the outside world until the late nineteenth century. If we look at China's frontiers, however, we constantly find interactions across the borders between those within and those beyond imperial boundaries. These interactions brought new elements to Chinese society that reshaped her core values. Traditions never stood still.

There is no one true description of China, of course, but today, many people are more likely to look for signs of dynamic evolution and creative mixing than to oppose two static entities of "tradition" and "modernity." Chinese nationalist historiography ironically shares with Western Orientalism the belief that a backward, complacent society was unable to respond to Western impact in the eighteenth and nineteenth centuries, even though it differs in blaming Western imperialism primarily for perpetuating a bankrupt regime.

Orthodox Marxist theory threatened to undercut this focus on China's uniqueness, by placing China in a universal pattern of six stages of social evolution. But many of the comparative possibilities opened up by the Marxist belief in universal stages were closed off by creating another version of dynastic history. Most Chinese Marxist historians defined the "feudal" stage as an essentially unchanging, self-sufficient economic and social structure lasting from the Qin unification in the third century BC through the end of the Qing in AD 1911. China's imperial "feudalism" turned out to be much longer than that of any other agrarian empire. Chinese historians debated intensively the timing and extent of "sprouts of capitalism" within the feudal structure, but they never referred to the possibility of "sprouts" in other non-European empires. Nearly all of them concluded that China, unlike Europe, never broke through to a new capitalist stage before 1911. Classifying China as "semi-colonial" in the nineteenth century once again set her off from the vast majority of the non-European world that was conquered by European imperialism.

The other Marxist option for China, that of the Asiatic Mode of Production, one endorsed by Marx himself, did place China alongside other non-European empires. Proponents of the Asiatic Mode aimed to break out of the linear straitjacket imposed by Stalin on orthodox Marxists, so as to assert variant routes to socialism and appropriate political strategies to realize it. But since the Asiatic Mode rested on a basic assumption of Asian stagnation, it was roundly rejected by nearly all Chinese analysts (Fogel 1988). In the view of most Marxist analysts, China's long bureaucratic history put her in a category all by herself.

Both Marxist and non-Marxist interpretations echoed the most common tropes of nationalism: victimization, teleology, and the invention of tradition. *Victimization,* the most emotionally charged trope, insisted on the horrors of massacres, poverty, famine, and invasion in the late nineteenth century, nationalists stressed the horrors of the Yangzhou massacre of 1645; the recent focus on the Nanking massacre is the most obvious recent example. *Teleology* interpreted history as moving inevitably toward the unification of people and state. Western national historians often invoked divine will; in the nineteenth century, Social Darwinism served a comparable goal in China by showing that irresistible impersonal forces, verified by modern science, inescapably supported victorious states. Chinese Marxists drew heavily on these evolutionary models to assert the inevitable victory of the revolutionary forces in class struggle. By *inventing traditions*, nationalist writers drew selectively on past practices to weave a common fabric for a people. Rejecting both Qing and Western clothing in favor of "native" dress, like the newly manufactured "Sun Yat-sen" suit, as part of broader campaigns to buy "national products" (*guohuo*), nationalists unified the consuming public and promoted Chinese business (Gerth 1999). Cutting the queue, as a symbol of Manchu oppression, and invoking myths of a unified Han resistance to barbarian oppressors, nationalists tore elements of China's past out of context in the service of mass mobilization.

But the very features of China that defined its uniqueness (*dida, renduo, lishichang*) created unresolvable paradoxes for a unified nationalist ideology. The Chinese had a surfeit of oppressors. Targets of the victimization charge included Manchu rulers, Western and Japanese imperialists, landlords and wealthy bourgeois classes. Yet each group was partly foreign and partly familiar. The Manchus occupied an especially puzzling and ambiguous position. Were they "Central Asian" barbarians, like the Mongols, long a hostile threat on China's northern frontiers, or were they assimilated ("cooked") barbarians, more like the native peoples of the Southwest and Taiwan, who voluntarily recognized China's superiority and even came to master important elements of the high culture. Calling the Manchus utterly alien ignored substantial evidence of their adaptation to Han Chinese ways over the course of the Qing dynasty. The Manchus were, in fact, frontier peoples on the edge of the Ming empire who creatively mixed agrarian and pastoral modes to create a new imperial synthesis. Many Han, especially those who served as "Chinese martial" bannermen (*Hanjun*), joined them. Mongols joined the Manchus also as key allies, with important military functions and kinship connections to the ruling elite. A frontier view replaces nationalist dualities with recognition of this hybrid character of the ruling elite.

The teleology of the nationalist narrative also ran into paradoxes, because of China's long and varied history. The vulgar Marxist model of clear sequential stages of slavery, feudalism, and capitalism fit very awkwardly with the period of great bureaucratic empires from Qin to Qing. Evidence of substantial dynamic commercial growth in Ming-Qing China makes it hard to identify specific features unique to Europe that define pre-industrial capitalism (Frank 1998; Pomeranz 2000; Wong 1997; Arrighi, *et al.*, this volume). The economic narrative of modern China can no longer trace a single unilinear path from self-sufficient rural economy to integrated industrialism; there appear to be early spurts, declines, and multiple pathways in both Europe and China. The center cannot hold together a single story line.

Similar paradoxes faced the issue of the transition from empire to nation. If the current territorial claims of the People's Republic resemble very closely the boundaries achieved by the Qing rulers around 1800, and China today includes within its borders fifty-six nationalities, contemporary China's ruling ideology and practice are as much imperial as national in content. It is hardly surprising, then, that uncanny echoes of Qing imperial rhetoric still ring in governmental prose. The controversies over the nomination of the Panchen Lama in 1995 and the escape of the Karmapa Lama in 2001, for example, are only the latest in a long line of events that reveal striking analogies to Qing efforts to intervene in Tibet. Once again, on the frontiers of the Qing and People's Republic, claims to incorporate clearly defined "nationalities" under a multinational nation-state have met great resistance.

Has the empire really become a nation at all? For Lucian Pye, China has only a "relatively inchoate and incoherent form of nationalism," because it is a "civilization pretending to be a nation-state," but we can be more historically specific (Pye 1993). The inadequacies of Chinese nationalist ideology derive from its inheritance of the claims of the Qing imperial rulers, without their legitimating appeal to a universal cosmology. Twentieth-century architects of a Chinese nation did not look to more Han-centered models of Chinese territory and polity, like the Song or Ming dynasties. Instead, nearly all of them, whether Guomindang, Communist, or independent intellectuals, took for granted that the boundaries and peoples included in the maximal period of the Qing should belong to the nation.The construction of the Han as a distinct "nationality" (*minzu*) in the late nineteenth century merged distinctive groups like the Cantonese, Hakka, Taiwanese, and Hunanese into a seamless whole, and the promotion of China as a "multi-nationality nation-state" (*duo minzu guojia*) in the twentieth century incorporated non-Han peoples under a single national ideal. Both ideologies tried to resolve the conflicting claims of empire and nation, legacies of the Qing's frontier expansion, but they could not remove all contradictions.

The contrasting perspectives of Zhang Binglin and Liang Qichao in the first decade of the twentieth century highlighted this contradiction clearly. Zhang, supporting a strictly racial construction of nationality, argued that the non-Han peoples could never be assimilated. He even once admitted that Muslims might hate the Chinese as much as Chinese hated the Manchus. Although he did not support independence for Muslims under Chinese rule, he did propose that China and Xinjiang could form an "alliance" against Russia if it suited Muslim interests. If not, he implied,

Muslims in Xinjiang could go their way separately from the Chinese state (Gasster 1969: 206).

Liang Qichao insisted on maintaining the Qing imperial territories, while transforming the empire and its peoples into citizens of a constitutional monarchy. For him, "protecting the race (*baozhong*)" was "not as critical as protecting the nation (baoguo)" (Shimada 1990: 105). Sun Yat-sen after 1905 converted from racialism to Liang's civic monarchy, because he could not allow the division of Chinese territory by claims for autonomy from separatists. The problem for Sun Yat-sen was that "the word 'Han' failed to accommodate the variety of ethnic communities now thought to comprise the 'race'." He constructed a "philosophically empty" vision of five nationalities unified under Han dominance so as to maintain China's claim to the frontier territories (Fitzgerald 1996: 122; cf. Crossley 1999a: 345, 351).

Contrary to many theorists of nationalism, East Asians have not had "homogeneous" societies that made it easier for them to develop nationalist ideologies than societies with more fractured histories.[1] Nationalist activists claimed that their peoples were a single entity, but the apparent "homogeneity" of Korea, Japan, or Vietnam, for example, is a product of successful myth creation, not social practice. Tokugawa Japanese, divided among over two hundred autonomous domains, and separated by rigid status barriers, hardly saw themselves as one people (Morris-Suzuki 1998). China's history, fractured among multifarious regional identities and divergent historical trajectories, did not form a smooth foundation for consistent nationalist ideology either.

The "invention of tradition" approach examines how nationalists deploy selected elements from a people's experience to create myths of unity. For example, the cutting of the queue was the most conspicuous, and nearly irreversible, mark of rejection of the Manchu regime. Since, during the Qing, the queue really did represent a conspicuous bodily marker imposed by a conquering elite, it served as an effective symbol of oppression. In the twentieth century, resurrecting accounts of the Yangzhou massacre of 1645 effectively demonstrated Manchu barbarity. At the same time, this revival created a myth of uniform Han resistance to Manchu conquest, belying the realities of negotiation, opportunism, and cooperation. Nearly all Han Chinese accepted the queue without protest, and Manchus were not the only troops who committed massacres. These invocations of selected elements of the past have often been more convincing to ordinary people than grand schemes of historical explanation. Hairstyles and clothing shape everyday life by altering the forms of the body. But we need to recognize that nationalists constructed not one single tradition, but many disparate elements for particular purposes. They did not necessarily form a coherent whole.

In sum, seeing China from a frontier perspective helps to replace the nationalist discourse with more productive metaphors. For victimization, we may substitute interaction and paradox: the mutual opportunism of the semi-colonial encounter. For teleology, substitute contingency. For invention of tradition, substitute the active construction of traditions in particular times, spaces, and social arenas.

Integrating China into world history: alternatives

Unlike the nationalist paradigm, several recent historical projects aim to connect China to the world by focusing on interactions of China with her neighbors, or by comparing China with other societies. A frontier perspective complements these new views. Joanna Waley-Cohen's survey, for example, argues that the Chinese have always been open to foreign influence; they have adopted institutions, religions, technology, and material culture from outsiders, and they have extended their influence outward (Waley-Cohen 1999). China's embrace of Buddhism, her eager adoption of mathematics and military technology from the Jesuits, and the incorporation of New World food crops, including chili peppers, into the Chinese diet, all demonstrate China's cultural openness. Trade and cultural interaction on China's borders brought these new elements into the interior. China has never been completely isolated nor essentially inward-looking. Her openness varies, to be sure, over time and by region and ethnic group, so that we cannot generalize about China as a whole. Xenophobia and the notion of Chinese resistance to external influence are products of particular situations, not inherent in Chinese tradition.

Two related approaches also highlight China's interaction with the East Asian region and the outside world. One is the "tributary system" of Hamashita Takeshi, the other is the "Southern model" promoted by a number of Hong Kong and Western scholars. (Hamashita 1990, 1994, 1999; Friedman 1995; cf. Lary 1996). Hamashita argues that long before the heyday of Western colonialism in Asia, East Asian inter-state relations were based on a "tribute trade system" with China at the center, oriented around ritual deference and presentation of gifts to the Chinese emperor in return for political legitimation and opportunities for trade. Just as foreign emissaries offered gifts in return for legitimation, so officials within the empire sent the emperor local products along with taxes and reports. Tribute relations were the underlying principle of a regional East Asian trading system that both linked Chinese localities to the center, and tied surrounding tributary states to the empire. John Fairbank outlined this concept in the 1950s, and his students developed it in the 1960s (Fairbank, 1968). Hamashita, however, does not separate ritualism from economic relations, but finds the two to be complementary. Also in contrast to Fairbank, Hamashita's research on nineteenth-century East Asia does not describe the destruction of an archaic tribute system by a Western system of equal states. Instead, East Asian states, especially China, Korea, Vietnam, and the Ryukyus, continued to conduct relations with each other by tributary norms, even as they also negotiated treaties with the West and with each other. He finds, in short, that China was not blindly clinging to obsolete notions of foreign relations in an age of "equal sovereign states." Rather, it was creatively modifying its inherited hierarchical principles to meet the challenge of *another* hierarchical system: one based on imperial domination. His chapter in this volume argues that Britain, the United States, and other Western powers sought to impose principles of free trade and equal diplomacy on Asia, but simultaneously recognized and upheld tributary relations in the China–Korea relationship.

I would note, however, that although major European powers, after the Peace of Westphalia in 1648, usually treated each other as having equal sovereign authority (with flagrant exceptions, like the elimination of the Polish state in the eighteenth century), they dealt with the non-Western world on different principles. As Europeans extended their reach into Asia, they created binary divisions between metropoles and colonies. Dutch control of Indonesia, followed by the British conquest of India in the eighteenth century, established strongly unbalanced power relations between the West and the East. By the nineteenth century, China no longer was an Enlightenment Utopia for Europeans; instead, it looked like another weak and backward Asian state. As James Hevia argues, the Chinese encounter with the British in 1793 was one of conflicting imperial modes, not equality vs. hierarchy (Hevia 1995). The Chinese tributary order was just as hierarchical, but more graduated than the European one. It was more sophisticated than the simple polarity of colonizer and colonized, as it contained many participants arranged conceptually in different degrees of distance from the center.

Hamashita explains Japan's actions in the late nineteenth century as a failed effort to displace China and put herself at the apex of the regional trading system. Elaborating on Hamashita's concept, Arrighi, Hui, Hung and Selden find links between modern inter-state relationships and the pre-nineteenth-century tributary system. Despite vast changes in economic and military technology, they argue that region formation without institutionalization was consistent with the historic legacy of maritime Asia (Arrighi *et al.*, this volume). Even though there can be no return to Sinocentric or Japan-centered dominance, the tributary system's legacy offers a model of a viable regional system quite distinct from that of the European Union.

These arguments reorient discussions of East Asian commercial relations in a more global and historical perspective. Other historians, rejecting a narrow focus on state-to-state diplomacy, have likewise made their field more inclusive by changing "diplomatic history" to "international history." This approach tries to integrate ritual, diplomatic, and political relationships at both the governmental and non-governmental levels. Like them, Hamashita looks at multiple interactions within East Asia. For example, instead of looking only at Western transmission to the East through treaty ports, he shows that trade between coastal treaty ports greatly exceeded each port's trade with Western powers, just as in contemporary East Asia. Instead of discussing Asia's "forced" opening from the "impact of the West," he views Asia "from a perspective that focuses on internal changes in the East Asian region." Thus he restores agency to Asian people, networks, and institutions (Hamashita, Chapter 1, this volume). Chinese merchants could take advantage of the treaty port system to extend their networks into the rest of Asia. Overseas and domestic Chinese played a critical role in forging links between different countries and between the newly arrived Westerners and China itself. Korea, the Ryukyu Islands, and Taiwan also acted as hinges between the representatives of colonial powers and the Chinese mainland.

Ultimately, it was Japan, not the Westerners, that rejected this hybrid treaty–tribute order, when it intervened to force Korea, Okinawa, and Taiwan exclusively into its sphere as prefectures and colonies and out of their accustomed dual roles. In this perspective, the main dynamics of change come from within East Asia; the Western impact is mediated by interactions of East Asian states with each other. Asians gain much more agency than the victimization, modernization, or teleological nationalist perspectives allowed them, and the East Asian region as a whole acts as an autonomous force.

Hamashita's perspective, however, still presumes that a political center in Beijing, in the end, made decisions about the direction of trade and diplomacy. Although Beijing could not directly determine all trade flows, his focus on tributary missions and diplomacy demonstrates the significant role of the court in influencing international trade. The "Hong Kong" or "Southern-centered" interpretation of the dynamics of Chinese history, also sees foreign trade as a powerful dynamic in China's development, at least from the Song dynasty to the present, but the main trade links are created by South coast private traders with Southeast Asia (Friedman 1995; Mazumdar 1998; Ngo 1999; Perdue 2000a; Arrighi et al., this volume). As the East Asia World System developed a commercially oriented society centered in Jiangnan and South China, merchants promoted trade within China and links to European and American trade routes in cooperation with local officials. Under this system, until the end of the eighteenth century, China achieved levels of living standards and commercialization approximately equal to those of early modern Europe (Wong 1997; Pomeranz 2000). In the view of some of these scholars, gains from colonialism, coinciding with the collapse of the Chinese empire, enabled European dominance. In the twentieth century Japan attempted to create its own East Asian world system, with itself as hegemon, but now much of the old system has been re-established, albeit with China and Japan as rival power centers. New features mark the late twentieth century, particularly the role of the USA as a regional military hegemon, and the greatly expanded role of transnational capital flows dominated by overseas Chinese, but many of the structural elements parallel the long-standing structures that have lasted since the year 1200. These include the economic predominance of the central and southern coasts, the key role of overseas Chinese and Hong Kong investment, and the close connections of local official interests in the south and the promotion of foreign trade.

I heartily endorse the efforts of these writers to look beyond national boundaries and to highlight the role of trading relationships, but I would caution against an exclusive focus on foreign trade as the engine of inter-state relations or economic development. Trade was only one of several factors driving the system as a whole. Military-geopolitical considerations, including diplomacy, power, and perception of outsiders, constantly shaped the scope of commercial networks. Sometimes the two imperatives conflicted. For example, the court often shut down official trade to put pressure on its foreign rivals, while merchants engaged in smuggling to preserve their profits. On the other hand, trade and security often supported each other. If conquest and openness generated wealth, wealth supported conquest. As states chose to direct their resources in particular directions, toward specific allies and enemies, these strategic choices strongly influenced trade flows.

In Charles Tilly's terms, the "marriage of Capital and Coercion" set the boundaries within which trading networks developed (Tilly 1990). Military activity has always been particularly prominent in the history of China's north and northwest frontier, because of the constant presence of nomadic horsemen who raided the borders and sometimes conquered the capital. In the nineteenth century military defense also became a key factor in inter-state and inter-regional relations on the Southeast and Northeast coasts. Wei Yuan, most famous in Western scholarship for recognizing the importance of coastal defense, in fact derived much of his strategic thinking from examining Qing military expansion in the northwest. In his Shengwuji (Account of Sacred Military Victories), he drew on the history of Qing expansion to derive lessons for responding to the Western incursions on the south coast (cf. Leonard 1984).

Viewing China from the frontier

Combining these elements – inclusion of military with trade and ritual diplomacy, and a regional focus – leads me to sketch a frontier perspective on China in the world. I use "frontier" here as a relational concept, not necessarily as a reference to a fixed geographical space.

We can analyze Imperial China profitably by looking at the relationship between two contrasting usages of "frontier," meaning either a zone or a linear border. The first usage is predominantly American; the second mainly Western European (Standen and Power 1998; Perdue forthcoming b). Frederick Jackson Turner defined the American frontier as a zone of transition between civilization and wilderness, focusing on the pioneers who pushed its boundaries outward as they integrated these undeveloped areas with the metropole. Although American historians now reject the assumptions of Anglo-Saxon racial superiority underlying Turner's concept, they have continued his analysis of incorporation. William Cronon, for example, in his study of Chicago entitled *Nature's Metropolis*, analyzed how the economic integration of the American Far West directed its agricultural commodities to Eastern consumption markets. While rejecting Turner's political and cultural biases, he retained Turner's process of progressive expansion. In opposition, American regionalists point out that areas beyond the Anglo-European settlement frontier did not contain wilderness or primitive barbarism, but distinctive cultures, each with dense social systems and historical memories, which cohabited, mixed and resisted incorporation into the center. For China, we can likewise note the imperial projects that promoted expansion of the civilized, settled realm against "barbarian" pastoralists on the northwest frontier, or mobile cultivators in the hills of the south. Regionalist perspectives stress the distinctive characteristics of these peoples and their drives to maintain autonomy against imperial pressure (Limerick 1987; Cronon 1991; White 1991a, 1991b; Faragher 1993; on China, cf. Giersch 1998; Perdue 2000b).

European stories of the frontier move in almost exactly the opposite direction, from inclusion to exclusion (Febvre 1973). Western European definitions begin with the frontier as a line, dividing two separate entities. This is the original meaning of the term "frontière" in French, closer to the modern word "border" than to "frontier zone." Out of the multiple sovereignties of the medieval period, when frontiers were the site of battle-fields, castles, and garrisons, new states in the early modern age developed fixed, negotiated boundaries. As they created more uniform internal structures, they drew sharper lines to divide them from their neighbors. In Western Europe frontier creation moved away from incorporation within a large empire toward division by borders in the era of absolutist states.

Many historians and political scientists single out the conclusion of the Thirty Years War in 1648 at the Peace of Westphalia as the origin of the "idea of sovereignty." In their view, this treaty marked a decisive turn toward recognizing the legitimacy of fixed state boundaries and the principle of non-interference in each state's internal affairs.[2] After the eighteenth century, nationalists asserted that geography had fixed "natural frontiers" for their states. Neighboring nations, like France and Germany, however, who disagreed on where the "natural" border ran, went to war with each other repeatedly. Only in the twentieth century did the damaging concept of "natural frontiers" begin to break down. The career of "frontier" as a dividing line is only now beginning to decline, as the European Union expands sovereignty across national borders.

The different connotations of the American and European usage of "frontier" – one as zone and one as border – reflect two different processes of state formation and territorial definition. Each, however, focuses primarily on the frontier as an element in the formation of new states and nations. China from the eighteenth to twentieth centuries, as an empire that first expanded, and then became a nation-state with nearly the same borders, combined both processes of incorporation and division. Incorporation meant attaching large territories of unprecedented size to the core administrative structure (the *junxian* system) by creating new forms of administration and economic exchange. Division meant drawing lines to prevent competing links of these territories across the newly defined borders, and defining their peoples as homogeneous entities. It also meant restricting their mobility and suppressing resistance.

All of China's frontiers have these dual characteristics, but the northwest region displays them most clearly. As the empire expanded, it drew progressively larger regions into its own administrative hierarchies and economic networks, detaching them from rival linkages. By the end of the eighteenth century, Xinjiang and Mongolia were inextricably linked to the imperial core by military and civilian administrative structures, and by flows of goods between the lower Yangtze valley and the Central Asian frontiers. At the same time, treaties, maps, and official discourse marked off the Kazakhs and Russians as outside the boundaries of the empire. Their trade was carefully supervised at guarded border crossings. The ambiguous "Western regions" were now delineated as fixed territories; they had "come onto the registers" (*ru bantu*). The culmination of this process was the designation of Xinjiang as a province in 1884 (Millward 1999).

China, of course, has many frontiers. On the largest scale, the imperial level, viewed from eighteenth-century Beijing, we may distinguish five inland and two maritime frontier regions, each with special characteristics: Manchuria, Mongolia, Xinjiang, Tibet, and Southwest China, plus the northeast and south-southeast coastal zones. On smaller scales, peripheries of macro-regions, frequently demarcated by mountains, lakes, or rivers, also display frontier characteristics. For simplicity, I will only discuss here the northwest and south-southeast frontiers. Many features of the maritime frontiers resemble those of China's interior. In both regions, diverse peoples traded with each other in specific economic niches, linking sites (oases, garrisons, or treaty ports) across several state boundaries. The coastal zone has its counterpart in the borderland between settled agriculture and the steppe. Chinese migrants moved to both frontiers and mixed with other peoples there: Arabs in coastal towns, Filipinos and Europeans in Manila, Mongols, Turkic and Tibetan peoples in the northwest. Much of Hamashita's discussion refers to common features of frontier regions, not exclusively maritime ones.

We can draw useful analogies between the structure of interactions on each of these frontiers. They share the characteristics of high costs of access from the center causing reduced central state control, greater autonomy for merchants, mobile peasantries, greater plurality of ethnic and religious identification (called "heterodox" by the center), and multiple cross-cutting networks of interaction, instead of a simple vertical link of one subject to one lord. Among these frontiers, the Northwest was always the most important one to Chinese rulers of the Ming and Qing, because they saw the greatest military threat to their rule there. As the main focus of imperial attention, it provided an arena of experimentation that often served as the model for other places. For example, the Canton trade system of regulated trade was first developed on the Russian border by the Qing in 1727, then extended to the Zunghars and Kazakhs in the mid-eighteenth century, and only then applied in the South. The first treaty recognizing extraterritoriality was negotiated with the ruler of Kokand, an oasis in the Ferghana valley, 200 km west of the Xinjiang border, in 1835. This agreement provided for Kokand to station political and commercial representatives in Xinjiang, to levy customs duties there on imports by foreigners. As Joseph Fletcher notes, "this was China's first 'unequal treaty,' and it paved the way in Peking for the later unequal treaties with the West" (1978: 378). This recent interest among historians in the study of frontiers represents a cycle of eternal return in Qing studies. An earlier generation of predominantly German and Russian scholarship on the Central Asian connections of Chinese rulers, represented in English, for example, by the early work of Franz Michael, is still carried on in Japan today. These scholars practiced meticulous philological analysis of texts in many languages to analyze each of the religions and cultures of Central Asia in depth. Classical Chinese civilization then appeared as only one among many traditions active in the region. The non-Chinese texts they studied supported the important thesis that Mongols, Tibetans, Turkic peoples, etc. each had their own distinctive, coherent values rooted in sacred texts.[3] Owen Lattimore picked up much of his outlook from this work, along with his personal experiences travelling across the Chinese frontier.

In the postwar US, by contrast, John Fairbank and most of his students focused on the political and intellectual response to the West, the structure of central imperial institutions, and local control in the interior. G. William Skinner's paradigm of macroregional analysis led many to focus on local socio-economic systems as bounded units. Now many recent works have either returned to the center, or looked at the peripheries, or revamped the closed Skinnerian models to include the impact of outside forces.

In China, the revival of interest in frontiers has a different lineage. Gu Jiegang, China's greatest twentieth-century historian, looked to the non-Han peoples of the Northwest in the 1930s to reinvigorate a decadent Han culture that he felt had grown impotent to resist Japanese and Western aggression. From the earliest times, he argued, Chinese civilization had been formed from a mixture of different cultures, in which those of the Northwest contributed the dynamic military elements that defended the core territories and established China's boundaries (Gu 1938a, 1938b; Schneider 1971; Lipman 1997). Gu's interests are carried on in China today by the Border Research Institute, where historians continue to explore the contributions of frontier peoples to China's national identity (Lü and Ma 1987).

But the new work, seen in important recent North American studies, takes a different angle of vision from its predecessors. First of all, the center now is a Manchu center. Pamela Crossley, Mark Elliott, and Evelyn Rawski have re-emphasized the importance of seeing the Qing state as controlled by a Manchu elite very conscious of its difference from the subject Han population, and constantly concerned to maintain that difference (Crossley 1990a, 1990b; Elliott 2000; Rawski 1996, 1998). Contrary to the dominant tradition of Chinese scholarship, the Manchus did not naturally assimilate to a "superior" majority Han culture. They maintained their distinctiveness, through the banners and imperial rituals, while at the same time they collaborated with Han officials to maintain legitimacy and ensure adequate tax collection. Even though they adopted the Chinese language and bureaucratic practices after settling down in China's major cities, they still maintained a consciousness of themselves as a separate ruling elite. Scholars may differ over exactly when and how the Manchus constructed their identity, but, Ho Ping-ti to the contrary notwithstanding, it is clear that they marked themselves off from the Han through the end of the Qing (Ho 1998; Rhoads 2000).

Second, the peripheries were of special concern to this ruling elite. Under the rubric of "Manchu colonialism," several scholars have examined the special characteristics of Qing rule in Mongolia, Xinjiang, and Tibet (di Cosmo 1998; Heuschert 1998; Millward 1998; Perdue 1998; Sperling 1998; Teng 1998; Waley-Cohen 1998). They suggest grounds for comparison of the Qing state to other colonial empires. Like the large agrarian empires of the Ottomans, Russia, or the Mughals, China faced problems with control, expansion, legitimacy, and revenue collection. Contrary to the nationalist narrative, it was not a unique victim of Western imperialism; or unique by virtue of its long-lasting bureaucratic and cultural tradition. China's distinctive characteristics are more like the "special features" of its current "socialist market economy": they are variations within a generic class of market economies, not a radically different type.

This new interest in frontier identities is found in much other historical writing as well. Many US historians have recently explored the borderlands of the American West, where European and indigenous, or Anglo and Hispanic cultures mixed together (Aron 1994; Adelman and Aron 1999). But this is not a peculiarly American obsession with multicultural interaction. The same issues have been investigated in Western Europe as well, and also in Japan. Hamashita Takeshi and Fuma Susumu have both focused on the Ryukyu Islands as a vital terrain for contacts between China, Japan, and Korea (Fuma 1999; Hamashita 1999). Such parallel trends indicate a global phenomenon. Words like hybridity, fluidity, and contingently constructed multiple identities are in the air everywhere.

How do these frontier perspectives complement other emerging critiques of nationalist history? I shall give a few examples below of new ways of thinking about China's military power, its commercial development, its economic history, and its state structures in a comparative framework. We now recognize that a network of constant interactions within East Asia persisted from the twelfth into the nineteenth and twentieth centuries. Seeing China from the northwest frontier, like the maritime perspectives, helps to insert China into world historical processes by moving away from the isolation of cultural essences. The frontier perspective incorporates both land and sea interactions, however, as variants of a single form, and it gives as much emphasis to the military power of the state and challenges to it as it does to trade, technology, production processes, and economic competition. In the north and northwest, China faced much more powerful and more sharply distinctive peoples than on other frontiers. Here it was very clear that the threat and use of force undergirded the trading-ritual order. The Qing could only seriously claim to be the uncontested central pole of a tribute system focused on Beijing after they had created military alliances with the Eastern Mongols, exterminated the rival Western Mongols, conquered Xinjiang, and secured formal suzerainty over Tibet. The expansion of the Qing into this region brought the Chinese into contact with new peoples in Central Eurasia. Administering each of them required new projects of intelligence gathering and cultural adjustment.

From this angle of vision, China looks comparable to other continental agrarian empires, in particular the "gunpowder empires" that rose in the sixteenth century in the wake of the Mongol empire's decline. The term "gunpowder empires" was applied by Marshall Hodgson to the three great Islamic empires: the Ottomans, the Safavids, and the Mughals, but it can also include the Qing and Muscovy/Russia. The term itself is somewhat misleading, since gunpowder *per se* was not really the critical element in their expansion. But all of these empires formed new, disciplined military forces and expanded rapidly across Central Eurasia from the sixteenth to eighteenth centuries. They originated in the steppe-frontier environment, and all of them faced acute crises on the frontier because of the unboundedness of the region. Nomads and mobile peasantries played crucial roles in providing military resources and in settling the conquered regions (Hodgson 1974; Bayly 1989; McNeill 1989).

Both military and economic mobilization played important roles in all these imperial expansions, but their relative weight varied. Looking at the balance of military and commercial power on both frontiers together helps to elucidate their commonalities and differences. On China's northwest land frontier, military forces led the way, followed by peasant settlers and officially sponsored merchants. Private traders supplied many of the garrison forces and settlers with goods from the interior after campaigns drove out the nomads. On the southeast coast, merchants usually led the way after the sixteenth century, without backing from Qing military forces, except for the conquest of Taiwan. Even though Qing forces did not protect merchants who went across the seas, however, they did provide for coastal defense, protecting the towns from which the merchants originated and where they maintained continual connections. Soldiers and merchants exchanged places in the driver's seat, but both rode the same vehicle.

Careful examination of the Northwest also helps to broaden our notions of the "tribute-trade" system (Fletcher 1968; di Cosmo 1998, 1999; Millward 1998). The claim that China followed enduring principles of tribute dividing the Middle Kingdom versus barbarian states, and lasting from "Tang through Qing" is true in a very broad sense, but it implies a static framework for foreign relations (Hamashita, Chapter 1, this volume). Hamashita's analysis in this volume and in other work focuses almost exclusively on the coastal tribute relationships, but for the court in Beijing, tributary relations with Inner Asia were even more salient, well into the nineteenth century. Qing rulers adapted the tributary framework to new situations. For example, in 1638, they created a distinctive new institution, the *Lifanyuan*, to manage the northwest peoples (Chia 1991; di Cosmo 1998). In fact, tribute trade was a very flexible form that allowed for many different kinds of political, commercial, and ritual relations, and the expansive Qing used it in a very different way from the defensive Ming. Relations with the Dutch, Russians, Kazakhs, Mongols, Koreans, Ryukyus, and later British, for example, all fit into the tribute system, but each had a separate political and commercial relationship to the Qing empire.

World system models that presume a stable structure over many centuries tend to ignore important regional and temporal variations in China's political relations with the outside world. We should not assume that there was one consistent, routinized form of tribute, and we should not confuse the ideals of ritual texts and imperial pronouncements with practice. What Chinese rulers wanted to believe was not necessarily what their neighbors actually thought (Fletcher 1968). Inner Asians exploited the rituals of tribute and trade for their own ends, without necessarily accepting Chinese pretensions of superiority. Some accepted their dependent position in return for political support; others had total autonomy, but pretended to obey the rituals for purely economic goals.

In fact, to put it starkly, a systematic form of tribute-trade relations could successfully enforce Chinese dominance only in the late eighteenth century. Before then, rival, equally powerful states and peoples challenged this hierarchical order. The Tang faced a major Tibetan empire which it could never defeat; the Sung could never claim to be the uncontested hegemon even in interior China; "tribute" was a very hollow shell masking huge protection payments to the northern dynasties. The Mongol rulers of the Yuan, who dealt with other Mongols across all of Eurasia, used the term "tribute" with a very different meaning from the Ming rulers, who never succeeded in subduing the Mongols of the northwest. Until they had exterminated the Zunghar Mongols and conquered Xinjiang in the mid-eighteenth century, the Qing also faced major rival states. This "system" was constantly under challenge, breaking down, being reconfigured and rebuilt. It was neither stable, fixed, nor uniform. In regard to some regions, like Korea, relations were fairly stable; elsewhere, particularly in the northwest, wide fluctuations occurred.

Rather than viewing tribute as a "system" or "cultural order," it is more useful to see the discourse of tribute and its associated ritual and economic practices as a particular kind of intercultural language, serving multiple purposes for its participants.[4] Like "pidgins," or trading languages in all multicultural contact zones, tribute discourse permitted extensive commercial exchange, masking the different self-conceptions of its participants with formal expressions, but allowing each, in different degrees, a measure of autonomy. Such flexible communication across cultural and disciplinary barriers is not in itself anti-modern; similar languages are even used in modern Big Science.[5]

As a vehicle for intercultural interaction, this language worked effectively to bring outsiders to the Central Kingdom, maintain diplomatic relations, and offer chances for profit to both sides. As it spread its influence beyond China itself, it became one of the principal frameworks for other Asian powers when they rose to military and economic dominance. It was never "hegemonic" in the sense of excluding all other modes of conceptualizing the world, even though China remained the dominant military and economic power through the end of the eighteenth century. Each state used the discourse for its own purposes. Even though they despised the Manchus as barbarians and remained secretly loyal to the Ming, Koreans sent many official missions to Beijing, which both legitimated the Korean rulers and supplied information and trade goods.[6] Tokugawa Japan sent no official tribute missions, but maintained a significant Chinese merchant colony in Nagasaki, and gained indirect access to Chinese markets through Satsuma and the Ryukyus. All the northwestern powers – Russia, the Zunghars, Tibetans, and Kazakhs – found tribute missions to be valuable sources of commodities and intelligence, as did the Vietnamese and Siamese. A kowtow was a small price to pay for legitimation, peace, and access to this giant neighbor's interior. Qing officials, knowing that tribute missions were costly to support and contained as many spies as merchants, tried to restrict their access, but at the same time the Qing learned much about their frontier from these visitors. Paying equal attention to China's many frontiers helps to enrich our understanding of the variety of transcultural relationships in which the empire was constantly involved.

In sum, the frontier perspective directs us to analyses that are both complementary and critical of world-system models, with their focus on the domination of cores and the predominant influence of economic incentives. In the borderlands, even of highly effective core states, languages of inclusion, exclusion, and exchange, along with acts of coercion, mattered as much as routine economic interactions. Processes look more fluid, interactive, and contingent than in the settled, prosperous core regions. At its edges (whether geographical border zones or technological "cutting edges"), well-established systems constantly grope their way into an uncertain future. The hazards of prediction, and unpleasant reversals, supplant the smooth rise and fall of cycles of social change.

Some other scholars have used the frontier metaphor in a different way to examine global economic relations. The economic historian Kawakatsu Heita, for example, used it to explain the rise of England and Japan in the nineteenth century (Kawakatsu 1993).[7] Inverting the common meanings of "core" and "periphery," he argues that both eighteenth-century England and Japan were "frontier" (henkyō) societies, highly dependent for vital consumption goods on "core" producing regions in Asia. England imported large amounts of cotton textiles from India, for example, just as Japan imported them from China. Determined to prevent the silver drain caused by these imports, both countries promoted "import substitution" policies designed to create indigenous industries to replace their Asian suppliers. This "escape from Asia" (datsu-A), however, followed two different paths. England took over India as a colony, restricted its handicraft textile production while promoting English industrialized manufactures, and later extended its global reach by drawing on raw cotton supplies from the southern United States. Japan, by contrast, sealed its borders, shut down its silver mines, and promoted its own domestic cotton textile production independently of global markets.

Kawakatsu's provocative argument correctly highlights the peripheral positions of England and Japan with respect to the large continental Asian producers, but it relies on an excessively static image of China, and neglects similarities between China and Japan. China, too, depended heavily on external suppliers: horses, obtained from Mongols and other nomads on the northwest frontier, and silver, supplied first from Japan and later from the New World. To overcome this dependency, China took both the English and Japanese paths: she conquered the Mongols, taking over control of their horse pastures, and developed domestic industries, so as to sell silks to the Kazakhs in exchange for horses, and tea to the British for silver. Highlighting how frontier dynamics figured in all three countries' economic development puts the global economic system in a new light.

This frontier perspective can also help to revise more general preconceptions about the structure of the Qing state. As I have noted, new research sharply criticizes the Sinicization thesis, which asserts that the Manchus governed China because they rapidly assimilated to the Chinese classical culture. We still lack an effective critique of another common assumption related to the Sinicization thesis, which we may call "the civilianization thesis," because scholars have not closely examined the military influence on Qing institutions. The impact of military conquest, the Manchus' most fundamental goal, endured long after the take-over of Beijing.

According to the civilianization thesis, military conquerors establish new dynasties, but to ensure long-term stability they must turn to civilian administrators (Chinese literati and bureaucrats). Over time, the rising prestige of scholar-bureaucrats downgrades the role of the military, as seen in the institutionalization of the civil examination system. Nationalists who portray China as an innocent victim of foreign invasion have argued that China was fundamentally a civilian, pacifist civilization, unlike the violent aggressive West. They echo their Western counterparts, from the eighteenth to the twentieth century, who saw in the literati officials of China the ideal alternative to a history of warfare and greed.

Like the Sinicization thesis, the civilianization thesis has some plausibility, but it is too easily exaggerated and simplified, and it can be subjected to a similar critique. Chinese rulers have, after all, fought a very large number of battles. Alastair Iain Johnston has demonstrated the persistence of a strategic culture in imperial China based on realpolitik, or what he calls a *parabellum* culture: if you want peace, prepare for war (Johnston 1995). Stressing the military factor allows us to compare China with other empires that faced similar security problems, and reveals the long-lasting impact of Qing military institutions on state structures, geopolitical behavior, political economy, and the writing of history.

Military history, however, should not merely recapitulate the heroic vision the emperors had of themselves, nor should it endorse a selective vision of the past to serve a modern nationalist agenda. To free history from the nation we have to do more than just look at narratives produced in the twentieth century, but also re-examine histories written by the Qing itself. The main theme of my current work is to pursue a frontier view of Qing history that incorporates the importance of the military experience. Qing territorial expansion was an event of great significance in recasting the terms of imperial rule, and in laying the foundations for China's reconstruction as a nation-state in the twentieth century. The expanded Qing empire did not assert a nationalist ideology, but its social and institutional structures formed the template for building China's "multi-nationality nation-state" (*duo minzu guojia*) (Perdue, forthcoming c). This emphasis highlights many aspects of Qing policy, but for the sake of brevity I will only list a few of them here. Military-security concerns can be found in the triple alliance of Manchus, Mongols, and Chinese banner-men (*Hanjun*) during the conquest; the promotion of peasant settlement of peripheral regions; development of the agrarian and commercial infra-structure of the frontier; the control and dissemination of vital informa-tion about grain prices, harvest, and weather reports; institutional reforms, like the creation of the Grand Council; new mappings and spatial categorizations of the empire; and new constructions of historical time, as seen in the new Qing genre of campaign histories (*fanglue*). As one example, I will briefly outline the last of these and conclude with a discus-sion of the implications of conquest for imperial and national identity.

Reviewing Qing history

By 1697, with the death of Galdan, the Zunghar Mongol leader, the Kangxi emperor could convincingly claim to have surpassed the military achievements of all previous dynasties. He claimed to have eliminated for all time the continual threat of steppe nomads to the imperial frontiers by conducting an unprecedented series of personal expeditions that pene-trated deep into Central Asia. After the victory, he commissioned an impe-rial history of the campaign under the supervision of several top Grand Councillors, entitled *Qinzheng Pingding Shuomo Fanglue* (History of the Emperor's Personal Expeditions to Pacify the Northwest). This history, published in 1708, described the emperor's victories as inevitably deter-mined by Heaven. Galdan deserved defeat because he had defied both the emperor's will and cosmic fate (Zhang 1708, j.48.21a).

The emperor thought that he had ended the Mongolian menace, but in fact the Zunghar state was not destroyed. It flourished for another sixty years until its final elimination by the Qianlong emperor. This emperor likewise commissioned another imperial campaign history (*fanglue*) to demonstrate that his achievements, too, were heavensent. But neither emperor could have predicted the ultimate outcome. Qing victory and Mongol defeat depended on "exogenous" factors like the weather, food supply, personalities, and psychology of panic among soldiers. The detailed historical materials contained in both *Fanglue* allow us to write an alternative, more contingent account than the explicit ideology that directed their compilation.[8]

Only after the fact were the victories made to seem inevitable. Wei Yuan's account in the *Shengwuji* (*Sacred Military Victories*), published in 1842, built upon the history projects sponsored by the Kangxi and Qianlong emperors. These accounts fixed in the minds of officials and ordinary Chinese the idea that the maximal boundaries achieved by Qing in 1760 were "natural frontiers," as Europeans would say, heavenly mandated definitions of imperial space. This definition of space determined the identity of the emperor, who claimed to incorporate multiple peoples under a single universal hegemon. He had many faces for many purposes: for Manchus he was the superior kinsman, for Mongols the inheritor of the imperial seal of Chinggis Khan (which he had captured), for Mongolian and Tibetan clergy the *chakravartin* (Buddhist wheel turning king), for Muslims the protector of Islam, and for Han the sponsor of the imperial version of neo-Confucian orthodoxy. This "multicultural" character of the Qing state rested first and foremost on military conquest and economic power, not on any natural superiority or "large-heartedness" of Han Confucian culture (Ho 1998: 151). Each of the peoples within the empire was assigned a single fixed identity, which became the basis for turning them into "nationalities" in the twentieth century.

This form of "multiculturalism" was a central legitimating ideology of the Qing state, but not everyone accepted the Qing claims. Each of the major Northwestern peoples – Mongols, Turkestanis, Chinese Muslims, Tibetans – generated repeated resistance movements, and in each case revolt was put down by force. These peoples were divided among themselves over resistance to the Qing, but they did not uniformly submit without protest. Apparent statements of voluntary submission to superior Chinese culture generally followed only upon military defeat. Each of these peoples also had alternative cultural foci. The Mongols maintained an autonomous link to Chinggis Khan's heritage, a steppe-centered focus, neither Manchu nor Han-centered. Mongolian state builders like Galdan used their Tibetan connection to uphold Buddhist universalism as a counter to Confucian claims. They also attempted to negotiate a Russian military alliance, which was prevented by Qing diplomacy. Under the terms of the Nerchinsk treaty of 1689 and Kiakhta trade treaty of 1727, the Russians were obliged to refuse support to Galdan's Mongolian state in order to maintain profitable trade with the Qing. Tibetan links to India opened up to them a broader realm beyond China. They viewed Mongolian Khans and Chinese emperors equally as Buddhist believers who supported the Lamaist institutions with alms. Even though the Qing destroyed their Mongolian alliances and lavished patronage on the monks, Tibetan sources provide evidence that Tibetans did not view their relationship to Qing power as simple submission to superior cultural might (Hevia 1993; Sperling 1998). Likewise, the Muslim peoples of Turkestan responded to Middle Eastern Islamic claims, as well as Turkic Central Asian ones; and localist identifications with their oasis communities.

Qing imperial relationships to these competing ties were nuanced and variable. Generally speaking, Qing rulers first concentrated on forcibly eliminating alternatives that could seriously challenge their political and military dominance. They promoted their own universalist claims to bring peace and prosperity to subject peoples as the most beneficial for their subjects. They did not, however, genuinely pursue a single "civilizing mission" that classified non-Han as primitive peoples who needed to be raised up to a uniform standard (cf. Harrell 1995). They claimed to respect Buddhism as an equally "civilized" force, and the Dalai Lama as having common ideals with the emperor. They left local elites in place, and did not try to replace local religious or cultural institutions. Qing toleration of diversity on the frontiers contrasts markedly with twentieth-century efforts by Chinese leaders and intellectuals to eliminate signs of "backwardness" through attacks on "superstition." The Qing did promote standardization and formalization of institutions and cultural forms, but it did not attempt the wholesale eradication of diverse cultures. Nevertheless, cultural normalization – the classification of peoples into distinct ethnic types – and security goals were closely tied together in the Qing imperial formation.

These Qing practices positioned the empire within a global state system, as the state which encompassed a multitude of peoples under its jurisdiction and embraced many foreign powers as tributary vassals. By fixing their boundaries, classifying their peoples, systematizing their trade and diplomatic practices, and extending commercial networks within and beyond the borders, the Qing by the eighteenth century had put in place the basic structures which all Chinese nationalists would struggle to preserve.

I have sketched here only a few links between military expansion and the culture of the Qing regime. By extending our scope to the Central Asian regions within and beyond the Chinese realm, and by including security concerns as major factors in the Qing state's formation, we can generate new insights that will help us place China's historical experience among the interconnected peoples of the world.

Notes

1 "China, Korea and Japan ... are indeed among the extremely rare examples of a historic state composed of a population that is ethnically almost or entirely homogeneous" (Hobsbawm 1990: 66).
2 Croxton (1999) questions the assumption that these ideas immediately took hold in 1648, but notes their gradual development during the period.
3 Scholars working in this tradition include Bernhard Laufer, Erich Haenisch, I.Ia. Zlatkin, Miyawaki Junko, Okada Hidehiro, Ishihama Yumiko, Saguchi Toru, and others.
4 On the multiplicity of practices encompassed by ritual language, cf. Bell (1992: 191):

> Ideology is not a coherent set of ideas, statements, or attitudes imposed on people who dutifully internalize them. Nor are societies themselves a matter of unitary social systems or totalities that act as one. Any ideology is always in dialogue with, and thus shaped and constrained by, the voices it is suppressing, manipulating, echoing.

Also cf. Hevia (1995); Zito (1997).
5 Peter Galison (1997) uses the concept of "trading languages" to describe the need for a common discourse between multiple sub-disciplines of twentieth-century physics.

6   Koreans believed that Confucian civilization was lost or at least greatly compromised in a barbarian dominated China [after the Manchu conquest], and that this civilization had to be safeguarded and transmitted in Korea ... Despite Korea's contempt for the Manchus, it had to remain under the hegemony of the Chinese empire performing to the Qing court the same diplomatic rituals of deference as a tributary state which it had performed to the Ming court.

(Haboush, forthcoming; cf. Chun 1968)

7 For critical discussion of Kawakatsu's theses, see Lee (1999), and Morris-Suzuki (1993).
8 Perdue (forthcoming c) discusses the rewriting of history in the compilation of the *Fanglue*, Oyunbilig (1999) gives a more detailed account of these editorial changes.

References

Adelman, Stephen and Jeremy Aron. 1999. "From Borderlands to Borders: Empires, Nation States, and the Peoples in Between in North American History," *American Historical Review* 104 (3): 814–44; 104 (4): 1221–39.

Aron, Stephen. 1994. "Lessons in Conquest: Towards a Greater Western History," *Pacific Historical Review* 63 (2): 125–47.

Arrighi, Giovanni. 1994. *The Long Twentieth Century: Money, Power, and the Origins of Our Times.* London: Verso.

Bayly, Christopher. 1989. *Imperial Meridian: The British Empire and the World, 1780–1830.* London: Longman.

Bell, Catherine. 1992. *Ritual Theory, Ritual Practice.* Oxford: Oxford University Press.

Chia, Ning. 1991. "The Lifanyuan and the Inner Asian Rituals in the Early Qing," *Late Imperial China* 14 (1): 60–92.

Chun Hae-jong. 1968. "Sino-Korean Tributary Relations in the Ch'ing Period" in J. Fairbank (ed.), *The Chinese World Order.* Cambridge, MA: Harvard University Press, pp. 90–111.

Cronon, William. 1991. *Nature's Metropolis.* New York: Norton.

Crossley, Pamela Kyle. 1990a. *Orphan Warriors: Three Manchu Generations and the End of the Qing World.* Princeton, NJ: Princeton University Press.

Crossley, Pamela Kyle. 1990b. "Thinking about Ethnicity in Early Modern China," *Late Imperial China* 11 (1): 1–35.

Crossley, Pamela Kyle. 1999. *A Translucent Mirror: History and Identity in Qing Imperial Ideology.* Berkeley, CA: University of California Press.

Croxton, Derek. 1999. "The Peace of Westphalia of 1648 and the Origins of Sovereignty," *International History Review* 21 (3): 569–91.

Di Cosmo, Nicola. 1998. "Qing Colonial Administration in the Inner Asian Dependencies," *International History Review* 20 (2): 287–309.

Di Cosmo, Nicola. 1999. "State Formation and Periodization in Inner Asian History," *Journal of World History* 10 (1): 1–40.

Elliott, Mark. 2000. *The Manchu Way: The Eight Banners and Ethnic Identity in Late Imperial China.* Stanford, CA: Stanford University Press.

Fairbank, John K. (ed.) 1968. *The Chinese World Order.* Cambridge, MA: Harvard University Press.

Faragher, John Mack. 1993. "The Frontier Trail: Rethinking Turner and Reimagining the American West," *American Historical Review* 98 (1): 106–17.

Febvre, Lucien. 1973. "*Frontière*: The Word and the Concept," in Peter Burke (ed.), K. Folca, trans. Lucien Febvre, *A New Kind of History.* New York: Harper & Row, pp. 208–18.

Fitzgerald, John. 1996. *Awakening China: Politics, Culture, and Class in the Nationalist Revolution.* Stanford, CA: Stanford University Press.

Fletcher, Joseph. 1968. "China and Central Asia, 1368–1884," in John K. Fairbank (ed.), *The Chinese World Order.* Cambridge, MA: Harvard, pp. 206–25.

Fletcher, Joseph. 1978. "The Heyday of the Ch'ing Order in Mongolia, Sinkiang, and Tibet," in John K. Fairbank (ed.), *The Cambridge History of China*, vol. 10: *Late Ch'ing, 1800–1911*, Part I. Cambridge: Cambridge University Press, pp. 351–408.

Fogel, Joshua. 1988. "The Debates over the Asiatic Mode of Production in Soviet Russia, China, and Japan," *American Historical Review* 93 (1): 56–79.

Frank, André Gunder. 1998. *ReOrient: Global Economy in the Asian Age.* Berkeley, CA: University of California Press.

Friedman, Edward. 1995. "Reconstructing China's National Identity," in Edward Friedman, *National Identity and Democratic Prospects in Socialist China.* New York: M.E. Sharpe, pp. 87–116.

Fuma, Susumu (ed.) 1999. *Shi Ryukyu Roku Kaitai oyobi Kenkyu* (Records of Missions to the Ryukyus). Okinawa: Yôju Shorin.

Galison, Peter. 1997. *Image and Logic: A Material Culture of Microphysics.* Chicago: University of Chicago Press.

Gasster, Michael. 1969. *Chinese Intellectuals and the Revolution of 1911.* Seattle: University of Washington Press.

Gerth, Karl. 1999. "Nationalizing Consumption, Consuming Nationalism: The National Products Movement, 1905–37," PhD dissertation, Harvard University.

Giersch, C. Patterson. 1998. "Qing China's Reluctant Subjects: Indigenous Communities and Empire along the Yunnan Frontier," PhD dissertation, Yale University.

Gu Jiegang. 1983a. *Xibei Kaocha Riji* (Diary of Investigations in the Northwest). Lanzhou Guji Shudian.

Gu Jiegang. 1983b. *Zhongguo Jiangyu Yangeshi* (History of Changes in China's Borders). Changsha: Shangwu yinshuguan.

Haboush, Jahyoun Kim. Forthcoming. "Contesting Chinese Time, Nationalizing Temporal Space: Temporal Inscription in Late Choson Korea," in Lynn Struve (ed.), *Time, Temporality, and a Change of Empires in East Asia: From Ming to Qing*. Honolulu, HI: University of Hawaii Press.

Hamashita, Takeshi. 1990. *Kindai Chugoku no Kokusaiteki Keiki* (The International Moment of Modern China). Tokyo: Daigaku Shuppankai.

Hamashita, Takeshi. 1994. "The Tribute Trade System and Modern Asia," in A.J.H. Latham and Heita Kawakatsu (eds), *Japanese Industrialization and the Asian Economy*. New York: Routledge, pp. 91–107.

Hamashita, Takeshi. 1999. "East Asia: Historical Perspectives on the Sinocentric Tributary trade," paper presented at conference, The Rise of East Asia: 500, 150, and 50 Year Perspectives, Johns Hopkins University Institute for Global Studies in Culture, Power, and History, 4–5 December.

Harrell, Stevan (ed.) 1995. *Cultural Encounters on China's Ethnic Frontiers*. Seattle: University of Washington Press.

Heuschert, Dorothea. 1998. "Legal Pluralism in the Qing Empire: Manchu legislation for the Mongols," *International History Review* 20 (2): 310–24.

Hevia, James L. 1993. "Lamas, Emperors, and Rituals: Political Implications in Qing Imperial Ceremonies," *Journal of the International Association of Buddhist Studies* 16 (2): 243–78.

Hevia, James L. 1995. *Cherishing Men from Afar: Qing Guest Ritual and the Macartney Embassy*. Durham, NC: Duke University Press.

Ho, Ping-ti. 1998. "In Defense of Sinicization: A Rebuttal of Evelyn Rawski's 'Re-envisioning the Qing'," *Journal of Asian Studies* 57 (1): 123–55.

Hobsbawm, Eric J. 1990. *Nations and Nationalism Since 1780*. Cambridge: Cambridge University Press.

Hobsbawm, Eric and Terence Ranger. 1983. *The Invention of Tradition*. Cambridge: Cambridge University Press.

Hodgson, Marshall. 1974. *The Venture of Islam: The Gunpowder Empires and Modern Times*. Chicago: University of Chicago Press.

Johnston, Alastair Iain. 1995. *Cultural Realism: Strategic Culture and Grand Strategy in Ming China*. Princeton, NJ: Princeton University Press.

Kawakatsu Heita. 1993. "Datsu A katei to shite no Nichi O no kinsei," (Modernity in Japan and Europe as an "Escape from Asia") *Rekishi Hyoron* 515: 43–58.

Kirby, William. 1997. "The Internationalization of China: Foreign Relations at Home and Abroad," *China Quarterly* 150: 433–58.

Lary, Diana. 1996. "The Tomb of the King of Nanyue: The Contemporary Agenda of History: Scholarship and Identity," *Modern China* 22 (1): 3–27.

Lee, John. 1999. "Trade and Economy in Preindustrial East Asia, 1500–1800," *Journal of Asian Studies*, 58 (1): 2–26.

Leonard, Jane Kate. 1984. *Wei Yuan and China's Rediscovery of the Maritime World.* Cambridge, MA: Harvard University Press.

Limerick, Patricia Nelson. 1987. *The Legacy of Conquest: The Unbroken Past of the American West.* New York: W.W. Norton.

Lipman, Jonathan. 1997. *Familiar Strangers: A Muslim History in China.* Stanford, CA: Stanford University Press.

Lü Yiran. 1990. *Zhongguo Beibu Bianjiangshi Yanjiu.* Heilongjiang: Heilongjiang Chubanshe.

Lü Yiran and Ma Dazheng. 1987. "Zhongguo bianjiang shidi yanjiu de jige wenti," *Xibei Shidi,* March: 79–82.

McNeill, William H. 1989. *The Age of Gunpowder Empires, 1450–1800.* Washington, DC: American Historical Association.

Mazumdar, Sucheta. 1998. *Sugar and Society in China: Peasants, Technology, and the World Market.* Cambridge, MA: Harvard University Press.

Millward, James A. 1998. *Beyond the Pass: Economy, Ethnicity, and Empire in Qing Central Asia.* Stanford, CA: Stanford University Press.

Millward, James A. 1999. "Coming onto the Map: The Qing Conquest of Xinjiang," *Late Imperial China* 20 (2): 61–98.

Morris-Suzuki, Tessa. 1993. "Rewriting History: Civilization Theory in Contemporary Japan," *positions* 1 (2): 526–47.

Morris-Suzuki, Tessa. 1998. *Reinventing Japan: Time, Space, Nation.* New York: M.E. Sharpe.

Ngo, Tak-Wing (ed.) 1999. *Hong Kong's History: State and Society under Colonial Rule.* London: Routledge.

Oyunbilig, Borjigidai. 1999. *Zur Überlieferungsgeschichte des Berichts über den persönlichen Feldzug des Kangxi Kaisers gegen Galdan (1696–1697).* Wiesbaden: Harassowitz.

Perdue, Peter C. 1998. "Boundaries, Maps, and Movement: Chinese, Russian, and Mongolian Empires in Early Modern Eurasia," *International History Review* 20 (2): 263–86.

Perdue, Peter C. 2000a. "China in the World Economy: Exports, Regions and Theories," *Harvard Journal of Asiatic Studies* 60 (1): 259–75.

Perdue, Peter C. 2000b. "Culture, History, and Imperial Chinese Strategy: Legacies of the Qing Conquests," in Hans van de Ven (ed.), *War in Chinese History.* Leiden: Brill, pp. 252–87.

Perdue, Peter C. Forthcoming a. "The Qing Empire in Eurasian Time and Space," in Lynn Struve (ed.), *The Qing Formation in World-Historical Time.* Cambridge, MA: Harvard University Press.

Perdue, Peter C. Forthcoming b. "From Turfan to Taiwan: Trade and War on Two Chinese Frontiers," in Bradley Parker and Lars Rodseth (eds), *Frontiers Through Space and Time.* Salt Lake City: University of Utah Press.

Perdue, Peter C. Forthcoming c. "The Qing Conquest of Central Eurasia," book manuscript. Harvard University Press.

Pomeranz, Kenneth. 2000. *The Great Divergence: China, Europe, and the Making of the Modern World Economy.* Princeton, NJ: Princeton University Press.

Pye, Lucian W. 1993. "How China's Nationalism was Shanghaied," *Australian Journal of Chinese Affairs* 29: 107–34.

Rawski, Evelyn. 1996. "Reenvisioning the Qing: The Significance of the Qing Period in Chinese History," *Journal of Asian Studies* 55 (4): 829–50.

Rawski, Evelyn. 1998. *The Last Emperors: A Social History of Qing Imperial Institutions.* Berkeley, CA: University of California Press.

Rhoads, Edward J.M. 2000. *Manchus and Han: Ethnic Relations and Political Power in Late Qing and Early Republican China, 1861–1928.* Seattle: University of Washington Press.

Schneider, Laurence. 1971. *Ku Chieh-kang and China's New History.* Berkeley, CA: University of California Press.

Shimada, Kenji. 1990. *Pioneer of the Chinese Revolution: Zhang Binglin and Confucianism.* Stanford, CA: Stanford University Press.

Sperling, Elliot. 1998. "Awe and Submission: A Tibetan Aristocrat at the Court of Qianlong," *International History Review* 20 (2): 325–35.

Standen, Naomi and Daniel Power (eds) 1998. *Frontiers in Question: Eurasian Borderlands 700–1700.* New York: St. Martin's Press.

Teng, Emma Jinhua. 1998. "An Island of Women: The Discourse of Gender in Qing Travel Accounts of Taiwan," *International History Review* 20 (2): 353–70.

Tilly, Charles. 1990. *Coercion, Capital, and European States, 990–1990.* Oxford: Basil Blackwell.

Waley-Cohen, Joanna. 1998. "Religion, War, and Empire in Eighteenth-century China," *International History Review* 20 (3): 336–52.

Waley-Cohen, Joanna. 1999. *The Sextants of Beijing: Global Currents in Chinese History.* New York: Norton.

Wei Yuan. 1984. *Shengwuji* (Record of Sacred Military Victories). Beijing: Zhonghua Shuju.

White, Richard. 1991a. *It's Your Misfortune and None of my Own: A New History of the American West.* Oklahoma: Norman: University of Oklahoma Press.

White, Richard. 1991b. *The Middle Ground: Indians, Empires and Republics in the Great Lakes Region, 1650–1815.* Cambridge: Cambridge University Press.

Wong, R. Bin. 1997. *China Transformed: Historical Change and the Limits of European Experience.* Ithaca, NY: Cornell University Press.

Zhang Yushu (ed.) 1708. *Qinzheng Pingding Shuomo Fanglue* (Chronicle of the Emperor's Personal Expeditions to Pacify the Northwest Frontier).

Zito, Angela. 1997. *Of Body and Brush: Grand Sacrifice as Text/Performance in Eighteenth-Century China.* Chicago: University of Chicago Press.

Chapter 3

The East Asian path of economic development

A long-term perspective

Kaoru Sugihara

Introduction

This chapter attempts to explain how and why East Asia's share in world GDP increased between 1500 and 1820, decreased between 1820 and 1945, and then increased rapidly over the last half century.

Table 3.1 suggests that between 1500 and 1820 there was only a marginal increase in the world's per capita GDP, while after 1820 there was both an accelerated increase in population and a dramatic rise in per capita GDP. The most plausible interpretation of the first shift is that the industrial revolution in Britain constituted a major watershed in global history, ushering in a deepening of the penetration of the modern world system, emanating from Western Europe and encompassing the rest of the globe from the nineteenth century.

The same table, however, reveals a significant increase in world GDP and a much slower increase in per capita GDP between 1500 and 1820. This is primarily because world population was on the rise, with much of this rise coming from Asia, particularly China and India. According to Maddison's 1995 data, as much as 52 per cent of world GDP in 1820 came from Asia, of which China contributed 29 per cent and India 16 per cent. Table 3.2 shows that in 1820 six East and Southeast Asian countries accounted for 35 per cent of world GDP, while the share of six advanced Western countries was 18 per cent. Angus Maddison's figures, drawing on the work of regional specialists, in my view, reflects the general trend of recent scholarship (for a summary of progress in demography, see Saito

Table 3.1 World economic performance, 1500–1995

	1500	*1820*	*1995*
World population (million)	425	1,049	5,664
World GDP per capita (1990$)	565	673	5,194
World GDP (billion 1990$)	240	706	29,412

Sources: Maddison (1995: 19) for the data for 1500, and Maddison (1998: 40) for 1820 and 1995.

Table 3.2 Relative economic performance: the West vs Asia, 1820–1992 (GDP in billion 1990$)

	1820	1913	1950	1992
Six advanced Western countries[a]	128	1,138	2,422	9,781
Six East and Southeast Asian countries[b]	243	435	603	7,487
China	199	301	336	3,616
Japan	22	69	157	2,415

Source: Maddison (1995: 19, 180–3 and 190–1).

Notes
a The UK, USA, France, Germany, Italy, Austria.
b Japan, South Korea, Taiwan, China, Indonesia, Thailand. Figures for South Korea, Taiwan and Thailand in 1820 are not available, but have been estimated as $5billion, $2billion and $3.5 billion respectively. Territorial boundaries are based as in the 1992 definition. For details, see Maddison (1995).

Osamu 1997). To take China as an example, recent work has confirmed findings, which originally emerged around the middle of the nineteenth century and were summarized by D.H. Perkins in the 1960s, that China's population increased rapidly during the eighteenth century. China's population, which had previously risen several times to a peak of 100 to 150 million only to fall, increased to nearly 400 million by the end of the eighteenth century. This was clearly a world demographic landmark (Perkins 1969; Liu and Hwang 1977; Naquin and Rawski 1987; Van de Ven 1996), and its impact on world GDP far outweighed that of post-industrial revolution Britain, whose share of world GDP in 1820 was less than 6 per cent. There is an important, relatively unexplored question of the 'Chinese miracle' here, that is, how China managed to escape Malthusian checks, and maintain such a vast population without serious deterioration in the standard of living. Essentially the same observation can be made with regard to developments in Japan in the seventeenth century, which, as will be argued below, took place under the influence of the China-centred international economy of East Asia.

Furthermore, during the eighteenth century the Japanese standard of living began to rise, if slowly, and the trend continued into the nineteenth. In addition, much of the economic progress made in East Asia during the second half of the nineteenth century was based on the indigenous development of labour-intensive industry rather than on the introduction of Western technology. How can one explain the sequence of population growth followed by a rise in the standard of living, both in the absence of any strong Western influence? This is the first question addressed, in the next section of this chapter.

Between 1820 and 1945 the West, including regions of recent European settlement in the Americas, Australasia and South Africa, achieved global dominance. The industrial revolution, the transport and communications revolution, the opening up of vast land areas in the new continents and the utilization of natural resources such as coal and oil, all benefited the Western population, whose per capita income increased enormously, resulting in a widening gap between the rich West and the poor non-West (see Table 3.3). The growth of trade between the West and Asia was often accompanied by colonialism, which tended to reinforce inequality, particularly between temperate and tropical zones (Lewis 1978: Chapter 8).

The third section of this chapter attempts to account for the ambiguous performance of East Asian economies during this period. On the one hand, the core of the region escaped Western colonialism and was able to pursue import-substitution industrialization. In China after 1870 and in Japan throughout, there was a slow but relatively steady rise in population without a deterioration in the standard of living. At the same time, East Asia was unable to catch up with the advanced Western countries, which went through a period of further technological advance (the second industrial revolution), and the gap in per capita income between the West and East Asia increased until about 1930. The Japanese standard of living did rise slightly, and the country's attempt to compete with Western manufacturers in the international market was widely viewed in the West as an example of unfair competition coming from a low wage economy. But the West continued to dominate the heavy and chemical industries, which required high technology, large amounts of capital and access to natural resources.

After 1945 the trend was reversed, and East Asia's GDP grew faster than that of the West. The precise timing of this reversal is difficult to determine, as the Great Depression and the Second World War make it hard to obtain reliable information on exchange (or other forms of conversion)

Table 3.3 Per capita GDP in selected countries, 1820–1992 (1990$)

	1820	1870	1913	1950	1973	1992
USA	1,278	2,457	5,307	9,573	16,607	21,558
Germany	1,112	1,913	3,833	4,281	13,152	19,351
France	1,218	1,858	3,452	5,221	12,940	17,959
UK	1,756	3,263	5,032	6,847	11,992	15,738
Japan	704	741	1,334	1,873	11,017	19,425
Taiwan			794	922	3,669	11,590
South Korea			948	876	2,840	10,010
China	523	523	688	614	1,186	3,098
Indonesia	614	657	917	874	1,538	2,749

Source: Maddison (1995: 23–4).

rates, or GDP itself for a number of countries. But, at some point in the middle of the twentieth century, and certainly by 1960, per capita income of East Asian countries began to grow faster than that of advanced Western countries as well as other developing countries. The growth of Japan's per capita GDP during the period from 1955 to 1973 was the most conspicuous example of this new trend. A sustained annual growth rate of around 10 per cent for this long a period had never occurred anywhere before (see Table 3.3). Furthermore, the same table suggests that the 'Japanese miracle' was in fact the beginning of an 'East Asian miracle' in which a number of other Asian countries have begun to participate (World Bank 1993). In the final decade of the twentieth century, East Asia's share in world GDP (as defined in Table 3.2) apparently exceeded that of the six largest Western economies.

Geopolitical considerations in the early stages of the Cold War were crucial to the changes in the American attitude towards Japan's economic future. In contrast to the pre-war situation, Japan was expected to use her economic strength to counter communist penetration in Asia, and was now able to import all necessary raw materials and resources, including oil, from the rest of the world (by contrast, the US ban on oil exports to Japan in 1941 was an immediate cause of the outbreak of the Second World War). In the post-war period Japan also enjoyed favourable opportunities to increase exports of manufactured goods to advanced Western countries. This change in international circumstances allowed Japan, and later a number of other Asian countries, to pursue the systematic introduction of capital-intensive and resource-intensive heavy and chemical industries to an economy with relatively cheap and disciplined labour. The fourth section discusses how the Western and East Asian paths of economic development fused to produce high-speed growth in East Asia.

The final section summarizes the argument, and attempts to place the 'East Asian miracle' in the context of global history. It will be argued that industrialization of the Western European variety, the mainstay of the growth of the world economy between 1820 and 1945, created the North–South divide, and failed to push up world GDP in a balanced way, until East Asia initiated an alternative pattern, emphasizing a more thorough utilization of human resources through labour-intensive technology and labour-absorbing institutions. The chapter will suggest that, while East Asia would not have industrialized without the West's impact, it was the East Asian path of economic development that made it possible for the majority of the world's population to benefit from global industrialization.

This chapter will not attempt to rigorously define the term 'East Asia'. Instead it concentrates on describing the experiences of the area or the country which led the technological and institutional innovations at each stage of development. The approach adopted here is to abstract a historically mobile but relatively autonomous core of economic development of the region (initially the Yangzi delta of China, subsequently primarily Japan), and identify the features common to the region but distinct from other regions of the world. I use country-based macro-data going as far back as 1820, for the purpose of a broad comparison between East Asia and Europe and cite data for 1500 in a more general way. I have also referred to the relatively developed areas of present East and Southeast Asia as 'East Asia' for the most recent period, for the sake of simplicity. But this should not suggest that all areas of East Asia have been influenced, throughout the period, by the pattern of development described below. Nor should it imply that accumulation of country-based studies is sufficient for understanding the region's long-term development (for comments on the limits of country-based historiography, see Sugihara 1996b). Rather, it is assumed here that a substantial degree of economic interaction has long existed in the region, for example between China and Japan, and that they influenced the region's long-term pattern of development in a fundamental way (Sugihara 1996b; for a full exposition of this position, see Sugihara 1996a). Other key terms such as Europe and the West are treated in the same spirit.

The development of labour-intensive technology

The industrious revolution path

As already stated, East Asia experienced a sustained period of population growth accompanied by a modest rise in the standard of living from the sixteenth to the eighteenth century. The argument of this section is that it did this because it successfully responded to natural resource constraints, particularly the scarcity of land, by developing a set of technological and institutional devices for full absorption of family labour. I shall call these devices labour-absorbing institutions and labour-intensive technology.

The term labour-intensive technology does not imply that East Asian technology developed in the scientific tradition so influential in the West. The great Chinese agricultural manuals, offering information, for example, on the methods of seed selection for different types of soil or on the use of a variety of agricultural tools, were transmitted in different languages and across cultures, for example, from China to Japan. They set the main pattern of dissemination of economic knowledge across East Asia. During the sixteenth and seventeenth centuries international contact in East Asia was driven by massive silver flows from Japan to China. Even during the eighteenth century, when intra-Asian bullion flows were reduced to insignificance and the volume of Japanese trade declined under the seclusion policy, the transfer of economic knowledge continued through written information. However, this knowledge consisted essentially of technical rules of thumb, wisdom rooted in the accumulation of experience.

Equally, in speaking of labour-absorbing institutions we do not imply the development of a set of institutions characteristic of a mode of production in a particular stage of economic development. Nor do we refer to feudalism or the emergence (or absence) of the nation-state when we talk of the key economic institutions which undergirded the East Asian path of economic development. What we have in mind is the development of much smaller units, namely the household (often, though not always, the family), and, to a lesser extent, the village community. In many cases these units survived political turmoil and changes in the mode of production and remained as the region's key institutions, underpinning the technological and institutional path. It is important to recognize this aspect of 'path dependency' in order to understand the rise of East Asia in a long-term perspective.

In his 1967 article Akira Hayami drew a figure, reproduced here as Figure 3.1, to describe the different paths which England and Tokugawa Japan followed, calling them the industrial revolution and the industrious revolution respectively (Akira Hayami 1967; for English versions see Akira Hayami 1986 and 1992). With their different mix of factor endowments, in this case of capital and labour, and assuming that no transfer of factor inputs took place between England and Japan, Hayami explained that it was natural for societies as economically-minded as these two countries to pursue different paths, and for Japan to exploit the potential benefit of increasing labour absorption. However, Hayami's graph has often been

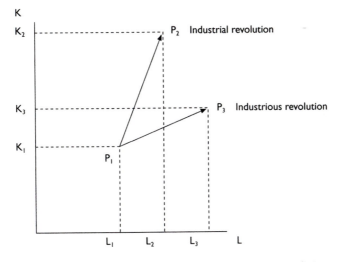

Figure 3.1 The industrial revolution and the industrious revolution

Source: Hayami Akira (1967: 13).

interpreted to imply that the industrious revolution did not lead to a rise in labour productivity of a magnitude comparable to the industrial revolution. It was drawn to explain how Japan was relatively well prepared for industrialization in the late nineteenth century.

It is possible to apply the industrious revolution theory to the Chinese case, for the purpose of comparing it with the Western European path. Well before 1500, probably during the twelfth and thirteenth centuries, China developed a set of highly advanced labour-intensive methods, involving seed selection, irrigation and water control, double cropping and the extensive use of agricultural tools. Central to this development was the opening up of land near the Yangzi River delta for rice cultivation. Of course, Chinese development had its ups and downs, and the commercialization of agriculture, the monetization of land tax, and the introduction of new world crops played an important part in the increase in population and agricultural output during the sixteenth to the eighteenth centuries. But the essential characteristics of small-scale production, centring on irrigated rice cultivation, established in the lower Yangzi region in the twelfth and thirteenth centuries (Shiba 1989), were extended to other parts of China and transmitted to Japan by the late sixteenth century. While adapting to ecological diversity and developing geographical specialization (see Buck 1937: 27), East Asian agriculture after the late sixteenth century nevertheless exhibited a clear tendency towards regional convergence, driven by the diffusion of intensive rice agriculture and several key commercial crops, notably cotton, silk and sugar.

The East Asian path of industrious revolution must be distinguished from that in Europe and North America with respect to labour-intensity. The size of land holdings was far smaller in East Asia than in, for example, Western European peasant society. The average farm size in East Asia in the nineteenth and early twentieth centuries ranged from 1 to 3 hectares (Bray 1986: 115–16; Buck 1930: 103). About 70 per cent of Japanese farms had 0.5 hectares of land or less, and nearly 90 per cent had 1 hectare or less at the time of industrialization in the late nineteenth century. In contrast, the average size of farm in France, a country with a strong peasant tradition, was 14 hectares in 1882 (Heywood 1996: 115).

Second, there were substantial differences in the degree of labour absorption within rice agriculture. Figure 3.2 highlights the importance of labour absorption at the initial stage of development of labour-intensive technology in rice agriculture (Ishikawa 1978: 34; see also Ishikawa 1967: Chapter 1; 1981: Chapter 1). Before mechanization, greater labour input was critical to raising land productivity. With the introduction of tractors and other inputs of capital, the size of holdings became larger, and labour inputs smaller. Thus the technology of land-use had two phases in terms of 'labour absorption'; first, land productivity rose with a proportionately greater input of labour, and then after a certain point it was improved

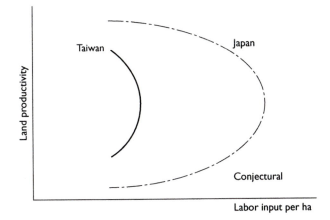

Figure 3.2 The Ishikawa curve

Source: Ishikawa (1968: 34).

with proportionately smaller input of labour. Booth and Sundrum (1984: Chapter 1) called this the 'Ishikawa curve'. On this path, labour productivity was unlikely to rise fast, if at all, at the initial stage of agricultural development (in Figure 3.2 this part of the Japanese path, mainly in the Tokugawa period, is shown in broken lines, indicating that it is conjectural). But it also meant that society could maintain a much greater number of people per unit area of arable land. This, essentially, was the East Asian answer to Malthusian checks, which applies to much of Japan and the wet-land farming areas of China.

Third, land productivity could be raised significantly prior to mechanization, and it is this supply-side change that was crucial to the industrious revolution. Table 3.4 suggests how advanced Japan's land productivity was by the late nineteenth century (for a historical comparison between India and Japan, see Sugihara with Yanagisawa 1996). A large part of the development of labour-intensive technology in Asian rice agriculture since then has been associated with the adaptation of Japanese rice technology to different soils and climates, first in Korea and Taiwan and later in other parts of East Asia. After the Second World War, the Ishikawa curve became the basis of a policy recommendation which emphasized labour absorption at the initial stage of development, and became one of the guiding principles behind the ILO programme for Asian agriculture.

An important conclusion we should draw from the above discussion, particularly from Figure 3.1, is that the industrious revolution path was much more successful in maintaining the region's large share in world GDP than the industrial revolution path was for England up to 1820. If

Table 3.4 Estimates of rice yields in Japan and other Asian countries

Country	Date	Tons per ha
Japan	1878–82	2.53
China	1921–5	2.56
India[a]	1953–62	1.36
Thailand[a]	1953–62	1.38
Indonesia[a]	1953–62	1.74
Malaya[a]	1953–62	2.24
Korea[a]	1953–62	2.75
Taiwan[a]	1953–62	2.93

Sources: Hayami and Yamada (1969: 108). For China, Buck (1930: 204).

Notes
The above Japanese figure is the revised official estimate. Other estimates range from 2.36 to 3.22 tons/ha.
a = FAO figures.

the world had ceased to exist in 1820, a hypothetical 'global historian' would surely have written an economic history centring on the industrious revolution path, with an important additional chapter on the recent rise of Western Europe. We should avoid accepting the nineteenth-century view, which was inclined to project European superiority, nor should we be unduly influenced by the observations on China by such well-known contemporary writers as Adam Smith and Thomas Robert Malthus. They were clearly handicapped by the lack of information, and believed that China's population was either stagnant or declining (Smith, A. 1776; Malthus 1798). By the time J.R. M'Culloch edited *A Dictionary of the Various Countries, Places, and Principal National Objects in the World* in 1868, people were much better informed. Indeed M'Culloch's dictionary included most of the relevant information on Chinese population which formed the basis of later studies (for example, Perkins 1969). Unfortunately, he, like such contemporaries as Karl Marx and Charles Darwin, was at a loss to interpret these enormous population figures and failed to see their global significance.

Sources of dynamism

Both Marxist historiography and the more recent literature of institutional economics have assumed the importance of the establishment of property rights as a condition of economic change (Marx 1867; North and Thomas 1973). Once property rights were clarified and land freely bought and sold, agriculture would become more efficient, as market forces would allocate resources, spread technology and select the optimum size of holding. Without the establishment of property rights, the transaction cost would not be lowered sufficiently to enable these developments. Moreover, on the basis of the establishment of the right to income from property, classical political economists in England saw the emergence of a class society and distinguished the main categories of income, with wages given to workers, profit to capitalists, and rent to landlords. This would enable the ruling classes to accumulate capital and develop more productive large-scale farming. Using this yardstick, East Asia does not fare well, as much of the most fertile land continued to be cultivated by family labour, and farming remained small-scale. And the traditional characterization of small-scale production has been that it lacked internal forces for change, because it neither faced constant pressure for technological improvement nor was driven by the capitalist principle of relentless profit maximization.

The argument against this view has been expressed in various forms whenever the dynamism of the peasant economy was recognized. A.V. Chayanov, for instance, tried to understand the behaviour of the peasant as if he were maximizing his earnings and welfare (Thorner 1966). Such an attempt can explain the responsiveness of peasant society to some extent, but stops short of pointing out some of the problems inherent in the Western (in this case more specifically English) model of class society. The East Asian peasant family worked a very small plot of land, and attempted to harvest the maximum amount of rice through a greater degree of labour input. They needed to perform a number of different tasks in accordance with the agricultural calendar, from transplanting to weeding to harvesting. They allocated family labour, and cultivated different varieties of rice to even out seasonal labour requirements and avoid hiring outside labour. They also exploited their own off-peak surplus labour for proto-industrial activities. Thus an ability to perform multiple tasks well, rather than specialization in a particular task, was preferred, and a will to cooperate with other members of the family rather than the furthering of individual talent was encouraged. Above all, it was important for every member of the family to try to fit into the work pattern of the farm, respond flexibly to extra or emergency needs, sympathize with the problems relating to the management of production, and anticipate and prevent potential problems. Managerial skill, with a general background of technical skill, was an ability which was actively sought after at the family level.

Looking at the separation of agricultural workers from management after the disappearance of peasant society in England from this perspective, it seems obvious that class division based on specialization had its own costs. Agricultural workers in England were deprived of the opportunity to share in managerial concerns, while specialist artisans came to despise the 'Jack-of-all-trades'. Division of labour, guided by the 'invisible hand', prevented the development of inter-personal skills needed for flexible specialization. The advantage of the 'visible hand' of the head of the peasant household was that he could allocate labour for production, distribute income among the members of the family for consumption and saving, and even control the number of children, hence the size of the family, all at the same time. Thus managerially independent farmers, even if they did not own land, had more reason than large-scale farm managers to increase output or income by linking effort to reward, not through the market, but directly.

The main institutional reinforcement of this dynamism came from the family and the village community, rather than from forces outside the village such as the nation-state's attempt to establish property rights. Effective sanctions were social rather than legal. Although the enforcement of paternalism and social cohesion could be as harsh as straight rejection or physical coercion, it did not necessarily imply the existence of nepotism and personal favours. On the contrary, rational, meritocratic, and market considerations all seem to have been as important for the East Asian peasant as for their European counterparts. Free from feudal restrictions, Chinese peasants were not rigidly tied to land, and could become local merchants. It was not unimportant that at least in theory, anyone could take the official examination to become a civil servant. Japanese peasants were less free, but in the course of the Tokugawa period (1603–1868) they enjoyed an unprecedentedly long period of peace, stability and political and economic independence from outside forces, perhaps more than anybody else did. Compared to China, the family system in Japan was less lineage-based (adoption was common) and more individualistically inclined (meritocratic concerns were taken seriously), and this helped make the peasant family an effective production, distribution and consumption unit (Macfarlane 1997). Their standard of living rose, if slightly, and many of them sent their sons to local schools to learn reading and abacus by the early nineteenth century (Dore 1965; Hanley 1997; but for criticism see Saito Osamu 1998). Under these circumstances it was natural for the East Asian peasant to become motivated to increase agricultural output or family income. So long as they observed social codes, the transaction cost of trade was small, and the risk involved in technical innovations was relatively low. While there was little room for big innovations or for investment in fixed capital or long-distance trade, these East Asian institutions provided the best opportunity for the development of labour-intensive technology.

Efficiency growth

In modern economics, a distinction has been made between extensive growth and intensive growth, to investigate whether growth occurred as a result of greater factor inputs or thanks to technological and institutional advance (Hayami Yujiro 1997: Chapters 5 and 6). The point about the industrial revolution was technological advance, with or without the corresponding accumulation of capital. But the idea of distinguishing between extensive (input-based) growth and intensive (efficiency) growth can be applied to the pre-industrial revolution economy. Was there efficiency growth in the industrious revolution path? Can we find output growth in spite of the exhaustion of factor inputs such as land and labour?

The best case for testing answers to this question is Tokugawa Japan from 1700 to 1850. By the end of the seventeenth century the possibilities for opening up new areas were exhausted, and a strong demographic pressure on land built up. The use of horses for cultivation and transport visibly declined, as the pressure on land left less and less available for raising animals. Already, in the 1734 official survey, the typical household illustrated in the 'model village' is assumed to cultivate less than a hectare of land. There was now very little chance to subdivide land among sons. It became increasingly difficult to get a new household 'approved' in the village, and, even if it was approved, its status was likely to be inferior to that of the existing households. Status mattered not just in village politics and ritual rights but in the allocation of water and sharing of labour. Thus there were good reasons for 'family planning' through infanticide and abortion. The former implied sex selection (in favour of males) as well as control of the number of children (Smith, T. 1977). Some economic historians suggest that this was the result of farmers' conscious attempts to raise their standard of living (Hanley and Yamamura 1977). But infanticide and abortion alone are unlikely to explain the low 'birth rate'. In some cases marital fertility itself was lower than the natural level, despite the fact that the average caloric intake was probably adequate. It is possible that the development of labour-intensive technology meant that women worked harder during their pregnancy in the eighteenth century, contributing to lower fertility (Saito Osamu 1992). In any case, Tokugawa demographic history lacked drastic Malthusian checks on a nationwide scale. Although there were some famines, catastrophes such as epidemics and warfare played little part in determining the overall trend, and mortality remained relatively low. Japan's population remained stable between 1721 and 1846 at a little over 30 million. In other words, there was no increase in the availability of either land or people.

Yet in Tokugawa Japan, per capita agricultural output stopped declining around 1730, and began to rise continuously thereafter. By 1850 it was 25 per cent higher than in 1730. The annual rate of increase is estimated to have been 0.38 per cent for 1730–50, 0.25 per cent for 1750–1800, and 0.08 per cent for 1800–50 (Hayami and Miyamoto 1988: 44). Clearly, more labour was absorbed for the cultivation of the same acreage of land. The trick was 'labour absorption' without population increase. The number of days a late Tokugawa peasant worked per year was greater than that in most other Asian countries in the late nineteenth century (Hayami and Yamada 1991: 251–2). However, if marginal labour productivity had declined considerably, it could have easily offset longer work days, and producers would soon have reached a point where further labour input would not be worthwhile. It was the development of labour-intensive technology and labour-absorbing institutions that overcame this Ricardian trap. To take a well-known example from the Meiji period (1868–1912), the development of summer–fall rearing of cocoons enabled farmers to combine rice production with sericulture, as, unlike the spring–summer rearing, it avoided the peak season of work in the rice fields (ibid.: 175–97). Progress in the Tokugawa period, if more modest than it was during Meiji, was clearly developing the East Asian technology path. While it would be hard to prove the presence of intensive growth in terms of output per day or per hour, the contribution of labour-intensive technology to the increase in per capita annual output is unmistakable. In other words, the East Asian path also had growth in efficiency without additional inputs of land and people. The difference from the Western path was that it mobilized human rather than non-human resources.

After the second half of the eighteenth century, major urban centres and castle towns in Japan declined, while rural industries began to grow. Rural merchants engaged in regional commerce, while feudal domains actively pursued policies to promote agriculture, commerce and industry to earn 'foreign' exchange. Both of these activities gave farmers a chance to exploit non-agricultural as well as agricultural economic opportunities. The rural household mobilized cheap labour, to produce more in response to the demand arising from the gradual rise in rural income. By the end of the eighteenth century the daughter of a rich farmer was likely to include a silk kimono in her dowry, but this did not have to be produced in the city of Kyoto where the most elaborate kimonos were made. Inter-regional merchants could bypass the merchant guilds in Osaka and Edo to cut their margins, which helped the expansion of the market for mass consumer goods.

From the point of view of the rural household, this proto-industrial work was merely an extension of their labour absorption strategy. For example, the rural merchant would bring a loom and yarn to the peasant household and collect the cloth a month later, thus providing a small income for the housewife-cum-weaver. Or cottage industries would bring workers together in one place to manufacture sake, using simple tools and waterpower. For the rural household, the 'main' agricultural work remained rice cultivation. Both non-rice cash crop production and proto-industrial work of all sorts were called 'additional' work, whether performed by household members or hired labour (Sugihara 1997a).

The growth of proto-industry in East Asia differed from the European pattern, where geographic specialization occurred and the household combination of agriculture and industry disintegrated. While geographic specialization did occur, proto-industry in East Asia grew as a further development of the peasant family economy. The division of labour between agriculture and industry occurred through the allocation of family labour, particularly in the form of the gender division of labour. The 'main' agricultural work was considered to be primarily a man's job, while women engaged in 'subsidiary' agricultural work as well as proto-industrial employment, particularly silk-reeling and cotton weaving (Saito Osamu 1983: 30–54). Farm family by-employment, carefully scheduled and organized around the agricultural calendar, constituted the bulk of East Asia's proto-industry. There was relatively little need for urban growth and rural–urban migration. In fact proto-industrialization brought about a relative decline of urban industry in late Tokugawa Japan. Thus in industry too, efficiency growth occurred without substantial inputs of land, people and capital.

The persistence of traditional industry is well noted in Chinese economic history, especially for the period after the middle of the nineteenth century (Oyama 1960; Feuerwerker 1970; Chao 1977). Figure 3.3 explains how the traditional sector, in this case the cotton weaving industry, survived in the face of competition from the modern power loom sector. When the modern sector was able to supply cotton cloth more cheaply, the traditional sector was able to respond by reducing prices, because of the nature of farm family by-employment. Insofar as one could find surplus labour, either at night or during off-peak periods, without disturbing the 'main' work of the

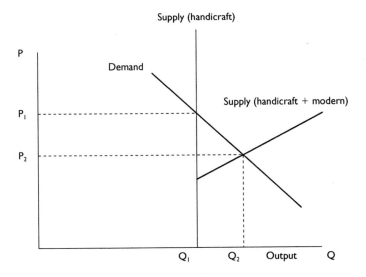

Figure 3.3 The survival of traditional industry
Source: Chao (1975: 200).

family, wages could come down to a very low level indeed, as there was virtually no extra cost involved in this employment. This was something which no modern factory could match.

The trap

Efficiency growth contributed to East Asia's relatively successful escape from Malthusian checks in the form of famine, epidemics and war, but failed to significantly increase labour productivity. If a society maintained a vast population without being able to improve the level of welfare for a long time, it could be argued that it fell into a 'trap', even if disasters were avoided. By the nineteenth-century Western standard, population pressure on land stifled East Asian growth, and the East Asian path fell into a Malthusian trap, often resulting in a significant degree of resource depletion. But it was a particular kind of Malthusian trap, because the society reached deadlock only after it had exhausted all the potential for efficiency growth. The higher the level of technical and institutional sophistication attained, the greater the degree of path dependence and the less flexibility.[1] Thus we get the sense that the trap resulted from dynamism rather than from stagnation.

Referring to China from the fourteenth to early nineteenth centuries, Mark Elvin called such a situation the 'high-level equilibrium trap' (Elvin 1996: Chapter 2). His point was that Chinese agriculture made various technological and organizational improvements aiming at high land productivity, but by the end of the period it had more or less exhausted the possibility of further improvements without the introduction of a radically new technology, such as that pursued by the Western path, which required a very different mix of factor inputs. Given the path dependency, the chances of such a radical change taking place from within progressively lessened. By this measure, Tokugawa Japan fell much more deeply into Elvin's trap than China during the same period. By the end of the Tokugawa period most Japanese entrepreneurs regarded Japan as the universe, and lacked the imagination to initiate big changes.

The government was powerless to tackle the issue too. Central and local governments played an important role, both in China and Japan, in reducing the risk of attacks from outside (the control of Japanese pirates was one such example) and maintaining internal peace. They also created a bureaucracy, and with it urban services and demand for food and clothing, in return for collecting land tax. Internationally, something of a balance of power was established in East Asia with the Chinese tributary-trade system in the centre, which helped maintain peace. But, as Chapter 7 by Arrighi et al. in this volume argues, there was no international order in East Asia, comparable to the one created in Europe by the treaties of Westphalia after 1648, that was able to back the growth of a commercial empire such as the one built by the Taiwan-based Zheng family in the seventeenth century. What was crucially missing in the region was the strong 'big' government of the nation-state in pursuit of territorial expansion and long-distance trade, willing to borrow heavily for that purpose and ready to promote big business and investment in fixed capital. Without such initiatives, there was no chance to develop the navigation and military technology, which in Europe prepared a scientific revolution and an industrial revolution.

Labour-intensive industrialization

Patterns of global industrialization

The standard understanding of the global diffusion of industrialization is that during the first half of the nineteenth century, Britain became the workshop of the world, while the rest of the world came to be specialized in the export of primary products. Countries in continental Europe and the regions of recent European settlement are thought to have achieved industrialization by learning new technology and/or by importing capital, labour and machinery with their export earnings (Hatton and Williamson 1994; Foreman-Peck 1995; Woodruff 1966; Kenwood and Lougheed 1999). In continental Europe, old barriers to trade and the transmission of knowledge were gradually removed, and an international regime which would facilitate, rather than hinder, the diffusion of industrialization emerged. The formation of the Customs Union in Germany in 1834 and the adoption of the gold standard by a number of countries of Western Europe in the late nineteenth century were among such moves.

Turning to the New World, the integration of vast natural resources into the international economy served as the engine of economic growth. Labour was scarce and land was abundant, and the difference in factor endowments between the old and the new worlds induced a growth of trade, migration and investment. Thus in the nineteenth century, the growth of the Atlantic economy dominated long-distance trade. Falling transportation costs were a crucial factor facilitating this process. This implied that the regions of recent European settlement had a greater incentive than Britain to raise labour productivity, using abundant natural resources and employing imported capital. The movement towards the development of labour-saving, capital-intensive and resource-intensive technology was most clearly observed in the United States (Habakkuk 1962; Saul 1970; David 1975). The need to save skilled labour led to standardization of industrial production such as the use of transferable parts, which in turn facilitated the transfer of technology across industries and mass production, as well as the 'deskilling' of labour. Industrialization became associated with the exploitation of economies of scale.

In recent ground-breaking work, Kenneth Pomeranz argued that this was not really the result of the accumulation of technology and institutions in Western Europe before 1800. Rather, the sudden rise of the West in the nineteenth century came from the incorporation by Western Europe of two highly contingent factors into its economic orbit: the availability of coal in the relatively developed regions of Western Europe; and (2) rich natural resources of the New World. Until the end of the eighteenth century, the core regions of Western Europe and East Asia were both exhibiting equally promising signs of development of commercial agriculture and proto-industrialization, and the standard of living of these regions were rising well above subsistence. Thus, for Pomeranz (2000), the West's rise during the nineteenth century was the 'great divergence' from the general pattern.

The American frontier was exhausted around 1890, and by the early 1920s migration from Europe ceased to be encouraged. But American technology continued to lead the world, by raising labour productivity through automation, the introduction of more systematic labour management and mass marketing. Looking back from the twenty-first century, the British industrial revolution only began to show the explosive power of labour-saving technology through the use of coal and steam engines, and merely paved the way for a fuller replacement of skilled labour by capital and technology. Therefore, although the 'industrial revolution path' may have been laid before 1800, the 'Western path', with an emphasis on capital-intensive and resource-intensive technology, arguably only became fully established, as a result of the 'great divergence'.[2]

Differences between East Asia and Europe became much clearer in the way industrialization occurred. In Asia the process started during the 1850s when India began modern cotton spinning in Bombay, and this was followed by Japanese efforts in the 1860s and the 1870s. In these cases the direct transfer of Western technology and institutions was the norm. By the 1880s, however, the Japanese government had developed an industrialization strategy quite different from its attempts in the preceding decades (for the significance of this change, see Sugihara 1995). Recognizing that both land and capital were scarce, while labour was abundant and of relatively good quality, the new strategy was to encourage active use of the tradition of labour-intensive technology, modernization of traditional industry, and conscious adaptation of Western technology to different conditions of factor endowment. The path Japan developed can be termed 'labour-intensive industrialization', as it absorbed and utilized labour more fully and depended less on the replacement of labour by machinery and capital than the Western path.

This pattern was essentially repeated in China and Korea, with state reinforcement, and the 'flying geese pattern of economic development' (Akamatsu 1962) emerged by the inter-war period. Both the development of labour-intensive technology, which occurred in East Asia in the previous period, and the colonial rule by Western powers in South and Southeast Asia which discouraged such a development in the subsequent period made East Asian producers of industrial goods competitive *vis-à-vis* those of other Asian countries. A number of relatively labour-intensive industries in East Asia proved to be internationally competitive. In particular, the Japanese cotton textile industry competed well in the Asian market with other Asian manufacturers as well as with Lancashire and other Western competitors. Thus there developed an industrialization-based international division of labour within Asia, and Japan, and to some extent China, was able to exploit the South and Southeast Asian markets for industrial goods. This was reflected in a much faster rate of growth of intra-Asian trade than of world trade between 1880 and 1939 (Sugihara 1996a: Chapters 1, 4; for English versions see Sugihara 1986a and 1998).

After 1945, in spite of the disruptions caused by the war, the growth in the international competitiveness of East Asia's labour-intensive industries continued. By the early 1950s, Japan had regained the position of the world's largest exporter of cotton textiles that it had held in the 1930s, and was replaced by China in the early 1970s. The chain of development of labour-intensive industries across other Asian countries has been impressive, starting from Hong Kong and spreading to Taiwan, South Korea, Thailand, Pakistan and Indonesia, and has by now reached many other countries, including those with the lowest levels of per capita income (Hayami Yujiro 1998). While the effects of this chain of diffusion cannot be seen as comparable to those of the global diffusion of high technology in a number of other respects (such as the effects on capital accumulation or on the international political and military order), it has surely been significant in terms of the creation of global employment. In fact, the majority of the world's industrial population must have been employed in those sectors primarily influenced by this kind of development. By now labour-intensive industrialization constitutes one of the two major routes to global diffusion of industrialization.

Going back to the period from 1820 to 1945, the fundamental difference with the period prior to it is that Western impact on the East Asian path of development became much more important. This is the case, in spite of the great influx of silver from the New World to China and the contribution of the Dutch East India Company to the growth of intra-Asian trade, particularly, though not exclusively, during the seventeenth century. By the middle of the nineteenth century the impact of industrialization had become world-wide. The key to the East Asian success was that the region was able to respond to the growth of resource-intensive and capital-intensive industries across the Atlantic resulting from the 'great divergence', by creating a resource-saving and labour-intensive path to industrialization. As a result, a new international division of labour emerged between advanced Western countries, with manufacturing competitiveness in 'high' (capital-intensive) technology industry, and East Asian and other developing countries, with manufacturing competitiveness in 'low' (labour-intensive) technology industry. Indeed, this was the only way in which the non-Western world could industrialize before 1945, given the international climate of imperialism, that is, by showing the West a new way of creating complementarity, which would increase world trade and output for mutual gain. By contrast, those Asian and African countries subjected to Western colonialism with a long tradition of labour-intensive technology, such as India, suffered from the imposition of technology and institutions associated with the Western path on an environment quite ill-suited to them.

The Japanese experience

Let us look now at the Japanese experience in the pre-Second World War period to see the origins of some of the characteristics of labour-intensive industrialization. First, it was rural-based. The first Japanese census conducted in 1920 found that the proportion of people living in cities was 18 per cent. Although this figure had risen to 38 per cent by 1940, it was still very small compared to most countries in Western Europe at a similar stage of development. The rate of urbanization in Britain exceeded 48 per cent by 1840 and 65 per cent by 1870, while the 'European norm' was 31 per cent in 1840 and 45 per cent in 1870. Put another way, the bulk of Japan's industry was a modernized version of the cottage industries, predominantly situated in rural areas. Between 1911 and 1915, 61 per cent of the population were engaged in agriculture, while the non-agricultural sector consisted of a large traditional sector (32 per cent) and a small modern sector (7 per cent). Cottage-industry production accounted for 51 per cent of total industrial production as late as 1909, and continued to grow in absolute terms. Takafusa Nakamura illustrated this process by showing the interdependence between traditional industry and modern industry (Nakamura 1983: 28 and 80. See also Figure 3.4). Thus, in its fully developed form in the early 1930s, the Japanese manufacturing industry had a relatively small, fast-growing modern urban sector and a large, slow-growing but steadily modernizing rural sector. Japanese manufacturing competitiveness, reflected in the rapid growth of exports to other Asian countries in the 1930s, came not just from the modern urban sector. The initiatives of the rural weaving industry played an important part in the expansion. In fact, it was more typically cooperation between the rural and urban sectors that was responsible for rapid export growth (Sugihara 1989).

Why was the modernization of rural industry so crucial? An obvious answer is that, given the technology gap, the relative abundance of cheap

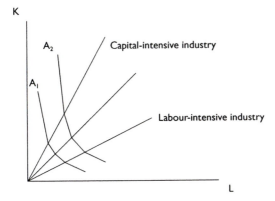

Figure 3.4 The choice of industrial structure
Source: Nakamura (1983: 69).

labour and the scarcity of capital, it was sensible for Japan to minimize the cost of building urban infrastructure, and specialize in the rural production of low-technology industrial goods. It was possible to produce many traditional commodities (such as ordinary kimono cloth and pottery) in bulk and mass-market them, provided the product was standardized and its quality was controlled. There were also attempts at production of transferable parts (Suzuki 1996). In the meantime, Western countries could supply capital and advanced machinery to Japan, so long as traditional commodities such as raw silk earned foreign exchange. Thus, the bulk of industrial goods produced in Meiji Japan were hybrid in character. Low-count yarn was produced in modern cotton mills in cities, while rural female workers hand-wove this machine-made yarn on improved traditional looms (and later power looms).

Second, a crucial factor in this process was the concerted efforts by local and central governments to foster rural entrepreneurship (Sugihara 1994). Rural promotion policies were first developed in the 1880s under French influence, with a heavy emphasis on agricultural protection. Following the Sino-Japanese War victory of 1894–5, however, the Ministry of Agriculture and Commercial Affairs staged a series of three supra-ministerial conferences between 1896 and 1898, in which a number of important policy proposals were made. By this time the priority was clearly on fostering internationally competitive export industries, while abandoning protection of uncompetitive branches of agriculture, such as raw cotton and sugar. With the exception of administrative reform (i.e. deregulation and reduction of the number of bureaucrats), most of the proposals were put into practice, though often in diluted forms and not immediately.

This rural orientation required the development of a set of policy tools quite different from the ones seen in Europe. It meant that there was a greater need to provide market information and technical assistance for the manufacture of local or regional industrial goods. Only those who were familiar with local consumer taste, societal values and peasant-worker mentality had a chance of identifying suitable markets and production methods, so members of the elite with a Western educational background or Westerners with good local knowledge needed a network of people who would cooperate with them. The government helped reorganize networks of local or regional merchants, and created a number of supporting institutions such as technical and commercial schools, commercial museums and regular exhibitions at the local, regional and national levels.

Third, turning to the development of modern industry, early government mills were ill-conceived and financially unsuccessful, but the success of the Osaka Spinning Company, which started production in 1883 with mules of more than 10,000 spindles, demonstrated the economic viability of modern factory operation. A few of the company's Japanese engineers managed to produce 15 to 20 count yarn, which was the suitable (low) count for the domestic market, without the presence of foreign engineers. Following the success of this company, many mills were established in the late 1880s. The ring frame, which was new and suited to the production of low count yarn, was imported through Mitsui Bussan, a general trading company, from Platt Brothers, and rapidly adopted within the industry. The invitation of foreign engineers was expensive, but the availability of Japanese-language manuals made it possible for local factories to operate new machines aided by the visits by Japanese engineers (Saxonhouse 1974). Short staple cotton suited for the production of low count yarn was initially imported from China, but in the 1890s direct links with Indian producers were established to secure a stable cotton supply. A cotton spinners association was formed partly to press the government to lift the import duty on raw cotton and provide freight subsidies for imports of cotton from India. In the 1890s, Japanese mills enjoyed extremely favourable circumstances for exports when Indian exports of cotton yarn to China were made difficult by the adoption of the gold exchange standard in British India, causing a rise in the value of the rupee against the silver-linked tael and yen. In the 1900s the ingenious technique of mixing short staple Indian cotton with a small amount of long staple American cotton was developed in Japan to cut costs and also to shift production gradually towards slightly higher count yarn. Some mills began to set up their own weaving operations, while the demand for improved handlooms (and eventually powerlooms) provided the basis for the development of the machinery sector (Nakaoka 1982: 54–61; Kiyokawa 1985; Sugihara 1990).

An overriding concern in this process was to minimize the cost of capital, which was scarce. The introduction of foreign machinery was thus accompanied by a variety of capital-saving devices. Along with the spread in use of the ring frame, which was relatively simple to operate, young country girls of 15 to 20 years of age were recruited from poor peasant households in relatively distant places, and were put into dormitories for the period of their stay (normally two to three years) as factory workers. The industry was able to save wage costs by selecting this section of the labour force, which was expected to play only a peripheral role in the maintenance and reproduction of the rural household. This was an effective way of recruiting and managing labour, albeit one whose long working hours, harsh working conditions and the prevalence of tuberculosis caused much concern. The dormitories also suited the night-shift system, which was another capital-saving device. To the extent that Japanese agriculture was labour-intensive, these girls were used to hard work and long working hours. This gave Japanese mills a distinct advantage over the competing Indian mills, which suffered from lack of discipline in their workers. Japanese workers understood the concept of loyalty and filial piety, both prevalent in rural society, and the knowledge that their performance in the factory would be reported to their parents and the village community at large, not only prevented them from running away from the factory when working conditions were harsh, but motivated them to compete with fellow workers to be designated a 'model worker'. Japanese mills took advantage of this strong rural societal base, and attempted to build on these traditional values to establish their authority (Sugihara 1986b).

In sum, the process involved complex interactions between the transplantation of Western technology (in cotton spinning, for example, which dramatically raised labour productivity) and the modernization of traditional technology (for example, in hand-weaving, which offered women in peasant households ample employment, due to the improvement in weaving methods). But a notable underlying characteristic was that, unlike most of its Western counterparts, East Asian technology aimed at the most effective use of labour wherever capital and labour were substitutable. This is the definition of labour-intensive industrialization adopted here.

The Chinese experience

China did not frame a systematic industrialization plan until the late 1920s and the 1930s, when the Nationalist government gained tariff autonomy, unified the currency and linked it to the international system, and announced comprehensive industrial policies. These plans were dashed by the Great Depression, the internal political struggles between nationalists and communists, and, above all, Japanese aggression and the Second

World War. Coble argues that the Nationalist government did little to help the Shanghai capitalists between 1927 and 1937, as it was preoccupied with the pressing short-term need to finance the war. The government failed to create an efficient bureaucracy, in part because officials often conflated their public duties with personal gain (Coble 1980).

On the other hand, there is strong evidence to suggest that a number of successful attempts were made by local, provincial and national governments to promote rural industries from the early twentieth century on. In Gaoyang, Hebei in north China, for example, a series of new policies, including a rural industrialization programme, were initiated in 1903 by Yuan Shikai, the newly-appointed Governor General:

> Inspection teams were sent to Japan where they discovered the semi-automatic iron gear loom. Prototype looms were imported and Japanese technicians invited to serve as instructors at a technical training school set up in Tianjin. Weavers in Gaoyang began to use the loom in 1908, and by 1910 Gaoyang had become the model for the new textile districts. By 1910, 20 per cent of the looms in use were iron gear looms, and by the middle of the next decade there had been a full conversion to the semi-automatic looms.
>
> (Grove 1993: 3)

There is no doubt about the resilience of Chinese rural industry for most of the pre-Second World War period (Rawski 1989: 76–7). The cotton trade between Shanghai and the rest of China grew rapidly, particularly in the 1920s. Raw cotton came to Shanghai where it was machine-spun; some of the yarn was sent to weaving centres in various regions of China, while some was woven there and the cloth sent to the countryside (Kose forthcoming). The interdependence between traditional and modern industries was clearly developing. An examination of various documents and periodicals published by the Nationalist government during the second half of the 1920s and the first half of the 1930s reveals that a large number of technical and vocational schools were being supported by local governments to improve production methods, with some notable results (for example, *Chinese Economic Journal* 1928: 609–11). A comprehensive industrial policy document, drafted by the Department of Industry and Commerce in 1928, included the promotion of inventions, the promotion of foreign trade, the establishment of commercial and industrial banks, the organization and reorganization of commercial and industrial trade associations, and the arbitration of management-labour relations (Mantetsu 1930: 81–4). H.H. Kung's manifesto in 1930 was in a similar spirit, and particularly emphasized the importance of industrial exhibitions and commercial museums.

Although these plans were only partially realized, the Nationalist government was able to control China's exchange rate reasonably well and raise import tariffs selectively to foster industrial development (Sugihara 2001). A series of boycotts against foreign (mainly Japanese) goods in the early decades of the twentieth century can be seen as part of this industrialization strategy (Goto-Shibata forthcoming). By the 1930s China effectively had become a 'rational shopper', importing machinery from many different countries, without necessarily being tied to capital imports from a particular country or affected by foreign pressures in ways experienced by the colonial states of Southeast Asia. For a country like China with a large rural population, it was difficult to determine whether to commit not only to import substitution but also to export-oriented growth. In the 1930s, however, there was a clear attempt at export promotion, with some success (Kubo 1999). In other words, the basic framework for economic nationalism was set, though industrial policies were pursued largely by local governments in a rather uncoordinated fashion.

Constraints on growth

Labour-intensive industrialization in East Asia contributed to a modest but notable rise in per capita GDP, but it did not match the growth of per capita income in advanced Western countries. This is because the region's developmental path was conditioned by both the international order dominated by Western powers and internal constraints on land.

As long as East Asia was willing to accept the international division of labour, in which the West specialized in resource-intensive and capital-intensive technology, and East Asia specialized in labour-intensive technology, the logic of complementarity worked. But when Japan attempted heavy and chemical industrialization in the 1930s, it faced the formidable problem of securing a supply of natural resources. It is well known that a variety of factors – investment, markets, emigration, and the availability of raw materials and other resources – motivated Japan's advance into Manchuria. However, in the 1930s at least, Manchuria, while absorbing vast amounts of capital and manpower, failed to become an adequate supply base for the raw materials and resources that Japan needed. In fact, the latter's need to import key raw materials from outside the yen bloc increased.

As Toichi Nawa has made clear, Japan's main economic motive for the advance into North China was to secure the American-type long-staple raw cotton produced there, and this was also one of the most important reasons why the Chinese spinners of Shanghai and the Nationalist government resisted it. Intra-East Asian competition in the cotton trade was the most important economic factor behind the outbreak of the Sino-Japanese War in 1937. Furthermore, the stronger China's resistance, the heavier Japan's burden became. Even if the conflict had been resolved,

Japan would still have been largely dependent on the West for raw fibres and for the raw materials for its heavy and chemical industries. With regard to the latter, Japan relied on British Malaya and Australia for iron ore, India for pig iron, Canada for aluminum and lead, Canada and Australia for zinc, British Malaya for rubber, and the United States and the Dutch East Indies for oil. In short, it was impossible to envisage autarky or even a significant reduction in resource dependency while at the same time pursuing rapid heavy and chemical industrialization (Sugihara 1998).

Even more important were the domestic difficulties, particularly the relative shortage of land. The level of agrarian rents was extremely high, and, in spite of high land productivity, labour productivity remained low by international standards (see Table 3.5). This set a ceiling for the rise in rural purchasing power and the standard of living of the peasant household. Because the bulk of industrial labour continued to come from the countryside, industrial wages were kept down as well. Under these circumstances, there was a limit to the expansion of the domestic market. The more East Asia industrialized in accordance with the new type of international division of labour mentioned above, the greater the productivity gap between East Asia and the West became. This constituted the background of the Japanese dilemma in the 1930s, which led to aggression and war (Sugihara 1997b).

Table 3.5 Land rent in different countries of the world *circa* the First World War

Country	Date	Type of field	Yen per ha
Japan	1921	Paddy field (one crop)	317.5
		(two crops)	396.0
		Dry field	97.1–109.4
		Mulberry field	232.8
England	before the First World War		25.0
Scotland	1912–20		20.0
Ireland	1881–1920		18.0
Germany	1913		19.2
Austria	before the First World War		24.6
France	before the First World War		12.0–16.0
USA	before the First World War		10.0–15.0

Source: Yasuba (1975: 67).

Note
Japanese data are taken from *Honpo Kosaku Kanko*. Other data are from Yasushi Sawamura, 'Nihon no Nogyo oyobi Nogyo Mondai (Agriculture and Agrarian Problems in Japan)' in Kamekichi Takahashi *et al.*, *Gendai Nihon Keizai no Kenkyu*, vol. 2, Kaizosha (1930: 635). The data included in this table has been assembled in this form in Moritaro Yamada, *Nihon Shihonshugi Bunseki* (The Analysis of Japanese Capitalism), Iwanami Shoten (1934: 188–9), and was cited in Yasuba's article in 1975. I have converted the figures from per tan to per ha, assuming that 10 tan equals one hectare.

The fusion of the two paths

The enlargement of the East Asian path

Figures 3.5 and 3.6 have been calculated from Maddison's work to show the changes in the patterns of global distribution of income. This is a 'Lorenz curve', originally designed to show the degree of income inequality for a particular society. If everyone in that society had the same income, the 'curve' would be a straight line from the bottom-left to the top-right corner. In reality some people are richer than others, so if we chart on the horizontal axis groups of people with different levels of income starting with the poorest group on the left corner and move from left to right, and plot the percentage of total income the poorest 10 per cent have earned, that the poorest 20 per cent have, and so on, we can

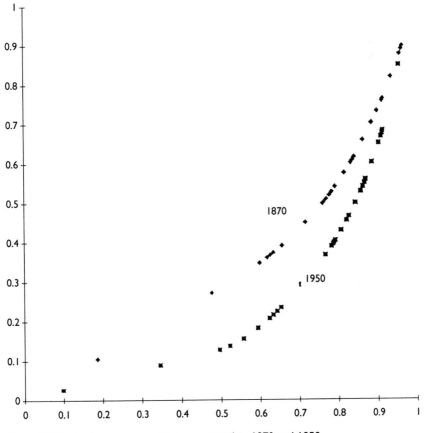

Figure 3.5 Global Lorenz curve (thirty countries) in 1870 and 1950

Source: Maddison (1995: 104–206).

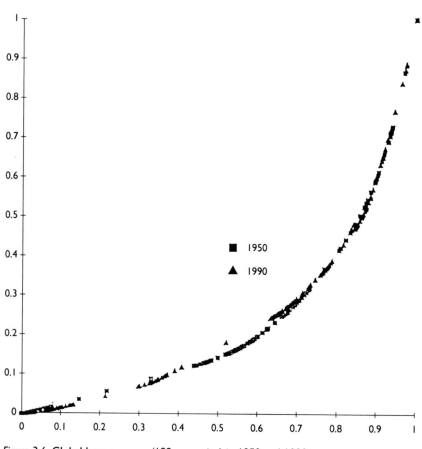

Figure 3.6 Global Lorenz curve (199 countries) in 1950 and 1990
Source: Maddison (1995: 104–206 and 217–21).

draw a curve which will have a downward bulge. The bigger the bulge, the greater the inequality.

Figure 3.5 differs from the normal Lorenz curve in that it represents global, rather than national, income inequality. It ranks thirty countries in terms of per capita GDP in ascending order, and allocates space for each country, proportionate to its population size, on the horizontal axis. Then the percentage of income the poorest 10 per cent had earned in global GDP, that the poorest 20 per cent had, and so on, is plotted. It is clear from Figure 3.5 that the bulge in 1950 was much larger that in 1870. In other words, between 1870 and 1950 there was a substantial increase in global income inequality. However, if we take 199 countries in 1950 and 1990 and do the same exercise, we see that the bulge in 1990 was about the same as that in 1950 (see Figure 3.6).

This change in the trend of the global Lorenz curve was largely the result of the 'East Asian miracle'. Tables 3.2 and 3.3 suggest that the sustained rise in per capita GDP in East Asian countries was the main cause of this change. First, Japan moved up the ladder of world ranking of per capita GDP, joining the high-income group. This move was then quickly followed by other countries in East and Southeast Asia, and eventually reached China. The overall effect of this on the curve was that a large number of East and Southeast Asian countries moved up the ladder from the low to the middle-income, as well as from the middle to the high-income groups, ironing out the bulge.[3]

In my view, this has a global significance which has not been well recognized. When Arthur Lewis wrote 'Economic Development with Unlimited Supplies of Labour' in 1954, he devoted the latter half of the article to the 'open economy model' and discussed why poor tropical countries were disadvantaged and the income gap persisted. His main message in the first half of the article was that economic development would be possible if poor countries were able to absorb labour from the countryside at subsistence wages. But in the latter half, he suggested that the equalization of global income distribution would be impossible unless agricultural (labour) productivity in poor countries was raised. He thought it unlikely that such an equalization was achievable in a short space of time. He had primarily tropical countries in mind, and the situation there, as well as the growing inequality between rich and poor countries, was too serious to make him feel optimistic about the future. In fact, it turned out that East Asia realized his dream, largely conforming to his vision of economic development. If the 'European miracle' was a miracle of production which initiated the transformation of the world economy, the 'East Asian miracle' has been a 'miracle of distribution', which brought the benefit of that transformation to the majority of the world's population.

If there was a missing element in Lewis' vision, it was the fusion of the two paths that enabled East Asia to overcome its resource constraints. In part, this was made possible by the Cold War regime and further development in the international division of labour. One of the most striking features of global development between 1945 and 1973 was the strong growth of capital-intensive and resource-intensive technology, both in the United States and the Soviet Union. One thing the two countries had in common was that they were able to translate abundant mineral resources into technological and military strength. Large-scale factories were built in the steel, aircraft, military, space and petro-chemical industries, and the technology race constituted a major element in the competition between the two with their different ideological stances the 1950s and 1960s.

This created room for a new international division of labour in which East Asia not only specialized in labour-intensive industries, but in the relatively resource-saving section of capital-intensive industries. After its defeat in the Second World War, the Japanese government was determined to pursue a programme of full economic modernization, primarily through expansion of the domestic market. But the problem of resource constraints mentioned above remained a critical bottleneck. The emergence of the Cold War offered the political background for a new American attitude towards Japan's economic future. By the late 1940s the USA viewed Japan as a country whose economic strength should be deployed to protect and further the 'free world' zone in East Asia, and it was allowed to pursue the systematic introduction of capital-intensive heavy and chemical industries. Although heavy and chemical industrialization was attempted in the 1930s and in some ways accelerated during the period of the wartime controlled economy, it was at this point that the character of Japanese growth shifted from labour-intensive industrialization to the fusion of the two paths, and its experiment began to assume global significance.[4]

Even after the Japanese 'miracle' was recognized, contemporary observers were slow to appreciate the economic potential of other Asian countries. This was in part because major political changes had taken place in Asia since the second half of the 1940s. Mainland China, India and some Southeast Asian countries either entirely or largely ceased to trade internationally, as a result of the policies of newly independent governments or as a consequence of the establishment of communist regimes and US-led embargoes. Some countries fought for their independence while others achieved it by political negotiation, and the 1950s saw the rapid progress of decolonization and a surge of nationalism. Although South Korea, Taiwan, Hong Kong, Singapore (collectively called newly industrializing economies, NIEs) and Malaysia came to be associated with the 'free world' at a relatively early stage, the clear entry of four ASEAN countries (the Philippines, Indonesia, Malaysia and Thailand) into the open economy zone had to wait until the middle of the 1960s. Then China, which had been heavily influenced by the Soviet model at the initial stage of the communist regime and had remained outside the 'free world' for thirty years, reopened the door to international economic contacts in the 1970s. By the early 1990s most East and Southeast Asian countries were participating in the dynamism of the Asian international economy.

East Asian growth was also closely related to the rise and demise of the Cold War regime. American hegemony provided an international framework in which NIEs and ASEAN countries pursued industrialization. They developed a variety of strategies, combining American technology and aid with cheap and relatively good quality labour. During the 1970s and 1980s some Asian countries such as South Korea and Indonesia gradually abandoned the heavy and chemical industrialization strategy, and tried to focus more on a thorough exploitation of human resources. What followed was the emergence of a new Asian international division of labour in which Japan specialized in relatively capital-intensive industries and the rest of Asia produced relatively labour-intensive goods. But a crucial change occurred when China changed its economic policy towards a more open and export-oriented outlook, as it dramatically broadened the region's labour-intensive industrial base. The fundamental problem of the Soviet model was that, with its emphasis on state allocation of resources, it lacked an effective incentive mechanism for production, distribution and consumption units (Hayami Yujiro 1997: Chapter 8). Therefore, China's re-integration into the regional dynamism of East Asia has inevitably been a gradual process. Nevertheless, in its fully developed form in the 1980s and the first half of the 1990s, the re-emergence of a powerful East Asian regional economy represented the fusion of the two paths, within the international order dominated by the United States.

In the 1950s and 1960s Japan chose to develop certain industries (such as automobiles and consumer electronics) which were neither too resource-intensive nor too labour-intensive, to achieve the fusion of the two paths. In this narrowly focused experiment, there was not much scope for a comprehensive fusion that would embrace the diversity of global economic allocation of resources. In the 1970s and 1980s, the range of industries which benefited from the fusion became broader, and it started to take place throughout Asia. Meanwhile, the success of the Cold War regime, that is, the retention of a period of 'long peace' (and this trend not only continued but was reinforced after the collapse of the Cold War regime in 1989), paradoxically reduced the importance of resource-intensive and capital-intensive technology. As a result, the relative influence of the two paths on the direction of global economic development became more equal. By the late 1980s, the transfer of Japanese technology was no longer confined to Asia. A large part of the recovery of the American automobile industry in the 1990s came from a conscious adaptation of Japanese production methods (Abo 1994). In this most recent period it appears that the sheer diversity of the Asia-Pacific region, in technological, institutional, and cultural terms, has offered the best opportunity to benefit from the fusion, enabling sustainable development on a global scale.

Japan's high-speed growth

The main source of energy for the Japanese economy in the immediate post-war period was coal, and the coal and steel industries were prioritized as the leading sectors for national economic rehabilitation. But it soon became clear that the domestic coal industry could not meet growing demand. Following the pre-war pattern, most oil firms in Japan depended heavily on capital and technology. The shift to oil began around 1954, and in the early 1960s the Ministry of International Trade and Industry (MITI) formulated a new policy for fostering the Japanese oil industry, in view of the vital importance of securing energy supplies. The biggest demand for oil in the 1950s came from the steel industry, but after 1960 the power stations became the most important consumers. The growth of demand in the transport sector and the petrochemical industry was also strong (Saito Tomoaki 1990). In 1953 oil accounted for 18 per cent of Japan's total energy consumption. Its share rose to 38 per cent in 1960 and to 71 per cent in 1970, all of it imported (Shimizu 1993).

Japan's domestic transformation into an oil-based economy involved fundamental structural changes. Pre-war Japanese industrialization was essentially based on coal, textiles and machinery and much of this activity was located in rural areas. The oil supply enabled Japan to expand its relatively small inorganic material-based sector into a leading sector of the economy. Major refineries and petro-chemical complexes were established along the Pacific coast, often using the sites of former arsenals and naval bases. Textile firms developed man-made fibre businesses. The steel industry invested heavily in large plants equipped with the latest technology, shifting its resource base from coal to oil. The machinery industry developed major new branches for the manufacture of transport machinery (tankers, trucks, passenger cars and railway carriages), electrical machinery (both industrial machinery and consumer electrical goods), heavy machinery (particularly for the construction industry) and precision machinery for industrial use. The shipbuilding and shipping industries were encouraged to build tankers and secure a level of tonnage sufficient to meet Japan's needs as well as to earn foreign exchange. Large ports and related facilities were built or renovated near major cities to meet the demand from the growth of trade.

It is absurd to view this development as an attempt to 'catch up' with or challenge the United States (or the Soviet Union for that matter), ignoring the fundamental difference in factor endowments between the United States and Japan. It is well known that the latter's heavy and chemical industries lacked a military side (Japan's aircraft and space industries were also weak). Although many parts of the heavy and chemical industries were related to the development of Japan's infrastructure and were capital-intensive, the bulk of the machinery (including shipbuilding and automobile manufacturing sectors), chemical and textile industries favoured labour-intensive processes, and it was these industries that eventually became internationally competitive. The Japanese automobile industry, for example, developed an efficient mass production system, with in-house programmes of skill formation and a well-organized network of subcontracting firms. These industries attempted to go beyond the constraints of Fordism, a technology which pursued automation, scientific labour management and economies of scale in a resource-rich and labour-scarce environment (Shimokawa 1994; Shiomi and Wada 1995). In the lower layers of the hierarchy of sub-contracting firms there was a growth of efficient small and medium-sized businesses, which offered the bulk of employment.

In other words, the fusion of the two paths occurred, not by attempting a direct articulation of the (originally labour-saving) imported technology and cheap labour (trained to replace capital) in any particular industry or factory, but through the development of inter-linked industries and firms with different factor inputs. The extremes at both ends, such as the space industry and traditional cottage industry, were abandoned and a balanced growth of industries in-between was attempted. Figure 3.4 was originally created by Takafusa Nakamura to demonstrate the rationality of the growth of traditional industry, and that, in fact, during the Meiji period modern industry and traditional industry coexisted and reinforced each other's development. But it can also be used to illustrate the process of fusion in which different types of industries simultaneously develop, linking and reinforcing one another, during the period of high-speed growth.

As such linkages formed, a massive rural-to-urban migration took place in the 1950s and 1960s. The proportion of city dwellers in the total population rose from 38 per cent in 1950 to 76 per cent in 1975. In addition to the demand for industrial workers, a huge demand for labour was created by the process of urbanization. The Japanese economy shifted its base from the rural household to the urban household, coinciding with a persistent rise in wages. But the standard of living did not necessarily rise as fast as nominal wages, since the urban infrastructure was poor, and living and environmental conditions were frequently appalling. On the other hand, the government made sure that social overhead capital, particularly goods and public transport, was able to cope with the demand arising from growth. Good communication networks also contributed to the diffusion of mass consumer culture. As a result, income distribution was kept remarkably egalitarian. At this time it was politically important to avoid creating a 'dual economy' of any kind. An effort was made to reduce regional inequality, while the growth of small and medium-sized businesses was encouraged.

While the increase in agricultural (labour) productivity, particularly in rice farming, contributed to containing the rise in agricultural imports, much of the new urban demand was absorbed by the growth of mass consumer goods. Initiatives ranged from the diverse attempts to mix elements of Western and Japanese food to the development of space-saving consumer electronics. In order to maintain the quality of labour with reasonable wage costs, it was necessary to form the stable urban household quickly and smoothly, and the management of big business sought to respond to this need. The diffusion of company housing and other welfare facilities, of occupational pensions and of 'companism' as an ideology all helped to fill the gap created by the rapid disappearance of the rural household and the village community.

Equally important was the rapid rise in the level of universal education. By the end of the period the majority of the core industrial workforce were recruited from high school graduates (at the age of about 18), rather than from junior high school graduates (at about 15). The investment in human capital was not confined to formal education. Large corporations adopted institutions such as lifetime employment, the seniority wage and the enterprise union, which suited their commitment to on-the-job training and their preference for multi-skilled workers. In the second half of the 1960s, the wage gap between white-collar and blue-collar employees narrowed, but what actually happened was that all workers increasingly came to be treated like salaried white-collar employees. Culturally and institutionally, class boundaries became very blurred.

The fusion in East and Southeast Asia

Coinciding with political splits arising from the surge of nationalism and the Cold War, fierce inter-Asian competition existed throughout the postwar period. Turning to the case of the cotton textile industry again, it was Chinese competition (and its price-cutting export strategy) that drove the rapid increase of labour productivity in Japanese industry in the 1950s (Sugihara 1999), and South Korea and Taiwan were Japan's main competitors in the man-made fibre market in the 1960s. More generally, relatively low wage industrializers competed well for their share in the world market for textiles, sundries and machinery, by using a technology similar to the more advanced countries. In this way, industrialization spread to low wage countries, encompassing a broad range of industries across East and Southeast Asia. As soon as wages in one country rose even fractionally, it had to seek a new industry which would produce a higher quality commodity to survive the competition, creating an effect similar to the 'flying geese pattern of economic development'. At the same time, successive entrance of new low wage countries ensured the lengthening of the chain of 'flying geese'. It is this aspect of industrialization, part of the enlargement of the East Asian path, that has been responsible for the increase in East Asia's share in world GDP.

As for income inequality, there has been an unmistakable rising trend in per capita income in lower to middle income groups among the participants in the 'East Asian miracle'. Although super-rich classes emerged in a number of Southeast Asian countries, the overall character of economic development was that of egalitarian income distribution. Under the environment of resource constraints, East and Southeast Asian countries invested heavily in human capital, which yielded a general rise in labour productivity. While there is a tendency for income inequality to increase to a peak before starting to improve as economic development occurs, the peak was reached in Asia when the level of per capita income was much lower than in the West. As a result, income distribution in East Asia has generally been more egalitarian than in advanced Western countries at similar stages of development (Oshima 1993: Chapter 9). Although like Japan, the rise in the standard of living lagged behind due to poor urban infrastructure, a 'law of rising expectations in the standard of living' has been set among the majority of the population. And, with high growth, expectations and living standards rose much faster than they had earlier in the case of Western populations. Even the informal sector came to look like a 'slum of hope' with a small proportion of people able to get out of the slum to move up the social ladder.

Another observation is that East Asian countries went through industrialization with a comparatively low level of energy intensity, because, in the early stages of industrialization, the region imported the bulk of its steel and heavy machinery from the West, and resource-intensive and capital-intensive industries never dominated the region's industrial structure. This was the case in spite of the wars in Korea and Vietnam, and despite the popularity of developmental authoritarianism and the influence of the Soviet model of heavy and chemical industrialization in some countries. If we take the period from the 1950s to the 1970s and compare the performance of Asian countries, those countries that placed more emphasis on heavy and chemical industries or did not promote agriculture and other labour-intensive sectors of the economy generally fared less well than those that pursued balanced growth with a more egalitarian profile of income distribution (Oshima 1987). Thus Taiwan in the 1950s and 1960s grew faster than South Korea, and China placed more emphasis on equality and education than India, with better results. Thailand outperformed the Philippines, and Malaysia fared better than Sri Lanka in terms of the improvements in agricultural productivity. As a result, the growth economies of East and Southeast Asia acquired a less resource-intensive profile than those following the Gerschenkronian 'catch-up' strategy or the Soviet model of economic development.

Clearly, the lack of proper infrastructure and dependence on cheap labour was a temporary solution to resource constraints with the serious consequences of pollution, poor urban health and congestion. And, as Table 3.6 suggests, many Asian countries were still going through the process of urbanization in this period. With the exception of Japan, a significant part of the building up of social overhead capital has been financed and/or guided by foreign resources. The East Asian regional economy has been conditioned by the development of a wider framework of the international division of labour, particularly in the Asia-Pacific. It would be wrong to assume that the growth of intra-Asian trade and a new

Table 3.6 The rate of Asia's urbanization in comparative perspective (%)

Country	1970	1993	1800	1870	1993
Japan	71	77			
South Korea	41	78			
Malaysia	34	52			
Thailand	13	19			
The Philippines	33	52			
Indonesia	17	33			
China	17	29			
India	20	26			
Bangladesh	8	17			
Britain			34	65	79
European norm			23	45	55

Sources: World Bank, *World Development Report 1995*, and Crafts *et al.* (1991: 112–13).

Note
The rate refers to the urban population as a proportion of total population. As the concept of urban population differs country by country, these figures should be taken as a rough guide. It is well known that the Japanese definition is too strict (hence the figures are too low) and the Chinese even stricter, ignoring the tens of millions of people living and working in cities without residence permits, confounding comparative analysis.

Asian international division of labour could have occurred without the simultaneous growth of Pacific and world trade and the enlargement of the region's resource base. The fusion in East and Southeast Asia was a truly global phenomenon.

The development of resource-saving technology

From the first oil crisis of 1973 Japanese technology showed a distinctive response to severe resource constraints. There was a concerted effort to diversify energy sources, the most important of which was an increased use of nuclear power stations. The exploitation of LNG (liquefied natural gas) also played a part. Furthermore, more efficient use of energy with the application of high technology and new industrial materials became a priority. Between 1975 and 1988 the oil intensity, measured by the ratio of oil consumption to GDP, fell by about 57 per cent (Hamauzu 1990: 50–1). Overall, energy intensity, the ratio of all energy consumption to GDP, declined substantially. In terms of the level of per capita energy intensity, Japan did far better than advanced Western countries.

Thus there was a significant shift from oil-using to energy-saving technology in the manufacturing industry, and a new industrial structure was built in the 1970s and 1980s. The relative importance of the steel, chemical, cement and aluminium industries declined. Within the machinery sector, the transport machinery and heavy machinery sectors shrank, while the electric (mostly electronic) machinery and precision machinery sectors grew. The automobile industry shifted its material base to harder and thinner steel as well as to plastics and other 'new materials', thus making cars lighter and more fuel-efficient, while the consumer electronics industry developed smaller and lighter products. The development of the machine tool industry enabled the production process in these sectors to become less energy-intensive as well.

At the core of this new economic structure was the development of the electronics industry. The computer, semi-conductor, telecommunications equipment and general electronic parts sectors interacted with one another, resulting in the creation of a sophisticated communications network to which many manufacturing industries could link their products and services. The dynamic growth of the service sector, not just in banking and distribution but in the new software industry as well as in medicine, education and management consulting, was also partly dependent on this new environment. Although the electronics industry was neither large in size nor always internationally competitive, it provided other industries with both vital technology and an informational infrastructure.

This application of the electronics industry's new products and knowledge to other manufactured goods played a significant part in enhancing the international competitiveness of Japanese industry. Exports of automobile and consumer electronics to the United States and the rest of the world grew rapidly, despite the appreciation of the yen from 1986. The strong yen adversely affected export industries, but also lowered the price of oil in yen terms. Equally important in this context was the survival of Japanese oil-using industries. The steel and shipbuilding industries attempted a reduction in energy consumption as well as a diversification into new fields on their own initiative (Hashimoto 1991: 71–143). They survived tough competition from other Asian countries by achieving productivity increases, partly through the application of high technology to the production process.

In other words, the Japanese path did not fully converge with the Western path, which had a much higher level of energy intensity. The Japanese level of energy consumption per capita per GDP remained among the lowest in advanced countries, and stayed at about half the American level, in spite of the latter's steady improvement in energy efficiency. Rather than finding new energy sources or financing new technology which would require inputs of additional natural resources, Japanese efforts were concentrated on developing new industrial linkages within the machinery sector, in the context of severely constrained factor endowments (Hashimoto 1996). Of course, as Japanese wages in dollar terms rose quite rapidly during this period, labour-saving technology advanced, and the simpler types of work were replaced by robots or transferred to other Asian countries. More importantly, however, Japanese industries (and society at large) attempted to increase labour productivity, not by deploying more capital and resources, but through the more efficient use of labour in manufacturing and service industries. It is in these areas that the recent transfer of Japanese technology to the rest of the world has been taking place. Furthermore, by the 1990s these tendencies came to be widely shared by other resource-poor Asian countries and city states, including Taiwan and South Korea. A combination of mechanical engineering and electronics helped them to build internationally competitive machinery industries (Zhou 1997). Of course, there remains a huge gap between the frontline technology and the reality of East Asian economies, and in some respects the gap may well be widening in recent years. But the innovative core of East Asian technology remains firmly in the resource-saving tradition of the East Asian path.

To some extent, the resurgence of the East Asian path was reinforced by the changes in the nature of the international division of labour itself. Between 1974 and 1985 Japan developed a huge trade deficit with all the oil-producing countries, especially of the Middle East, and settled it with an equally large trade surplus with the rest of the world, especially advanced Western countries. Faced with strong competition from Japan and other East Asian countries in the international automobile and consumer electronics markets, the United States and Western Europe were inclined to focus on exporting arms and military-related equipment, especially to the Middle East. This 'oil triangle', consisting of Japanese imports of oil from the Middle East, Western imports of Japanese manufactured goods and Middle Eastern imports of Western arms, constituted the largest single pattern of multilateral trade settlement in this period (Sugihara 1993). This development reinforced the new international division of labour where the West specialized in military-related technology and Japan specialized in high-technology mass consumer goods, maintaining the difference in the level of energy intensity, particularly between the United States and Japan. While East Asia depended critically on the United States for the region's security, American hegemony in turn depended increasingly on it's ability to monitor the changing international division of labour, as East Asia's share in global manufacturing output increased. This explains why the US–Japan trade conflict, on the face of it no more than a bilateral trade imbalance, became an issue of global significance.

Conclusion

In the standard literature on the evolution of the modern world system, industrialization is understood to have emanated from Western Europe and spread to the rest of the world, and all industrialization is simply taken as a chain of technological diffusion. In this chapter, we looked at the East Asian experience, and argued that in fact there were two paths of economic development, the industrial revolution path, which started in Western Europe, and the industrious revolution path, which developed in East Asia.

From this perspective, global development consisted of three phases. In the first period, from about 1500 to 1820, the two paths developed independently of each other, but with broadly similar results. There were significant connections between these regions, for example, through world silver flows, but they did not result in the convergence of the two paths. We have emphasized the fact that the East Asian path was more successful in maintaining the region's large share in world GDP, as it was able to increase the size of the population through the development of characteristically labour-intensive technology and labour-absorbing institutions. Core regions of East Asia, notably Japan and coastal China, matched the West in per capita GDP as well.

The second phase was led by British industrialization, particularly during the first half of the nineteenth century, and it is generally accepted that it spread principally to Europe and the regions of recent European settlement. This is a model based on the growth of the Atlantic economy. In particular, the growth of the US economy brought Western technology to a new height, exploiting abundant resources, economies of scale and a liberal political order backed by superior military technology. In fact, we suggest, there were two routes of global industrialization, one represented by the American experience which developed capital-intensive and resource-intensive technology, the other represented by the East Asian experience which developed labour-intensive and resource-saving technology.

The West European variety of industrialization did not spread into the non-European world in its original form, as the man–land ratio was very different there, and the straightforward introduction of Western technology proved to be problematic. Thus Japan, as well as China and Korea, pursued an alternative pattern of industrialization, with greater labour inputs relative to capital. This we call labour-intensive industrialization. Beginning in the 1880s, Japan created a wide range of modern Asian industrial goods such as cheap cotton textiles and noodle-making machines, to accommodate Asian cultural needs. Japan also reactivated traditional Asian local institutions, which eventually emerged as modern corporations committed to raising the quality of labour. During the first half of the twentieth century other East Asian countries followed suit. However, despite an increase in land productivity, and the growth of labour-intensive industries, during this second phase of global development East Asia's labour productivity lagged behind that of the West, and the region's share in world GDP decreased.

In the second half of the twentieth century, Japan underwent heavy and chemical industrialization, and acquired the highest level of Western technology while retaining the East Asian institutional framework, which permitted a more thorough exploitation of human resources than had been possible following the American path. By this time the mass consumer goods Japan produced (small cars and fax machines, for example) were no longer targeted at Asian cultural needs alone. It was not the industrial revolution in Britain or the subsequent Western technological advance alone, but the fusion between such technology and East Asian human resource exploitation that produced the very high rate of economic growth in East Asia.

This fusion did not occur easily. Although heavy and chemical industrialization began before the Second World War, it was not until after it that full interaction between the two paths occurred across the Asia-Pacific region. This fusion turned out to be much more powerful than the development of labour-intensive industrialization, involving deeper clashes and articulations of technology and institutions. It represents the third phase of global development.

Strictly speaking, the three phases sketched above are neither mutually exclusive nor geographically separate. The two paths both attempt to utilize capital and labour efficiently, and create institutions to do so. Depending on ecological and cultural endowments, different institutions are created at different times in different places, and they set the pattern and pace of economic growth. What has not been well recognized is that the greater the difference in the nature of the two paths, the greater the potential for generating growth. The different technological paths followed by Europe (and its offshoots) and East Asia between 1500 and 1945 created the best opportunity for explosive growth, especially in the Asia-Pacific region.

The development of the third phase has had major implications for global history. First, it suggests the possibility of a move to end worsening global income inequality. The possibility of labour-intensive industrialization is now a real one for the majority of developing countries. If the 'European miracle' was a miracle of production which initiated the transformation of the world economy, the 'East Asian miracle' has been a miracle of distribution which brought the benefits of global industrialization to the majority of the world's population. Second, the resurgence of the East Asian path has contributed to the diffusion of industrialization by retaining and promoting energy-saving technology. In spite of the rising concern about environmental destruction as a result of the diffusion of industrialization and the very high level of energy consumption in advanced countries, few would argue for a complete halt of this process. The only way to make global industrialization possible is a further improvement in energy efficiency on a global scale. In order to allow the miracle of distribution to continue, the Western path must converge with the East Asian path, not the other way round.

Acknowledgements

This chapter was originally presented at the conference 'The Rise of East Asia: 50, 150 and 500 year Perspectives', on 27–29 June 1998, at the Chinese University of Hong Kong, and was further discussed at the follow-up conference at Johns Hopkins University on 4–5 December 1999. I am grateful to the organizers and participants of these conferences, as well as to Gareth Austin, Mark Elvin, Yukio Ikemoto, Alan Macfarlane, Angus Maddison, Gerry Martin, Patrick O'Brien and Osamu Saito, for their useful comments. I have been able to respond to their comments and criticisms only at a very superficial level. None of them should be accused of not pointing out the factual errors or missing references that remain.

Notes

1 Much has been made of the fact that most proto-industrial regions of Western Europe failed to initiate the industrial revolution (Pollard 1981; Wrigley 1988). Even so, they must have had a greater chance than their East Asian counterparts in initiating one, if only because land intensity was less thoroughly exploited there, and the dependence on labour-intensive technology and labour-absorbing institutions was that much weaker.

2 Although Pomeranz acknowledges that capital accumulation and the scientific revolution were both necessary conditions for the industrial revolution, he does not see the 'divergence' between East Asia and Western Europe occurring before 1800. He argues that, far from escaping from the Malthusian trap, Western Europe after 1750 was heading towards the vicious circle of population growth, diminishing returns from land and the tendency towards labour-intensive technology, in the same way as East Asia had been. Thus the West could only be rescued by the contingent factors (coal and the New World). I substantially agree with his view, but wish to retain my emphasis on the important differences in the man–land ratio between the core regions of East Asia and those of Western Europe before 1800 (see Pomeranz 2000: 16–17, for his comments on my work). The core regions of Western Europe never experienced the type of land scarcity seen in eighteenth-century Japan, and it was in Japan, not Europe, that land productivity rose to the extreme and the perception of work was most systematically moulded around labour-intensive technology (Takemura 1997). It is as crucial to formulate the concept of the industrious revolution on the basis of the typical East Asian (Japanese) experience as to formulate the concept of the industrial revolution on the basis of the typical European (English) experience. It is surely possible to plot both the European experience of the industrious revolution (for a conceptualization of the European experience with emphasis on demand-side changes, see de Vries 1993, 1994) and the East Asian experience of capital accumulation (see Pomeranz 2000: Chapter 4) in the broadly Smithian–Malthusian comparative perspective suggested by Pomeranz (see also Wong 1997), without denying the notable divergences in factor endowments in Japan and England emphasized in this chapter. Pomeranz (Chapter 4, this volume) observes a similar pattern emerging in the Jiangnan region of China.

3 It is likely that the shape of global Lorenz curves for the period from 1500 and 1820, if they could be drawn would look more egalitarian than that in 1950 or

even in 1870, because the amount of global surplus over and above global sub-sistence needs must have been smaller. Certainly the East Asian societies in the earlier period looked more egalitarian. If that is the case, the post-war 'East Asian miracle' was a correction of temporary imbalance on a global scale, arising from the 'European miracle'.

4 If Pomeranz is correct in suggesting that the industrial revolution was unlikely to occur anywhere in the world without the presence of highly contingent factors, a similar sentiment can be expressed with regard to the fusion of the two paths. On the face of it, when world resources came to be freely allocated through trade and the pressure on land eased, East Asia could have converged with the West, as simple 'convergence' theory predicts. In practice, however, the popu-lation of East Asia and the rest of the developing world was so large that it would have been impossible to raise their standard of living to the Western level, given the level of technology and available world resources. In any case, American technology was so heavily biased towards resource-intensive and capital-intensive technology that it was ill-suited to the needs of developing countries. But to lower Western standards of living for a more egalitarian world would have been politically unacceptable to the population of advanced Western countries. Thus, a much more likely scenario would have been the persistence of the North–South divide, and the continued struggle for a greater share of income and resources among nations, leading to military and political tension. Fusion only took place because of the presence of two highly contingent factors; the Cold War regime fortuitously creating a vacuum which allowed Japanese indus-trial growth, and the Japanese determination to achieve economic moderniza-tion using the fewest possible external resources, which was an instinctive reaction to the self-inflicted consequences of the Asia-Pacific War.

References

Abo, Tetsuo (ed.) 1994. *Hybrid Factory: The Japanese Production System in the United States*. Oxford: Oxford University Press.

Akamatsu, Kaname. 1962. 'A Historical Pattern of Economic Growth in Develop-ing Countries', *Developing Economies*, Preliminary Issue 1: 1–23.

Booth, Ann and Sundrum, R.M. 1984. *Labour Absorption in Agriculture: Theoretical Analysis and Empirical Investigations*. Oxford: Oxford University Press.

Bray, Francesca. 1986. *Rice Economies: Technology and Development in Asian Societies*. Oxford: Basil Blackwell.

Buck, John L. 1930. *Chinese Farm Economy*. Chicago: University of Chicago Press. Reprinted by Gerald Publishing, New York, 1982.

Buck, John L. 1937. *Land Utilization in China*. Nanking: University of Nanking. Reprinted by Paragon, New York, 1964.

Chao, Kang. 1975. 'The Growth of a Modern Cotton Textile Industry and the Competition with Handicrafts', in D.H. Perkins (ed.), *China's Modern Economy in Historical Perspective*. Stanford, CA: Stanford University Press.

Chao, Kang. 1977. *The Development of Cotton Textile Production in China*. Cambridge, MA: Harvard University Press.

Chinese Economic Journal 1928. 'Technical and Vocational Schools at Foochow', *Chinese Economic Journal*, 3–1: 609–11.

Coble, Parks M. 1980. *The Shanghai Capitalists and the Nationalist Government, 1927–1937*. Cambridge, MA: Harvard University Press.

Crafts N.F.R., Leybourne S.J., and Mills, T.C. 1991. 'Britain', in Richard Sylla and Gianni Toniolo (eds), *Patterns of European Industrialization: The Nineteenth Century*. London: Routledge.

David, Paul. 1975. *Technical Choice, Innovation and Economic Growth: Essays on American and British Experience in the Nineteenth Century*. London: Cambridge University Press.

de Vries, Jan. 1993. 'Between Purchasing Power and the World of Goods: Understanding the Household Economy in Early Modern Europe', in John Brewer and Roy Porter (eds), *Consumption and the World of Goods*. London: Routledge.

de Vries, Jan. 1994. 'The Industrial Revolution and the Industrious Revolution', *Journal of Economic History* 54–2: 249–70.

Dore, Ronald P. 1965. *Education in Tokugawa Japan*. London: Routledge and Kegan Paul.

Elvin, Mark. 1996. *Another History: Essays on China from a European Perspective*. Australia: Wild Peony, Broadway.

Feuerwerker, A. 1970. 'Handicraft and Manufactured Cotton Textiles in China, 1871–1910', *Journal of Economic History* 30–2: 338–78.

Foreman-Peck, James. 1995. *A History of the World Economy: International Economic Relation since 1850*, 2nd edn. Brighton: Wheatsheaf.

Goto-Shibata Harumi forthcoming. 'Japanese and British Perceptions of Chinese Boycotts in Shanghai: With Special Reference to the Anti-Japanese Boycotts, 1928–1931', in Kaoru Sugihara (ed.), *The Growth of the Asian International Economy, 1864–1945: The Chinese Dimension*. Oxford: Oxford University Press.

Grove, Linda. 1993. 'North China Textile Markets in the Prewar Period: Native Products vs. Foreign Imports', paper presented at the workshop on China in Asian International Economic History, 1850–1945, May 1993, Osaka.

Habakkuk, H.J. 1962. *American and British Technology in the Nineteenth Century: The Search for Labour-saving Innovations*. Cambridge: Cambridge University Press.

Hamauzu, Tetsuo. 1990. 'Japan's trade with the Gulf States', *Arab Affairs* 43–51.

Hanley, Susan B. 1997. *Everyday Things in Premodern Japan: The Hidden Legacy of Material Culture*. Berkeley, CA: University of California Press.

Hanley, Susan B. and Yamamura, Kozo. 1977. *Economic and Demographic Change in Preindustrial Japan, 1600–1868*. Princeton, NJ: Princeton University Press.

Hashimoto Juro. 1991. *Nihon Keizairon* (Studies in the Japanese Economy). Kyoto: Minerva Shobo.

Hashimoto Juro. 1996. 'Daitenkanki no Kozo Chosei to ME Gijutsu Kakumei (Structural Adjustments during the Period of Great Transformation and the Technological Revolution in Micro-electronics)', in Hashimoto Juro (ed.), *20-seiki Shihonshugi 1* (Capitalism in the Twentieth Century 1). Tokyo: Tokyo Daigaku Shuppankai.

Hatton, Timothy and Williamson, Jeffrey (eds). 1994. *Migration and the International Labor Market, 1850–1939*. London: Routledge.

Hayami Akira. 1967. 'Keizai Shakai no Seiritsu to sono Tokushitsu (The Emergence of Economic Society and its Characteristics)', in Shakai Keizaishi Gakkai (ed.), *Atarashii Edo Jidaizo o Motomete* (In Search of a New Image of the Edo Period). Tokyo: Toyo Keizai Shinposha.

Hayami Akira. 1986. 'A Great Transformation: Social and Economic Change in

Sixteenth and Seventeenth Century Japan', *Bonner Zeitschrift für Japanologie*, 8: 3–13.

Hayami Akira. 1992. 'The Industrious Revolution', *Look Japan* 38–436: 8–10.

Hayami Akira and Miyamoto Matao. 1988. 'Gaisetsu (An Overview)', in Hayami Akira and Miyamoto Matao (eds), *Keizai Shakai no Seiritsu, Nihon Keizaishi 1* (The Emergence of Economic Society: An Economic History of Japan, 1). Tokyo: Iwanami Shoten.

Hayami, Yujiro. 1997. *Development Economics: From the Poverty to the Wealth of Nations*. Oxford: Oxford University Press.

Hayami, Yujiro (ed.) 1998. *Toward the Rural-based Development of Commerce and Industry: Selected Experiences from East Asia*. Washington DC: World Bank.

Hayami, Yujiro and Saburo Yamada. 1969. 'Agricultural Productivity at the Beginning of Industrialization', in K. Ohkawa, B. Johnston and H. Kaneda (eds), *Agriculture and Economic Growth: Japan's Experience*. Tokyo: University of Tokyo.

Hayami, Yujiro and Saburo Yamada. (eds) 1991. *The Agricultural Development of Japan: A Century's Perspective*. Tokyo: University of Tokyo Press.

Heywood, Colin. 1996. 'Agriculture and Industrialization in France, 1870–1914', in Peter Mathias and John A. Davis (eds), *Agriculture and Industrialization: from the Eighteenth Century to the Present Day*. Oxford: Blackwell.

Ishikawa, Shigeru. 1967. *Economic Development in an Asian Perspective*. Tokyo: Kinokuniya.

Ishikawa, Shigeru. 1978. '*Labour Absorption in Asian Agriculture*', Bangkok: International Labour Office.

Ishikawa, Shigeru. 1981. *Essays on Technology, Employment and Institutions in Economic Development: Comparative Asian Experience*. Tokyo: Kinokuniya.

Kenwood, A.G. and Lougheed, A.L. 1999. *The Growth of the International Economy 1820–2000: An Introductory Text*, 4th edn. London: Routledge.

Kiyokawa Yukihiko. 1985. 'Nihon Menboshi-gyo ni okeru Ringu Boki no Saiyo o Megutte: Gijutsu Sentaku no Shiten yori' (On the Introduction of the Ring Frame into the Japanese Cotton Spinning Industry: A Study of Technology Choice), *Keizai Kenkyu* 36–3: 214–27.

Kose, Hajime forthcoming. 'The Impact of Industrialisation on Foreign and Internal Trade: A Statistical Analysis of Regional Commodity Flows in China, 1899–1931', in Kaoru Sugihara (ed.), *The Growth of the Asian International Economy, 1864–1945*. Oxford: Oxford University Press.

Kubo Toru. 1999. *Senkanki Chugoku Jiritsueno Michi: Kanzei Tuka Seisaku to Keizai Hatten* (A Road to Independence in Inter-war China: Tariff and Monetary Policy and Economic Development). Tokyo: Tokyo Daigaku Shuppankai.

Lewis, W. Arthur. 1954. 'Economic Development with Unlimited Supplies of Labour', *Manchester School* 22–2: 139–91.

Lewis, W. Arthur. 1978. *Growth and Fluctuations, 1870–1913*. London: George Allen and Unwin.

Liu, Paul K.C. and Kuo-shu Hwang. 1977. 'Population Change and Economic Development in Mainland China since 1400', *Proceedings of the National Science Council*, ROC, 1–11: 143–55.

Macfarlane, Alan. 1997. *The Savage Wars of Peace: England, Japan and the Malthusian Trap*. Oxford: Blackwell.

Maddison, Angus. 1995. *Monitoring the World Economy, 1820–1992*. Paris: Development Centre, OECD.

Maddison, Angus. 1998. *Chinese Economic Performance in the Long Run*. Paris: Development Centre, OECD.

Malthus, T.R. [1798] 1993. *An Essay on the Principle of Population*. Oxford: Oxford University Press.

Mantetsu Chosaka. 1930. *Kokumin Seifu no Sangyo Seisaku* (Industrial Policy of the Nationalist Government). Japanese translation.

Marx, Karl. [1867] 1990. *Capital: A Critique of Political Economy*, Vols 1–3. London: Penguin Books.

Nakamura, Takafusa. 1983. *Economic Growth in Prewar Japan* Tokyo: University of Tokyo Press.

Nakaoka, Tetsuro. 1982. 'The Role of Domestic Technical Innovation in Foreign Technology Transfer: The Case of the Japanese Cotton Textile Industry', *Osaka City University Economic Review* 18: 45–62.

Naquin, Susan and Rawski, Evelyn S. 1987. *Chinese Society in the Eighteenth Century*. New Haven, CT: Yale University Press.

North, Douglas C. and Thomas, Robert Paul. 1973. *The Rise of the Western World*. Cambridge: Cambridge University Press.

Oshima, Harry. 1987. *Economic Development in Monsoon Asia: A Comparative Study*. Tokyo: University of Tokyo Press.

Oshima, Harry. 1993. *Strategic Processes in Monsoon Asia's Economic Development*. Baltimore, MD: Johns Hopkins University Press.

Oyama Masaaki. 1960. 'Shinmatsu Chugoku ni okeru Gaikoku Men Seihin no Ryunyu' (The Import of Foreign Cotton Textiles to China in the Late Qing), Kindai Chugoku Kenkyu I'inkai (ed.), *Kindai Chugoku Kenkyu* No. 4, Tokyo Daigaku Shuppankai (reprinted in Masaaki Oyama, *Min-Shin Shakai Keizaishi Kenkyu*. Tokyo: Tokyo Daigaku Shuppankai, 1992).

Perkins, Dwight H. 1969. *Agricultural Development in China 1368–1968*. Chicago: Aldine.

Pollard, Sydney. 1981. *Peaceful Conquest: The Industrialization of Europe, 1760–1970*. Oxford: Oxford University Press.

Pomeranz, Kenneth. 2000. *The Great Divergence; China, Europe, and the Making of the Modern World Economy*. Princeton, NJ: Princeton University Press.

Rawski, Thomas G. 1989. *Economic Growth in Prewar China*. Berkeley, CA: University of California Press.

Saito, Osamu. 1983. 'Population and the Peasant Family Economy in Proto-Industrial Japan', *Journal of Family History* 8: 30–54.

Saito, Osamu. 1992. 'Infanticide, Fertility and 'Population Stagnation': The State of Tokugawa Historical Demography', *Japan Forum* 4–2: 369–81.

Saito Osamu. 1997. 'Ajia Jinko-shi Tenbo' (A Survey of Asian Demographic history), *Keizai Kenkyu* 48–1: 59–79.

Saito Osamu. 1998. 'The Context of Everyday Things', *Monumenta Nipponica* 53–2: 257–63.

Saito Tomoaki. 1990. 'Sekiyu (Oil),' in Yonekawa Shinichi, Koichi Shimokawa and Yamazaki Hiroaki (eds), *Sengo Nihon Keieishi*, vol. 2. Tokyo: Toyo Keizai Shinposha, 209–77.

Saul, S.B. (ed.) 1970. *Technological Change: The United States and Britain in the 19th Century.* London: Methuen.

Saxonhouse, Gary. 1974. 'A Tale of Japanese Technological Diffusion in the Meiji Period', *Journal of Economic History* 34–1: 149–65.

Shiba Yoshinobu. 1989. *Sodai Konan Keizaishi no Kenkyu* (Studies in the Economy of the Lower Yangzi in the Song). Tokyo: Tokyo Daigaku Toyo Bunka Kenkyusho.

Shimizu, Hiroshi. 1993. 'Japanese Trade Contact with the Middle East: Lessons from the Pre-Oil Period', in Kaoru Sugihara and J.A. Allan (eds), *Japan in the Contemporary Middle East.* London: Routledge.

Shimokawa, Koichi. 1994. *The Japanese Automobile Industry: A Business History.* London: Athlone.

Shiomi, Haruhito and Kazuo Wada (eds). 1995. *Fordism Transformed: The Development of Production Methods in the Automobile Industry.* Oxford: Oxford University Press.

Smith, Adam. [1776] 1974. *The Wealth of Nations*, Books I to III. London: Penguin Books.

Smith, Thomas C. 1977. *Nakahara: Family Planning and Population in a Japanese Village, 1717–1830.* Stanford, CA: Stanford University Press.

Sugihara Kaoru. 1986a. 'Patterns of Asia's Integration into the World Economy, 1880–1913', in Wolfram Fischer *et al.* (eds), *The Emergence of a World Economy, 1500–1914, Beiträge zur Wirtschafts- und Sozialgeschichte*, vol. 33, 2, Franz Steiner, Wiesbaden, pp. 709–28.

Sugihara Kaoru. 1986b. 'The Transformation of Young Country Girls: Towards a Reinterpretation of the Japanese Migrant (Dekasegi) Industrial Labour Force', in Janet Hunter (ed.), *Aspects of the Relationship between Agriculture and Industrialisation in Japan.* London: STICERD, London School of Economics.

Sugihara Kaoru. 1989. 'Japan's Industrial Recovery, 1931–36', in Ian Brown (ed.), *The Economies of Africa and Asia in the Inter-war Depression.* London: Routledge.

Sugihara Kaoru. 1990. 'Japan as an Engine of the Asian International Economy, *ca.*1880–1936', *Japan Forum* 2–1: 127–45.

Sugihara Kaoru. 1993. 'Japan, the Middle East and the World Economy: A Note on the Oil Triangle', in Kaoru Sugihara and J.A. Allan (eds), *Japan in the Contemporary Middle East.* London: Routledge.

Sugihara Kaoru. 1994. 'The Development of an Informational Infrastructure in Meiji Japan', in Lisa Bud-Frierman (ed.), *Information Acumen: The Understanding and Use of Knowledge in Modern Business.* London: Routledge.

Sugihara Kaoru. 1995. 'Keizai Hatten no Kiban Seibi' (Laying the Foundations for the Development of (Japanese) Business), in Miyamoto Matao and Abe Takeshi (eds), *Nihon Keiei-shi 2: Keiei Kakushin to Kogyoka.* Tokyo: Iwanamai Shoten.

Sugihara Kaoru. 1996a. *Ajiakan Boeki no Keisei to Kozo* (Patterns and Development of Intra-Asian Trade). Kyoto: Minerva Shobo.

Sugihara Kaoru. 1996b. 'The European Miracle and the East Asian Miracle: Towards a New Global Economic History', *Sangyo to Keizai* 11–2: 27–48.

Sugihara Kaoru. 1997a. 'Agriculture and Industrialization: The Japanese Experience', in Peter Mathias and John Davis (eds), *Agriculture and Economic Growth.* Oxford: Basil Blackwell.

Sugihara Kaoru. 1997b. 'Economic Motivations behind Japanese Aggression in the late 1930s: Perspectives of Freda Utley and Nawa Toichi', *Journal of Contemporary History* 32–2: 259–80.

Sugihara Kaoru. 1998. 'Intra-Asian Trade and East Asia's Industrialisation, 1919–1939', in Gareth Austin (ed.), *Industrial Growth in the Third World, c.1870–c.1990: Depressions, Intra-regional Trade, and Ethnic Networks*. LSE Working Papers in Economic History, 44/98. London: London School of Economics and Political Science.

Sugihara Kaoru. 1999. *International Circumstances Surrounding the Japanese Cotton Textile Industry*. Discussion Papers in Economics and Business, 99–6. Osaka: Graduate School of Economics, Osaka University.

Sugihara, Kaoru. 2001. 'Higashiajia ni okeru Kogyoukagata Tsuka Chitujo no Seiritsu' (The Emergence of an Industrialisation-promoting Monetary Regime in East Asia), in Akita Shigeru and Kagotani Naoto (eds), *1930-nendai no Ajia Kokusai Chitsujo*. Hiroshima: Keisuisha.

Sugihara Kaoru with Haruka Yanagisawa. 1996. 'Internal Forces of Change in Agriculture: India and Japan Compared', in Peter Robb, Kaoru Sugihara and Haruka Yanagisawa (eds), *Local Agrarian Societies in Colonial India*. Richmond, Surrey: Curzon.

Suzuki Jun. 1996. *Meiji no Kikai Kogyo* (The Machinery Industry in Meiji Japan). Kyoto: Minerva Shobo.

Takemura, Eiji. 1997. *The Perception of Work in Tokugawa Japan*. New York: University Press of America.

Thorner, Daniel *et al.* (eds) 1966. *A.V. Chayanov on the Theory of Peasant Economy*. Manchester: Manchester University Press.

Van de Ven, Hans. 1996. 'Recent Studies of Modern Chinese History', *Modern Asian Studies* 30–2: 225–69.

Wong, R. Bin. 1997. *China Transformed: Historical Change and the Limits of European Experience*. Ithaca, NY: Cornell University Press.

Woodruff, William. 1966. *Impact of Western Man: A Study of Europe's Role in the World Economy, 1750–1960*. London: Macmillan.

World Bank. 1993. *The East Asian Miracle: Economic Growth and Public Policy*. Oxford: Oxford University Press.

World Bank. 1995. *World Development Report*. Oxford: Oxford University Press.

Wrigley, E. Anthony. 1988. *Continuity, Chance, and Change: The Character of the Industrial Revolution in England*. Cambridge: Cambridge University Press.

Yasuba, Yasukichi. 1975. 'Anatomy of the Debate on Japanese Capitalism', *Journal of Japanese Studies* 2–1: 63–82.

Zhou (Shu) Muzhi. 1997. *Mekatoronikusu Kakumei to Shin Kokusai Bungyo: Gendai Sekai Keizai ni okeru Ajia Kogyoka* (The 'Mechatronics' Revolution and the New International Division of Labour: Asia's Industrialisation in the Contemporary World Economy). Kyoto: Minerva Shobo.

Chapter 4

Women's work, family, and economic development in Europe and East Asia

Long-term trajectories and contemporary comparisons

Kenneth Pomeranz

Scholars seeking explanations of the differences in East Asian and Western European development have often focused on family structure and gender roles. The earlier literature, dating back at least to the nineteenth century classics of Western social theory, argued that psychological differences caused in part by kinship organization inhibited capitalist development in Asia. These theories have now been largely discarded, undermined by both the success of various East Asian economies since the 1960s and a growing historical literature showing how various non-Western ideas could serve as functional equivalents of the "Protestant ethic."

More recently, scholars perfectly willing to concede that East Asian households sought economic advancement have shifted the grounds of discussion, arguing that East Asian family structures powerfully influenced the ways in which families deployed their labor – especially female labor – and that these patterns in turn help explain the economic divergence of these two regions over the past 200 years, and (to a lesser extent) the prominent role of low-wage female labor in much of China, Taiwan, Korea (and for some authors, Southeast Asia as well) today.[1] For reasons that will become clear below, most of this literature has focused on China; and most has combined, in varying ways, a set of arguments about Chinese culture in particular with a set of arguments about the supposed characteristics of peasant households in general. And to one degree or another, all compare East Asia with an ahistorical "Western" ideal type drawn largely from the household economics of Gary Becker (1981), rather than with the increasingly rich literature on the changing historical patterns of family labor allocation in Europe.[2] Consequently, they tend to contrast a Europe which was – for better or worse – relatively "liberal" in the ways that it thrust both men and women into the market with a China and Japan that were less so. But a closer examination will show that this dichotomy does not hold up well.

Meanwhile, at least some social scientists more interested in the role of women in contemporary East Asian development have been drawn precisely to this historical literature on early modern Europe (which, for our purposes, might better be thought of as "late pre-industrial"), and see strong similarities between these two cases – albeit 200–400 years apart.[3] We are confronted, then, with both models of enduring difference and models of stages and/or convergence.

This chapter questions arguments that rely on stable cultural differences (or even "essences") to explain economic divergence on the one hand, and claims for either long-run convergence or a common set of stages, on the other. Instead it emphasizes the flexibility of economically relevant gender roles in both Europe and East Asia, while also arguing that economic development is sufficiently path-dependent that cultural differences as they exist at any one moment can have a lasting impact. Differences in gender norms during the seventeenth to twentieth centuries did matter, but not necessarily in the ways cited in the literature. Very crudely, I will emphasize three patterns – one from Europe, one from China, and one from Japan – while acknowledging that the reality of all three places is far more complex and varied. (Other parts of East Asia are omitted both for brevity and because of my limited knowledge.) My emphasis in each case will be on relatively advanced "core" regions. These patterns are:

1   A Western European pattern in which there was *relatively* little difference in the geographic mobility of men and women, and in which the vast majority of women worked, both for the market and in production for domestic use, but in which (especially from the late eighteenth through the mid-twentieth century) families were encouraged to *seek* a situation in which women (and children) did not work for the market.

2   A Chinese pattern in which it was continually expected that women would produce for the market, as well as for domestic use, and this was viewed as desirable as well as necessary. However, different types of remunerative labor were gendered as male (e.g. ploughing) or female (e.g. rice transplanting or weaving); the extent to which households conformed to those preferences varied dramatically across time, space, and class, and some of the preferences themselves varied across time and space. Meanwhile, there were also very significant differences in the geographic mobility of men and women: differences which may be eroding now, but have proved quite durable and fairly consistent across regions.

3   A Japanese pattern, in which the idea of women producing only for domestic consumption existed, but was far less influential than in Europe (until the twentieth century), while ideas about the *types* of

market-oriented work thought to be "womanly" and compatible with nurturing one's husband and children were often quite important; and in which differences in geographic mobility generally mattered far less than in China.

All three of these cases, however, involved patterns of development and change, rather than fixed notions of the relationship between domestic life and production for the market. All three have, at various critical junctures, facilitated capital accumulation by appropriating a particularly large share of the product produced by women; and all three have, at various times, both promoted and interfered with the commodification of goods, services, and factors of production. But they have not done so in the same ways, and important differences remain. While Japanese and Western European patterns have converged to a significant degree in the twentieth century, significant differences remain, and Chinese patterns remain very different from either of the others. Analogies between Chinese patterns and those in earlier periods of European or Japanese development are sometimes illuminating, but more by highlighting peculiarities of those other pasts than by providing a template or model that we can see China now moving through.

Some general background: regions and patterns of economic change

This chapter takes as its backdrop a revisionist account of the origins of modern economic growth that I develop at length in a recent book: in many, but not all ways, that account dovetails with the argument presented by Professor Sugihara in Chapter 3, in this volume. Like him, I argue that much of East Asia consisted of a loosely linked set of heavily commercialized economies,[4] the most advanced core regions of which were quite comparable to the most advanced areas in Europe. I establish rough comparability between these cores as late as 1750 in life expectancy, levels of consumption, the efficiency of product and factor markets, and the degree to which market dynamics shaped the strategies of households. Perhaps most surprisingly, I find that, despite their very dense populations, East Asian cores were no worse off ecologically than Western European ones in the sixteenth to eighteenth centuries: i.e. both ends of Eurasia faced environmental challenges to their ability to continue supporting population growth without a decline in standards of living, but the problems of East Asian cores were not necessarily more intractable than those faced by their European counterparts at that time.

The East–West divergence that followed, I would argue, stemmed largely from (a) a series of discontinuous technological shifts in Northwest Europe (about which few would argue) and (b) a set of favorable resource shocks that allowed European technology and investment to develop in labor-saving, land and energy-gobbling directions at the very moment when the intensification of resource pressures previously shared by all core regions were forcing East Asian development along ever more resource-saving, labor-absorbing paths. These were paths which Europe too, had *begun* to travel, and would have continued to follow without this combination of dramatic shifts in both technology and accessible resources. (It is worth emphasizing, though, as Sugihara does in his chapter, that Europe had not yet gone nearly as far in this direction as some parts of East Asia: thus there was a rather large difference in relative factor endowments between East and West on the eve of industrialization, which became much larger still as parts of Europe adopted highly capital- and energy-intensive methods of production before there was much mechanization in East Asia. It is only in the twentieth century that the gap has closed to any significant degree).

One of the favorable resource shocks that allowed European divergence involved the shift to fossil fuels (partly a product of fortunate geography), which greatly relieved pressure on ecologically crucial forest acreage and on timber supplies. Another, which I discuss in more detail, concerned relations between core and peripheral regions in the Atlantic world which differed in crucial ways from those between cores and peripheries in East Asia (e.g. between the cloth-producing Lower Yangzi and interior regions that sold it rice and timber). Peculiar global conjunctures made the Americas a greater source of needed primary products than any Old World periphery: this allowed Northwestern Europe to grow dramatically in population, specialize further in manufactures, and remove labor from the land, using increased imports rather than maximizing yields. But in East Asia, various hinterlands boomed after 1750, both in population and in their own handicraft manufacturing. This reduced primary products exports to core regions: their growth essentially stopped, while labor and capital were redeployed out of manufacturing to manage land and fuel more intensively. It took fossil fuels, New World resources and the New World as an outlet for migrants (many of whom then produced primary products for export) to move Northwest Europe onto a completely new development path, and avert an ecological cul de sac like the Yangzi Delta's.

I recap this argument here not only because it informs many of the claims made below, but because it shapes the way in which the East Asian "region" is treated here. For the most part, this will not be an argument about either East Asia or Europe as a unit, but about a set of core regions in each area (above all the Yangzi Delta and England), which have economically important relations with a shifting set of hinterlands; larger regions are treated as artifacts, not facts, with a coherence that comes and goes over time. In fact, one argument that will be stressed repeatedly below is that at times the further articulation of a gender division of labor in both China and Japan has been an alternative to the further development of greater regional inter-dependence, whether across East Asia or within the politically unified realm of China; at times during the past 250 years, a further elaboration of the gender division of labor within certain Chinese regions has, in fact, been connected with a trend toward greater regional self-sufficiency that tended to *reverse* earlier patterns of inter-regional inter-dependence. (This contrasts quite sharply with the European/Atlantic world. There extensive inter-dependence, as measured by long-distance trade in staples, actually developed rather late; but once it did, we never see any substantial reversion toward regional autarchy.) But in spite of these limits on the usefulness of "East Asia" as a term to denote a functionally integrated region, there clearly was some important exchange – both economic and cultural – and I do see some shared characteristics which (as long as we remember to compare cores with cores and peripheries with peripheries) at least in Qing/Tokugawa times give its development a distinct cast. In elaborating these patterns, I share with the other authors of this volume a desire to avoid treating East Asia as a deviation from "normal" Western development, whether in family gender roles, or anything else: it seems more useful to see the region as embodying another development path that has also created significant successes, and which has enough similarities and differences with European development that each can be used to illuminate the peculiarities of the other within a more general family of intensely commercialized economic systems.[5]

The literature

Perhaps the most influential account of how gender roles have shaped Chinese economic development is that of Philip Huang. Central to Huang's argument is the notion that due to "cultural constraints," women were almost totally excluded from labor outside the home.[6] These constraints encouraged families to treat women's labor within the home as costless, and since the women had to be fed anyway, it made sense to keep them working within the home as long as that labor produced *something* (either in products to be sold or in items for domestic use that could substitute for purchases), even if the implicit wage rate per hour fell far below subsistence. Thus, Huang argues, the expansion of Chinese production and exchange between 1368 and 1978 rested on a non-market, "involutionary" dynamic. Such earnings helped the household meet its more or less fixed consumption needs, but did not allow for dramatic breakthroughs: indeed, the combination of low profits and a near-zero implicit wage made it pointless for the family to invest in labor-saving machinery, kept people locked in low-productivity tasks, and left but a small market for other than subsistence products.[7] Thus, "this was the commercialization of small-peasant production and subsistence";[8] it was radically different from Western capitalism, in which both male and female labor were sold on the market, and employers relentlessly sought ways to use labor only to the extent that it produced a marginal product greater than its marginal cost.

More recently, Jack Goldstone has offered an argument which at first seems to resemble Huang's, since it emphasizes the cheapness of home-bound female labor (in this case focusing on teenagers) as a deterrent to mechanization; but it is in fact significantly different. Goldstone points out that what Huang calls involution was not absent from Western European development: indeed, the same pattern of increased mobilization of family labor (and rapid population growth) to meet a relatively fixed consumption target amidst falling per hour wages characterized early modern Europe as well.[9] He also doubts that the implicit wages for adult Chinese women ever actually fell below subsistence, and grants that cultural constraints on women's mobility varied considerably across time and space in Chinese history. He does, however, accept Huang's claim that the wage gap between men and women in China was unusually large, because respectable women were not supposed to leave the home to work. He then posits that this reserve of very low-cost weavers and spinners was an impediment to the development of factories in China, since any mills that were built would have had to compete with home-based production, while using more expensive male labor.[10]

Hill Gates (1995) has meanwhile offered a different account of the intersection of gender roles and economic development in China. Essentially, she argues that the state in a "tributary mode of production" – in which surplus was extracted outside the market by an overweening state – forged an alliance with the heads of patriarchal families. Social stability and loyalty to the state were gained in return for confirming the dominance of the family head, including his ability to treat junior and female members of the family as commodities: forcing them to produce for the market while withholding the fruits of their labor from them, selling them in disguised fashion (through bride price) or even selling them outright. Since these same families were forced into commodity production by the heavy tax demands of the tributary state, the result was a "petty capitalism" of "patricorporations." Like Huang, then, Gates argues that an important part of China's story is that women's products entered the market, but women did not sell their labor power in a competitive market; they were always "owned" by one or another patricorporation which mediated all their exchange relations. However, while in Huang's scenario this resulted in the production of very cheap goods and no substantial accumulation (the benefits of women's cheap labor essentially being turned into subsidies for the continued subsistence of an ever-growing population),

Gates' argument does allow for substantial accumulation by the families that deploy their women. (What keeps this from becoming capitalism rather than petty capitalism, according to Gates, are aspects of the environment beyond the family: the insecurity of property and unenforceability of contracts once one moves beyond the kin network and confronts a state indifferent or even hostile to development.)

This is not the place to engage in an extended discussion of any of these views; I have written about all of them elsewhere[11] and Huang's work in particular has been shown to rest on a number of empirical and methodological errors.[12] But they do form an important backdrop for the rather different discussion of related issues that follows. For current purposes, three points will suffice. First, both Huang and Gates treat Chinese gender norms, family structure, and the basic institutions of the Chinese political economy as essentially static over a very long period of time (from the fourteenth century until quite recently for Huang, and from the twelfth century on for Gates); yet all of these things turn out to have been quite changeable. Even Goldstone, who focuses much more precisely on one period and allows for more variation in gender norms, seems to me to underestimate its extent, and not to take full account of the flexibility of these norms in response to changing economic incentives in particular. Second, both Huang and Gates contrast China, not with the socio-historical realities of European development, but with an ideal type of capitalist development, as if Adam Smith had been a chronicler of the actual institutions of early modern Europe. Thus both of them (Goldstone largely avoids this trap) treat any sign that state, family, or gender norms interfered with the abstract market as signs that China (and for Gates, Japan, too) was on a definitively different path from that which led to capitalism: they never ask whether comparable "imperfections" existed in Europe, and so can neither determine which East–West differences were real nor which were important. Third, Huang's attempts to measure the earnings of women and compare them with earnings from farming, on which Goldstone also relies, turn out to be based on very dubious data, and on a basic arithmetic mistake (a misplaced decimal point). These result in a mis-statement of earnings from weaving by over ten times, and of earnings from textile production overall of over 5 times.[13]. In fact, it turns out, that, at least in the crucial eighteenth and early nineteenth centuries, the earning power of women in China was much closer to that of their husbands than was the case in Europe, or probably Japan.[14] That the price at which families sold their cloth did not reflect an exceptionally low implicit wage makes Huang's story, in which the gains from under-compensating female producers are dispersed among millions of impoverished consumers in the form of very cheap cloth, untenable. On the other hand, it makes Gates' conjecture – that the labor of under-compensated women served accumulation by the producing patricorporations – plausible. However, she makes no attempt to measure the size or significance of this particular mechanism of accumulation, to compare it with others, or with the exploitation of women in different institutional settings.

General attitudes

In all these societies, one found cases in which powerless women were forced to work unusually hard for unusually little return; in all three, one also found families that could afford to do so attempting to "invest" in their daughters by giving them womanly skills. There was, however, a crucial difference. In China many of these womanly skills were (perhaps coincidentally) the same skills that moved a rural family up the value-added ladder toward better-paying kinds of production (textile production rather than farming, and within textile work a hierarchy from cotton production to silk production to silk embroidery). In Japan and especially Europe, however, the skills and knowledge that made a woman suitable for upward mobility were more likely to be purely domestic in orientation, rather than being skills that enabled either her natal or her marital family to move into more lucrative kinds of market-oriented activities. To that extent, what separates our cases seems less a matter of women's status – i.e. of one society being particularly oppressive of women, creating a pool of super-cheap labor – and more one of gender roles: how varying ideas of what *sorts* of work helped one fulfill true womanhood (or manhood) shaped a household's adaptations to the changing economic returns of various activities.

Most of the time, most people had to work, regardless of how their toil was regarded. It is significant, however, that in Western Europe, much more than either China or Japan, abstaining from market-oriented labor, and particularly having the women of the family do so, has long been associated with higher social status. Such attitudes were, of course, most often put into practice among the aristocracy, but they appear to have also exercised considerable sway among the early modern bourgeoisie and to some extent even among better-off landed commoners.[15] In a later, "bourgeois," era, this notion would become far more sharply gendered. The males of the new elite would distinguish themselves from their aristocratic predecessors (or at least what they imagined their aristocratic predecessors to have been) by emphasizing their *dedication* to work[16] – an identification reinforced by the fact that few except the very rich seem to have had either the inclination or the means to turn their businesses over to their sons when they grew up[17] – but paired with this was an idea that "true womanhood" required not working outside the home for pay. In nineteenth-century France, for instance, it appears (though the evidence is fragmentary) that middle-class men preferred taking two jobs to having their wives work, and fairly clear that working-class families generally preferred having children work rather than wives.[18]

By contrast, idleness was never prestigious in China, even for the elite: as David Keightley notes, even the aristocratic dead were imagined as working in the other world.[19] And this value applied to both males and females, at least from the Song on: even women whose families could easily afford to forego any income from them encouraged them to engage in productive, as well as reproductive, labor. What made for womanly virtue was diligence and skill at particular *kinds* of work (especially weaving and embroidery), and performing that work within the confines of the family compound:[20] but it was a badge of honor, not dishonor, for a woman to contribute to the family income through such work, and was thought to enhance, rather than detract from, her ability to serve as a moral guide to her children. Thus, as we shall see later, Chinese families with rising incomes tended not to withdraw their women from market-oriented labor (as occurred in nineteenth-century Europe), but instead to change the *type* of productive labor they engaged in.

Japanese patterns seem to have fallen between European and Chinese ones, though closer to the Chinese end. As Uno puts it "society scorned idleness in women of all ages, save perhaps the wives of nobles, feudal lords, and their top retainers"; "the emergence of (female) domesticity as a cultural ideal can be traced to the turn of the [twentieth] century."[21]

Four to five hundred years ago

Jan De Vries has argued forcefully for the origins in early modern Western Europe of what he calls (using a term coined for slightly different purposes by Akira Hayami) the "industrious revolution": a process in which, well before the mechanization of production, households in at least Northwestern Europe had begun to work more hours, and perhaps more importantly, to allocate more of their labor time to the production of goods for the market, while saving time for that labor by purchasing more things that they used to produce for themselves. The industrious revolution, then, is both a process of increasing labor (a result of a changing set of preferences which favored various kinds of goods over leisure) and of Smithian specialization, with the expected gains from increased efficiency.[22] As I have argued at length elsewhere, the same process can be seen, beginning even a bit earlier, in the more economically advanced areas of both China and Japan – and with similar results.[23]

De Vries proposes his industrious revolution, among other things, to resolve a paradox. If you measure the buying power of Europeans' per hour or per day wages in terms of grain – their basic staple – those wages fall dramatically between about 1430 and 1550, and do not return to 1350 levels until 1840 or later.[24] Yet at least after about 1650, inventories taken at death show a fairly steady rise in what ordinary people own – clothes, pots and pans, jewelry, furniture, decorations, and what have you. These two trends could occur together because people spent more and more hours per year working for the market (the decline of saints' days being one prime example), generating income that paid for these things above and beyond the large number of hours they needed to work for subsistence. In the process people may have decreased their leisure time; they certainly reduced the amount of time that they spent making things for their own households. The process is one of specialization, in which people stopped, say, making their own candles, and put more hours into weaving cloth for sale, buying candles with some of the income. (The process has a logical conclusion of sorts in contemporary two-income families who even contract out much of their child-rearing and food preparation.) Thus the industrious revolution combines an increase in the amount of labor, in the orientation of labor toward the market, *and* in the specialization of labor.

The same thing was happening in East Asia (and maybe elsewhere too). The rice-buying power of Chinese day laborers' wages generally fell from about 1100 on,[25] but nutritional standards do not seem to have fallen; nor did they clearly fall below those of Europe until well into the nineteenth century.[26] Meanwhile the earnings per day worked of much larger social groups, including both male peasants (whether renters or owners) and their textile-producing wives probably rose slightly between the mid-Ming and mid-Qing, at least in the advanced Yangzi Delta region; but because the ratio of (lower-earning) female to male labor days also rose, peasant families probably achieved their income gains at the cost of a larger increase in days worked.[27] There is also powerful evidence of an increase in consumption of "non-essentials" even by peasants, especially between about 1500 and 1750. Once you look for the literary evidence it is plentiful, from travelers' accounts to elite complaints about popular consumption, to gazetteer lists of products available in rural markets. In a recent book, I make an initial effort to quantify this, and find that for tea, silk, sugar and cloth, Chinese per capita consumption was actually significantly *higher* in 1750 than in Europe in 1800. The most advanced region of China, the Yangzi Delta, probably trailed somewhat behind English and perhaps Dutch consumption, but exceeded that of the rest of Europe. But for current purposes it is less important whether China was really as well off as Europe than it is to simply note that rural families in the Lower Yangzi, Lingnan, and other relatively advanced macro-regions were buying a great deal from the market, and paying for it by providing increasing amounts of goods to the market: the dynamic fits De Vries' industrious revolution much more closely than it does Huang's involution. The case is still stronger for the more developed parts of Japan, which may have had the highest standards of living anywhere in the seventeenth- and eighteenth-century world.[28] In general, increased marketization of the household in core regions of both Western Europe and East Asia was propelling them toward unusually high standards of living for pre-industrial societies.

What can we say about the deployment and the compensation of female labor in particular? Both in Europe and in East Asia, sixteenth- to eighteenth-century farm women and men both worked in the fields, though often not at the same tasks. The pattern is well known for early modern Europe.[29] It is also well established for Japan.[30] While women were generally paid less than men for farm work – even when the tasks were the same – the size of the wage gap seems to have narrowed during the course of the Tokugawa (1600–1868),[31] while, as we shall see, it was growing sharply in Europe.

It is often thought that Chinese women were kept out of the fields by pollution taboos, bound feet and/or concerns for their modesty; this is a great exaggeration. Though the Chinese phrase "man plows, woman weaves (*nan geng nu zhi*)" is extremely ancient, it co-existed with the phrase "husband and wife work together (*fufu bing zuo*)," and there is little evidence to suggest that it represents the actual division of labor in any rural region until fairly recent times. Indeed, Li Bozhong's survey of gazetteers and farming handbooks suggests that accounts of rural life describing men and women working at the same tasks do not disappear until the nineteenth century, and even then only in the silk-producing regions of the Lower Yangzi.[32] This position may be a bit extreme. Accounts stressing a fairly sharp sexual division of labor were common even before the nineteenth century, and the presence of a few counter-examples Li cites could sometimes reflect the copying of earlier textual models rather than lived experience. In the Yangzi Delta, it does appear that farming had become overwhelmingly masculine by mid-Qing times, but women were clearly involved in agricultural labor (at least at peak seasons) in most of the rest of China throughout the late imperial (1368–1912) period.

Where Chinese gender norms were far more restrictive than either Japanese or Western European norms was in the strong pressures on women to remain at home. Women – except for the senior generation – were expected to remain under family supervision as much as possible; even the brief overnight stays elsewhere that were a necessary part of religious pilgrimage were strongly discouraged. Consequently, there could be little in the way of a physical market (i.e. a place where people congregated to compete for work) for the labor of single females, as there was for males; this is part of what has led Huang, among others, to assume that families set the opportunity cost of having a woman do an extra hour of either productive or reproductive labor in the home at zero.

Moreover, the sort of life-cycle service that was an important part of work in both Japanese and English households (and which Goldstone sees as preparing those societies for allowing their daughters to enter factories once they appeared) was essentially absent in China. A teenage girl in England or Japan who was sent to a more prosperous household as a servant would return home afterwards, and was on a normal path to a proper marriage after that – she was probably both accumulating her dowry and learning skills that she could not learn at home but would need if she were to succeed in marrying up. (These might range from more refined deportment – particularly important, it seems in the Japanese case[33] – to kinds of household production that her parents could not teach her because only better-off households engaged in them (e.g. preserving fruits from an estate's orchard).[34]

By contrast, a Chinese family that sent its teenage daughter to another household was relinquishing her once and for all, and abandoning hopes of what Wolf and Huang (1980) call a "major," or proper, marriage for her. To invest in a daughter's future earning power and marriage prospects, one kept her home while she mastered womanly work. The term "invest" here is not merely an anachronistic nod to contemporary notions of "human capital" formation: the sums required to carry out this strategy could be substantial. In addition to feeding the daughter and providing her dowry, it cost money for her to learn the skills needed for a good marriage. A clean, light, and well-ventilated workplace was needed for more demanding crafts; more expensive kinds of weaving required rather expensive looms;[35] and plenty of valuable cotton – or for better-off households, even silk – would have to be purchased (and might sometimes be ruined) as she slowly learned spinning, weaving, or (most prestigious of all) embroidery.[36] Thus, though the simple equations that both Huang and Gates draw in different ways between limited physical mobility, economic exploitation, and barriers to development are questionable, this strong preference for keeping women within the family compound may indeed have had important influences on Chinese development.

In handicrafts, the early modern period shows roughly similar trends in Europe and East Asia, though the trends become evident earlier in China and Japan. Handicraft production for home use involved both sexes everywhere; the issue is the division of labor in handicraft production for the market. Here, if we look back far enough, we find an alliance everywhere between political authorities and some urbanites who attempted to make market-oriented crafts the hereditary monopoly of certain groups of male city-dwellers (except for the occasional widow); and everywhere, we find some people attempting to circumvent this monopoly by mobilizing cheap, and often female, rural labor. In China, this latter project succeeded quite early. Ming statutes set the compensation for hereditary artisans at such artificially low rates that these workers deserted in droves, and the system was essentially a dead letter by the late 1400s;[37] production of all but the fanciest and most specialized crafts moved to the countryside instead, with women becoming a large part of the workforce, especially in textiles. But the increased dominance of women in textile production for the market did not mean that men abandoned this field. Not only did men hold on to many of the most prestigious and remunerative kinds of luxury production; in areas such as North China, where weaving was by far the best-paid occupation available during the long agricultural slack season (and perhaps all year round), rural men as well as women continued to weave.[38] The only rural economic sphere from which women seem to have been systematically excluded was commercial activity that involved extensive travel. And overwhelmingly, this participation in the market economy seems to have been something sought, financed, and managed by rural families themselves (rather than, as in many parts of Europe, by a "putting-out" system controlled by merchants).

In Japan, urban and shogunal efforts to keep crafts in the hands of privileged city artisans collapsed along with the rest of the "medieval" social structure during the wars of the fifteenth century; both men and women in the countryside moved into all but a few crafts. While the Tokugawa tried – at least on paper – to re-"peasantize" the countryside, these efforts were at best a temporary success, at least in the more developed parts of the country.[39] And where craft production settled in the countryside, women were almost always heavily involved. In towns and cities, too, "it seems likely that women's economic participation in merchant and artisan households was more extensive than scholars have previously imagined."[40] Summing up patterns of "proto-industrialization" for Japan and England, Saito Osamu argues that the English pattern featured a sharper geographic division of labor, and the Japanese a sharper gender division of labor.[41] While this conclusion differs from the East–West comparisons that have been emphasized here, it is noteworthy that the complex division of labor Saito describes certainly did not exclude women from production for the market, nor mark either farming or handicrafts (as broad categories) as exclusively male or female. Instead, more specific products and tasks were gendered, and – particularly since, given the limited interregional division of labor in a flourishing domestic economy, each area produced many products – this was a division of labor in which both men and women participated in a wide variety of agricultural and handicraft activities (including some very lucrative ones).[42]

In Europe, putting-out merchants were quick to note the potential profits to be made by tapping rural labor supplies. However, a political system that empowered urbanites and (in some cases) prevented rural families from making their own decisions about labor allocation meant that the ruralization of industry proceeded more slowly than in core regions of China and Japan.

Urban artisans were widely agreed to have a legitimate property right in the monopoly rights associated with their craft; this could be regulated, but not simply ignored.[43] Enlightenment thinkers began to question the legitimacy of this sort of property, but not until after 1789 (in some cases long after) did legal codes reflect their views. Partly because of this, European governments – which tended to be preoccupied with keeping order in *cities*[44] – were well aware that any rapid dissolution of urban monopolies would lead to massive unrest, and frequently enforced bans on rural production. In much of Germany, the state moved – though not always successfully – to *strengthen* urban monopolies in the seventeenth and eighteenth centuries, guilds remained able to exclude rural competition even as late as 1848.[45] In spite of such efforts, rural industry continued to spread through much of Western Europe during the early modern period, and some masters turned from trying to exclude rural laborers to employing them. Nonetheless, millions of other country-dwellers were still legally blocked from industrial activities by the power of urban privileges.

Meanwhile, rural families seeking to produce textiles for the market might face barriers from within the countryside, too. The Dukes of Rutland, for instance, apparently concluded (with some justice) that the spread of rural knitting led to competition for agricultural workers, higher birth rates, and ultimately higher assessments on the land to support the poor: and as owners of three-quarters of the village of Bottesford and buyers of most of its marketed output, they were able to prevent the development of such evils. As late as 1809 (and this in England, heartland of both liberalism and European textiles), Pitt described their policy thusly: "A numerous and able-bodied peasantry is here supported, no stockingers, and care taken there shall be none." Not surprisingly, historians of Leicestershire have found that while textile development boomed in the county in general, it was often absent in villages that were dominated by a single noble family, and weak in areas of concentrated landownership.[46] In some parts of Germany (especially outside Prussia) guild restrictions effectively barred many workers (especially women) from participating in textile production well into the nineteenth century.[47]

Perhaps most striking – and directly contrary to the involutionist interpretation of female labor and Chinese development – the earning power of Western European women appears to have trailed that of their menfolk by much more than was the case in China, at least in the eighteenth century. Moreover, that gap was growing, as we shall soon see. By contrast, the earnings of a hypothetical Lower Yangzi woman working 200 days a year would in fact exceed those of a male agricultural laborer, even if the latter somehow found twelve months of work per year at unusually high pay rates. (They lagged behind the daily earnings of her husband if he was a tenant farmer, as tenants netted much more per day than proletarians – which no doubt mattered to power within the family, among other things – but for present purposes that is less crucial.) Thus, there is no reason to think, as Huang does, that Chinese peasant families would always prefer making their wives continue to produce goods for home consumption to purchasing goods that saved time and allowed them to devote more of their labors to specialized production for the market; on the contrary, the potential gains from doing just that would have been (as we will see) as large as in Europe. Moreover, any claims that female-made products were delivered to the market in this period at a below-subsistence implicit wage by "self-exploiting" peasant families is empirically untenable. If the women themselves were receiving a below-market return on their labor because they could not easily leave their homes, it would appear that it was the males in their families (and/or a senior, more powerful female) who were pocketing the difference, not the merchants who dealt in their wares.

At least to this extent, Gates' notion of a petty capitalist Chinese family exploiting its womenfolk has more basis than Huang's notion of a Chayanovian family whose underpaid female labor merely depresses prices for all. (We should be careful, however, about assuming that the crucial variable is always gender rather than generation: see Mann, 1992, 1997, on the power of senior women over the earnings of both son and daughter-in-law.) Chinese farm families may indeed have been extracting surplus value from the labor of their womenfolk in particular; but this claim requires evidence that, despite their relatively equal earning power (at least in textile regions), women consumed much less above their basic energy requirements than men; and what little evidence we have is mixed. At any rate, as we will see in the next section, the evidence for sharp differences in consumption is actually stronger in eighteenth- and nineteenth-century Europe. Gates' suggestion[48] that Chinese families have continually subordinated their women more ruthlessly to the goals of survival and accumulation by the family than could families in the more individualistic West rests on little evidence.

Two hundred to one hundred years ago

It is in the core of late eighteenth-century Western Europe, not China, that we find the largest and fastest-growing male-female wage gap. In the mid-eighteenth century, women's wages in agriculture were typically about half of those for men,[49] which was probably about the same as in the Yangzi Delta, but the gap grew thereafter; so did a gap in the amount of time worked.[50] By the turn of the nineteenth century, the differences were very large indeed. Horrell and Humphries' work on England,[51] for instance, shows the contribution of women to the household budgets of various samples of workers between 1790 and 1865 varying from under 1 percent (for households headed by miners and by high-wage agricultural workers in certain periods) to a high of 24.3 percent (for households of factory workers after 1846; otherwise the highest figure is 11.6 percent). In most cases even the contribution of children exceeds that of adult women (presumably because more than one working child was often involved), and that of women and children together reached 30–40 percent only for the poorest groups.

Even the highest of these figures for women is well below the ranges that would be plausible for either Japan or the more developed parts of China. Unfortunately, we do not have fully reliable figures on per day or per hour earnings; but given what we know of how much eighteenth- and early nineteenth-century women were involved in production for the market, figures like this must indicate far larger wage differentials than what we see in either China or Japan. (If we take just the 1787–1815 period in England, for instance, the multiple of men's earnings over women's for various occupational groups varies from 8 to 1 to 26 to 1;[52] nobody has ever suggested a gap in hours worked during this period that would bring the per hour wage gap down to even 2 to 1.) The little bit of gendered wage data we have that *is* standardized by time units confirms this. It appears, then, that Chinese women, despite being severely limited in where they could work, were closer to pay equity with their menfolk than were their European sisters;[53] the same to have been true (somewhat less surprisingly) for their Japanese peers.

It is harder to know how to estimate and assess gendered differences in consumption. Rural Chinese men do seem to have eaten *much* more than women. Agricultural manuals, for instance, suggest that adult females ate only half as much as adult males, and such a difference in consumption levels is logically necessary in order to square the manuals' figures for adult male consumption with the average figures for the population as a whole that we find elsewhere.[54] By contrast, adult women in nineteenth-century England ate about 70 percent as many calories as their husbands. But a fair amount of this difference may be due to differences in energy requirements: labor-intensive agriculture demands an astonishing amount of energy.[55] (Certainly nobody has suggested that this was a very fat group of male peasants.) Unfortunately, we have no gendered estimates of grain consumption in eighteenth-century *urban* Chinese families, where the energy demands of male and female work would have been much more equal; but the earliest such figures I have found (from Shanghai in the 1930s) yield a ratio between adult male and female calorie intake (1.36:1) that is almost precisely that found in most developed countries today.[56] And it is worth noting that many of the goods which we know the English working class was consuming in much larger amounts during the eighteenth century – particularly tobacco and liquor, which are most often cited as evidence of increased purchasing power – were overwhelmingly consumed by males; the same is true of the forms of commercialized leisure (boxing, horse-racing, etc.) that reached the popular classes before the mid-nineteenth century. In both China and Japan, it appears that goods which were less gendered, or even tilted toward women – medicines, cosmetics, textiles, etc. – made up a somewhat larger share of increased consumption. (They figure very prominently in elite complaints about popular consumption – though this may reflect a particular hostility to female adornment on the part of Confucian moralists – and in lists of specialized goods available in local markets.) These fragments are nowhere near enough to make a confident comparison of how males and females shared the household budget in East Asia and in Western Europe, but they at least place the burden of proof on anyone who wishes to argue that women in pre-industrial East Asia saw the relative equality of their contributions to the family pot turn into a greater disadvantage in what they drew from that pot than their European sisters suffered.

But just as important as the huge earning differentials *ca.*1800 that Horrell and Humphries point to are their arguments about what happened over the next several decades. Over the course of what we might call the long nineteenth century (and the first half of the twentieth century), labor force participation rates of both women and children tended to fall, except during a few periods of exceptional hardship.[57] Indeed, the phenomenon is sufficiently clear that De Vries[58] marks a period beginning around 1800, accelerating after 1850, and continuing until roughly 1960 as a distinct phase of his industrious revolution, in which households moved from a "labor-supplying" strategy to a "labor-withholding strategy." (He then sees another labor-supplying phase beginning in the 1960s and continuing through the present.) He sees this period as one in which households increasingly valued jointly consumed goods, both purchased (e.g. home furnishings) and self-produced (e.g. increased household cleanliness), while devoting less of their purchasing power to individually consumed goods (e.g. meals away from home, tobacco, etc.).

Even more important, De Vries argues that the labor-withholding strategy was compatible with increased investment in human capital in a way that the industrious revolution was not. At least English literacy rates had stagnated during the later eighteenth and early nineteenth century,[59] but improved dramatically from the mid-nineteenth century on as children went to school; health improved as fewer young people worked long hours, food was more carefully prepared, and homes were kept cleaner; and so on. De Vries ends his summary of this period with a sweeping though (as he admits) speculative statement:

> Indeed, I would go so far as to claim that it was more through the household productive system than the larger formal economy that the major achievements of industrial society – lower morbidity and mortality, better nutrition and higher educational levels, greater domestic comfort – were achieved. None of these "goods" could be bought off the shelf.

(1994: 264)

Since no comparable labor-withholding phase is evident in Japan before the early twentieth century, or in China until very recent times (if at all), De Vries' formulation poses at least three inter-related challenges for us. First, how are we to explain this striking divergence? Second, can we draw a compelling causal relationship – in either direction – between this divergence and the enormous divergence in living standards, technology, and capital accumulation between East and West during the nineteenth and early twentieth centuries? (It is worth remembering here that while substantial industrialization began in Japan in the 1870s, and in a few parts of China after 1895, even in Japan living standards did not approach those of Western Europe and North America until well after 1945.) Third, it has often been noted that early industrialization in Japan relied heavily on female workers who were unusually poorly paid even by the standards of the time. For instance, women in Osaka textile mills in the early twentieth century were more poorly paid than their counterparts in Shanghai or even Bombay,[60] though general living standards in Japan were certainly higher than in either China or India; and very low-paid female workers have been quite important in China's more recent industrial boom, particularly its most export-oriented sectors.[61] Can these patterns – in contrast to the labor-withholding pattern that became increasingly prominent in early European industrialization – be somehow linked to a fundamental difference in kinship and gender norms? We have seen that it is hard to credit notions that China or Japan had always under-compensated women's work more than more "individualistic" Western Europe did; but might it nonetheless be the case that such a pattern has been pronounced and important in the nineteenth and twentieth centuries?

Explaining labor withholding

There is no single, straightforward, explanation for the decline in the participation of married women and children in the English labor force. De Vries notes that both the first (fifteenth to eighteenth, especially eighteenth century) and second (late twentieth century) periods in which households supplied increased amounts of labor to the market were periods of stagnant or declining real wages,[62] but we cannot attribute the intervening labor withholding phase entirely to rising adult male wages, as he seems to suggest.[63] Temporally, the decline in female labor force participation starts too early, since real wages did not unambiguously turn upwards until the late 1840s.[64] Sociologically, the situation is complicated by the fact that the share of family income contributed by women behaved in roughly parallel fashion among families of high wage and low wage agricultural workers, outworkers, and tradesmen. Horrell and Humphries note, unsurprisingly, that women were more likely to remain in the paid labor force when their own wages were holding up well, and more likely to exit it when their husbands' wages rose and theirs did not;[65] in other words, it seems to be trends in the male–female wage *differential*, rather than rising male wages alone, that drive the story. (And, in a few specific but important cases, there was a drying up in demand for certain kinds of women workers at any price: the collapse of hand-spinning, and the switch to agricultural tools which required greater upper body strength, come to mind.) In light of this pattern, it is worth thinking about how important it may have been that this wage differential seems to have already been quite large in comparative terms *before* mechanization. Certainly we need to invoke something besides industrialization *tout court* to explain labor withholding, and this unusually large "gender gap" and/or the elite cultural ideal of not working for pay seem the obvious candidates. Given how thoroughly that ideal was overturned in the case of males, with nineteenth-century working hours reaching what were probably all-time highs even among men who had significant amounts of property, I would be inclined to place greater weight on the wage gap than enduring cultural ideals in explaining labor withdrawal. This, of course, still leaves the size of the wage gap itself unexplained; and at least in this chapter, it will remain so.

East Asian parallels and differences

By contrast, we see no nineteenth-century signs of increased labor withholding in either China or Japan; on the contrary, the labor-supplying phase of their industrious revolutions seems to continue unabated, at least in some regions. Indeed, the marked expansion of silk production in much of Meiji Japan and in the post-Taiping Lower Yangzi and Guangdong (largely in response to soaring Euro-American demand) involved a substantial increase in female labor for the market in both places.[66] The total number of workdays per year in Japanese agriculture rose 30 percent from 1880 to 1920, and the number of days worked per year by the average worker in agriculture by about 45 percent.[67] No comparable figures are available for China, but the trend in most of the country appears to have been upward. Xu Xinwu cites an early twentieth-century work year for Jiangnan women making cloth of 305 days, which far exceeds the 180–220 days that various scholars have suggested for these women 100–150 years earlier.[68]

Thus, measured against European expectations, it may seem that we have a non-story: with little growth in male real wages (Japan) or even a decline (much, though not all of China), there is no change away from a labor-supplying strategy. But at the same time, there are changes in the allocation of female labor *between* sectors that command our attention.

Before going any further, it is important to look a bit more closely at what was probably happening to real incomes in late eighteenth- to early twentieth-century China. The overall trend in per capita consumption of most goods other than grain seems to have been flat or declining. Grain consumption in average years seems to have held steady,[69] though disasters became more frequent and more devastating as the state became less willing and able to assist in rural crises.[70]

When we take the apparent decline in non-grain consumption apart regionally, we find something more complex than any simple tendency to sink back to mere subsistence. Average levels of consumption in the three richest Chinese macro-regions – the Lower Yangzi, Southeast Coast, and Lingnan – appear to have held up rather well, albeit with significant fluctuations. What is most striking, though, is that these affluent regions came to include a much smaller portion of China's population. The Yangzi Delta alone (the core of the Lower Yangzi region) fell from perhaps 20 percent of China's population ca.1750 to barely 9 percent in 1850, and roughly 6 percent ca.1950. The relative declines in Lingnan and the Southeast Coast were not as sharp, but the pattern is similar: the three regions together had perhaps 40 percent of China's population ca.1750 and under 25 percent in 1930. Moreover, within each of these macroregions, most of what population growth there was appears to have been in the regional peripheries.

Meanwhile, most of China's post-1750 population growth occurred in regions which, in the eighteenth century, had been major exporters of primary products to the Yangzi Delta in return for manufactured goods (especially cloth): North China (raw cotton), the Middle and Upper Yangzi (rice and timber), Manchuria (soybeans and timber), and, to a lesser extent, the Northwest and Southwest (mostly timber). As they filled up, all of these regions, except for Manchuria, exported far less to China's core regions. This partly reflected genuine ecological constraints, as their own growing populations eliminated forests and/or cut into earlier rice surpluses. In the Middle and Upper Yangzi and North China, it also reflected substantial growth of handicraft industry (mostly cottonspinning and weaving); this both reduced the market for cloth from older cores and meant that additional (mostly female) labor that might have otherwise been used to further expand agricultural output was re-directed toward handicrafts. In North China, worsening shortages of land and water were such that the marginal returns to additional labor in agriculture must have fallen steeply, but this was much less true in the Middle and Upper Yangzi. Qing officials in Hunan, for instance, were quite struck by how few peasant families (even with substantial government encouragement) chose to double-crop their grain fields, often attributing it to "laziness."[71] Instead it seems quite likely that as average farm size shrank in these areas, while cloth production soared, what was happening was a reallocation of female (and to some extent child) labor: rather than farm their smaller plots more intensively by utilizing all the family labor they had once used on larger plots, households utilized this labor for handicraft production. Given that the terms of trade were generally shifting against handicrafts during this period (the value in rice of a piece of cloth may have fallen as much as 50 percent in Jiangnan, where our data is best[72]), this may at first seem curious, though we must remember that labor used to produce a second (or third) crop on a given piece of land generally yields much less per hour than the labor used to produce the first crop.

It is probably still more important, though, that, in China, producing textiles at home was the epitome of what Francesca Bray has called "womanly work":[73] i.e. activities thought to nurture feminine virtue and to *contribute* to the increasingly central female role of raising proper children. Indeed, the same state that was hoping to see more double-cropping in the Middle and Upper Yangzi also made a systematic effort to show people there how to plant cotton, how to spin and weave it, and to promote the normative ideal of the "man plows, woman weaves" family.[74] Thus, an *increasingly* sharp gender division of labor within these regions can be seen as the increasing conformity of families to a long-established and heavily promoted notion of the proper family, brought into reach for more families by technological change (increased knowledge of cotton growing and its use in the Middle and Upper Yangzi, and the spread of spinning cellars, which trapped enough humidity to allow cotton-spinning during the long semi-arid season in the North[75]), and – in the Middle and Upper Yangzi, though not North China – by what were probably continued, though slight, increases in per capita income.[76]

Meanwhile, the declining ability of advanced regions to export cheap cloth and import primary products was one important reason for the very limited population growth in these regions. (In the early twentieth century, this constraint was somewhat reduced by the rise in rice imports from Southeast Asia, as Chinese and Indian laborers settled newly-drained "rice bowls" in the Mekong, Irrawaddy and Chaophraya Deltas; after imports more or less dried up from 1937 to the late 1970s, under the influence of foreign invasion, civil war, and then cold war, they have now again become important to these very dynamic regions.) A combination of out-migration and relatively efficient birth control kept population down, and helped these areas protect their standards of living,[77] which were still the highest in China.

Another part of protecting this standard of living under worsening trade conditions (at least in respect to the rest of China) was a move up the value-added ladder in handicrafts: as hinterland regions produced more low and medium grade cloth in the late eighteenth and early nineteenth century, coastal regions increasingly concentrated on higher-end cotton fabrics requiring more skill,[78] and (especially after 1860) on silk. These more expensive products were sold to an even more far-flung market (but with fewer potential buyers in each locale), including a number of areas beyond China. While this move up the value-added ladder is small compared to the kinds of advances we use as an index of whether contemporary developing countries are really entering the ranks of the prosperous (e.g. moving from textiles to auto parts or electronics), and thus easily overlooked, it is important to free ourselves from such anachronistic biases: and once we do, this appears as a perfectly normal adjustment of a sophisticated, though non-mechanized, industrial region responding to changes in the larger East Asian world of which it was a part.

In terms of gender roles, such a pattern of development had the effect of making the gendered division of labor in the most advanced coastal areas much sharper, just as it was coming to be in the newly (proto-) industrializing Middle and Upper Yangzi. As previously noted, Li Bozhong has argued that it is in the nineteenth century that references to men and women working together in the fields essentially disappear from the Lower Yangzi record.[79] The separation became particularly clear where silk production came to dominate, since silkworm raising, silk-reeling, and silk weaving all generally took place in separate buildings: in the case of both reeling and weaving, often buildings that were at some distance from the family's farm.[80] Under the circumstances, women could usually play little role in agriculture, and men little role in sericulture; moreover, as women's work became more skilled, it made more sense, from the perspective of maximizing household income, for both men and women to specialize. It is worth noting in this connection that in North China – where people were generally less prosperous, the agricultural season was shorter, and the cloth people produced generally coarser – both men and women continued to weave during the off-season.[81] Thus women did not leave the paid labor force in late eighteenth- to early twentieth-century East Asia as they did in Europe – quite the contrary – but they did tend, with some exceptions (such as the tea country, where there seems to have been almost no cloth production, and men and women worked side by side in the fields[82]) to leave agriculture and concentrate more on "womanly work."

Thus, when compared to European patterns of proto- and early industrialization, the Chinese pattern moved very decidedly in the direction emphasized by Saito for Tokugawa Japan. There was less geographic division of labor – though I would emphasize that this was decline from a very high base – as Chinese hinterlands and Japanese outer *han* imitated the textile and other industries that had first taken root in advanced regions; meanwhile there was a deepening and spread across space of the division of labor within the family, as families in more areas could afford to direct their wives and daughters into womanly work, while improved earnings for farmers relative to spinners and weavers (and in Jiangnan rising skill requirements) kept men out of such work. In Japan, rapid factory-based industrialization, urbanization, and revolutionary changes in transportation broke these patterns in the twentieth century, so that the country's new division of labor looked increasingly "Western." In China, however, where machine-based industry grew much more slowly,[83] the pattern became steadily more entrenched, and was widely assumed to be "traditional" by 1949 (even where it was actually fairly new); this would have important consequences for policy in the People's Republic.

Migration

Before moving to the post-1949 period, however, it is worth considering one other way in which gender and kinship norms may have had an important effect on economic dynamics: namely, through its effects on patterns of migration. Very crudely, poor people in a crowded region have two basic migration paths open to them. They can either move to where land/labor ratios are more favorable to them (e.g. a frontier) or to some place where capital/labor ratios are more favorable (and where there are likely to be industrial or service jobs, for which the supply of land is not crucial). In some cases, potential migrants may find a destination where both land and capital are more plentiful relative to labor than back home: for instance, post-1865 North America and Australia (for most migrants), and perhaps the southern cone of Latin America (for, say, Italian, though not German emigrants), or contemporary Western Europe (for South and Southeast Asians). But for most purposes, particularly before the surge in capital-intensive industry and farming that made the sparsely populated "neo-Europes" exceptionally rich, one can treat these pulls as distinct.

From the sixteenth to the eighteenth century, Chinese institutions had been remarkably effective at encouraging people to move toward available land, often over very long distances: we see just how effective when we consider that Chinese migration to Sichuan alone in the eighteenth century far exceeded all European migration to the New World in the three centuries from 1500 to 1800. This was due to the absence of various artificial barriers important in the West (e.g. one could move to the Chinese frontier while remaining free, while a poor Western European seeking the relatively under-populated land of the Ukraine or Hungary would have had to become less free, and two-thirds of whites seeking the free lands of North America had to indenture themselves[84]), to the presence of *hui guan* and other institutions that efficiently transmitted information about migration opportunities, and to a state that often provided seed money, loans, and either *de facto* or *de jure* tax holidays for people reclaiming new land.[85] But once empty and fertile land to move to had become scarce in the nineteenth century (except in Manchuria, Mongolia and overseas), it is striking to notice that relatively few migrants from poor regions moved toward the densely populated but high average income regions along the East and South China coasts.

The phenomenon of China's richest regions receiving few migrants and still sending many requires some explanation, since there were not the sorts of internal passports or other legal barriers that barred these flows in Tokugawa Japan and Maoist China. After all, despite its nineteenth-century troubles, the Lower Yangzi still had a much higher per capita income than the Middle Yangzi or North China, and as more and more people in those regions found it hard to get access to enough land, one could imagine them migrating toward the handicraft and service jobs of the Yangzi Delta; restarting its population growth, lowering its wages, improving the competitiveness of its cloth, and moving living standards in different parts of the country closer to the rough equality that an abstract model would predict for a society in which people, money, and goods could move fairly freely[86] and information about opportunities elsewhere seems to have been widely available. That is, one could imagine it if single women had been able to migrate alone (toward textile-making jobs) without stigma, had weaving not been seen as ideally done by women in a household in which the husband had land to farm (as a tenant or owner-occupier) and so on.

But in fact migration by unaccompanied women was extremely rare in pre-twentieth-century China: in part for that reason, Chinese cities (in sharp contrast to most early modern European ones) were almost always heavily male.[87] And if female potential weavers were only supposed to migrate as part of households with a male head seeking access to land, no such reverse migration back to the coast was likely to occur, even once interior areas had become pretty full. Even tenants in the Yangzi Delta generally earned more than owner-operators upriver, but the initial rent deposits that landlords required would have been a significant obstacle for poor farmers coming from inland regions. It took the rise of urban factory-based industry (some of which came with dormitories for single women workers attached) and a proletariat in the European sense in the twentieth century to create a significant flow of female migrants toward richer coastal regions. (This process was then halted again, as we shall see, by the CCP's ban on migration to the cities from roughly 1960 to the 1980s.) The restrictions on the geographic mobility of Chinese women – the one area in which they do seem to have been much more restrained than either Japanese or Western European women – may then have placed important limits on the ability of families to deploy that labor for maximum income before the 1920s: with important consequences for the geography of proto-industry, poverty, and development in modern China.

It is worth noting here, however, that even this story is perhaps not best told as one powered by a specific cultural restriction on women, particularly insofar as the counter-factual we are imagining is women moving from the hinterlands to Jiangnan to take up exactly the same work as before. The point seems to be at least as much a family division of labor which was normative for men as well as women (particularly striking if weaving really did pay better than farm work in the eighteenth century) and which went along with strong preferences (both on the part of the state and among individuals) for at least some tie to the land. As Charles Tilly and others have noted, the age of rural industry in Europe saw the growth of a rural proletariat (couples of two textile workers, or a textile worker and a hired hand), and, in some places, villages full of such couples. These rural proletarians often reproduced themselves for several generations, but were then relatively easily moved to the cities when entrepreneurs found concentrated factories preferable to dispersed putting out.[88] By contrast, the bulk of Chinese proto-industry was carried out in families in which one member still had strong ties to the land, and which often supplied their own raw materials (rarer in Europe, and virtually non-existent after the switch to cotton for fiber and coal for fuel). Such families were slower to move to cities even once urban factories existed: in part no doubt because they felt more secure and closer to the family ideal than even a wealthier family of two wage earners would be. Or, to put the matter in terms closer to those chosen by Sugihara, a household economic strategy based on participating in many kinds of production, on being able to extend the labor year to maximize income, and on the role of the household head as allocator of labor across these varied tasks may have made risking proletarianization seem particularly unattractive, even if this risk went along with moving to an area with higher average incomes. Again, then, a strongly defined gender division of labor seems to have been a partial alternative to a sharpening of the geographic division of labor.[89]

The past fifty years

The West and Japan

For Europe and North America, the most striking development in the gender division of labor since 1945 is what De Vries calls a new industrious or labor-supplying phase. After a huge surge in hours worked by married women during World War II, the late 1940s and 1950s saw a pronounced return to labor-withholding strategies, which were soon taken to be normal even for many working-class families. But since 1960, there has been a new and prolonged rise in hours worked by married women and, to a lesser extent, by teenagers, with only a very slight decline in hours for married men. Fourteen percent of married US women were in the paid labor force in 1940; 60 percent were in 1990. Labor force participation by 16–19 year olds rose more modestly, from 45 percent in 1960/65 to 55 percent in 1980/89, but even this relatively small increase is striking in an era in which school attendance was also rising markedly.[90] European patterns are not quite so stark – hours for males have fallen more than in the USA, and hours for women and teenagers have risen less – but the general direction of change is similar. The same is true with regard to the social and cultural accompaniments of the new industrious household: the decline of value added in the home and the increased use of fast and frozen foods, organized day care, professional tutoring services, and so on. There are also broad similarities across Europe and North America (though with some important differences, too) in the differing types of jobs men and women get: the greater (though of late probably declining) likelihood that men will have long-term job security, substantial benefits, and so on. (Of course many benefits are much less tied to jobs in Europe or even Canada than in the USA.)

Japanese married women are still slightly less likely to work outside the home than wives in most of Europe or North America, though the way in which data are categorized makes direct comparisons difficult. The far more striking contrast, however, is in types of work. Married Japanese women are far less likely than their Western counterparts to be found in well-paid or managerial jobs[91] and trail much further behind their male compatriots in the degree to which they enjoy security and benefits.[92] A surprisingly large percentage of married women do paid *manual* labor from within their homes, which is quite rare in other advanced industrial societies. Japanese society also emphasizes a female role as home-based contributors to the human capital of others, but without the strong prejudice against combining this with some sort of income-producing work that one found in the West from roughly the Victorian era through the 1950s.[93] The result is that the fairly high rate of participation in the paid labor force for Japanese women is not matched by either an emphasis on income-earning as an activity for women that is as important as domestic responsibilities or a sense that it is important that women have relatively equal access to the better-compensated and more secure parts of the job market. To put it in other terms, the labor-withholding phase that followed early industrialization in the West was never as marked in Japan, despite a parallel growth in the male/female earnings gap[94] and a comparably strong preference for a gendered division of labor (though not quite the same one as in the West).

Certainly Japanese households today, like their Western counterparts, are in a labor-supplying phase – except during the period when the family has young children. And, if anything, the recent stagnation of wages in Japan seems likely to keep many women in the paid labor force somewhat longer. The big difference is that Japanese women seem significantly more excluded from the better-paid and more secure parts of the labor force than their North Atlantic counterparts, and the current stagnation of real wages may well increase male resistance to changing that. On the other hand, the unusually high dependency ratios in Japan (due in part to exceptional longevity) seem likely to continue to rise, and since Japan seems far less inclined than either the United States or most of Western Europe to allow immigration substantial enough to counter-act this trend, there may be some erosion of the barriers keeping women out of the more skilled and permanent parts of the workforce.[95] Under the circumstances it seems possible that Japan will come to look more like the North Atlantic countries in many of these respects – and that Europe and North America will continue to move away from the nineteenth-century gender ideas that caused them (and, more tentatively, Japan) to deviate from Tokugawa-like "industrious" patterns. Since the ideal of the wife who did not work for pay came rather late to Japan in the first place, and has long been honored in the breach even by many middle-class families, it seems destined to mark a rather brief period in the country's history.

China: the collective era

The Chinese situation from 1949–78 looks very different from either Japan or pre-1949 China, and different again from developments since 1978. I begin with a brief analysis of the Maoist period, but will focus on the reform era.

On the one hand, most of the leadership of the People's Republic was quite determined to have all adults in the labor force, and was generally able to make this a reality.[96] Thus huge numbers of women entered the paid labor force (or the full-time paid-labor force) who were not there before, both in cities and in the countryside. This change was particularly pronounced in certain poor areas that had had few commercial handicrafts and where women were often either not needed in the fields or were not thought to belong there.

On the other hand, the new regime came over the course of the 1950s to think of what was essentially a two-sector model of the economy: agriculture and mechanized industry. This had fateful consequences for gender relations in the countryside; we will begin with them, and then turn to the urban and state sectors.

Rural handicrafts, like other "sidelines," were increasingly squeezed out of existence.[97] In the many parts of the country in which women had become increasingly specialized in handicrafts over the previous centuries, huge numbers of rural women found themselves effectively de-skilled,[98] and consigned to a crowded agricultural sector where they often faced both serious disadvantages (in, for instance, tasks requiring upper body strength) and serious discrimination, including various taboos. While attempts were made to train some women in the use of new agricultural equipment (in the favored areas where such equipment was available), they do not seem to have been very successful. In part, this was because of long-standing taboos against women being away from home, especially overnight, since tractor stations were few and had to serve large areas.[99] While women – especially older women – often retained control of such family-controlled sidelines as vegetable gardening and poultry-raising, which, during more liberal periods, could yield a large share of a family's income,[100] such work was not always possible, and was rarely highly valued by the official culture.

Meanwhile, the work-point system seems to have placed both a floor and a ceiling on rural women's earnings, so that they generally earned 60–80 percent (more often probably closer to 60 percent) of what males doing comparable work earned. Since most income was apparently paid to the household (represented by its head) as a unit, rather than to individuals, it is not clear how relative wages translated into individual access to goods; but for families in which relative influence, respect, or comfort were at least roughly related to the visible financial contributions of each member, work-points would probably have been the most relevant measure.

Thus, Maoism changed the economic significance of gender in both city and countryside, but in very different ways. Urban women seem to have moved much closer to economic equality with men. Birth rates, the hazards of pregnancy, and the incidence of poverty so severe that it forced neglect with the result that family members (usually girls) all decreased sharply in the cities; educational attainments converged at least through high school; wages were paid to individuals; and in many (though certainly not all) occupations, at least pay rates for the same work were equalized.[101] While the post-1978 era has seen disproportionate job losses among women[102] and some attempts to promote a "return to the household" for women as a positive program,[103] the bulk of the pre-1978 gains seem likely to be retained, and the one child policy (which has been far more successful in the cities than the countryside) has strongly encouraged families to invest as much in the future of their daughters as they would in their sons.

By contrast, though rural women also made gains (especially in life expectancy), many aspects of the re-gendering of work affected them negatively. The main path for rural women seems to have been from a pre-revolutionary world of very different kinds of labor force participation, with female work usually but not always less well compensated, and backed by an ideology of complementarity, to a more uniform world of paid work, with women more poorly paid for doing the same kinds of work as men (and bearing most of the responsibility for domestic work, too). Coupled with unprecedented population growth, a near-ban on migration after 1960,[104] and (at least much of the time) formal discouragement of traditional sidelines, this probably made the 1950s to 1970s the period of

Chinese history in which the involutionary model of the economy was closest to being accurate: however, the unit that disposed of "surplus" labor was no longer the family but the work team or brigade.[105] And in a situation in which nobody (except a few cadres) traveled much, prejudices against unaccompanied women traveling were not likely to be challenged. Thus, while we should not forget all the positive ways in which the early PRC laid a basis for the growth that has occurred since 1978 – providing unprecedented levels of public health, literacy, political stability, and water control, for instance – it also did much to freeze (or even create) both geographic and gender patterns in the countryside that have much to do with the extremely unequal experience of the post-1978 boom.

Gender and development in post-Mao China

For purposes of this chapter, three inter-related features of China's post-1978 development are particularly noteworthy: (1) the prominence of women (mostly young women) in export-oriented assembly-line plants; (2) the feminization of agriculture in many of the more dynamic parts of rural China, as men move into better-paid industrial and service jobs (though in some of the best-off areas, both men and women now disdain field work, which is done either by the elderly or by "guest workers" from the Chinese interior[106]); and (3) the ways in which many township and village enterprises (TVEs), which both need to make profits and to please local cadres, have simultaneously utilized limits on female mobility to increase their rates of accumulation, while assigning more desirable jobs in ways that tend to reinforce male leadership in the household.

The first of these patterns is found around the world, especially in export-processing zones; it thus requires no special explanation in terms of East Asian or Chinese characteristics. What may be somewhat unusual is the extent to which women go to these jobs without breaking with their families, continue to send money home, and so help stabilize the country-side.[107] Meanwhile, that these women can work away from home and then return to their villages as respectable adults separates them from the relatively immobile women of the Qing, and also from the rural-born women workers in Republican cities, who rarely returned to their natal places (unless they broke their contracts, in which case they probably did not return home to great respect). This may partly reflect changing gender norms, though it is also true that many factories today, like their Republican predecessors, house their female workers in dormitories and supervise them closely. Meanwhile, an important question for the future is whether these jobs, like employment opportunities for young women in many other times and places, will erode the control of seniors over juniors and males over females in rural Chinese families.

The second feature, though it shows again the remarkable flexibility of

Chinese gender norms under changed socio-economic circumstances (and thus casts still further doubt on any notion that they were binding on economic actors in the past, either), does not seem particularly surprising. Those who are more socially and culturally empowered are of course likely to move first into better-paying jobs; and farming is generally more compatible with child care and housework than many of the better-paying jobs (which often involve substantial commutes, or even a migratory existence). A more complex issue, though, is whether women experience this feminization of agriculture as ghettoization, and whether they implicitly compare this new division of labor to a gender-neutral one, or to one with a different gender division of labor (such as that of 1949–78).

There is evidence that some married women, even if they are being left further behind by their menfolk in terms of both income and connections to the wider world, may experience the combination of increased earnings in absolute terms (especially in peri-urban areas) and relative freedom from supervision as a positive development. Greenhalgh provides the following summary of attitudes in a market-gardening village near Xi'an, in which the men have largely moved out of agriculture: "Although [married women's] economic opportunities remained limited to family horticulture, they loved the open air of the fields and cherished the opportunity to make important contributions to the family economy."[108] Judd, describing a Shandong village where reform has had less impact than most, but where many men are nonetheless now in industry or working elsewhere,[109] notes that it is now common for women to retire from agricultural labor when their sons marry, while the daughter-in-law takes their place in the fields; later they will provide much of the child care, so that the daughter-in-law can continue to earn money. According to Judd, the mothers-in-law generally welcome this arrangement while for the daughters-in-law "the period between a woman's marriage and the birth of her first child may be one of the pleasantest periods of her life."[110]

If this were a common situation, it would represent a remarkable contrast to the picture provided in classic ethnographies of rural China, in which these were generally presumed to be the most miserable years of a woman's life (and had the suicide rates to prove it).[111] On the other hand, the women quoted above may be putting the best possible face on their situation for benefit of their foreign interlocutors; most women are presumably aware of the advantages of non-farm employment, and many of them must find exclusion from such work disturbing, even if they also agree that their lot within agriculture has improved. With only anecdotal evidence, I see no way to tell how common any given reaction is.

Little of this needs to be explained in terms of particularly Chinese or East Asian patterns; but the feminization of farming, particularly insofar as some women do find it acceptable, may provide an interesting perspective on Chinese gender roles. As Susan Mann has recently noted,[112] when asked to think about Chinese gender roles, most of us immediately think about male–female interactions in the family. Yet millions of Chinese have always passed much of their time in unisex environments, including work environments: the "inner quarters" of well-off households, the *huiguan* and other social clubs of overwhelmingly male cities, and many of the work teams of the collective era were all essentially unisex. And while some work environments are becoming more integrated today, the agricultural example above suggests that new unisex workplaces are also appearing. With both short- and long-term travel still much easier for men, a state that still enforces links to the land for millions of families, and a long-standing practice of high labor force participation rates for women, it seems likely that economic change for women will primarily involve changing definitions of what work belongs within "women's sphere," and the conditions and compensation for "women's work," rather than a breakdown of the separation of spheres. And while the two spheres are clearly unequal, some women may welcome the autonomy that this division makes possible, especially since the generational inequalities that once made many homosocial environments extemely hierarchical have weakened considerably since 1949.

But in places more industrialized than the villages surveyed by Judd and Greenhalgh, the life-cycle and locational patterns of rural Chinese women's work have changed dramatically; and they may now resemble either Europe or Japan in the proto-industrial and early industrial periods more than they do earlier Chinese patterns. Unmarried women in relatively developed villages, as we will see, often do work outside the home, usually in low-skilled jobs in local factories, just as unmarried young rural women in Japan and Western Europe often did either handicraft work or service. Many married rural women work for the market, but they are mostly still part of household enterprises rather than earning wages: in Hare's Guangdong samples, 54.6 percent of single women worked for wages, but only 1.3 percent of married women.[113] (There is also some resemblance here to Brinton's account of working wives in contemporary Japan, cited above.)

Moreover, in both the early-modern cases elsewhere and the rural Chinese case today, married women with young children are apparently more likely to participate in work for the market than women with older children. The reasons, to be sure, differ sharply. In early modern and early industrial Europe the woman with a young child was likely to have more than one young child, so that her family's consumption needs were at their life-cycle peak; she stayed in the paid labor force (often while continuing to be the principal child-care provider) to earn necessary money until at least one child could replace her.[114] The rural Chinese woman today is likely to have two children at most and a mother-in-law who is still relatively young and vigorous; her labor force participation is thus a rather different phenomenon. In some cases, these women may leave the paid labor force when a daughter enters it, but it is at least as likely that she will wait until she has a daughter-in-law to do so.

The daughter, except in particularly poor areas, is likely to at least begin middle school; but she is also likely to have some time when she has stopped going to school but has not yet married. A large percentage of these young women work outside the home (and often outside the village), as we have seen. Many others, though, take over domestic and agricultural chores for their natal families when they leave school. Moreover, there is a growing question about a sub-set of these women who are leaving school early. While older women who are taking on housework to allow their daughters-in-law to earn money may not mind this (as Judd suggests), teenage girls who are being relegated to a domestic role (as opposed to either school or paid work) are probably losing out quite seriously. Estimates of the number of school-age children not in school vary widely from study to study, but in every sample, the large majority of those not in school are girls; in one Zhejiang study, school-age girls not in school outnumbered boys by three to one. Girls also far outnumber boys among child laborers, both within family enterprises and in others.[115]

It is unclear how widespread the phenomenon of keeping girls out of school to work for family enterprises or do domestic labor is. In a survey of reasons for not attending school in 1990, most of the difference between rural boys and girls was accounted for by the answers "financial," "not allowed to," and "too much housework." Hare also cites evidence which suggests that significantly more girls than boys are withdrawn from school to meet family labor requirements, and that this is particularly common in families that have a relatively large amount of land (and thus farm tasks) per worker.[116] Young men are much less likely to forgo finishing school, in spite of the generally higher wages available to them and the lack of correlation between education and earning power in most of rural China.[117] Moreover, approximately 10 percent of rural females aged 18–19 were reported in a 1993 survey to have never attended school: a lower figure than for older cohorts, but still significant.[118] These young women – even more than those who do the less desirable jobs in TVEs, about whom more in the next section – seem to be being sacrificed for the good of others. They are being deprived of the opportunity to accumulate human capital in narrowly economic terms, and of cultural resources, in order to aid the accumulation of a unit they will not remain part of.

There is no obvious analogy for such a phenomenon in the experience of earlier industrializers, since the first labor-supplying phase in Japan and Western Europe preceded universal middle school attendance, and the current one has not interfered with it. Nonetheless, the resemblance to earlier female life cycle patterns elsewhere is suggestive, and provides a context in which to consider our last topic: the relationship between women and TVEs, which have been the prime motors of rural Chinese development over the past two decades, and employ the largest numbers of the rural young women who work outside the family fields and courtyard.

TVEs, gender norms and strategies of accumulation

TVEs are – at least in theory – enterprises that are officially owned by the village or township government and *leased* to private entrepreneurs, rather than purely private businesses; and contrary to what often appears in journalistic accounts, they have thus far been much more important as sources of output, employment, revenue, and capital accumulation than private enterprises *per se* in most of China.[119] State firms generally pay better than TVEs and provide various other benefits to the individuals who work for them, but they are few and far between outside large cities, and declining in numbers everywhere.

Though the entrepreneurs running TVEs may wish to maximize profits, the institutional role of the local government that owns the firm allows them to impose a number of restrictions which meet the political goals of local cadres and to some extent reflect the norms of their constituents: preferential hiring for local residents, guarantees of local reinvestment, donations for social services and local infrastructure, and (perhaps most interesting for our purposes) limits on income inequality among employees.[120] Some of them are even compelled to hire from families that have no members in non-agricultural employment so long as such people are available.[121] Such a policy spreads better-paid non-farm work relatively evenly among households, but that is not all. In areas where little truly private enterprise exists, it also has the effect of insuring that there will be one person in each household (usually a male) with higher income than the rest of the family, thus propping up a principal breadwinner role in circumstances in which firms seeking the cheapest possible labor (often female) might otherwise tend to undermine it.

Whether consciously or not, such policies continue an important pattern that runs through most of the history of the People's Republic, in spite of numerous policy switches: the tendency to couple certain kinds of economic radicalism with gender conservatism, appealing especially to rural males by offering them an environment in which – in sharp contrast to the pre-revolutionary situation – every peasant male could realistically aspire to be head of a "normal" family.[122] (This guarantee is, however, likely to become increasingly empty for poorer men as birth control policies, cultural preferences, differences in earning power and the availability of amniocentesis combine to produce a surplus of male children over females. The long-term consequences of this trend for the status of women, the problems of poor men, and the legitimacy of the state are still far from clear.)

When this is judged in a still longer historical perspective, we again see a pattern in which limits on geographical division of labor (TVEs often depend on local government protection of various sorts to avoid being undersold by "imports" from other parts of China, as well as to secure re-investment of profits) go along with the elaboration of a gender division of labor that sustains an incompletely proletarianized rural industrial workforce. While the government's announced goal of having people "leave the land but not the countryside"[123] has certainly not been completely achieved – as witness the huge "floating population," at least some of which now seems to be permanently urbanized – it has tended to have a number of effects, which in some ways continue trends of middle and late Qing political economy in a world whose technologies are often thought to link development inexorably to both proletarianization and urbanization.[124] Once again, an impressive share of industrial production remains in the countryside, and many households that participate in it also have one foot in agriculture (and even in subsistence agriculture), with guaranteed access to land. Indeed, there are often pressures on families to continue to do some farming even where there are enough non-farm jobs that everybody could have one;[125] and both state policy and the policies of TVEs that are influenced by local norms tend to put men in jobs that are better paid, involve more travel and/or contact with non-kin,[126] and thus tend to buttress their positions as heads of the households. (This includes, ironically, a reconceptualization of agriculture as "inside work," when for generations it was seen as male and "outside" compared to home-based textile production.) In geographic terms, economic policy remains poised between an idea of economic growth premised on the development of a national market and division of labor and another which envisions the replication of a series of largely self-sufficient cells. Despite a commitment to growth, the state still treats rural to urban migration as an unfortunate necessity, and the migrants themselves are subject to various official and unofficial discouragements.[127]

Gender, mobility, and accumulation revisited

If the gender division of labor again has women producing for the market while limiting the physical sites and types of work they can do – preventing the women themselves from being fully in the market – it makes sense to consider a contemporary version of a hypothesis we rejected for the Qing: that Chinese development has been fundamentally driven by the commercial exploitation of women working for artificially low returns (and working more hours than they would be hired for in a profit-seeking firm that had to pay competitive wages to potentially mobile workers). This time, however, such arguments center primarily on the village, not the family, and see the process leading, not to involution at a subsistence level, but to substantial capital accumulation. In part, because of this difference, such arguments seem to me to invite a more useful set of comparisons between China and Europe than do the arguments discussed in our earlier literature review: one which finds similarities and differences (and so invites some re-thinking of European stories), rather than stressing differences alone in a way that essentializes divergent "Eastern" and "Western" paths.

Not all jobs at TVEs are equally desirable, and there is a strong tendency for males to get the better ones. Women are, for instance, almost completely excluded from management of TVEs, and especially from sales and procurement – among the best paid work, and work that is most likely to foster the connections needed to further any private business initiatives – because of the need for unaccompanied travel, social contact with unrelated men, and drinking that are required.[128] Production work involving high-tech skills is also disproportionately given to men, though with some significant exceptions.[129] There is a strong tendency for young women in particular (who are the majority of women employed in TVEs) to be given the least remunerative work, and the ones in which they will gain the fewest skills, even when their educational and other qualifications resemble those of males; nonetheless, they are generally regarded as better workers than young unmarried men.[130] Married women are often excluded entirely,[131] which of course also reinforces the tendency not to give younger women work in which they will acquire valuable skills: better to reserve those for males who will continue to be part of both the enterprise and the village for many years to come. In light of these tendencies, Judd concludes that for the firms which are the principal motor of rural Chinese accumulation:

> This accumulation should be seen as substantially consisting of the appropriation of the product of women's labor, and especially young women's labor. Similar appropriation of young women's labor has been reported for nearby Taiwan (Diamond 1979) and Hong Kong (Salaff 1981).
>
> At a slightly greater remove of time and space, it is also similar to processes observed for Europe, in which socio-economic changes in capitalist modernization were facilitated through a reliance on young women's labor. Their relative powerlessness enabled their labor to fuel capitalist economic growth and to reconcile it to a domestic economy. The encapsulation of domestic economy within capitalist economy stabilized the latter.
>
> (1994: 105)

The analogies are provocative, and Judd's analysis of how the state (which, among other things, makes the "household" rather than the individual the crucial unit for so many economic and social purposes) has helped *create* this situation (rather than simply "failing" to dislodge an age-old, domestically anchored patriarchy) is quite helpful. But this point suggests some further differences, both from other East Asian cases and from early modern Europe (and Japan).

First of all, it is noteworthy that despite the pervasiveness of various sorts of sexism, the wage gaps between men and women doing the same work do not appear very large: in a study of TVEs in three relatively prosperous townships (one in Jiangsu, one in Guangdong, and one in Jiangxi), gender made a 14 percent difference in pay once other variables were controlled for.[132] Hare (1999: n. 2) cites two studies which found a 20 percent intra-occupational difference between men and women (without controlling for other factors) and one study that found a 40 percent gap. Even the 40 percent gap seems relatively small compared to many other societies, including the early modern European case we looked at earlier; certainly the 20 percent gap (and the 14 percent gap after controlling for other variables) are historically fairly small. Rural China may indeed be building its capital stock at the expense of young women, but if so it seems likely that the allegedly less familistic and "traditional" Europeans did so even more.

Second, there are again questions about who is doing the accumulating at women's expense, and how. Salaff's (1995) and Diamond's (1979) analyses concern women working for profit-maximizing firms in Hong Kong and Taiwan and turning over at least some of their pay to parents, even if they do not live with them; they thus raise the same question as before about whether the surplus generated by these women's labors are going to the firm or to the women's families. Both authors argue that the firms receive the lion's share, but that the pecuniary benefit to these women's families is still significant. It is not significant because these households are doing any substantial accumulating of their own, but because the little bit they do receive is enough to align their interests with those of their daughters' employers – both benefit from labor discipline and worker frugality – and so to add the pull of family affections to the other pressures leading these women to acquiesce in their exploitation. Tsurumi makes a roughly similar argument for early Japanese factory women.[133] It is, in Judd's phrase, one way in which "the encapsulation of a domestic economy within a capitalist economy stabilized the latter."

Ching-Kwan Lee considers similar issues in a comparative study of women in Shenzhen and Hong Kong factories – but with a difference that is important for us. In Hong Kong, she suggests, gender ideology and filiality are very important parts of labor discipline: but in Shenzhen they are much less so, with more direct coercion, backed by the state, playing a more significant role.[134] It is, of course, possible that the young women of Shenzhen, who are often quite far away from their parents, feel the tug of filiality less than most women. Nonetheless, Lee's emphasis on coercion in the Shenzhen case suggests the possibility that the ideological weight of the family in TVE labor discipline may also have been overestimated.

It is also worth noting that the locus of accumulation in the case of TVEs is somewhat different than with the factories (or putting-out merchants) employing underpaid women in our other cases. While the entrepreneurs in TVEs clearly benefit from the surplus young women workers generate, much of the profit from TVEs accrues to the village as a collectivity.[135] Indeed, because of the peculiar tax structure of rural China, profits and contributions from TVEs are by far the most important way of funding local services. As a result, Bird and Gelb found that while a Jiangsu township with many TVEs had an average per capita income seven times that of one with few TVEs (though both were in areas of fairly well-developed agriculture), the public spending per capita of the more industrialized township was 140 times that of the more agrarian township.[136] More recently, West and Wong found that per capita revenues varied among townships in one county (Penglai, Shandong) from a low of 23 *yuan* to a high of 294 (a ratio of 13:1), while the variation among counties within the province was over 16:1.[137] While these differences are less extreme than those suggested by Bird and Gelb (and variations in expenditures are narrower still, thanks to subsidies from higher levels of government[138]), they are still quite substantial. To the extent that village exogamy is still practiced, the males and married women of a village (along with its officials) have an interest in favoring this kind of social accumulation over the payment of higher wages to their soon-to-be-departed daughters.[139] Thus, indeed, capital is being accumulated at the expense of young women in particular, and the social restrictions that make it hard for them to leave the village before marrying also serve to keep this cheap labor pool available.

Yet because the village accumulates much of this capital, the situation does seem different from our other cases. First of all, women will marry into the village, too, and they and their children will benefit from schools, sewers, and so on built with the profits wrung from their sisters-in-law. And to the extent that these profits do fund essential public services that would otherwise not be provided, we can see the artificially low wages paid women as a forced diversion of private (female) income to investment in human capital. The beneficiaries are the workers' nephews and nieces rather than their own children, but it is nonetheless significant that the increased mobilization of women for commodity production is here being made to serve the production of human capital – while, at least in De Vries' account, it was the partial withdrawal of women from such work that allowed such improvements in the nineteenth and early twentieth century, after likely stagnation in the labor-supplying eighteenth and early nineteenth.[140]

Some final thoughts: gendered development and human capital

TVE profits, which depend heavily on cheap female labor, are indeed crucial for funding rural (and urban) services, particularly education and public health.[141] This does not, of course, justify making young women bear most of the costs of this forced investment in the next generation. It does, however, suggest some important ways in which China's gendered accumulation is not simply that of Japan, Western Europe, or even Taiwan and Hong Kong at an earlier date. First, it may well be restrictions on physical mobility (which are at this point, still both customary and legal) that are central here, not power or sentiment within the family itself. Second is the political control over profits – and the fact that they are crucial to human capital formation in rural China. (Whether these profits will be enough to support the badly needed improvements in rural education and infrastructure is another issue; so is the matter of what the increasing privatization of former TVEs will entail.) Third, the especially strong link between TVE profits in particular and social services is in large part an artifact of a particular tax code, which can be changed, rather than rooted in a deeper level of structure. Were that system to change, so would the connection between social accumulation and employment policies which disadvantage women (in ways and for reasons different from those we might expect in purely private profit-making firms).

Finally, this suggests that the emergence of a "domestic ideology" prizing female labor-withholding – which has, among other things, been touted periodically by some Chinese officials as a way to combat underemployment – would be very unlikely to play the socially stabilizing role that it played in certain periods of European, American, Japanese and other histories. It has relatively little historical resonance, since female virtue never meant abstaining from paid work, and it is no longer associated with a prestigious foreign way of life (as it was when Japan moved in that direction a century ago). On the contrary, women's employment is widely associated with the highly desired goal of "modernity," and the Women's Federation provides an institutional base for opposition to attempts to have women "return to the home":[142] phenomena with no close parallels in either the North Atlantic countries or Japan at the onset of their labor-withholding phases.

Moreover, to the extent that TVE profits are the prime source of local educational funds, a domestic ideology might imperil rather than encourage the (re)production of a labor force suited for moving up the value-added ladder. (By the time state budgets became a crucial part of human capital formation in most of the West, factories had long since supplanted putting out households as crucial sites of work and accumulation.) If the story of the industrious revolution and the current permeation of families by market-oriented individualism in the West reminds De Vries of Schumpeter's verdict on the bourgeois family – "the capitalist order rests on props made of extra-capitalist material (and) derives its energy from extra-capitalist patterns of behavior which at the same time it is bound to destroy"[143] – then a partially, but only partially, parallel set of claims might be made about China. China's development may not be fully capitalist, but it has been as market-driven as the West's – for much of our period, probably more so. It has its own set of "external props," which should be seen as such, rather than as barriers that kept its capitalism "petty." Some of these props have gendered its development – by, for instance, shaping migration patterns and choices among different kinds of remunerative work (at least among those who could afford some choices). This does not make Chinese development more gendered than Europe's, in which women were, at some times, more likely to be outside the market economy altogether than they ever were in China; it makes it differently gendered, in shifting ways that in turn shaped specific, non-recurring, historical junctures.

Notes

1 See Huang (1990); Goldstone (1996); Gates (1995).
2 For example, Tilly and Scott (1978, 1989); Horrell and Humphries (1995).
3 For example, Judd (1994).
4 On this point, see also Hamashita (1990), Kawakatsu (1991).
5 For a prior example of this strategy of *balanced* comparison, and an account of proto-industrial development largely compatible with mine, see Wong (1997).
6 Huang (1990: 110).
7 This part of Huang's argument closely resembles that in Chayanov's *Theory of Peasant Economy*.
8 Huang (1990: 91, 112).
9 Goldstone (1996); and see Levine (1977), Kriedte *et al.* (1980).
10 In a follow-up discussion (personal communication 5/9/01) Goldstone has rightly pointed out that, because the costs of capital in early textile mills accounted for a much smaller percentage of total production costs than labor did, relatively small differences in the price of labor could make a huge difference to the rate of return on the owner's capital. This would make access to labor at rates close to those earned by women working at home important if the differences in output per worker between home and factory were modest (50 percent in Goldstone's example), and that may have been the case for weaving. It was not, however, the case for spinning, where the gains in productivity from even early mechanization (Crompton's mule) were roughly 25-fold, with a gain of more than 300-fold by 1825 (Chapman 1987: 17). In that case, it would take very large wage differentials to make factory development unprofitable. Thus any argument that not being able to have

young women working away from home hindered the development of spinning mills in particular would have to rest on some other characteristic of these workers, such as their supposed docility. This seems to me much less likely to have been crucial than the near absence of fuel, very limited animal traction, and near absence of water power in the coal-less, densely populated, and nearly flat Yangzi Delta.

11 Pomeranz (1998, 2000, 2002, 2003).
12 See particularly Wong (1990, 1992, 1997); Myers (1991); Pomeranz (2002, 2003).
13 Pomeranz (2002: 555–64).
14 Pomeranz (2000: Appendix E); Pomeranz (2002).
15 Earle (1989).
16 See e.g. Daumard (1963: 629, 649–50) on Paris, a place where the bourgeoisie is often thought to have been more drawn to a "noble" lifestyle then in England or Holland. See also Troyansky (1989: 92), who points out that for French bourgeois before the Revolution, retiring was seen as taking the opportunity to act like a noble – an ideal that lost its appeal for many bourgeois in the nineteenth century.
17 Daumard (1963: 341).
18 Tilly and Scott (1978: 128–9). See Stansell (1982: 132, 138–41) on how this made working-class females inherently "deficient" as women. But note also (Stansell 1982: 72–3) how a partial exception was made for seamstresses working at home, so long as they remained isolated. The principal difference from the Chinese formulation is that in Stansell's US case, paid work done at home was viewed as an acceptable compromise with economic realities, while in China it was viewed as good in itself, regardless of economic circumstances.
19 Keightley (1993: 46; 1999: 37, 45).
20 Mann (1992, 1997); Bray (1997).
21 See Uno (1991: 28, 18–19); see also Walthall (1998: 94–5).
22 De Vries (1994: 249–70).
23 Pomeranz (2000: Chapter 2).
24 Braudel (1982: I: 134–5); Abel (1980: 121, 136, 161, 199); Clark (1991: 446).
25 Zhao Gang (1983: 54–7).
26 This conclusion is supported by both efforts to reconstruct actual diets and by evidence concerning life expectancy and death rates. For a summary, see Pomeranz (2000: Chapter 1).
27 Li (1998: 133–55); Pomeranz (2003).
28 Hanley (1983: 183, 190–2; 1997).
29 For one among many standard texts that take this for granted, see Goubert (1986: 105).
30 Hanley (1991); Hayami Akira (1989).
31 Walthall (1991: 57).
32 Li (1996: 102–6).
33 Walthall (1991: 47–9; 1998: 94–5).
34 For Tokugawa Japan, see, e.g. Tsurumi (1990: 191). For Europe, see e.g. Tilly and Scott (1978: 114).
35 Bray (1997: 203).
36 Keeping a daughter at home could, of course, have the opposite impact, that is, being a way for her natal family to exploit her earning power at her expense. This would be more likely, though, in poorer families – who might otherwise sell the daughter into concubinage rather than arrange a proper marriage – and even in such families a portion of the retained daughter's

earnings, and her actual physical products (especially cloth) were likely to go into her dowry.

37 Mann (1992).

38 See citations in Zhang Gang (1985: 100–1) and Grove (1975).

39 Smith (1959); Smith (1977); Nakamura (1990); Hanley and Yamamura (1977) with the latter suggesting that castle town monopolies may have been much more effectively enforced in some peripheral domains.

40 Uno (1991: 25).

41 Saito (1983: 40–3).

42 It is worth noting the congruence between this point and Sugihara's emphasis on an East Asian labor force in which people were used to moving among a variety of tasks – and remained so even as they produced more and more for the market.

43 Sewell (1980: 117–21), on France; Walker (1971), on Germany.

44 Wong (1997) makes this point very forcefully, and explores its implications for how the kinds of economic dislocations European states would and would not respond to differed from those in China.

45 Kellenblenz (1974: 59); Walker (1971: 88–107); Ogilvie (1996).

46 Levine (1977: 19–20).

47 Ogilvie (1996b: 128–9).

48 Gates (1995: 94–102, 112, 223–4, 273–9).

49 Bowden (1990: 280).

50 Snell (1985: 15–66, 155–8); Allen (1992: 216–17).

51 Horrell and Humphries (1995: 102–3).

52 Horrell and Humphries (1995: 102–3).

53 See the discussion in Pomeranz (2000: 101–6, 316–26).

54 See the discussion in Pomeranz (2000: 39 n. 47).

55 Pan forthcoming.

56 Shanghai shehuiju (1935: 183); Clark *et al.* (1995: 226 n. 25).

57 Horrell and Humphries (1995: 98–100); see also Lindert and Williamson (1983: 19).

58 De Vries (1994: 262–4).

59 Schofield (1973: 446).

60 Tsurumi (1990: 48, 153).

61 See e.g. Lee (1995: 379, 381).

62 De Vries (1994: 264–5).

63 De Vries (1994: 263).

64 See, e.g. Mokyr (1988: 69–91, especially 90–1).

65 Horrell and Humphries (1995: 105–6).

66 Huang (1990: 121–2, 126–7); So (1986: 69–73, 88–9); Bell (1999: 117–25); Vlastos (1986: 92–112), on p. 112 noting the increase in silk production after 1859.

67 Hayami Yujiro (1973: 24).

68 Xu (1992: 469). For some estimates of the work year for home textile producers in the Qing see Li Bozhong (1998: 152–3), and Pomeranz (2000: 101).

69 Perkins (1969) was the first to assert this, though without much evidence. Fang Xing (1996) makes a good case for slight improvements in diet in the Lower Yangzi between the seventeenth and nineteenth centuries; Lee and Wang (1999: 30–4) assemble scattered evidence for stability or slight improvements in the diet of various Chinese populations in the nineteenth and early twentieth centuries; and most surveys of early twentieth-century Chinese diet suggest reasonable average food availability, though with large and often devastating fluctuations. Most of this work can tell us little about the distribution

of food supplies, though Fang's work is based on reconstructions of the budgets of agricultural laborers

70 See, e.g. Will and Wong (1991), Pomeranz (1993).

71 Perdue (1987: 131–5).

72 See Pomeranz (2000: Appendix E).

73 Bray (1997: 5, 47).

74 Mann (1992; 1997: 161–5).

75 On spinning cellars, see Bray (1997: 217).

76 For further analysis of regional income trends, see Pomeranz (1998) and Pomeranz (2000: 123–4, 243–5).

77 The population of Jiangnan, and of the Lower Yangzi in general, in 1953 was roughly the same as that on the eve of the Taiping, despite the enormous growth of Shanghai. See Ho (1959: 240–6), and Skinner (1987) which suggests slightly lower 1850 figures, but still figures which would produce zero population growth for the region as a whole over this period. The nineteenth century population figures for Fujian are particularly dubious, but the 1787 figure seems much more reliable, and the 1953 figure is only 9.4 percent above that level (see Ho 1959: 54, 287). Among the relatively rich provinces of Southern and Eastern China, only Guangdong grew significantly during the century after 1850 (a bit over 50 percent – see Marks 1997: 280), and even that was probably mostly in interior regions. All of these provinces were major sources of emigrants, both to the rest of China and overseas: see Lee and Wang (1999: 116–19) for a summary. On Chinese fertility and birth control generally see Lee and Wang (1999: 83–100, 105–13); on the Lower Yangzi in particular see Li Bozhong (1994: 37–56). For some rough but revealing numbers on the changing share of various provinces in the overall population, see Zhao and Xie (1988: 472–3, 512–13).

78 Li Bozhong (1998: 107–8).

79 Li (1996).

80 Li (1996); see also Stockard (1989: 142–3, 150–3, 158–9).

81 See Zhang Gang (1985: 100–1), and Grove (1975).

82 See Gardella (1994).

83 The reasons for this divergence are far too complex to discuss here. I sketch a few of them that are particularly relevant to the concerns of this in Pomeranz (2000: 285–97), but say little about some others that are obviously important: state policy, directions in science and technology, and so on. For the latter, I have found Morris-Suzuki (1994) particularly stimulating.

84 Galenson (1989: 56–64).

85 The most complete account of the ways in which the Qing encouraged migration is J. Lee, forthcoming. See also Sun (1997).

86 We know little about inter-regional flows of funds in pre-twentieth-century China and there do not seem to have been very efficient institutions for facilitating it, but there were not important barriers to it either. At any rate, labor mobility should narrow regional inequalities significantly even with limited flows of capital.

87 See Skinner (1977) on Ming-Qing cities, De Vries (1984: 178, 186) on early modern European ones.

88 Tilly (1984: 23–6, 42–53).

89 For more on the comparison of Chinese and European proto-industry (though with a different emphasis) and proletarianization, see Wong (1997: 33–8).

90 See. e.g. Schor (1991: 25–6). More recent Department of Labor data, which does not separate married and unmarried people is nonetheless interesting:

while the labor force participation rate for men over 20 has fallen from 85 percent in 1960 to 76 percent in 1985 (presumbably due both to increased college attendance and to the fact that there is no upper age limit on these data, and post-retirement lifespans are increasing), the numbers for women have risen from 37 percent to 61 percent over the same period. See http://146.142.4.24/cgi-bin/surveymost.

91 Making up, for instance, only 13.8 percent of "executive, administrative and managerial workers" in 1980, versus 28.8 percent in the US in 1984. See Brinton (1993: 61).

92 See, for instance, Ogasawara (1998: 27–38); Brinton (1993: 3–10, 14, 41, 52, 61, 65, 169–71).

93 Brinton (1993: 6, 10, 12–13, 36, 91–6, 232–3).

94 See Brinton (1993: 120), citing 1930 figures giving the mean female wage as 34 percent of the mean male wage. At that time, the industrial labor force was still almost 53 percent female (Garon 1987: 13). It is noteworthy, though, that the male/female wage gap seems to have reached such a large scale somewhat later in the process of mechanization than in England: in 1882, when textiles (which had an even more heavily female labor force in Japan than in the West) were still the dominant industrial sector in Japan, the mean female wage was 59 percent of the mean male wage.

95 Brinton (1993: 234).

96 See, e.g. Ho (1995: 378–9).

97 See for instance, Friedman *et al.* (1991: 127–9, 143, 175, 229).

98 See, e.g. Chao (1977: 267–71).

99 For example, Friedman *et al.* (1991: 168).

100 M. Wolf (1983: 104–6).

101 See, for instance, Wang Zheng (2000: 63–4).

102 Tan and Peng (2000: 157).

103 Wang Zheng (2000: 66–8, 76–8).

104 Cheng and Selden (1994: 666–7).

105 For a general discussion of the work team and brigade as "public patriarchs" in Mao's China, see Stacey (1983: 217–43).

106 See e.g. Chan *et al.* (1992: 297–8).

107 See e.g. Hung (1995), cited in Hare (1999) and Wang Zheng (2000: 79), and compare with Tilly and Scott (1978: 108–10).

108 Judd (1994: 23).

109 Ibid.: 12.

110 Ibid.: 191, 190.

111 See e.g. M. Wolf (1972: 32–41) and M. Wolf (1975: 117–29) on suicide.

112 Mann (forthcoming).

113 Hare (1999: 11).

114 See, e.g. Tilly and Scott (1978: 130–5).

115 Billard (2000: Chapter 3).

116 Hare (1999: 5, 20).

117 Ibid.: 14, 17, 20.

118 Survey cited in Tan and Peng (2000: 156).

119 See e.g. Byrd and Lin (1990: 14); West and Wong (1995: 81); Ho (1995: 365–70); Brown (1998: 24–30). In practice, the term is sometimes loosely applied, including enterprises *jointly* owned by a township or village and private investors, and even some firms that are really privately owned. This makes precise quantitative statements about this sector rather shaky; but so long as the bulk of TVEs are township or village owned, I think the claims that follow can stand.

120 Byrd and Gelb (1990, esp. p. 362); Ruf (1998: 140, 142); Ho (1995: 387–90); Clegg (1998: 66–82).
121 Ruf (1998: 142).
122 See, e.g. Stacey (1983: 108–94); Friedman *et al.* (1991: xiii, 111, 114–15).
123 Quoted in Ho (1995: 360).
124 For a similar argument, see Wong (1997).
125 Jacka (1997: 134).
126 Ibid.: 135, 166–7.
127 On the awkward status of rural–urban migrants see Solinger (1999).
128 Judd (1994: 89).
129 For example, Judd (1994: 98–9).
130 Ibid.: 160.
131 Jacka (1997: 166–7).
132 Gelb (1990: 292).
133 Tsurumi (1990: 77, 191).
134 C.K. Lee (1995: 383–9).
135 Judd (1994: 246).
136 Byrd and Gelb (1990: 368).
137 West and Wong (1995: 79).
138 Ibid.: 80.
139 Judd (1994: 246).
140 De Vries (1994: 294).
141 West (1997: 217, 222–3, 241–6, 259, 262–3); West and Wong (1995: 77, 80–1); Ruf (1998: 139–41).
142 Wang Zheng (2000: 66–72); Rofel (1999: 41–9, 71–5).
143 Schumpeter (1942: 162); quoted in De Vries (1994: 265).

References

Abel, Wilhelm. 1980. *Agrarian Fluctuations in Europe from the 13th to the 20th Centuries.* New York: St. Martin's Press.
Allen, Robert. 1992. *Enclosure and the Yeoman.* Oxford: Oxford University Press.
Becker, Gary. 1981. *A Treatise on the Family.* Cambridge, MA: Harvard University Press.
Bell, Lynda. 1999. *One Industry, Two Chinas: Silk Filatures and Peasant-Family Production in Wuxi County, 1865–1937.* Stanford, CA: Stanford University Press.
Billard, Elizabeth. 2000. "Women, Literacy, and Liberation in Rural China." Melbourne University PhD dissertation.
Bowden, Peter (ed.) 1990. *Economic Change: Wages, Profits, and Rents, 1500–1750.* Vol. 1 of Joan Thirsk (gen. ed.), *Chapters from the Agrarian History of England and Wales.* Cambridge: Cambridge University Press.
Braudel, Fernand. 1981. *The Structures of Everyday Life.* Trans. Sian Reynolds. New York: Harper and Row.
Brinton, Mary C. 1993. *Women and the Economic Miracle: Gender and Work in Post-war Japan.* Berkeley, CA: University of California Press.
Brown, George P. 1998. "Budgets, Cadres, and Local State Capacity in Rural Jiangsu," in Fleming Christiansen and Zhang Junzuo (eds), *Village, Inc.: Chinese Rural Society in the 1990s.* Richmond, Surrey: Curzon Press, pp. 22–47.
Byrd, William A. and Alan Gelb. 1990. "Why Industrialize? The Incentives for Rural Community Governments," in William A. Byrd and Lin Qingsong (eds),

China's Rural Industry: Structure, Development, and Reform. Oxford: Oxford University Press, pp. 358–87.

Byrd, William A. and Lin Qingsong. 1990. "China's Rural Industry: an Introduction," in William A. Byrd and Lin Qingsong (eds), *China's Rural Industry: Structure, Development, and Reform.* Oxford: Oxford University Press, pp. 3–18.

Chan, Anita, Richard Madsen, and Jonathan Unger. 1992. *Chen Village Under Mao and Deng.* Berkeley, CA: University of California Press.

Chao Kang. 1977. *The Development of Cotton Textile Production in China.* Cambridge, MA: Harvard University Press.

Chapman, S.D. 1987. *The Cotton Industry in the Industrial Revolution.* London: Macmillan.

Cheng, Tiejun and Mark Selden. 1994. "The Origins and Social Consequences of China's *Hukou* system," *China Quarterly* 139: 644–68.

Clark, Gregory. 1991. "Yields per Acre in English Agriculture 1250–1860: Evidence from Labour Inputs," *Economic History Review* 44 (3): 445–60.

Clark, Gregory, Michael Huberman and Peter H. Lindert. 1995. "A British Food Puzzle, 1770–1850," *Economic History Review* 48 (1): 215–37.

Clegg, Jenny. 1998. "Multi-Stakeholder Cooperation in China – Changing Ownership and Management of Rural Enterprises," in Fleming Christiansen and Zhang Junzuo (eds), *Village, Inc.: Chinese Rural Society in the 1990s.* Richmond, Surrey: Curzon Press, pp. 66–82.

Daumard, Adeline. 1963. *La Bourgeoisie Parisienne de 1815 à 1848.* Paris: S.E.V.P.E.N.

Davin, Delia. 1998. "Gender and Migration in China," in Fleming Christiansen and Zhang Junzuo (eds), *Village, Inc.: Chinese Rural Society in the 1990s.* Richmond, Surrey: Curzon Press, pp. 230–40.

De Vries, Jan. 1984. *European Urbanization: 1500–1800.* Cambridge, MA: Harvard University Press.

De Vries, Jan. 1994. "The Industrious Revolution and the Industrial Revolution," *Journal of Economic History* 54 (2): 249–70.

Diamond, Norma. 1979. "Women and Industry in Taiwan," *Modern China* 5 (3): 317–40.

Earle, Peter. 1989. *The Making of the English Middle Class: Business, Society, and Family Life in London 1660–1730.* Berkeley, CA: University of California Press.

Fang Xing. 1996. "Qingdai Jiangnan nongmin de xiaofei," *Zhongguo jingji shi yanjiu* 11 (3): 91–8.

Friedman, Edward, Paul Pickowicz, and Mark Selden. 1991. *Chinese Village, Socialist State.* New Haven, CT: Yale University Press.

Galenson, David. 1989. "Labor Markets in Colonial America," in David Galenson (ed.), *Markets in History.* Cambridge: Cambridge University Press, pp. 52–96.

Gardella, Robert. 1994. *Harvesting Mountains.* Berkeley, CA: University of California Press.

Garon, Sheldon. 1987. *The State and Labor in Modern Japan.* Berkeley, CA: University of California Press.

Gates, Hill. 1995. *China's Motor: One Thousand Years of Petty Capitalism.* Ithaca, NY: Cornell University Press.

Gelb, Alan. 1990. "TVP Workers' Incomes, Incentives, and Attitudes," in William A. Byrd and Lin Qingsong (eds), *China's Rural Industry: Structure, Development, and Reform.* Oxford: Oxford University Press, pp. 280–98.

Goldstone, Jack. 1996. "Gender, Work and Culture: Why the Industrial Revolution Came Early to England but Late to China," *Sociological Perspectives* 39: 1–21.

Goubert, Pierre. 1986. *The French Peasantry in the Seventeenth Century.* New York: Cambridge University Press.

Greenhalgh, Susan. 1994. "Controlling Births and Bodies in Village China," *American Ethnologist* 21 (1): 1–30.

Grove, Linda. 1975. "Rural Society in Revolution: The Gaoyang District, 1910–1947." PhD dissertation, University of California, Berkeley.

Hamashita Takeshi. 1990. *Kindai Chugoku no kokusaiteki keiki: choko boeki shisutemu to kindai Ajia.* Tokyo: Tokyo Daigaku shuppan kai.

Hanley, Susan. 1983. "A High Standard of Living in Tokugawa Japan: Fact or Fantasy," *Journal of Economic History* 43 (1): 183–92.

Hanley, Susan. 1997. *Everyday Things in Premodern Japan.* Berkeley, CA: University of California Press.

Hanley, Susan and Kozo Yamamura. 1977. *Economic and Demographic Change in Pre-Industrial Japan, 1600–1868.* Princeton, NJ: Princeton University Press.

Hare, Denise. 1999. "Women's Economic Status in Rural China: Household Contributions to Male–Female Disparities in the Wage Labor Market," forthcoming in *World Development* 27: 6 (June).

Hayami Akira. 1989. "Kinsei Nihon no keizai hatten to Industrious Revolution," in Hayami Akira, Saito Osamu and Sugiyama Chuya (eds), *Tokugawa shakai kara no tenbo: hatten, kozo, kokusia kankei.* Tokyo: Dobunkan, pp. 19–32.

Hayami, Yujiro. 1975. *A Century of Agricultural Growth in Japan.* Tokyo:/Minneapolis: University of Tokyo Press with University of Minnesota Press.

Ho Ping-ti. 1959. *Studies on the Population of China.* New York: Columbia University Press.

Ho, Samuel P.S. 1995. "Rural Non-agricultural Development in Post-Reform China: Growth, Development Patterns, and Issues," *Pacific Affairs* 68 (3): 360–91.

Horrell, Sara and Jane Humphries. 1995. "Women's Labour Force participation and the Transition to the Male-Breadwinner Family, 1790–1865," *Economic History Review* 48 (1): 89–117.

Huang, Philip. 1990. *The Peasant Family and Rural Development in the Lower Yangzi Region, 1350–1988.* Stanford, CA: Stanford University Press.

Jacka, Tamara. 1997. *Women's Work in Rural China.* Cambridge: Cambridge University Press.

Judd, Ellen. 1994. *Gender and Power in Rural North China.* Stanford, CA: Stanford University Press.

Kawakatsu Heita. 1991. *Nihon bunmei to kindai seiyo: "sakoku" saiko.* Tokyo: Nippon hoso shuppan kyokai.

Kellenblenz, Herman. 1974. "Rural Industries in the West from the End of the Middle Ages to the Eighteenth Century," in Peter Earle (ed.), *Essays in European Economic History 1500–1800.* Oxford: Clarendon, pp. 45–88.

Knight, John and Song Lina. 1993. "Workers in China's Rural Industries," in Keith Griffin and Zhao Renwei (eds), *The Distribution of Income in China.* New York: St. Martin's Press, pp. 173–215.

Lee, Ching Kwan. 1995. "Engendering the Worlds of Labor: Women Workers, Labor Markets and Production Politics in the South China Economic Miracle," *American Sociological Review* 60 (June): 378–97.

Lee, James. Forthcoming. *The Political Economy of China's Southwest Frontier: State Building and Economic Development.* Cambridge, MA: Harvard University Press.

Lee, James and Wang Feng. 1999. *One Quarter of Humanity: Malthusian Mythologies and Chinese Realities.* Cambridge, MA: Harvard University Press.

Levine, David. 1977. *Family Formation in an Age of Nascent Capitalism.* Academic Press.

Li Bozhong. 1994. "Kongzhi zengchang yi bao fuyu – Qingdai qian, zhongqi Jiangnan de renkou xingwei," *Xin shixue* 5 (3): 25–71.

Li Bozhong. 1996. "Cong 'fufu bing zuo' dao 'nan geng nu zhi' " *Zhongguo jingji shi yanjiu* 11 (3): 99–107.

Li Bozhong. 1998. *Agricultural Development in Jiangnan, 1620–1850.* New York: St. Martin's Press.

Lindert, Peter H. and Jeffrey Williamson. 1983. "English Workers' Living Standards During the Industrial Revolution: A New Look," *Economic History Review* 36 (2nd series): 1–25.

Mann, Susan. 1992. "Household Handicrafts and State Policy in Qing Times," in Jane Kate Leonard and John Watt (eds), *To Achieve Security and Wealth: The Qing State and the Economy.* Ithaca, NY: Cornell University Press.

Mann, Susan. 1997. *Precious Records: Women in China's Long Eighteenth Century.* Stanford, CA: Stanford University Press.

Mann, Susan. 2000. "AHR Forum: The Male Bond in Chinese History and Culture," *American Historical Review*, December 2000.

Marks, Robert. 1997. *Tigers, Rice, Silk, and Silt: Environment and Economy in Guangdong, 1250–1850.* Cambridge: Cambridge University Press.

Mokyr, Joel. 1976. *Industrialization in the Low Countries, 1795–1850.* New Haven, CT: Yale University Press.

Mokyr, Joel. 1988. "Is There Life in the Pessimist Case? Consumption during the Industrial Revolution, 1790–1850," *Journal of Economic History* 48 (1): 69–92.

Morris-Suzuki, Tessa. 1994. *The Technological Transforation of Japan: From the Seventeenth to the Twenty-First Century.* Cambridge: Cambridge University Press.

Myers, Ramon. 1991. "How Did the Modern Chinese Economy Develop? A Review Article," *Journal of Asian Studies* 50 (3): 604–28.

Nakamura, XT. 1990. "Development of Rural Industry," in Chie Nakane and Shinzaburô Oishi (eds), *Tokugawa Japan*, pp. 81–96.

Ogasawara, Yuko. 1998. *Office Ladies and Salaried Men: Power, Gender, and Work in Japanese Companies.* Berkeley, CA: University of California Press.

Oi, Jean. 1992. "Fiscal Reform and the Foundations of Local State Corporatism in China," *World Politics* 45 (October): 99–126.

Pan, Ming-te. 1994. "Rural Credit Market and the Peasant Economy (1600–1949) – The State, Elite, Peasant, and Usury," PhD dissertation, University of California, Irvine.

Pan, Ming-te. Unpublished. "Who Was Worse Off?" Paper delivered at 1998 meeting of Chinese Historians in the United States.

Perdue, Peter. 1987. *Exhausting the Earth: State and Peasant in Hunan 1500–1850.* Cambridge, MA: Harvard University Press.

Pomeranz, Kenneth. 1993. *The Making of a Hinterland: State, Society, and Economy in Inland North China, 1853–1937.* Berkeley, CA: University of California Press.

Pomeranz, Kenneth. Unpublished (1998). "Re-thinking the Late Imperial Chinese

Economy: Development, Disaggregation and Decline in the 18th and 19th Century," paper presented at UC Berkeley Economic History Workshop, May, 1998.

Pomeranz, Kenneth. 2000. *The Great Divergence: China, Europe, and the Origins of the Modern World Economy.* Princeton, NJ: Princeton University Press.

Pomeranz, Kenneth. 2002. "Beyond the East–West Binary: Resituating Development Paths in the Eighteenth Century World," *Journal of Asian Studies* 61 (2): 539–90.

Pomeranz, Kenneth. 2003. "Facts are Stubborn Things: A Response to Philip Huang," *Journal of Asian Studies* 62 (1): 539–90.

Rofel, Lisa. 1999. *Other Modernities: Gendered Yearnings in China After Socialism.* Berkeley, CA: University of California Press.

Ruf, Gregory. 1999. *Cadres and Kin: Making a Socialist Village in West China, 1921–1991.* Stanford, CA: Stanford University Press.

Saito Osamu. 1983. "Population and the Peasant Family Economy in Proto-Industrial Japan," *Journal of Family History* 8 (1): 30–54.

Saito Osamu. 1985. *Puroto-Kogyo no jidai: Seio to Nihon no hikakushi.* Tokyo: Nihon Hyoronsha.

Salaff, Janet. 1995. *Working Daughters of Hong Kong.* New York: Columbia University Press.

Schumpeter, Joseph. 1942. *Capitalism, Socialism, and Democracy.* New York: Harper.

Schor, Juliet. 1992. *The Overworked American.* New York: Basic Books.

Sewell, William. 1980. *Workers and Revolution: The Language of Labor From the Old Regime to 1848.* Cambridge: Cambridge University Press.

Shanghai shehuiju. 1934. *Shanghai zhi shangye.*

Skinner, G. William. 1977. "Cities and the Hierarchy of Local Systems," in G. William Skinner (ed.), *The City in Late Imperial China.* Stanford, CA: Stanford University Press, pp. 275–351.

Smith, Thomas. 1958. *The Agrarian Origins of Modern Japan.* Stanford, CA: Stanford University Press.

Smith, Thomas, Rober Eng, and Robert Lundy, 1977. *Nakahara: Family Farming and Population in a Japanese Village.* Stanford, CA: Stanford University Press.

Snell, K.D.M. 1985. *Annals of the Labouring Poor: Social Change and Agrarian England, 1660–1900.* Cambridge: Cambridge University Press.

So, Alvin. 1986. *The South China Silk District: Local Historical Transformation and World-System Theory.* Albany, NY: SUNY Press.

Solinger, Dorothy. 1999. *Contesting Citizenship in Urban China: Peasant Migrants, the State, and the Logic of the Market.* Berkeley, CA: University of California Press.

Stacey, Judith. 1983. *Patriarchy and Socialist Revolution in China.* Berkeley, CA: University of California Press.

Stockard, Janice. 1989. *Daughters of the Canton Delta.* Stanford, CA: Stanford University Press.

Sun Xiaofen. 1997. *Qingdai qianqi de yimin zhen Sichuan.* Sichuan daxue chubanshe.

Tan Lin and Peng Xizhe. 2000. "China's Female Population," in Peng Xizhe (ed.), *The Changing Population of China.* London: Blackwell, pp. 150–66.

Tilly, Charles. 1984. "Demographic Origins of the European Proletariat," in David Levine (ed.), *Proletarianization and Family History.* New York: Academic Press, pp. 1–85.

Tilly, Louise and Joan Scott, 1985. *Women Work and Family* (2nd edition).

Troyansky, David. 1989. *Old Age in the Old Regime*. Ithaca, NY: Cornell University Press.

Tsurumi, Patricia. 1990. *Factory Girls: Women in the Thread Mills of Meiji Japan*. Princeton, NJ: Princeton University Press.

Uno, Kathleen. 1991. "Women and Changes in the Household Division of Labor," in Gail Lee Bernstein (ed.), *Recreating Japanese Women, 1600–1945*, Berkeley, CA: University of California Press, pp. 17–41.

Vlastos, Stephen. 1986. *Peasant Protests and Uprisings in Tokugawa Japan*. Berkeley, CA: University of California Press.

Walker, Mack. 1971. *German Home Towns: Community, State, and General Estate, 1648–1871*. Ithaca, NY: Cornell University Press.

Walthall, Anne. 1991. "The Life Cycle of Farm Women in Tokugawa Japan," in Gail Lee Bernstein (ed.), *Recreating Japanese Women, 1600–1945*. Berkeley, CA: University of California Press, pp. 42–70.

Walthall, Anne. 1998. *The Weak Body of a Useless Woman: Matsuo Taseko and the Meiji Restoration*. Chicago: University of Chicago Press.

Wang Zheng. 2000. "Gender, Employment, and Women's Resistance," in Elizabeth J. Perry and Mark Selden (eds), *Chinese Society: Change, Conflict, and Resistance*. London: Routledge, pp. 62–82.

West, Loraine A. 1997. "Provision of Public Services in the Rural PRC," in Christine P.W. Wong (ed.), *Financing Local Government in the People's Republic of China*. Hong Kong: Oxford University Press, pp. 213–82.

West, Loraine A., and Christine P. Wong. 1995. "Fiscal Decentralization and Growing Regional Disparities in Rural China: Some Evidence in the Provision of Social Services," *Oxford Review of Economic Policy* 11 (4): 70–84.

Will, Pierre-Etienne and R. Bin Wong. 1991. *Nourish the People: The State Civilian Granary System in China, 1650–1850*. Ann Arbor, MI: University of Michigan Press.

Wolf, Arthur and Chieh-shan Huang. 1980. *Marriage and Adoption in China, 1845–1945*. Stanford, CA: Stanford University Press.

Wolf, Margery. 1972. *Women and the Family in Rural Taiwan*. Stanford, CA: Stanford University Press.

Wolf, Margery. 1975. "Women and Suicide in China," in Margery Wolf and Roxanne Witke (eds), *Women in Chinese Society*. Stanford, CA: Stanford University Press, pp. 111–42.

Wolf, Margery. 1985. *Revolution Postponed: Women in Contemporary China*. Stanford, CA: Stanford University Press.

Wong, R. Bin. 1992. "Chinese Economic History and Development: A Note on the Myers–Huang Exchange," *Journal of Asian Studies* 51 (3): 600–11.

Wong, R. Bin. 1997. *China Transformed: Historical Change and the Limits of European Experience*. Ithaca, NY: Cornell University Press.

Xu Xinwu (ed.) 1992. *Jiangnan tubushi*. Shanghai shehui kexueyuan chubanshe.

Zhang Gang. 1985. "Qingdai Zhili shangpin jingji fenxi," *Hebei shiyuan xuebao* 3: 9–104.

Zhang, Weiguo. 1998. "Rural Women and Reform in a North China Village," in Fleming Christiansen and Junzuo Zhang (eds), *Village, Inc.: Chinese Rural Society in the 1990s*. Richmond, Surrey: Curzon Press, pp. 193–212.

Zhao Gang (aka Chao Kang). 1983. "Zhongguo lishishang gongzi shuiping de bianqian," *Zhongguo wenhua fuxing yuekan* 16 (9): 52–7.

Chapter 5

The importance of commerce in the organization of China's late imperial economy

Gary G. Hamilton and Wei-An Chang

Asian business networks have been much in the news. For the past decade or so, many observers of Asia's rise to prominence have written about the importance of these networks to Asian economic success. The Japanese *keiretsu*, the Korean *chaebol*, and the Chinese family-owned conglomerate – these business groups, many writers believe, lie at the core of Asia's capitalist transformation. To explain these groups, the same writers touted the significance of the government in creating and making them flourish. In the Asian business crisis of 1997–8, reportage about these networks abruptly switched from praise to damnation. All types of Asian business groups and the government/business relationships supporting them suddenly became examples of cronyism and crony capitalism and were seen to be the harbingers of Asia's unanticipated economic collapse.

In most of these writings, regardless of their tone, there is a tension between accounting for the origins of these business groups, on the one hand, and explaining how these groups organize the economy and with what effects, on the other hand.[1] Many analysts seem to think that by explaining why groups form, they have also explained how groups operate economically. The nurturing of these groups ostensibly explains their nature. For instance, a significant number of writers explain the present configurations of business groups in terms of proximate causes – a government policy, an alliance based on old school ties, the lack of adequate capital markets – all happenstance or historical preconditions for their emergence. Another set of analysts makes business networks arise from a timeless culture. They are the embodiments, respectively, of Japanese or Korean or Chinese ways of life, in which the past is refurbished for use in the present. Either way, these analysts imply that the social or political origins of such groups simultaneously summarizes their economic roles and economic consequences. For example, groups with once and continuing political ties are judged as examples of political intervention into the marketplace and, in the extreme, cronyism. Groups founded on social connections among owners, managers, or employees may be seen as examples of embeddedness, a condition where shared values increase trust among participants and reduce the cost of doing business.

The reason that it seems so natural to conflate the origins and operations of economically active groups is typically due to the presence of an underlying theory of economies that would seem to explain the connection between the two. For instance, when analysts demonstrate the political origins of groups, they, implicitly or explicitly, contrast this observation with an essentialized neo-classical theory of capitalist markets, and thus reach the conclusion that the organization of the economy in these societies does not reflect market forces and hence market outcomes must be politically influenced, if not mandated.

This ongoing comparison between the origins of groups and an underlying theory of economies produces a curious outcome when it comes to doing a historical analysis of economies.[2] The organization of economic groups becomes coterminous with the types and duration of economies in which they are active. In the case of modern Asian business groups, most writers make them historical outcomes, but provide no actual histories of their origins or functioning before the capitalist era began. In most accounts, business groups, except for those in Japan, started after World War II. Occasionally a writer will push the timeline further back, as far back as the late nineteenth century, but at this point the writer is really examining the source, the headwaters of the capitalist river that has flowed forth in the late twentieth century. By this logic, capitalism in Asia, including capitalist economic organization, could have no possible history apart from the history of Western capitalism. With a lineal conception of history, how could it be otherwise?

The same logic extends to the period before Western capitalism spread to Asia. The history of pre-capitalist economic organizations typically ends with the coming of capitalism, in whatever guise it appears: colonialism, imperialism, dependent development, or commercial capitalism. For imperial China, some crude versions of this thesis are found in Marxian theories of pre-capitalist economies. The despotic state dominated the weak economy, making merchants an appendage of the state and subject to the arbitrary power of China's patrimonial bureaucracy. The organization and operation of the economy are subsumed within and understood to be a part of China's pre-capitalist classifications: "Asiatic mode of production," "Oriental despotism," and "hydraulic societies." This characterization immediately stops when Western capitalism enters the scene at which time China's economic organization is shaped by the global economy and becomes classified as semi-colonial and is subject to the withering effects of Western imperialism.

Although not so blatant, quite sophisticated interpretations of China's pre-nineteenth-century economy make the same leap from origins to organization via a theory of capitalism.[3] As we outline below, most interpretations of China's economy before the capitalist era are based on a comparison between ideal-typical models of markets derived from the analysis of European capitalism and abstracted forms occurring historically in China. Several writers (Hamilton 1985; Wong 1997) have argued that this approach – attempting to understand China's late imperial economy through applying theories of capitalist origins derived from the Western experience – is, in methodological terms, questionable and often produces pernicious results, but no one has made the point earlier or more clearly than Perry Anderson:

> Asian development cannot in any way be reduced to a uniform residual category, left over after the canons of European revolution have been established. Any serious theoretical exploration of the historical field outside ... Europe will have to supersede traditional and generic contrasts with it, and proceed to a concrete and accurate typology of social formations and state systems in their own right, which respects their very great differences of structure and development. It is merely in the night of our ignorance that all alien shapes take on the same hue.
>
> (1974: 549)

As Anderson's "procedural lesson" implies, the methodological problems arise when the pre-modern, non-Western economy becomes a negative case, a case stereotyped negatively against the positive components of theories explaining the rise of Western capitalism (Hamilton 1985). According to this approach, the Chinese economy is not treated as an independent case that has an organizational logic grounded in the subjective understanding of the participants. The classificatory schemes generated by Western capitalism bestow the nature, organization, and economic effects on whatever organized forms might appear within the pre-modern economy.

In opposition to this type of historical interpretation, recent work in economic sociology demonstrates that the way economies are organized and operate on a day-to-day basis directly reflects the way societies themselves are organized. Today's capitalist economies are quite different from one another. For instance, the organizational foundations of capitalism in Germany differ from that in France, and consequences of those differences are substantial (Hollingsworth and Boyer 1997). Even the organizational differences in two parts of the same national economy, say, between Silicon Valley and East Coast high technology firms in the 1980s (Saxenian 1994), can also lead to sizeable differences in economic outcomes. In order to explain these differences, it is not helpful to argue that France is more or less capitalistic than Germany or that West Coast firms are more or less market-oriented than East Coast firms. Instead, one should argue that capitalism has neither an inherent nature nor essential features and that these examples indicate substantively different versions of how industrial economies in the modern world can be effectively organized.[4]

This perspective has implications for the historical analysis of economies as well. The divide between capitalist and pre-capitalist economies may be more theoretical than empirical and more conceptual than real. How economies are organized and operate are institutionally rooted in ongoing societies. Societies do not stop suddenly and start again when some innovations, however momentous, appear. Instead people integrate those new ways of doing things into fully packed, ongoing, subjectively understood patterns of existence. Without a doubt, from the sixteenth century forward, the economies of Western Europe, expanding beyond the borders of Europe, spearheaded a still-continuing transformation of economies round the world. But essentializing the capitalist transformation, giving it conceptual exactitude beyond time and place, masks the continuities in the social organization of economic activity, even in Europe. In fact, it is one of those paradoxes of history that the continuities in society – those things that we hold dear or cannot change or do not even recognize because they are so much a part of our taken-for-granted existence – these things give direction to changes. Long-term transformation may have very subtle beginnings, for it is often the organization of ongoing activity and not the subtle beginnings that leads society along one trajectory or another and that nurtures and accelerates the change.

What are some of these continuities in the Chinese economy? We argue that there are significant parallels between the organization of the late imperial economy and the organization of the modern capitalist economies in Taiwan and Mainland China (cf. Ka and Selden 1986). This parallel cannot be explained as a function of some linear sequence of events – of one thing coming after another. In fact, these parallels that we describe are disconnected in time and, to some extent, even in space. We should think of these parallels instead as having emerged from similar (but by no means identical) shared understandings of social organization and from similar (but by no means identical) structural conditions confronted by economically active participants, such as relations of power and authority. Framed in this manner, we believe that a comparison between modern and pre-modern, between capitalism and non-capitalist economies, can help solve some persistent problems in the understanding of both modern and pre-modern economies. In particular, we show that an analysis of the organizational patterns in the late imperial Chinese economy helps to clarify some key theoretical issues in the analysis of global capitalism today. Unsurprisingly, the reverse is also true. The bundle of theoretical concepts created to explain today's economic transformations is very useful in interpreting some of the most significant characteristics of China's own extraordinary imperial economy, many organizational patterns of which continue to shape China's economic development today.

Let us begin with a summary of our thesis: In late imperial and early modern China, commercial organization, that is the organization of marketing products, shaped the patterns of commodity production, in our case the production of cotton textiles. Using Gary Gereffi's commodity chain approach (Gereffi and Korzeniewicz 1994), we argue that the production and distribution networks represented by cotton textiles approximate that of a "buyer-driven chain" and that the production end of this chain can be accurately characterized as a "flexible production system." Substantiating this claim for historical China forces us to reassess those "up-to-the-minute" factors that most theorists view as the essential causative elements in today's global economy, namely information and work process systems, high technology, and global merchandising. Such factors may not prove to be as decisive as they are touted to be after all, but merely contributory to the economic patterns that we observe today. Our conclusions points to an alternative explanation, in line with the embeddedness approach for which Granovetter (1985) and others have argued: Recurring patterns of social organization shape the ways that people come together to engage in economic activities, and, in our case, we show that these patterns of "doing things together" (Becker 1986) shape both modern and pre-modern Chinese economies.

I

One of the most persistent and complex debates about the Chinese economy in imperial times is whether it exhibited capitalistic characteristics. There are two important versions of this debate. One version features scholars from the People's Republic of China,[5] who argue whether "feudalistic" China harbored nascent capitalist tendencies. This is known generically as the "sprouts of capitalism" debate, but the second version might as well be called that too, because the basic issues are very similar. The second version rages primarily among Western scholars (Elvin 1973; Huang 1991; Myers 1991; Feuerwerker 1992; Wong 1992, 1997; Brook and Blue 1999; Pomeranz 2000). Wanting to put some distance between themselves and the Marxist slant taken by the first group, the second set of scholars address a Smithian version of the question, by asking whether or not the commercial expansion of the Chinese imperial economy constitutes "genuine" economic development.[6] As academic disagreements go, both versions of the debate are quite heated.

The debate hinges on a paradox. On the one hand, by any measure, the late imperial Chinese economy was an extraordinarily large economy.

Remember that, based on "purchasing-power parities," the International Monetary Fund ranks the mainland Chinese economy in the late 1990s as the third largest GDP in the world. By comparison, the imperial economy through much of Ming and Qing times (1368–1911) was undoubtedly the largest domestic economy in the world well into the nineteenth century. Absolute size of this economy is, however, not so indicative of development if the economy was based primarily on household and village self-sufficiency. All disputants in the debates, however, agree that this was not the case, though they differ on the levels of commercialization and commodification and on whether these levels differ from those in Western Europe in the same period (e.g., Wong 1997; Pomeranz 2000). As the starting point in the debate, they recognize that the imperial economy contained exceedingly sophisticated and organizationally complex economic regions. In this regard, nearly everyone acknowledges Skinner's (1964, 1977, 1985) research in defining the major regions in the late imperial economy. These regions consisted of densely integrated marketing structures that connected all parts of the region to a hierarchy of urban marketing centers. At the imperial level, all the regions were integrated by means of a vibrant inter-regional trade in both luxury goods and many basic commodities, such as rice, salt, tea, sugar, and the inputs to make clothing (including the raw cotton and silk, dyed and undyed yarn, and bolt cloth) (Rowe 1984: 54–62; Mazumdar 1998). As Mazumdar (1998: 51–9) stresses, we should not overstate the amount of China's internal trade. Although "the domestic market for all commodities remained restricted" and although the average peasant family consumed few traded commodities, the absolute level of trade was nonetheless very high.[7]

Wu Chengming (1985) gives one of the best-informed, though still very rough, estimates of the scale of this trade, as shown in Table 5.1.[8] From Table 5.1, it is difficult to interpret the level of consumption that this internal trade represents. Wu gives an added indication that about 14.3 percent of the total output of cotton cloth was internally traded in the mid-nineteenth century (cited by Mazumdar 1998: 57). Mazumdar (ibid.: 57) notes that Wu's calculations understate the level of domestic trade because they exclude commodities sold for tax payments. Moreover, if we add trade in cotton and cotton yarn, which most peasant families had to purchase in the marketplace in order to weave their own cloth and make their own clothes, then this level of trade is very substantial. If we also add to these figures the extraordinary maritime trade in which Chinese merchants engaged and for which peasant produced goods (see Hamashita, Chapter 1, in this volume), then we must conclude that the domestic trade was a very large and very significant component of China's late imperial economy. In fact, Pomeranz (2000: 165) argues that China's internal trade rivaled, and perhaps even exceeded Europe's trade as late as the late eighteenth century.

Table 5.1 Estimates of the important commodities in China's internal trade in 1840[a]

Commodity	Volume	Value (1,000 taels)	Percent of total value
Grain	24.5 billion catties (JIN)	16,333.3	42.14
Cotton	2,555,000 piculs (DAN)	1,277.5	3.30
Cotton fabric	315,177,000 bolts (PI)	9,455.3	24.39
Silk	71,000 piculs (DAN)	1,202.3	3.10
Silk fabric	49,000 piculs (DAN)	1,455.0	3.75
Tea	2,605,000 piculs (DAN)	3,186.1	8.22
Salt	3.22 billion catties (JIN)	5,852.9	15.10

Note
a Wu (1985). During the late imperial period, China's weights and measures were not standardized, but rather varied widely throughout China. See, for instance, Abstract of Information (1889–90), and Morse (1908). We can obtain only the roughest idea of the amounts represented by Table 5.1 with the figures provided by Mazumdar (1998: 413–17). A catty equals about 1.32 pounds; a picul equals 100 catty or 133.3 pounds. A tael equaled approximately one avoirdupois of silver. At the time, three taels equaled US $4.00.

Despite such a huge volume of internal trade in basic commodities, the late imperial economy showed, on the other hand, very few signs of advanced production techniques for any commodity, including the production of cotton cloth. In fact, outside of the imperial workshops, where fine porcelains and silks were manufactured, the levels of technological sophistication in many areas of production did not approach the levels one finds in Europe and Japan during the same period, a point made by a number of scholars (Elvin 1973; Jones 1981, 1988; Huang 1985, 1990; Goldstone 1996).[9] Their general argument is that cheap peasant labor, supplied by rapidly expanding population, drove out the possibility of technical advances, and thus removed the possibility of an independent origin to industrial capitalism. As Mark Elvin (1973) put it, despite being the largest economy in its day, the Chinese economy was unable to get out of its population-induced "high-level equilibrium trap," a Malthusian condition that resulted in "quantitative growth and qualitative standstill."

This debate and, in particular, the concept of "high-level equilibrium trap" epitomize the use of Western models of capitalism to characterize China's late imperial economy. The participants in the debate argue about the causes of China's perceived lack of economic development in contrast to a catalog of factors causing capitalist development in Europe.[10] This contrast makes China into a negative case, where the focus of explanation is the absence of something, in this instance, the absence of increasing levels of centralized, factory-based production. The absence in China of what was present in eighteenth-century Europe is then explained by evoking the opposite of what was present in the positive case. The "high-level equilibrium trap" is an unexamined assertion for China of a supposed opposite truth in Europe, namely that the aggregate effects of population density diminish wages and reduce demand to the point that there is no incentive to centralize production, as occurred in Europe. Therefore, the verdict on China's late imperial economy is rendered "quantitative growth and qualitative standstill."

Cotton textiles, by far the largest handicraft industry in late imperial China, form the most significant point of reference in this debate. According to Philip Huang:

> Cotton lies at the heart of the story of commercialization in the Ming-Qing Yangzi delta. In 1350, no one in China wore cotton cloth; by 1850, almost every peasant did. The dramatic spread of cotton, replacing hemp, affected every household and powered a host of related changes. Its story dwarfs those of all other crops and industries in importance for this period.
>
> (1990: 44)

Those who argue for economic dynamism suggest that cotton production illustrates the roots, if not the actual sprouts of capitalism. In the course of the Ming and Qing dynasties, cotton textile production expanded tremendously and became increasingly rationalized, with substantial differentiation in the chain of production (Dietrich 1972). Growing, spinning, weaving, dyeing and calendering, wholesaling, and retailing – all became separate steps in the manufacture and distribution of cotton textiles. Different people predominated at different stages in the production process, a process characterized by a sophisticated division of labor that required considerable skills in some stages of production and relatively simple skills in other stages. Whole regions became known for their cotton production and entire villages for their specialization in one or another of the stages. As the production of cloth became rationalized, the system of distribution widened, so that an integrated, highly competitive market in cotton textiles existed throughout the empire (Myers 1991: 615).[11] This cotton trade extended into Southeast Asia, and some Chinese-manufactured cotton cloth, called Nankeen, even made it to Europe and the Americas in the eighteenth and early nineteenth centuries as one of the export items in the China trade. The presence of a vibrant textile industry in late imperial China is indisputable.

On the other side of the debate, however, are some other equally indisputable points. Despite considerable sophistication in the marketing of cotton textiles, at the production end of the process, especially in growing, spinning, and weaving, there is a well-documented devolution in production technology (Elvin 1972) and an "involution" in economic development (Huang 1990). The critics show that, as commercialization increased and distribution widened, the technology of production did not advance and, in fact, even simplified. For these writers, the Song dynasty is the high-water mark of China's economy, a point in time when China's technology was advanced beyond that of contemporary Europe (Elvin 1973; Jones 1988). Despite technological sophistication, China's economy did not take off; economic development did not occur. Mark Elvin (1972, 1973) argues, for example, that China, as late as the fourteenth century, possessed water- or animal-powered spinning machines that were in wide use and technologically more advanced than anything in Europe before the eighteenth century. Yet, by the beginning of the seventeenth century, these machines had disappeared in China. Replacing these more complex machines were simpler, more labor-intensive devices suitable for use by women and children inside the household. As a result of this devolution, Elvin further argues, China moved in the opposite direction, away from a large, integrated factory system, as occurred in Europe and the United States, and toward the asserted "high-level equilibrium trap."

To these critics, a growing sophistication of production (i.e. where "output expands faster than labor input," Huang 1990: 11) is the essence of capitalist development. Without such sophistication, they argue, no industrial revolution, no genuine sprouts of capitalism, occurred in China. Instead, with commerce serving "as a substitute for management" (Elvin 1973), China supposedly experienced only a long steady devolution into increasing poverty and immiseration.

Although this debate is considerably more varied and the argumentation more complex than we have portrayed here, it is nonetheless obvious that some of the aspects of the debate seem very similar to some of the issues confronting observers of modern global capitalism. Is the only type of industrialization one that is indicated by the presence of large factories? To this question, analysts today would quickly and resoundingly answer no. Complex forms of industrialization (defined here as the "ization" of industry, namely the development and systematization of an area of production) occur outside of large-scale, technologically sophisticated factories, as many studies in contemporary Asia, Europe and the United States clearly reveal. The catchall label for such non-vertically integrated systems of production is "flexible production" or "flexible specialization."

II

Given the fact of flexible production systems in modern capitalism, can we argue that late imperial China is an example of industrialization in the absence of factories, an example of flexible specialization on a mammoth scale? The first reaction to such a suggestion is that the idea is absurd. Neither the literature on flexible production systems in the contemporary times nor the literature on late imperial China would support such an implication.

In their seminal book, *The Second Industrial Divide,* Piore and Sabel (1984) do connect premodern craft traditions to the development of flexible specialization. But their argument is that Fordism, in the form of large-scale vertically integrated factories, drove out craft industries in most societies except in peripheral industries where the markets were "too narrow and fluctuating to repay the specialized use of resources of mass production" (ibid.: 206). In a few places, however, such as in northern Italy, a craft tradition persisted, and in the wake of a crisis in Fordist production, this craft tradition revitalized and was so transformed that it became the leading edge of a totally new form of capitalist production. What made flexible specialization new and different from both Fordist production and the pre-industrial craft tradition was the ability to use the most advanced technology, to create complex subcontracting arrangements to match product specification and product demand, and to develop new products using the flexible production techniques (ibid.: 215). As a consequence of these innovations, modern small firm networks shifted "toward greater flexibility [in] provoking technological sophistication – rather than regression to simple techniques" (ibid.: 207). Although there is a substantial literature criticizing various aspects of Piore and Sabel's conception of flexible specialization,[12] critics do not argue that this shift from a pre-industrial craft tradition to the small firm networks in the world economy today was anything other than an economic transformation. From this literature, therefore, it seems difficult to argue that textile industry in late imperial China is an instance of flexible production, because this is a clear example of a regression toward simpler technology.

The literature on cotton production in imperial China offers no help in rebutting this conclusion. The descriptions of textile production in the Ming and Qing periods show that the initial steps in production, namely spinning and weaving, were not concentrated in cities, but rather in the countryside (Xu 1981, 1988, 1992). Moreover, despite some examples to the contrary, these descriptions also make it clear that these initial steps, including growing cotton, were largely subsidiary agricultural industries, which supplied additional income to peasant households. Women and children who did most of the spinning and weaving within the households were themselves scattered throughout the cotton-growing regions and beyond. What this literature shows is that the initial steps in production were so decentralized and, seemingly, so uncoordinated that it is difficult even to speak of a "system" of textile production. Hence, the only conclusion that seems possible is that this is not only not an example of flexible production, but also not even a good example of a "craft" industry, if by that term we mean, following Piore and Sabel (1984), a sophisticated artisan-based handicraft tradition that draws on cooperative community traditions.

III

This is where most analysts end the discussion: late imperial production is simply labeled as "traditional," and despite a few insignificant continuities, modern production is entirely different in spirit, in organization, in all regards. Our examination of imperial China's textile industry, however, raises some problems with the old formula that radically severs the past from the present.

The first thing we notice is that there are too many similarities between the organization of economic activity in late imperial China and the post-World War II industrialization process in both Taiwan and now the PRC to simply brush them aside. Outside the state-controlled sectors in both economies, the industrialization process has been concentrated in the countryside in small and medium-sized firms, and, in the initial phases at least, draws on subsidiary household labor. In Taiwan, the household, in the form of family firms, was and remains, the basic unit of production, and the technology of production matches the resources of the producers, and hence is different, if not simpler, than it would have been in large economy-of-scale factories (Hamilton and Biggart 1988; Hamilton and Kao 1990; Orrù *et al.* 1997). Even in Taiwan, in some areas of production, particularly in intermediate goods, such as plastics and chemical, where the firms have grown very large and have become diversified business groups, the businesses remain fundamentally family owned and con-trolled. In the PRC, restrictions on private ownership still favor some form of collective ownership, but even in this context, township enterprises contain some of the dynamics of family-controlled firms, especially in regard to personalized and centralized decision-making and the necessity to cultivate inter-personal ties (Lin 1995; Wank 1999).

These and other similarities would be superficial ones were it not for a more fundamental parallel between modern and pre-modern Chinese economies that makes the economies in the two different periods organizationally very similar. Examining how the economies in both periods actually operate in both economic and organizational terms reveals that the distribution sectors of the economies drive the entire structures. These economies are organized "backwards" from distribution rather than "forward" from production.

Our understanding of the significant effects of commerce on commodity production builds on a widespread agreement among the disputants in the "greater" sprouts-of-capitalism debate that, from at least the middle Ming into the twentieth century, the commercial sectors of the imperial Chinese economy steadily developed and reached considerable levels of organizational complexity, so complex in fact that some analysts simply write the whole commercial system off as being confusing, particularistic, and detrimental to economic growth.[13] The same writers (Huang 1990;

Myers 1991), however, acknowledge that the commercialization of the late imperial economy resulted in remarkably efficient markets in those basic commodities that were widely traded.[14] A curious aspect of this literature is, however, that none of the disputants causally connects what happens at the production end with what happens at the distribution end. It is as if the two ends of the production chain bear no causal relationship to one another.

This omission is less pronounced in the most recent and richly detailed discussions of commodity production that builds on a dialogue with the literature on proto-industrialization in Europe (Wong 1997; Mazumdar 1998; Bray 1999; Pomeranz 2000). These scholars consider at length the conditions of peasant producers of sugar, cotton, and silk who are incorporated in merchant-led putting-out systems, and recognize that "small peasant producers were not able to set prices any more than they were able to choose which market to sell in" (Mazumdar 1998: 329). Even so, the most recent work still does not connect the effects of regional merchant groups, whose economic power also control the national distribution of these commodities, back on the conditions of production. For example, in Pomeranz's extended analysis (2000) about why the economies of late imperial China and early modern Europe diverged from each other in the late eighteenth and early nineteenth centuries, he barely touches on merchants or merchant organization. Concerning primarily the macro-economic factors, he instead draws a linear and non-reflexive relationship between production and distribution, thus concluding that production of goods amounted to nothing more than a

> proto-industrial cul de sac, in which even with steadily increasing labor inputs, the spread of the best known production practices, and a growing commercialization making possible an ever-more efficient division of labor, production was just barely staying ahead of population growth.
>
> (2000: 207)

At the theoretical level, this omission can be explained in large part because the literature on economic theory and economic history, on which they draw heavily, exhibits the same reluctance to connect distribution and manufacture. From Marx and Smith to Coase and North, economic theorists have been predominantly theorists of production. Distribution, marketing, and consumption are relegated to a secondary position.[15] Only in the most recent economic theorizing does the distribution end of the process start to have a backward effect on the production end.

One of the clearest characterizations of these linkages is found in Gary Gereffi's formulation of global commodity chains (1994a and b; also Gereffi and Hamilton 1996).[16] Gereffi argues that production should not be analyzed in the absence of knowledge about the entire chain – from the basic inputs to the final consumption of a product. Using a wealth of empirical data, Gereffi shows that the organization of production is very different if it is "driven" from the distribution rather than from the manufacturing ends of the chain. By "driven," Gereffi means that, in some but certainly not all cases of commodity production, a firm or a set of firms is able to coordinate the most significant steps in the production of a product, directly through ownership or indirectly through its economic power in controlling some aspect of production or distribution. The crucial determinants in whether firms are able to control multiple steps in commodity chains are the barriers to entry at any point in the production and distribution process.

For some products that are very difficult to produce because, for instance, of the level of technology or required capital, the firm that controls the production is often able to coordinate most steps in the chain. Commercial aircraft manufacturers, such as Boeing, and automobile manufacturers, such as Toyota and General Motors, are examples of what Gereffi calls "producer-driven commodity chains." Some firms vertically integrate the entire production sequence inside the firm, thereby owning and authoritatively controlling the significant steps in a commodity chain. Other larger producers, such as the Toyota group, form very large networks of independent firms, some of which the Toyota group partially owns and some of which they do not. Those firms that the group does not own, however, are still eager to produce under Toyota's direct guidance simply because of Toyota's great economic power.

The organizing influence of large vertically integrated firms and interfirm networks is easy enough to envision. Alfred Chandler (1977, 1990), for one, has described the very great influence of large firms to integrate forward in the chain to control distribution or backward in the chain to control production, and in so doing to reshape the organization of entire economies. It is the absence of such firms and of the tendency to develop such firms that prompts many analysts of late imperial China to reject any claims of a nascent form of capitalism in late imperial China.[17]

Gereffi's research, however, shows the equally important, but very different effects of merchandising on production. Using many examples of consumer non-durables, such as footwear and garments, Gereffi shows that in the past several decades large-scale retailers and brand name merchandisers, which he collectively calls "big-buyers," have begun to dominate their respective sectors. Toys "Я" Us, Home Depot, Office Max, Ikea, Costco, Sam's Club are all examples of discount retailers that do not own or directly control the firms that supply their goods, but that have such large-scale purchasing power and the ability to shape buyer preferences as to be able to exert tremendous influence over quality and pricing of the goods they buy. Nike, Reebok, The Gap, Liz Claiborne, The Limited,

Gateway Computers, and Dell Computers are example of brand name retailers that do not own or directly control the factories that make the goods they sell. The brand name merchandisers are

> technically ... not "manufacturers" because they have no factories. Rather, these companies are "merchandisers" that design and/or market, but do not make, the banded products they sell. These firms rely on complex tiered networks of overseas production contractors that perform almost all their specialized tasks. Branded merchandisers may farm out part or all of their activities – product development, manufacturing, packaging, shipping, and even accounts receivable – to different agents around the world.
>
> (Gereffi 1994b: 221)

As Gereffi (ibid.) makes clear, both sets of companies do not make their profits from "scale, volume, and technological advances" but rather from "unique combinations of high-value research, design, sales, marketing, and financial services that allow the buyers and branded merchandisers to act as strategic brokers in linking overseas factories and traders with evolving product niches in their main consumer markets." Product differentiation is the key strategy of merchandising, a strategy aimed at creating niche markets for specialized products in which the merchandisers can reduce competition and approach monopolistic control. The economic power of mass retailers and brand name merchandisers is achieved by creating such barriers to entry at the marketing end of the commodity chain that the actual producers of goods have no choice but to fall in line with the demands of these firms. The backward organization of production then, assuming equal quality, goes to the least cost providers of the product. If there are multiple providers of a product, then the big buyers drive the production cost down by playing one producer off against the others. The backward power of commercial organization on producers competing in the same markets forces these producers to create ever cheaper and therefore simpler forms of production, given acceptable levels of quality.

Not every location is equally suited for this low-cost production. It is, therefore, no coincidence that big buyers have had a clear preference for subcontracting in economies dominated by small and medium-sized independent firms, which outside the PRC are typically family-owned. Research makes it clear that the industrialization of modern Taiwan, Hong Kong, and the PRC (after 1978) has resulted mightily from export production of batch-manufactured products purchased by big-buyers.[18] From bicycles, footwear, and garments to components for computers and televisions, networks of small and medium-sized Chinese firms have led their respective economies in the production of items sold around the world under the brand names of one kind of merchandising firm or another (Chen 1994; Hamilton 1997). It is also clear that this form of production has become increasingly rationalized so that these small-firm economies progressively get better at being efficient, flexible producers (Gereffi 1994b; Chen 1998; Kao and Hamilton forthcoming). Indeed, modern Chinese economies are among the best examples of flexible production systems in the world today.

IV

What do such buyer-driven chains have to do with late imperial China? Surprisingly, the answer is, we believe, about the same as it is for China in the late twentieth century.[19]

The economy in late imperial China was not only vastly larger than in either medieval Europe or pre-industrial Japan, but it was also organized differently along three important dimensions: (1) the social structural conditions of consumption; (2) the affinity between these conditions and the development of a system of mass merchandising; and (3) the organization of the distribution end of the commodity production. Before the mid-eighteenth century in both Europe and Japan, the buying power of a relatively small, disproportionately wealthy aristocracy directed the efforts of the best craftsmen. In Japan, the samurai class, constituting about 10 percent of the total population, was largely urban based and set the standards for consumption until they became increasingly impoverished in the late eighteenth and nineteenth centuries (Hanley 1997). In Europe, again before the eighteenth century, aristocratic families, which were becoming increasingly urbanized from the sixteenth century on, also established the fashions of the day, and had the power to exclude most other classes from imitating their style of life (McKendrick *et al.* 1982; Campbell 1987). The hereditary upper strata in both locations also directly or indirectly controlled the economic decisions of many handicraft and agricultural producers, as well as resident merchant groups (Hanley and Yamamura 1977; Pratt 1999). Hereditary elites and their agents vied over and controlled much of the land and most economically active towns and trading routes. In both Japan and Europe, urban-based merchants and artisans gained some independence, primarily by organizing in trade and handicraft associations (Sheldon 1958; Pratt 1999), so much so that Weber referred to European cities as being illegitimate enclaves in the midst of the *oikos* economies of the Middle Ages (Weber 1978: 1212–338). Free peasants in Western Europe did not emerge until the rise of great monarchies after the devastating Thirty Years War, and did not rise at all in Central and Eastern Europe until nearly the twentieth century. In Japan, until the mid-eighteenth century, peasants were tied to the land and largely cut off from participation in regional and national markets. After that time, a largely rural elite emerged that began to link rural areas to national markets, but this elite also controlled peasant participation in proto-industrial activities (Smith 1959; Pratt 1999). Therefore, indirectly through their buying power and demands for conspicuous consumption, and sometimes directly through incorporating artisans in their patrimonial households, the upper strata in Europe and Japan shaped the efforts of handicraft producers, pulling them toward a system of production based on creating finely made, one-of-a-kind products. This is a handicraft tradition of relatively few buyers, restricted markets, and conspicuous products.

By contrast, starting as early as the sixteenth century, Chinese peasants and artisans produced for impersonal mass markets for which they made the ultimate decisions about what they produced and how they produced it. The major consumers for peasant-produced agricultural and handicraft products included a wide range of people from non-hereditary landowning and administrative elites to even rather poor peasants. The elites, however, were clearly the principal consumers. However, elite status was not hereditary, and because of partible inheritance, the landowning wealth was constantly being reshuffled. Tenure as an imperial administrator was short-lived, was based on merit in the examination system, and could not be directly passed on to one's heirs. Unlike the Japanese and European counterparts, the consuming elites in China were located in urban areas and small marketing centers scattered throughout imperial China and not concentrated in disproportionately huge primary cities, such as Paris, London, or Tokyo. Contending for power and privilege, Chinese elites needed to consume conspicuously in relation to peers in their locale, but not so sumptuously as to separate themselves in status from others in local society with whom they maintained alliances.[20]

We have simplified the differences between China, on the one hand, and Japan and Europe, on the other hand, in order to suggest that the social structure in late imperial China created an affinity, an opening if you will, for a pre-modern equivalent of mass merchandisers. In order to illustrate this affinity, we want to cite Alexis de Tocqueville's comparative model to explain the differences in manufacturing he observed between aristocratic Europe and democratic United States (which not coincidentally contained, as did late imperial China, a significant landowning elite in the midst of a fluid class system).

> Craftsmen in aristocratic societies work for a strictly limited number of customers who are very hard to please. Perfect workmanship gives the best hope of profit. The situation is very different when privileges have been abolished and classes intermingled and when men are continually rising and falling in the social scale ... [The fluctuation in family fortunes creates] a crowd of citizens whose desires outrun their means and who will gladly agree to put up with an imperfect substi-

tute rather than do without the object of their desire altogether. The craftsman easily understands this feeling, for he shares it. In aristocracies he charged very high prices to a few. He sees that he can now get rich quicker by selling cheaply to all. Now, there are only two ways of making a product cheaper. This first is to find better, quicker, more skillful ways of making it. The second is to make a great number of objects which are more or less the same but not so good. In a democracy every workman applies his wits to both these points ... Craftsmen in democratic ages do not seek only to bring the useful things they make within the reach of every citizen, but also try to give each object a look of brilliance unconnected with its true worth.

(1969: 466–7)

Tocqueville's mental experiment is useful here in understanding the complex social structural differences between the late imperial Chinese economy and other pre-modern economies with which it is usually compared. Tocqueville clearly sees the backward linkages between the consumption and production of goods, and recognizes that the consumption of goods is directly shaped by the awareness of consumers whose situational logic reflects their positioning in the social order. Knowing Europe of his day well, he saw that craft production in the United States appeared to have a very different orientation in relation to the consumer. We would extend this model one step further by suggesting that the activities of merchants (literally "merchandising") built on and accentuated the same structurally induced situational logic.

Tocqueville's portrait of the United States has a number of features in common with late imperial China, although they are obviously very different societies. First, both late imperial China and nineteenth-century America were societies with ambiguous class structure, with few legal or formal barriers to class mobility. Both societies had considerable intergenerational mobility, as is well illustrated by land divisions in China (Rowe 1985), and in both locations there were powerful socially embedded logics that prevented freezing class boundaries. Second, both societies were strongly decentralized with vibrant regions and with elites integrated into the status structure at local and regional levels, more so than at the national levels. Third, both societies had vast domestic economies, and moreover, outside of the American South, the orientation of both economies was toward domestic and not exports markets, unlike Britain and to a lesser degree France. These conditions set the stage for the development of an economic system oriented to producing differentiated products for mass markets. In late imperial China, these affinities encouraged a handicraft tradition to produce for impersonal mass markets. In the United States, these same affinities provided the entrepreneurial conditions for creating, after the Civil War, large vertically integrated firms –

producer driven commodity chains – to produce products for mass markets.

The similarities between China and the United States are broad structural ones, which helps specify some of the distinctive features of China. One of the key points of difference between the economic organization in China and the US concerns the ability to create and maintain large businesses in the private sphere. Large businesses in the USA emerged only in the post-Civil War period, when the courts interpreted shareholding companies as a legal "person," which limited the liability of owners to assets of the company. This legal change coincided with the organizational revolution that transformed every sphere of American society. Administered bureaucratically, large groups in both public and private spheres became the order of the day. By contrast, in late imperial China, only the state and political contenders (e.g., the Taiping rebels) could organize large centrally controlled groups. Outside of the political sphere, the family was the primary medium for setting groups boundaries (Fei 1992). In late imperial China, and to a large extent in modern China as well, the combination of partible inheritance shaping property owning and property "rights" (which undermined the formation of large groups outside of those created by the state) and the aggressiveness and success of non-family based economic organizations, such as merchant associations, limited the size of businesses and pushed these businesses toward commodity production based on merchandising, that is, on pre-industrial equivalents of buyer-driven commodity chains. The ever-present tendency to segment property holdings across generations and the presence of effective long-term networks controlling trade meant that the crucial "barrier to entry" in producing commodities for China's vast domestic economy was the distribution of those commodities to mass markets, instead of their actual manufacture.

To better understand how such barriers to entry operated in the Chinese economy, one needs to examine both the products being sold and the organization of buying and selling, or what is termed in Chinese, the organization of *maimai*. The products themselves were genuine commodities in the modern sense of that term. Increasingly from the mid-Ming on, most widely traded commodities were differentiated products, in the sense that they were distinguished from like products through brand names and other differentiating markers. The use of brand names has been verified for a wide range of products, including cotton cloth, garments, porcelain, boots, tea, wine, medicine and herbs, scissors, needles, copper locks, copper mirrors, gold and silver bullion, hair ornaments, jewelry, jade items, writing brushes, writing paper, ink sticks, ink stones, lacquerware, books, and bank drafts. Widely available throughout the empire, many of these branded products were associated with their regional origins, including, for example:

Shaoxing wine, Jianzhou tea, Luchou silk piece goods, Xiangxiu (Hunan embroidery), Yuexiu (Guangdong embroidery), Shuxiu (Sichuan embroidery), Suxiu (Suzhou embroidery), Shujin (Sichuan cotton cloth), Huizhou ink stones and brushes, Fuzhou paper, Suzhou New Year prints, Yixing teapots and cups, and Jingdezhen porcelains (*Quanguo Mingtechanpin*, 1982). Such regional distinctions are not simple area designations. These products were widely available in most large urban centers, and in the richer regions of China, many could be found even in small markets.

(Hamilton and Lai 1989: 258)

This kind of product differentiation was minutely developed for cotton textiles as well for other goods. The cotton fabric production was mostly centered in Songjiang prefecture, which is located in the Yangzi River delta. According to Ye Mengzhu (1981: 157–8), a native scholar of Songjiang living in the seventeenth century, Songjiang cloth was classified into three categories by width. The widest cut of cloth, called *biaobu*, was shipped to Shaanxi, Shanxi, and the capital, Beijing. The middle category of cloth, labeled *zhongji*, was made for markets in Hunan, Hubei, Jiangxi, Guangdong, and Guangxi. The narrowest cut, measuring about one foot (*chi*), was called *xiaobu*, and it was marketed only in Raozhou and other districts in Jiangxi. Besides being classified by width, Songjiang cloth was also differentiated by various types of woven patterns and by merchant seals. Even in remote areas, such as Guizhou, some cloth included advertisements (e.g., "A fine product circulated in Beijing") woven directly into the fabric itself (Lai and Hamilton 1986). According to the 1512 edition of *Songjiang fuzhi*, the prefectural gazetteer, "As for cotton cloth ... every (manufacturing) village and market town has its own varieties and names; the list is inexhaustible" (quoted by Nishijima 1984: 49). The edition goes on to list, in a special section on cloth, fifteen different types. Within the distinctions made by producing regions, there was also an additional variation based upon the quality of the weave. The most expensive cotton weave was known as "three shuttle cloth." One bolt of this cloth could be exchanged for one bolt of silk, both of which sold for about two taels per bolt. Ordinary cotton cloth sold from 0.3 to 0.4 taels per bolt (Wiens 1976; Nishijima, 1984).

In addition to these distinctions made by producing communities, there were also those made by distributors. Cloth merchants, usually buying from producers in local market towns, were known by the quality of cloth they handled. To certify the cloth they would sell, in turn, to long-distance merchants, they made a mark, known as a *jitou* (loom-head), at the end of each bolt of cloth they collected for resale.

The importance of these *jitou* brand names, and how they worked, can be gleaned from a late Qing novel, *Sanyi Bitan* (1827). In the story, Wang Yimei was one of the largest cloth distributors among the famous Xinan merchants (i.e., merchants from Huihou, Anhui Province). On his firm's signboard, he used his given name, *Yimei*, and he paid *jihu* (families involved in textile production) to place "*Yimei*" at the end of each bolt. Using this method, Wang developed a national market for his product and sold one million bolts annually. Although fictitious, the example is backed up by stone inscriptions showing that for the late imperial period, long-distance cloth merchants made their decisions about which cloth to buy based on merchant marks; firms having a reputation for honesty and quality would have their mark accepted above those of uncertain reputation (Shanghai beike 1980: 84–8). Undoubtedly, because cloth marked with certain merchant chops would bring higher prices, the stone inscriptions also record complaints that some merchants using fraudulent marks would try to sell inferior cloth (ibid.: 202–3). Considering this sort of brand name proliferation, it is not surprising that, according to one source for late Ming (cited by Fu 1957: 15–16; Li Renpu 1983: 199), there were forty-two different kinds of cotton cloth available in the market of Yanshan, a small town in Jiangsu.

A contrast with Europe accentuates the extraordinary character of brand names in China. Very few students of industrializing Europe mention the presence of commodities bearing brand names. What little research has been done is primarily in marketing and advertising research (e.g., Borden 1947; Coles 1949; Davis 1967) and in historical studies of patents and trademark laws (e.g., Schechter 1925; Dutton 1984). More recently, however, a few historians and social scientists have started looking more closely at patterns of consumption in Western societies (e.g., Jones 1973; Ewen 1976; McKendrick *et al.* 1982; Fox and Lears 1983; Marchand 1985). The uniform conclusion of these studies is that analysts regard the origin and widespread use of brand names as being an aspect of capitalist development.

Two types of studies are particularly important in this regard. First, several scholars mention the absence of brand names in medieval Europe. The most cited study is that by Schechter (1925). Schechter explains in his history on trademark laws that merchant and artisan marks were not brand names in the modern sense of the term. Instead:

> the characteristics of the typical craftsman's mark of the Middle Ages were: (1) that it was compulsory, not optional; (2) that its purpose was the preservation of gild standards of production and the enforcement of gild or other local monopolies rather than the impressing on the mind of the purchaser the excellence of the product in question and thereby the creation of a psychological need for that product; (3) that, consequently, while the modern trademark is distinctly an asset to its owner, the medieval craftsman's mark was essentially a liability.
>
> (1925: 78)

Schechter explains that the difference between modern and medieval commodity marks results from differences in production and distribution systems between the two eras, particularly in the relations between producers and consumers. For the majority of people in medieval society, "wants were comparatively few and unchanging." People "were supplied by neighboring craftsmen; consumer and producer stood in direct relation with one another." Each town of any size had its own merchants and artisans, who in turn organized guilds through which they sought to monopolize production and trade. The guilds "strove by every means at their disposal to prevent 'foreigners' – as the merchants coming from a town five miles away might be described – from competing with their gild" (ibid.: 41–2). Merchant and artisan marks were the devices by which guilds sought to exclude outsiders and to control the economic activities of insiders. Although Schechter's thesis is dated and rather simplistic,[21] historians of marketing and advertising (e.g. Borden 1947; Coles 1949; Davis 1967), based largely on references to Schechter's study, argue that brand names start only in the modern era.

This thesis largely coincides with recent scholarship on patterns of consumption in modern society. A growing number of studies discuss the appearance, in the eighteenth century, of differentiated consumer products and the importance of these products for the success of Western capitalism. Mokyr (1977), Jones (1973), McKendrick et al. (1982) and Brewer and Porter (1993) argue that the eighteenth-century English economy became commoditized in response to changing patterns of consumption. An expanding middle class, according to their analyses, began to require affordable items of fashion and comfort in order to emulate the accouterments of the elite. McKendrick in McKendrick et al. (1982: 13) believes that this shift in demand is of such importance as to proclaim a "consumer revolution" in eighteenth-century England. "[C]onsumer behavior was so rampant and the acceptance of commercial attitudes so pervasive that no one ... should doubt that the first of the world's consumer societies had unmistakably emerged by 1800" (ibid.). This demand for fashionable products created an opportunity for manufacturers to explore ways to streamline their production and to market their products. Accordingly, such individuals as Josiah Wedgwood, the mass producer of English porcelains, began to create and to advertise brand name products designed to distinguish their wares from similar lines produced by competitors (Jones 1973; McKendrick et al. 1982; Brewer and Porter 1993; Fine and Leopold 1993).

Research on later periods of Western capitalism (e.g., Ewen 1976; Fox and Lears 1983; Marchand 1985) uniformly emphasizes the interrelations of mass consumers markets, the growth of large corporations, and advertising and marketing based upon products having brand names.

Consumerism and brand names, so the theory goes, went hand in hand to produce capitalist production as we know it today.

Even though their significance can certainly be debated,[22] that brand names are an important feature of modern Western capitalism can hardly be disputed. It is certain, however, that England was not the world's first consumer society and that consumerism does not occur only under conditions of capitalism.

V

Widespread distribution of differentiated commodities in late imperial China implies vast merchandising networks. As described elsewhere (Hamilton 1985), these merchandising networks certainly existed. Moreover, they emerged without the institutional support of the late imperial state. The Ming and Qing state did not standardize weights and measures, support a fixed currency, create commercial codes, or guarantee contracts – all of which formed the bedrock of Western economies. This absence of state-supported economic institutions helps to explain why there were such formidable barriers to entry at the distribution end of commodity chains. What the state did not provide, the merchant and artisan groups did, and in so doing they restricted access to marketing products. It was only through these merchant groups that China's vast domestic economy actually worked. But, more than that, the control over commerce established by merchants and artisan groups not only shaped trade, but also moved backwards to structure commodity production as well.

How were these merchants groups organized so that they created these backward effects on production? A contrast with Europe and Japan is again revealing. Merchant associations in Europe and Japan were divided between resident guilds and non-resident traders. The guild structure in most urban areas allowed resident merchants exclusively to control the commerce of the locale. Non-resident merchants were, in essence, wholesalers but not retailers. The ability of guilds to restrict commercial competition meant that such guilds could limit the widespread distribution of common products and could force consumers to buy what was locally produced or distributed. This situation prevailed until the guild structure broke up in the seventeenth and eighteenth centuries. The division between local and non-local merchants remains, even to this day, in the form of the distinction between wholesale and retail.

In China, however, the resident/non-resident categorization did not serve as the foundation for merchant and artisan organizations. Regardless of their length of residence in a locale, when merchants and artisans defined themselves collectively, they did so in terms of some combination of occupational specialization and regionality. This regionality, loosely linked to a lineage homeland somewhere outside their city of business, was very flexibly defined, and could be expanded or contracted based on the situational needs of the group (Hamilton 1985).

These economic groupings provided the institutional underpinning of Chinese commerce. These commercial activities were centered in *huiguan* or *gongsuo*, which were places, much like club houses, set aside for anyone who came from a defined region in China to meet and to do business. Every *huiguan* and *gongsuo* had its own rules, rules that applied to fellow-regionals or to people in that line of business. These were rules of personal conduct, as well as rules for the businesses in which the fellow regionals specialized. These groups specified such things as the weights and measures for the line of business, the type of currency accepted, the quality and price of the products or services that they sold. Those who did not abide by the rules, the leaders would sanction, sometimes by fines, but they could go so far as to drive violators into bankruptcy and out of business.[23]

By serving all these functions, regional groups created the institutional environment in which trade flourished. From the point of view of individuals, these merchant associations provided a structure of restraint and coercion to which individuals had to conform in order to realize their economic opportunities. From the point of view of the economy as a whole, these groups created an institutional environment in which buying and selling (*maimai*) was made into predictable and routine activities (Hamilton 1985).

Day-to-day normality and predictability were socially manufactured through the operation of trading networks. To an extent not appreciated by most scholars today,[24] Chinese merchants and artisan networks promoted competition within and among networks. These networks form the interpersonal structure of merchants and artisan associations.[25] Economically, however, they created an equivalent of a commodity market in which buyers and sellers met repeatedly, made deals, and set prices self-consciously and reflexively in the company of other buyers and sellers of the same or similar products. In this context, transactors tried to make the best long-term deals for themselves. Short-term maximization, in which fellow regionals and their regular consumers would short-change each other, would not serve as well as long-term deals that would insure longevity for all transacting parties. In his account of the activities of Chinese traders in Indonesia, Geertz describes the manner in which Chinese merchants in China also traded. The merchant, he said, typically wants

> to spread (himself) thin over a very wide range of deals rather than to plunge deeply in any one. Putting all one's eggs in a single basket is not a favored mode of procedure ... As a result, large, or even moderately large, single deals with only two people involved are very rare,

even in cases where the traders are large enough to handle such deals alone. Both large and small transactions usually involve a multiplicity of people, each making a small contribution and each taking out a small return. A trader contracting even a fairly petty agreement will look for others to go in with him; and, in fact, there is widely felt normative obligation on the part of traders to allow other people to cut into a good thing ... The individual trader, unless he is very small indeed, is the center of a series of rapidly forming and dissolving one-deal, compositely organized trading coalitions.

(1963: 40)

As Geertz describes, each investment is split into many parts and distributed to others in the network.

Merchants and artisans formed similarly organized groups at each step in the final production and distribution of a product. Such groups created mini-clearing houses for goods and services, which assured everyone in the group that no one person could dominate the group and that the general rules of trade would be fair, mutually agreed upon, and collectively enforced.[26] The groups, in effect, created price-efficient markets in goods and services at each step in a commodity chain, effectively segmenting each chain and encouraging different groups of people to handle each step. The segmentation maximized leverage at the merchandising end of the chain.

VI

We can set these organized economic activities into motion by showing how the textile trade worked. The important point to emphasize here is that the organization of the late imperial economy is not a static system, but rather an evolving one. We will divide our discussion of late imperial commercial organization between the period before and after 1850. Before 1850, China was a net exporter of commodities (e.g. teas and silks) and an importer of bullion. Although both the exports and imports had important effects on China's economy, the internal organization of trade was largely insulated from the diffusion of Western goods. After 1850, with China's defeat in the Opium Wars, Western products, technologies, and organizational forms were introduced into China, where they began to reshape the organization of the Chinese economy.

Long before 1850, Chinese merchants had gained control of both the collection of textiles from producing areas and their final dispersion to local sellers throughout the area of distribution. The same is true for other products as well. While it is the case that, in the mid-nineteenth century, long-distance trade was in the hands of different sets of merchants in different places, all the merchant groups seemed to work in much the same way (Rowe 1984; Hamilton 1985). The groups specializing in textiles, for instance, would attempt to make connections in particular producing regions and would concentrate their distribution in other areas. Merchants typically went to regional markets in the producing areas and bought cloth from commission agents or petty merchants who had collected the cloth in smaller markets from producing households in the region. Merchants then delivered the cloth to groups specializing in finishing the cloth though dyeing and calendering. According to Craig Dietrich (1972: 130), the merchants would give the cloth, together with "calendering contracts," to a set of people called *pao-tou*, or bosses. These bosses, in turn, would hire independent artisans, who rented their equipment from the bosses and worked under their supervision:

> The merchants exercised considerable control over the calendering industry without assuming any direct managerial responsibility . . . The whole organization resembled a modified putting-out system, wherein merchants entrusted raw material (cloth) to laborers through the intermediary of bosses. After processing, the laborers returned it, through the same intermediary, to the merchants. The importance of merchants was not confined to the calendering industry. Since the activities of the innumerable spinners and weavers were not integrated with one another in any organizational structure, it was the merchants, both local and regional, who held the industry together and allowed it to function as a system.
>
> (ibid.: 131)

As nearly as we can tell, over the course from mid-Ming to the late Qing periods (1500 to 1850), regional merchant networks gained a progressively stronger hold of China's economy, and then after 1850 these networks spread to Southeast Asia where they also dominated the domestic economies in the region. The data are not sufficient to say whether these early changes in networks occurred gradually or whether they occurred in spurts. But it is clear that the organization of commerce changed during the 350-year period. At the start of the era, and perhaps for the duration of the Ming period, local markets were controlled by local brokers (*ya hang*) who had licenses from the government to act as intermediaries between peasants selling goods in official markets and long-distance merchants who would bring in goods to sell and who would buy local products to sell elsewhere (Mann 1987). In large cities, brokers set up branches (called *shu chuang*) in the countryside to deal with peasant producers more directly, but such branches could only sell to licensed brokers. Even during the Ming period, however, non-local regional merchant networks had the resources and the connections to final markets and therefore probably had the upper hand in dealing with market brokers. A Ming dynasty poem says as much: "Brokers treat outside merchants like kings, because to oppose them means war."

By the start of the Qing dynasty in the mid-seventeenth century, the balance of power had swung decisively toward long-distance trading networks (Xu 1992). In early Qing, peasants could sell directly to long-distance merchants without going through market brokers. As a consequence, long-distance merchants began to patronize buyers in the countryside (*zuo chuang*) who collected goods directly from peasant producers. Such collection strategies put regional merchants directly into competition with market-based brokers.

By mid-Qing, the economic power of non-local merchants had overwhelmed locally based merchants (Xu 1992). The brokerage system, which was relatively powerful in the Ming, had lost its significance and had been largely replaced by non-local merchants, the most successful of whom began to establish brand name stores (*zihao*). At the same time, specialization in the textile trade occurred so that different steps in the production of cotton cloth were now systematically farmed out to different groups. Local traders or local representatives of regional networks would collect raw cloth that had been woven by peasant households and would sell it to brand name stores. Very similar to OEM (original equipment manufacturing) production today, where branded products (e.g., Nike, Dell) indicate the merchandiser and not the maker of products, the merchant owners of these stores would farm out the cloth to dyeing mills. The mills would return the dyed cloth to the brand name stores with the brand name dyed into each bolt of cloth. A typical brand name would read "Manufactured by the Lin Family." At this point, the merchandiser had become by far the most powerful link in the chain, powerful enough to shape all the backward links.

By late Qing, the regional merchant networks controlled all the links in the cotton textile commodity chain (Hamilton 1977a; Xu 1992). The broker system declined over the long term and eventually disappeared. The local merchants who had previously been brokers gradually became long-distance traders themselves. Capitalizing on their local connections, they extended their trading networks to other locations. By late Qing, the great bulk of China's commerce was handled by regionalized trading networks, which in any one urban setting might have sufficient density to be represented by merchant associations that had been established by non-local merchants from this or that region. By late Qing, the invidious distinction between local and non-local merchant and artisan groups had all but disappeared, when virtually all groups became enmeshed in one or another form of non-local grouping (Hamilton 1985). Moreover, by the late nineteenth century, as Mark Elvin (1973) and Ho Ping-ti (1966) show, these regional merchants had greatly expanded; regionally organized migrants had gained control not only of commerce but also of most occupations in China's cities, everything from sailors to barbers; even the beggars in Beijing (Burgess 1928) had a regionally based organization.

VI

In the 1840s, losing the first round of skirmishes with Western states, China was forced to open its borders to Western traders and Western commodities. By 1850, British cotton textiles began to flood Chinese markets. Eyeing China's millions, the British had expected Chinese consumers to buy great quantities of British-made cotton goods, as had so many other consumers in other parts of the world. In fact, Sir Henry Pottinger, the British representative at the signing of the Treaty of Nanking in 1842, had forecast that "even the total output of Lancashire would not be sufficient to satisfy consumption in a single province in China" (Chao 1977: 168). This prediction matched the belief in Europe, echoed by Marx (1959: 11) that, "Cheap commodity prices are the heavy artillery with which (the bourgeoisie) batters down all Chinese walls and forces the barbarians' intensely obstinate hatred of foreigners to capitulate." This perception colored the interpretation of the Western impact on China for years, as many analysts (e.g., Isaacs 1961) reported that Western imports had destroyed China's handicraft industries. That view, however, has now been thoroughly revised (Feuerwerker 1970; Chao 1977; Hamilton 1977). But what is less understood is the role played by China's merchants in creating a new system of handicraft cotton textile production that competed successfully with Western cotton textile imports. The new system, based on the importation of foreign yarn, unambiguously shows a continuation of the backward linkages of merchandising on cotton textile production.

From 1850 to the 1930s, when the Great Depression and the Japanese invasion irrevocably disrupted daily life in China, Chinese handicraft cotton textile production not only survived the onslaught of Western and Japanese imported textiles, but also thrived as well. This, in fact, was the heyday of China's handicraft production. Chinese hand-made textiles not only supplied most of the domestic market with cloth, but also became a flourishing export commodity. As Table 5.2 shows, the export of Chinese native cloth grew about eighty-fold between 1870 and 1925, and millions of households were engaged in making cloth from yarn, and, in addition, thousands of small factories emerged to weave, dye, and finish the cloth (Chao 1977: 169–217; Xu 1992).

The impetus for this remarkable growth in China's cotton handicraft industry was the ready availability of large supplies of cotton yarn imported largely from India and Japan between 1860 and 1920, and subsequently provided by mills in China as well. China's pre-1850 cotton handicraft production had been concentrated in the cotton-growing regions in the lower reaches of the Yangtze River. The demand for cotton textiles was in part

Table 5.2 Exports of Chinese native cloth, 1871–1930 (5-year total)[a]

Period	Quantity (piculs)	Value (1,000 haikwan taels)
1871–5	3,903	193
1876–80	9,328	487
1881–5	12,917	526
1886–90	28,086	1,037
1891–5	88,528	3,289
1896–1900	139,188	5,855
1901–5	129,932	6,124
1906–10	178,346	8,548
1911–15	221,917	11,454
1916–20	258,596	15,698
1921–5	315,516	19,737
1926–30	201,486	13,494

Note

a Table 5.2 is reproduced from Chao (1977: 173). The data for Table 5.2 are found in Yen (1963: 83). For approximate conversions of piculs and taels to Western measures, see note to Table 5.1.

limited by the supply of cotton and, more importantly, by the control of merchant networks whose economic power structured the whole system of production. Although competitive within networks, only a few regional merchant networks had access to raw cotton, these, in turn, had control over the national distribution of cotton cloth. When Chinese markets were opened to foreign trade, different sets of merchants all across China could suddenly purchase cotton yarn cheaply and could promote and manage their own production networks. Demand for yarn boomed. After 1850, every province in China began to produce hand-made cottons (Chao 1977), and cotton-growing areas began to produce more cotton as well. In an effort to explain the dismal reception of British cotton cloth in China (Britain did not sell yarn overseas, only cloth), troubleshooters from Lancashire reported that even in the peripheral provinces of Yunnan and Guizhou yarn imported from India had created thriving handicraft industries where none had existed before. Women even attended classes to learn how to weave (Neville and Bell 1898: 261–6).

What remained crucial for the expansion of production was the ability of merchants successfully to merchandise and sell hand-made cloth in competition with Western and Japanese imported cloth. Here, too, the Western opening of China, which introduced new and cheaper means of transporting goods (e.g., railways and steamships) greatly enhanced the ability of Chinese merchants to distribute their goods and hence to compete with Westerners. But it was organization of commerce that created the potential and led the system of handicraft production to new levels.

In the post-1850 period, increasing opportunities to participate in the cotton trade led Chinese merchants to rationalize the existing system of production and distribution, but not to transform it. The number and size of putting-out systems of production greatly increased, as did the efforts to merchandise finished cloth, but each step in the chain of production remained segmented, as it had before 1850. Chao (1977) gives several examples that causes one to realize that handicraft production was not a throwback to a traditional system, but rather was a competitive alternative to a factory-based system. One example he gives is of the emergence of a new handicraft industry in Wei district in Shandong province. In the early years of the twentieth century, Wei district was linked to Qingdao, a new treaty port opening in 1899, by a railroad built in 1904. Taking advantage of this new opportunity, a number of merchant firms organized a putting-out system based on providing credit to households to buy simple hand-looms and cotton yarn and return cotton cloth. In ten years, they had organized over 100,000 looms producing cotton cloth:

> During the peak years about 150,000 persons were involved in the production of native cloth, with a maximum annual output of ten million bolts ... Although gray goods and bleached cloth remained as the prominent products throughout, the quantities of colored and patterned cloth were sufficiently large to justify the establishment of factories specializing in various finishing processes. According to a survey made in the early 1930s, there were 30 dyeing factories, 7 calendering factories, and 3 packing companies. The products of Wei Xian enjoyed a nationwide market.
>
> (ibid.: 196)

As is the case with most analysts, Chao describes the system of production in greater detail than the system of merchandising and distribution, but he does recognize the importance of the merchant end of the endeavor (ibid.: 206–17). Arguing that merchants decisively affected the rise and fall of centers of handicraft production, he cites some examples of merchant organization. For instance, a study of cotton handicrafts in Hebei province in 1934 showed that "a total of 25.7 million bolts of native cloth were produced in 89 xian (districts) in the province, of which 89 percent were sold to other places through cloth merchants." These cloth merchants were not consolidated into huge firms, but were rather divided into many small firms, each handling, calculates Chao (ibid.: 204), about one hundred weaving households. The largest firms he came across managed 4,000 looms. These putting-out firms organized production in the following ways:

(1) buying factory yarn in large quantities from big cities, (2) distributing the yarn to individual hand weavers and setting specifications

for the products, (3) collecting cloth from weavers and performing finishing works if necessary, and (4) transporting the goods to other cities for sale.

(ibid.: 204)

A recent book by Xu Xinwu (1992: 365–8) substantiates that the same patterns that were observed in the Ming and early Qing continued in the 1920s.[27]

VII

The interpretation of China's handicraft industry travels the same path as the greater "sprouts of capitalism debate." Historians have not viewed China's handicraft production in the Ming, Qing, and Republican eras – right up to the Japanese invasion in 1936 – as an example of capitalism, of industrialization, or even of modernization. Most analysts see it as evidence of continuing traditionalism and of spreading commercialization without genuine development. As such, most conclude that China's handicraft tradition at last came to an end with destruction caused by World War II and the post-war economic reorganization that occurred as a consequence of the Communist Revolution on the Mainland.

The thesis in this chapter is different. By overemphasizing the capitalism/no capitalism, development/no development debate, analysts ignore the organizational features, and particularly the strength and dynamism, of the Chinese economy as well as the evolution of the system over the past 500 years. If we push our analysis back to an even earlier period, to the economically sophisticated, but rigidly stratified Song dynasties (Northern and Southern Song Dynasties), we see that the economic organization of the Song differed greatly from what emerged in the Ming and Qing periods. Song commerce was urban-based with relatively little penetration of the rural areas (Shiba 1970). Merchants were rooted to urban locales. They were urban resident merchants and not non-local regional merchants, and commodity production was equally urban and not rural. The economic organization of Song China was more similar to that in late medieval Europe and Tokugawa Japan than to what emerged in Ming and Qing China, in large part because the social organization of society promoted that form of economy.

The commercial transformation of late imperial China grew out of the intense reorientation of Chinese society that occurred at the end of the Yuan and beginning of the Ming dynasties. In the Ming, a relatively decentralized, rural-based society emerged. Elites were centered in and mainly circulated in local society, grounded there, in part, by the growth of powerful, local lineage groups. Centered on the mobility of households, the class structure became "fluid," as Ho Ping-ti (1964) put it. The commercial system that developed in mid-Ming reflected the features of that society. Although the society certainly changed during the last 500 years, from the sixteenth century to the early twentieth century, the changes were largely matters of degree rather than of kind, and consisted of systematizing the patterns that were already prevalent and important. By late Qing, the commercial system of China was the tail that wagged the entire structure of China's economy outside of the state sector, and for much of this period, the state sector was concerned with taxation and the redistribution of grain through the granary system that the Qing state developed (Will and Wong 1991). Although the state sector collapsed in the final decades of the nineteenth century, the economic organization of the private was not transformed into some other economic stage or system when Western and Japanese powers forcibly opened China, but rather grew along a trajectory established in the pre-1850 period. The opening of China's markets to Western traders merely quickened this earlier process of change by expanding the range of economic opportunities that Chinese people could grasp, a conclusion echoed by Sherman Cochran (1980, 2000) as well. This outcome occurred despite the changes wrought by Western and Japanese imperialism (Brandt 1989).

The advances in this commercial system during the late imperial period directly contributed to the simplification of technology when contrasted with production of the same products elsewhere around the world, particularly Europe and the United States. There is no culprit in this process, no direct or indirect agency that blocks economic development in China, no high-level equilibrium trap that Mark Elvin (1973) discussed, no economic involution that Huang (1985, 1990) talks about, and no peasant-induced barrier to development that Mazumdar (1998) ends up with. The merchandising power at the commercial ends of China's economy pushed the deployment of simple technology at the production end of the economy; and as production became centered in the household, then gender and kinship dynamics controlled the labor force. Often confined to households, women and young girls became primary producers of many handicraft goods.[28] But population pressure and cheap labor are not the reasons for these developments. What happened in the large picture also happened in the small. "A puzzling fact" that Chao (1977: 182) noted is that in the early part of the twentieth century when both foreign yarn and a range of alternative looms were readily available, the first ones to disappear were the "native spinning wheels with 3 or 4 spindles." The most common loom in use was also the most primitive one, a "single spindle wheel so simple that a girl of seven or eight would learn to operate it."

As we argue here, China's system of production and distribution was an alternative to Fordist systems of production that emerged in the nineteenth and early twentieth centuries, systems with well-organized producer-driven commodity chains. But the absence of these types of chains does not mean that China's economy was antagonistic to capitalism. Quite the contrary, China embraced the new economic order. China's economy was extensively and intensively organized and was rooted deeply in Chinese social institutions. The buyer-driven features of the economy gave the economy momentum and direction, and as economically active Chinese took advantage of new opportunities introduced by the opening of China to the outside world and as they incorporated Western organizational forms (e.g., limited liability companies) and material technologies, they simply reinvented their traditions. A large part of the Chinese economy, especially the coastal areas, seamlessly became integrated into global capitalism, and indeed became a competitive form of capitalist production. This is simply to say that the Chinese ways of doing business were sophisticated, were oriented to profit, and could compete successfully in almost any market. Even in the late nineteenth and early twentieth centuries, in the struggle for economic success, Chinese merchants and industrialists usually came out on top (MacPherson and Yearley 1987; Hamilton 1996; Cochran 2000).

If one were to examine the organization of the textile industry in Taiwan and China in the past decade or the footwear industry or the garment industry or the bicycle industry or even the high technology industries, as we have done elsewhere (Orru *et al.* 1997; Hsing 1998; Kao and Hamilton forthcoming), it would be apparent that the economic organization in all of these sectors share organizational features of putting-out systems of production that existed a century earlier. This observation does not imply that there is a lineal chain of events that connects the two eras. At this particular historical moment, the big buyers pulling the greater Chinese economies are the same big buyers that now shape the global economy, and these are not predominantly Chinese-owned firms. Instead, the globally oriented discount houses and brand-name merchandisers (e.g., Walmart, Home Deport, the Gap, Nike, Timberland, even Dell and Gateway) are largely, but not exclusively Western owned. Like a century ago, the production networks shaped by these big buyers emphasize piecework (called batch-production system) and flexible work routines. These factors give advantages to factories with low overhead (such as small and medium-sized family-owned firms) and to flexibility in organizing production networks that can expand or contract with changing demand (Shieh 1992; Chen 1995). The technology used in such factories must necessarily match the manufacturing jobs being done and the resources available to those running the businesses. Inevitably, the technology used in such circumstances is simpler and less costly than that deployed in large vertically integrated factories. To be sure, some differences currently exist between the organization of Taiwan's and the Mainland's economies, but in the vibrant export sector of the Mainland economy, productions systems intermingle Taiwanese, Hong Kong, and PRC firms, often resulting in even greater flexibility than is found solely in Hong Kong or Taiwan. Indeed, the boundary lines between the economies of Hong Kong, Taiwan, and the PRC have virtually disappeared, creating what Barry Naughton (1997) calls "the China circle."

The point is that the technology in use reflects the way the economy is socially organized, as well as the product being made. That young girls made cloth on single-spindle looms a century ago or that the women (and often men too) in households gather around the dining table to assemble computer parts today does not indicate economic involution or capitalistic ineptitude of any kind. But it does indicate that we cannot understand how economies work unless we understand how they are organized in some holistic way.

Acknowledgment

This chapter was written with the assistance of Lai Chi-Kong, Department of History, University of Queensland, Brisbane, Australia.

Notes

1 For a more developed discussion of the theme of this paragraph, including the pertinent literature, see Hamilton *et al.* (2000) and Feenstra and Hamilton (forthcoming).

2 Recently a number of scholars have made similar observations, including Brook and Blue (1999), Wong (1997), and Pomeranz (2000).

3 Much the same can be said for many interpretations of the rise of capitalism in other locations in Asia, in Southeast Asia and especially Japan. In the Japanese literature, however, there is also an equal effort on the part of some scholars to discover the pre-modern origins of Japanese capitalism in functional equivalents to the prerequisites for Western capitalism, as for instance Bellah (1957) did a number of years ago and as Collins (1999) did very recently.

4 There are, of course, limits to this type of comparison. Clearly, European nations are more oriented to capitalism than most African nations are. But the point is that many economic differences result from differences in the how economic activity is organized and institutionalized in a particular social environment, and not whether the economic configuration is more or less capitalistic. The latter makes capitalism into an ideal condition, the difference from which can be measured precisely.

5 For reviews of this literature, see Rawski (1991), Feuerwerker (1992), and Brook (1989).

6 In his discussion of China's economy, Bin Wong (1997) uses the adjective "Smithian" to describe the market dynamics of an essentially agricultural economy. He opposes Smithian markets with commercial capitalism. Our use of Smithian conforms to the more orthodox economic connotations of Adam Smith's work to mean market dynamics, whether capitalist or not (Hamilton 1985). We argue in this chapter that Wong's distinction between Smithian commerce and capitalistic commerce is not particularly meaningful when applied to nineteenth- and twentieth-century China.

7 For an excellent comparison of the levels of consumption in China and Western Europe in the nineteenth and twentieth centuries, see Pomeranz (2000: 114–65).

8 Also see Pomeranz's more recent estimates (2000: 138–41; 327–38), which appeared after this chapter was in a finished version.

9 Literati paraphernalia are exceptions, but even these were often modest in contrast to the finery and accoutrements of Western and Japanese elites.

10 The most recent and thorough participant in this debate is Pomeranz (2000), whose book is an extended analysis of "The Great Divergence" between China and Western Europe.

11 Wu Chengming (1985: 260–2) has shown that in the Ming Dynasty, cotton production was centralized in Jiangsu Province. "The main types of cloth produced [in this region] was called *biao* and *leng* [later called *shi* cloth]. About 150 to 200 million bolts of this cloth were shipped and marketed throughout a wide region of China connected by means of long-distance trade. In the Qing Dynasty, the areas of cotton production expanded, to include cloth from Sung-jiang, Chang-shou, Wu-shi, all of which was collectively called the Su-sung production area. Apart from these, there were also some smaller centralized production regions in north and central China. The long-distance shipping and marketing of this cloth increased over that which occurred in the Ming dynasty." For similar description, see Nishijima Sadao (1984: 526).

12 For some of the more recent contributions to the assessment of this literature, see Lazerson and Lorenzoni (1999), Storper and Salais (1997), and Vallas (1999).

13 The interpretation of this commercialization is, however, disputed. The Marxian advocates of the sprouts of capitalism view commercialization as evidence of the bourgeoisification of feudalism, a necessary step for the eventual revolution. The critics of this interpretation argue that, despite commercialization, no independent merchant class developed, and hence no capitalism. The Smithian advocates of a sustained economic development in late imperial China see commercialization as evidence for the creation of price-setting markets that allowed industrious peasants gradually to raise their standard of living through participation in the market. The critics of the Smithian interpretation argue that no improvement in the standard of living resulted from this commercialization, but instead involution and peasant immiseration.

14 In opposition to evidence given by Rawski (1989) and Brandt (1989), Wong (1997: 66) questions how efficient China's markets really were, but without giving any evidence to support his contention.

15 Some might be inclined to think of Adam Smith as the theorist who connected both ends of the commodity chain together in his concept of supply and demand. Although he theorized demand, Smith's work transformed thinking about production. To some extent neo-classical economics, as a production-led theorization of markets, has followed this lead ever since.

16 The concept of global commodity chains was first suggested by Terence Hopkins and Immanuel Wallerstein (1986), but Gereffi (Gereffi and Korzeniewicz 1994) is most responsible for its recent re-emergence and importance.

17 It is worth noting the Western bias in the thinking of many analysts of the imperial Chinese economy, who assume that vertical integration, whether backward or forward, naturally occurs in the process of industrialization, when in fact many writers, including Chandler, show different outcomes occurred in different locations.

18 It is worth noting that significant portions of the PRC's export economy are organized through the direct investments and involvement of entrepreneurs

from Hong Kong and Taiwan, who have moved their firms or branches of their firms to the Mainland and who have subcontracted portions of their production to local firms.

19 This section draws heavily on the arguments made in Hamilton and Lai (1988).

20 For more detail on these patterns of consumptions, see Hamilton (1977a).

21 Recent research on medieval markets (e.g., Berger 1980; Hilton 1985; Biddick 1985) show greater market penetration into the countryside than previously believed, but they do not fundamentally alter Schechter's characterization.

22 The economic literature on brand names is largely confined to marketing research (e.g., Pilditch, 1970). There are, however, relevant economic studies about product differentiation. Economists (e.g., Scherer 1970; Chamberlin 1950) have investigated theoretically the conditions producing product differentiation. According to Scherer (1970: 324), brand name differentiation occurs when producing firms "strive to differentiate their goods and services from rival offerings." Given this competition, firms rationally plan strategies to create products that consumer will buy.

23 It is significant to note that *huiguan* and *gongsuo* all but disappeared during the Mao era in the PRC. After the economic reforms in the late 1970s, they have started to reappear.

24 We are struck by the tendency to interpret Chinese merchant associations as examples of collusion, monopoly, cronyism, and cartels without really examining how these associations operated economically. This tendency is reminiscent of the 1879 civil suit by Western merchants against the Swatow Opium Guild in which the Westerners brought charges of unfair trade, collusion, and conspiracy against Chinese merchants. The Chinese merchants defended themselves successfully by showing that Westerners had imposed their own conceptions of guilds onto Chinese behavior. Not only was there no collusion, there was also no guild, merely a place where fellow-regionals meet to discuss business and enjoy each other's companionship (Hamilton 1977a; also see Hamilton 1985).

25 It should be emphasized that merchant groups in late imperial China, the *huiguan*, were unlike Western guilds in which a person either belonged or not. *Huiguan* are meeting places and not formal organizations. As places, they fostered economically active networks that rested on common social relationships. The commonality allowed the network to be socially binding, because normative rules existed on how one should treat others bound by a *guanxi* tie. Merchants associations of out-of-towners formed for many reasons, such as when the critical mass of fellow regional was sufficient to support building a meeting hall, when the competition among networks was great enough to promote greater coordination, or when local opposition to non-local merchants merited a common front. But merchant networks, resting on both economic opportunity and some social basis for moral, if not physical, coercion operated whether a physically located *huiguan* existed or not.

26 The structural similarity between trading in a commodity market and trading in a situation where transactors engage in long-term repetitive trading is striking. For a detailed analysis of commodity, bond, and equity markets that are very similar to the account of Chinese traders given by Clifford Geertz, see Abolafia (1997).

27 Xu (1992) concludes that brand name products were crucial to how the cloth market functions. Much of the cloth business revolved around the ability to obtain credit, and the better known the brand, the easier it was to obtain the credit essential for creating a putting-out system and the easier it was to sell the

cloth to merchants who would resale the cloth in other places. Cloth merchants would grade their cloth and give a different brand name to each grade. The merchants would, in turn, register their brand names with the cloth merchants' trade associations, which would protect the brand names and take such actions as were necessary to punish violators. Xu reports that then, as now, brand name piracy was a problem.

28 It is worth noting that the large spinning factories that emerged in Shanghai during the 1920s and 1930s, producing cheap yarn, partially supported the spread of handcraft production.

References

Abolafia, Mitchel Y. 1997. *Making Markets: Opportunism and Restraint on Wall Street.* Cambridge, MA: Harvard University Press.

Abstract of Information on Currency and Measures in China. 1889–90. *Journal of the China Branch of the Royal Asiatic Society*, New Series 24: 48–135.

Anderson, Perry. 1974. *Lineages of the Absolutist State.* London: New Left Books.

Becker, Howard S. 1986. *Doing Things Together: Selected Papers.* Evanston, IL: Northwestern University Press.

Bellah, Robert. 1957. *Tokugawa Religion: The Cultural Roots of Modern Japan.* New York: The Free Press.

Berger, Ronald M. 1980. "The Development of Retail Trade in Provincial England, *ca.*1550–1700." *The Journal of Economic History* 40, 1 (March): 123–8.

Biddick, Kathleen. 1985. "Medieval English Peasants and Market Involvement." *The Journal of Economic History* 45, 4 (December): 823–31.

Brewer, John and Roy Porter. 1993. *Consumption and the World of Goods.* London: Routledge.

Borden, N.H. 1947. *The Economic Effects of Advertising.* Chicago: Richard D. Irwin.

Brandt, Loren. 1989. *Commercialization and Agricultural Development in East-Central China, 1870–1937.* Cambridge: Cambridge University Press.

Bray, Francesca. 1999. "Towards a Critical History of Non-Western Technology," in Timothy Brook and Gregory Blue (eds), *China and Historical Capitalism: Genealogies of Sinological Knowledge.* Cambridge: Cambridge University Press, pp. 158–209.

Brook, Timothy (ed.) 1989. *The Asiatic Mode of Production in China.* Armonk, NY: M.E. Sharpe.

Brook, Timothy and Gregory Blue. 1999. *China and Historical Capitalism: Genealogies of Sinological Knowledge.* Cambridge: Cambridge University Press.

Burgess, John Stewart. 1928. *The Guilds of Peking.* New York: Columbia University Press.

Campbell, Colin. 1987. *The Romantic Ethic and the Spirit of Modern Consumerism.* Oxford: Basil Blackwell.

Chamberlin, Edward H. 1980. *The Theory of Monopolistic Comptetition.* Cambridge, MA: Harvard University Press.

Chandler, Alfred D., Jr. 1977. *The Visible Hand: The Managerial Revolution in American Business.* Cambridge, MA: Harvard University Press.

Chandler, Alfred D., Jr. 1990. *Scale and Scope: The Dynamics of Industrial Capitalism.* Cambridge, MA: Harvard University Press.

Chao, Kang. 1977. *The Development of Cotton Textile Production in China.* Cambridge, MA: East Asian Research Center, Harvard University Press.

Chen, Chieh-hsuan. 1994. *Xieli wangluo yu shenhuo jiegou: Taiwan zhongxiao qiye de shehui jiji fenxi* (Mutual Aid Networks and the Structure of Daily Life: A Social Economic Analysis of Taiwan's Small- and Medium-sized Enterprises). Taipei: Lianjing.

Chen, Chieh-hsuan. 1995. *Huobi wangluo yu shenhuo jiegou: Difang jinrong, zhongxiao qiye Taiwan shisu shehui zhi zhuanhua* (Monetary Networks and the Structure of Daily Life: Local Finances, Small and Medium-sized Enterprises, and the Transformation of Folk Society in Taiwan). Taipei: Lianjing.

Chen, Chieh-hsuan. 1998. Taiwan change de shehuixueyanjiu (Sociological research on Taiwan's industries), Taipei: Lianjing.

Cochran, Sherman. 1980. *Big Business in China: Sino-Foreign Rivalry in the Cigarette Industry, 1890–1930.* Cambridge, MA: Harvard University Press.

Cochran, Sherman. 2000. *Encountering Chinese Networks: Western, Japanese, and Chinese Corporations in China, 1880–1937.* Berkeley, CA: University of California Press.

Coles, J. 1949. *Standards and Labels for Consumer Goods,* New York: Ronald Press.

Collins, Randall. 1999. *Macrohistory: Essays in Sociology of the Long Run.* Stanford, CA: Stanford University Press.

Davis, A. 1967. *Package and Print, The Development of Container and Label Design.* New York: C.N. Potter.

Dietrich, Craig. 1972. "Cotton Culture and Manufacture in Early Chng China," in W.E. Willmott (ed.), *Economic Organization in Chinese Society.* Stanford, CA: Stanford University Press, pp. 109–36.

Dutton, H.I. 1984. *The Patent System and Inventive Activity During the Industrial Revolution, 1750–1852.* Manchester: Manchester University Press.

Elvin, Mark. 1972. "The High-Level Equilibrium Trap: The Causes of the Decline of Invention in the Traditional Chinese Textile Industries," in W.E. Willmott (ed.), *Economic Organization in Chinese Society.* Stanford, CA: Stanford University Press, pp. 137–73.

Elvin, Mark. 1973. *The Pattern of the Chinese Past.* Stanford, CA: Stanford University Press.

Ewen, S. 1976. *Captains of Consciousness.* New York: McGraw-Hill.

Faure, David. 1989. *The Rural Economy of Pre-liberation China.* Hong Kong: Oxford University Press.

Faure, David. 1994. *China and Capitalism: Business Enterprise in Modern China.* Hong Kong: Hong Kong University of Science and Technology.

Feenstra, Robert C. and Gary G. Hamilton. Forthcoming. *Emergent Economies, Divergent Paths: The Organization of Development in South Korea and Taiwan.* Cambridge: Cambridge University Press.

Fei, Xiaotong. 1992. *From the Soil: The Foundations of Chinese Society.* Trans., Introduction, and Epilogue by Gary G. Hamilton and Wang Zheng. Berkeley, CA: University of California Press.

Feuerwerker, Albert. 1970. "Handicraft and Manufactured Cotton Textiles in China: 1871–1910." *Journal of Economic History* 30: 338–78.

Feuerwerker, Albert. 1992. "Questions about China: Early Modern Economy History that I Wish I Could Answer," *Journal of Asian Studies* 51 (4): 757–69.

Fine, Ben and Ellen Leopold. 1993. *The World of Consumption.* London: Routledge.

Fox, R.W. and T.J.J. Lears (eds) 1983. *The Culture of Consumption: Critical Essays in American History 1880–1980.* New York: Pantheon Books.

Fu Yiling. 1957. *Mingdai Jiangnan shimin jingji shitan* (Exploratory Essay on the Urban Economy of the Kiangnan Area during the Ming Dynasty). Shanghai: Shanghai Renmin Chubanshe.

Geertz, Clifford. 1963. *Peddlers and Princes: Social Development and Economic Change in Two Indonesian Towns.* Chicago: University of Chicago Press.

Gereffi, Gary. 1994a. "The Organization of Buyer-Driven Global Commodity Chains: How U.S. Retail Networks Shape Overseas Production Networks," in Gary Gereffi and Miguel Korzeniewicz (eds), *Commodity Chains and Global Capitalism.* Westport, CT: Greenwood Press, pp. 95–122.

Gereffi, Gary. 1994b. "The International Economy and Economic Development," in Neil Smelser and Richard Swedberg (eds), *The Handbook of Economic Sociology.* Princeton, NJ: Princeton University Press, pp. 206–33.

Gereffi, Gary and Gary G. Hamilton. 1996. "Commodity Chains and Embedded Networks: The Economic Organization of Global Capitalism." Unpublished paper presented at the Annual Meeting of the American Sociological Association.

Gereffi, Gary and Miguel Korzeniewicz. 1994. *Commodity Chains and Global Capitalism.* Westport, CT: Praeger.

Goldstone, Jack. 1996. "Gender, Work and Culture: Why the Industrial Revolution Came Early to England and Late to China," *Sociological Perspectives* 39 (1): 1–21.

Granovetter, Mark. 1985. "Economic Action and Social Structure," *American Journal of Sociology* 91: 471–510.

Hamilton, Gary G. 1977a. "Chinese Consumption of Foreign Commodities: A Comparative Perspective," *American Sociological Review* 42: 877–91.

Hamilton, Gary G. 1977b. "Nineteenth Century Chinese Merchant Associations: Conspiracy or Combination? The Case of the Swatow Opium Guild," *Ch'ing-shih wen-t'i* 3: 50–71.

Hamilton, Gary G. 1985. "Why No Capitalism in China," *Journal of Developing Societies* 2: 187–211.

Hamilton, Gary G. 1996. "Competition and Organization: A Reexamination of Chinese Business Practices," *Journal of Asian Business* 12 (1): 7–20.

Hamilton, Gary G. 1997. "Organization and Market Processes in Taiwan's Capitalist Economy," in Marco Orrù, Nicole Woolsey Biggart, and Gary G. Hamilton (eds), *The Economic Organization of East Asian Capitalism.* Thousand Hills, CA: Sage Publications, pp. 237–96.

Hamilton, Gary G. and Cheng-shu Kao. 1990. "The Institutional Foundations of Chinese Business: The Family Firm in Taiwan," *Comparative Social Research* 12: 95–112.

Hamilton, Gary G. and Chi-kong Lai. 1988. "Consumerism without Capitalism: Consumption and Brand Names in Late Imperial China," in Benjamin Orlove and Henry Rutz (eds), *The Social Economy of Consumption.* New York: University Press of America, pp. 253–77.

Hamilton, Gary G., Robert C. Feenstra, Wong Choe, Chung Ku Kim, and Eun Mie Lim. 2000. "Neither States Nor Markets: The Role of Economic Organization in Asian Development," *International Sociology* 15 (2): 291–308.

Hamilton, Gary G. and Nicole Woolsey Biggart. 1988. "Market, Culture, and Authority: A Comparative Analysis of Management and Organization in the Far East," *American Journal of Sociology* 94 (Supplement): S52–S94.

Hanley, Susan B. 1997. *Everyday Things in Premodern Japan: The Hidden Legacy of Material Culture.* Berkeley, CA: University of California Press.

Hanley, Susan B. and Kozo Yamamura. 1977. *Economic and Demographic Change in Preindustrial Japan, 1600–1868.* Princeton, NJ: Princeton University Press.

Hilton, R.H. 1985 "Medieval Market Towns and Simple Commodity Production." *Past and Present* 109 (November): 3–23.

Ho, Ping-ti. 1964. *The Ladder of Success in Imperial China.* New York: John Wiley and Sons.

Ho, Ping-ti. 1966. *Zhonghuo huiguan shilun* (A Historical Survey of Landsmann-schaften in China). Taipei.

Hollingsworth, J. Rogers and Rober Boyer. 1997. *Contemporary Capitalism: The Embeddedness of Institutions.* Cambridge: Cambridge University Press.

Hopkins, Terence K. and Immanuel Wallerstein. 1986. "Commodity Chains in the World-Economy Prior to 1800," *Review* 10 (1): 157–70.

Hsing, You-tien. 1998. *Making Capitalism in China: The Taiwan Connection.* New York: Oxford University Press.

Huang, Philip C.C. 1985. *The Peasant Economy and Social Change in North China.* Stanford, CA: Stanford University Press.

Huang, Philip C.C. 1990. *The Peasant Family and Rural Development in the Yangzi Delta, 1350–1988.* Stanford, CA: Stanford University Press.

Huang, Philip C.C. 1991. "Reply to Ramon Myers," *Journal of Asian Studies* 50 (3): 629–633.

Isaacs, Harold R. 1961. *The Tragedy of the Chinese Revolution.* Stanford, CA: Stanford University Press.

Jones, E.J. 1981. *The European Miracle: Environments, Economies, and Geopolitics in the History of Europe and Asia.* Cambridge: Cambridge University Press.

Jones, E.L. 1973. "The Fashion Manipulators: Consumer Tastes and British Indus-tries, 1660–1800," in L.P. Cain and P.J. Uselding (eds), *Business Enterprise and Economic Change.* Ohio: The Kent University Press.

Jones, Eric. 1988. *Growth Recurring: Economic Change in World History.* Oxford: Clarendon Press.

Ka, Chih-Ming and Mark Selden. 1986. "Original Accumulation, Equity and Late Industrialization: The Cases of Socialist China and Capitalist Taiwan," *World Development* 14 (10/11): 1293–310.

Kao, Cheng-shu and Gary G. Hamilton. Forthcoming. "Reflexive Manufacturing: Taiwan's Integration in the Global Economy," *International Studies Review* 3, 1.

Lai Chi-kong and Gary G. Hamilton. 1986. *Jinshi Zhongguo shangbiao yu quanguo dushi shichang* (Trademark and National–Urban Market in Late Imperial China). *Proceedings of the Conference on Regional Studies of Modern China.* Taipei: Institute of Modern History, Academia Sinica.

Lazerson, Mark H. and Gianni Lorenzoni. 1999. "The Firms that Feed Industrial Districts: A Return to the Italian Source," *Industrial and Corporate Change* 8 (2): 235–66.

Li Renpu. 1983. *Zhongguo gudai fangzhi shigao* (A Draft History of the Premodern Chinese Textile Industry). Hunan: Yuelu Shushe.

Lin, Nan. 1995. "Market Socialism and Local Corporatism in Action in Rural China," *Theory and Society* 24: 301–54.

McKendrick, N., Brewer, J., and Plumb, J.H. 1982. *The Birth of a Consumer Society: The Commercialization of Eighteenth Century England.* Bloomington, IN: Indiana University Press.

MacPherson, K.L. and C.K. Yearley. 1987. "The 2½% Margin: Britain's Shanghai Traders and China's Resilience in the Face of Commercial Penetration," *Journal of Oriental Studies* 25 (2): 202–34.

Mann, Susan. 1987. *Local Merchants and the Chinese Bureaucracy, 1750–1950.* Stan-ford, CA: Stanford University Press.

Marchand, R. 1985. *Advertising the American Dream: Making Way for Modernity, 1920–1940.* Berkeley, CA: University of California Press.

Marx, Karl. 1959. *Basic Writing on Politics and Philosophy.* New York: Anchor Books.

Mazumdar, Sucheta. 1998. *Sugar and Society in China: Peasants, Technology, and the World Market.* Cambridge, MA: Harvard University Press.

Mokyr, J. 1977. "Demand vs. Supply in the Industrial Revolution," *Journal of Economic History* 37: 98–100.

Morse, Hosea B. 1908. *The Trade and Administration of the Chinese Empire.* Shanghai: Kelly and Walsh.

Myers, Ramon H. 1991. "How Did the Modern Chinese Economy Develop? – A Review Article," *Journal of Asian Studies* 50 (3): 604–28.

Naughton, Barry. 1997. *The China Circle: Economics and Technology in the PRC, Taiwan, and Hong Kong.* Washington, DC: Brookings Institution Press.

Neville, N. and Bell, H. 1898. *Report of the Mission to China of the Blackburn Chamber of Commerce, 1896–7.* Blackburn: The Northeast Lancashire Press.

Nishijima, Sadao. 1984. "The Formation of the Early Chinese Cotton Industry," in Linda Grove and Christian Daniels (eds), *State and Society in China: Japanese Perspectives on Ming–Qing Social and Economic History.* Tokyo: University of Tokyo Press, pp. 17–77.

Orrù, Marco, Nicole Woolsey Biggart, and Gary G. Hamilton. 1997. *The Economic Organization of East Asian Capitalism.* Thousand Hills, CA: Sage Publications.

Pilditch, James. 1970. *Communication by Design: A Study in Coporate Identity.* London: McGraw-Hill.

Piore, Michael J. and Charles F. Sabel. 1984. *The Second Industrial Divide: Possibilities for Prosperity.* New York: Basic Books.

Pomeranz, Kenneth. 2000. *The Great Divergence: Europe, China, and the Making of the Modern World Economy.* Princeton, NJ: Princeton University Press.

Pratt, Edward E. 1999. *Japan's Protoindustrial Elite: The Economic Foundations of the Gono.* Cambridge, MA: Harvard University Press.

Quanguo chanpin (Famous Native Products in China). 1982. Shanxi: Shanxi Renmin Chubanshe.

Rawski, Evelyn S. 1991. "Research Themes in Ming–Qing Socioeconomic History – The State of the Field," *Journal of Asian Studies* 50 (1): 84–111.

Rawski, Thomas G. 1989. *Economic Growth in Prewar China.* Berkeley, CA: University of California Press.

Rowe, William. 1984. *Hankow: Commerce and Society in a Chinese City: 1796–1889.* Stanford, CA: Stanford University Press.

Rowe, William. 1985. "Approaches to Modern Chinese Social History," in Oliver Zunz (ed.), *Reliving the Past: The Worlds of Social History.* Chapel Hill, NC: The University of North Carolina Press.

Saxenian, Anna Lee. 1994. *Regional Advantage: Culture and Competition in Silicon Valley and Route 128.* Cambridge, MA: Harvard University Press.

Schechter, F.I. 1925. *The Historical Foundations of the Law Relating to Trade-marks,* New York: Columbia University Press.

Scherer, F.M. 1970. *Industrial Market Structure and Economic Performance.* Chicago: Rand and McNally.

Shanghai beike ziliao xuanji (Selected Epigraphic Materials from Shanghai). 1980. Shanghai: Shanghai Renmin Chubanshe.

Sheldon, Charles David. 1958. *The Rise of the Merchant Class in Tokugawa Japan, 1600–1868.* Locust Valley, New York: J.J. Augustin Incorporated.

Shiba, Y. 1970. *Commerce and Society in Sung China.* Ann Arbor, MI: Center for Chinese Studies, University of Michigan.

Shieh, G.S. 1992. *"Boss" Island: The Subcontracting Network and Micro-Entrepreneurship in Taiwan's Development.* New York: Peter Lang.

Skinner, G. William. 1964–65. "Marketing and Social Structure in Rural China," *Journal of Asian Studies* 24 (1): 3–43; 24 (2): 195–228; 24 (3): 363–99.

Skinner, G. William (ed.) 1977. *The City in Late Imperial China*. Stanford, CA: Stanford University Press.

Skinner, G. William. 1985. "Presidential Address: The Structure of Chinese History," *Journal of Asian Studies* 46 (2): 271–92.

Smith, Thomas. 1959. *The Agrarian Origins of Modern Japan*. Stanford, CA: Stanford University Press.

Storper, Michael and Robert Salais. 1997. *Worlds of Production: The Action Frameworks of the Economy*. Cambridge, MA: Harvard University Press.

Tocqueville, Alexis de. 1969. *Democracy in America*, Trans. J.P Mayer. New York: Doubleday.

Vallas, Steven P. 1999. "Rethinking Post Fordism: The Meaning of Workplace Flexibility," *Sociological Theory* 17 (1): 68–101.

Wank, David L. 1999. *Commodifying Communism: Business, Trust, and Politics in a Chinese City*. Cambridge: Cambridge University Press.

Weber, Max. [1921–22], 1978. *Economy and Society*. Trans. and ed. G. Roth and C. Wittich. 3 vols. Berkeley, CA: University of California Press.

Wiens, Mi Chu. 1976. "Cotton Textile Production and Rural Social Transformation in Early Modern China," *The Journal of the Institute of Chinese Studies of the Chinese University of Hong Kong* 7 (2): 515–34.

Will, Pierre-Etienne and R. Bin Wong. 1991. *Nourish the People: The State Civilian Granary System in China, 1650–1850*. Ann Arbor, MI: Center for Chinese Studies.

Wong, R. Bin. 1992. "Chinese Economic History and Development: A Note on the Myers–Huang Exchange," *Journal of Asian Studies* 51 (3): 600–11.

Wong, R. Bin. 1997. *China Transformed: Historical Change and the Limits of European Experience*. Ithaca, NY: Cornell University Press.

Wu Chengming. 1985. *Zhongguo zibenzhuyi yu guonei chichang* (Chinese Capitalism and the Internal Market). Beijing: Zhongguo Shehui Kexue Chubanshe.

Xu Xinyu. 1981. *Yapian zhanzheng qian Zhongguo mianfangzhi shougongye de shangpin shengchan yu zhibenzhuyi mengya wenti* (Commodity Production and the Sprouts of Capitalism in China's Handicraft Weaving Industry before the Opium War). Nanjing: Jiangsu renmin chubanshe.

Xu Xinwu. 1988. "The Struggle of the Handicraft Cotton Industry against Machine Textiles in China," *Modern China* 14 (1): 31–49.

Xu Xinwu (ed.) 1992. *Jiangnan tubushi* (The History of Native Cloth in Jiangnan). Shanghai: Shanghai shehui kexueyuan.

Ye Mengzhu. 1981. *Yueshibian*. Reprint. Shanghai: Shanghai guji shubashe.

Yen Zhongping. 1963. *Zhongguo mianfangzhi shikao* (Draft History of China's Cotton Textile Industry). Beijing.

Chapter 6

Japan, technology and Asian regionalism in comparative perspective

Peter J. Katzenstein

Since the middle of the nineteenth century on questions of technology Japan and Asia have been in a subordinate position in the international system. This chapter argues that during the second half of the twentieth century, Asia's technology order has also been defined by a relatively hierarchical regional division of labor even though first Japan and other Asian states later have improved rapidly their technological profiles. Focusing on the Japanese technological challenge, this chapter shows how governments and corporations seek to respond to and appropriate the effects of international technological developments through distinctive institutions, and how they attempt to project their preferences, in the form of national policies and corporate strategies, into the region of which they are a part. Although the technological leads and lags that separated Japan from the USA and other Asian political economies have changed over time, the underlying order has not. As different producers in Japan and Asia rapidly mastered the leading technologies of different industrial sectors, Asia's technological order has remained defined by the search for enhanced national autonomy and corporate profitability.

Even in realms where they led the field internationally Japanese producers did not dictate developments. Networks organized around overseas Chinese commercial and technological elites operating in Southeast Asia and in Silicon Valley have at times linked up with US producers thus offering plausible alternatives for Asian producers seeking to reduce their technological dependence on Japan. The process of change in regional hierarchies thus is relatively fluid and offers chances for absolute and relative advancement to weak states and corporations in peripheral economies which are clever to exploit the competition between larger states and core economies. Yet this has done little to change the hierarchical, national and market-oriented character of Asia's technology order.

The contrast with Germany and the European technology order is instructive. In Europe technology is only one among many sectors in which the process of regionalization plays itself out. National governments are partially pooling state sovereignties and corporations seek to gain resources from that process to improve their competitiveness in world markets.

Regions are both geographically given and politically made. Geographic proximity matters for a broad range of economic, social and cultural interactions. So does politics which can redraw maps by shaping collective identities. Karl Deutsch (1981: 54) defines regions succinctly as a group of countries markedly interdependent over a wide range of different issues when compared to other groups. Regions are shaped by both economic and social processes of regionalization and by structures of regionalism (Fishlow and Haggard 1992; Fawcett and Hurrell 1995; Grugel and Hout 1999). Regionalization describes the geographic manifestations of global processes. Regionalism characterizes formal or informal political structures that shape the strategies of actors. Asia is marked primarily by regionalization processes, a relative weakness in formal political structures, and the existence of a variety of informal network structures. In Europe, on the other hand, regional structures tend to be formal rather than informal while regionalization processes have grown less sharply than in Asia in the 1980s.

At the beginning of the twenty-first century the situation in Asia is extremely fluid. Is Japan in the process of consolidating a new technology paradigm uniquely well suited to its changing institutions? Or has Japan reached the political and economic limits of institutions no longer adequate for the information technologies that promise both large economic returns and important social change in the coming decades? Nobody knows for sure the answers to these questions. Just as the optimism about Japan's technological prowess was overblown a decade ago, so is today's pessimism. Technological orders endure longer than moments of excessive optimism or pessimism. They express evolving political solutions that resolve unavoidable tensions between ideological visions and institutional practices.

Technology in historical perspective

Technology is important for the rise and decline of nations. Since the beginning of the nineteenth century first Britain and then the United States have parlayed their technological prowess into positions of world power. And through technological imitation and innovation Japan and Germany, among others, have at various times sought to consolidate their leading positions in Asia, Europe and the global system. Because of its direct relevance to both military strength and economic competitiveness, technology matters politically to both leaders and followers.

National economies, often closely linked to their regional and global environments, are central in creating technological change. Britain was the dominant technological power during the first half of the nineteenth century. In the second half, together with Germany, the USA quickly came to compete successfully with Britain especially in the new fields of chemistry and electrical engineering (Nelson 1990: 4–6). In the decades leading up to World War I Germany moved into a position of scientific leadership. But in mass-production industries US corporations eventually established a position of leadership over both Britain and Germany (Chandler 1990). By the turn of the century the United States had established itself as the world's leading technological power even though in some fields (organic chemical products, chemical process equipment and electronics) it probably lagged behind Germany (Yakushiji 1985). For a series of case studies of technology transfers see Jeremy (1991 and 1992).

Changes in technological power were also evident in Asia. After the Meiji restoration Japan's modernization was driven by the need to quickly create an independent army and navy (Seki 1994: 36). Government and corporations paid heavily for foreign technical expertise as "Meiji Japan imitated, borrowed from, and modified techniques from the West" (Nafziger 1995: 45). Between 1868 and 1892 the central government spent 1.9 percent of its total budget on hiring thousands of foreigners and sending thousands of Japanese students and government officials abroad (ibid.: 37–8). This position of backwardness has, for more than a century, made the Japanese government not waver from its commitment to enhance the country's technological autonomy, even though, in recent decades, Japan has become a technological leader in many international markets. And it has generated widespread societal consensus on the need to enhance the country's economic security (Katzenstein 1996: 113–15). Many other Asian states including Korea and China, have followed in Japan's footsteps.

Technological autonomy is central to Japan's developmentalist strategy and its sense of moving up in the international division of labor. "Japan's technology and security ideology," Richard Samuels writes, "has evolved to serve the nation across a diverse set of structural conditions" (1994: 42). Directly and indirectly throughout the twentieth century military considerations ranked high in Japan's technology policies. In the 1980s some observers dubbed this "techno-nationalism." It is a constant in Japan's approach, modified only marginally in recent times. A 150-years' perspective thus underlines this chapter's focus on the last half-century.

In Prussia and Germany technological backwardness was not overcome by the determined modernization push of the state. Instead what proved to be decisive was the gradual emergence of the technical institutes as sites of applied and practical learning. Against the opposition of the "German Mandarins" (Ringer 1969) ensconced in the universities, the technical universities used the technological advances of the 1860s to improve their academic standing and gain additional resources. Within a few decades they had become the backbone of Germany's technological ascendance to leadership in new industries such as chemicals and electrical engineering.

Creating the conditions for military strength and economic competitiveness through technology was one thing, having the political capacities to deploy power prudently was quite another. Both Germany and Japan moved quickly to close the technological gap that had defined their status as industrial latecomers in the nineteenth century. But their systems of government proved woefully inadequate to fashion coherent and feasible strategies serving their newly-found military strength and economic competitiveness. The technological dynamism of these two economies and societies became the vehicle for an aggressive nationalism and military expansion that by 1945 had proved to be disastrous for them, Asia and Europe. The result was total military defeat and unconditional surrender in 1945.

Germany's scientific and technological prowess was sapped not only by the loss of two world wars but also by the self-inflicted wounds of anti-Semitism that murdered or sent into exile a very large number of the country's scientific and technological elite. Germany's vaunted strategy of diffusing widely and quickly technologies developed elsewhere rather than becoming an innovator itself in key industries such as electronics is partly a consequence of its own policy. So is the quick rise of the United States to a position of scientific and technological pre-eminence after 1945.

In sharp contrast to Germany, Japan's military defeat did not decimate its scientific and technological elite. It did, however, eliminate all traces of a political role for the military and, under the defense umbrella provided by the United States, freed the country's talents for a dynamic commercial expansion in world markets. Chalmers Johnson (1982) has shown how the formidable organizational capacities of Japan's economic bureaucracy, without the constraints imposed by the military, came after 1945 to focus directly and primarily on economic objectives. In cooperation with business, the government's economic strategy soon yielded impressive results. Completing its process of rapid catch-up industrialization, in the early 1980s, Japanese producers began to challenge the position of the United States in leading areas of high technology such as computers, electronic chips, robotics and new materials. In the mid-1980s Japanese production moved off-shore with amazing speed, spreading technology in a carefully controlled manner to other Asian economies. By the 1990s Japanese firms had become a world leader in important technologies and had succeeded in making deep inroads into areas in which US firms held unassailable positions only two or three decades earlier (Yakushiji 1986; Taylor and Yamamura 1990; Hatch and Yamamura 1996: 97–8).

Japan and Asia – Germany in Europe

Asia's and Europe's emerging regional orders differ (Katzenstein and Shiraishi 1997a; Katzenstein 1997b). European regionalism is formal. It is reflected in collective political institutions operating at the regional level, including a common court, a Commission issuing thousands of binding regulations a year, a Parliament, a common central bank and currency, and, soon, a limited collective military capacity for peace-keeping and peace-enforcement operations. Asian regionalism is informal. Despite institutions such as ASEAN and the Asian Development Bank (ADB) it operates predominantly through market institutions. Specific to Asian markets are networks that are partly competing and partly complementary, as, for example, in Japanese and Korean corporate networks and Chinese family, clan and ethnic networks. While Asia's multilateralism is at best incipient, especially since the 1970s, informal networks have contributed to creating new regional links and altering the pattern of Asian trade.

On questions of technology, Europe's and Asia's regional orders differ. The main explanation lies in Japan's and Germany's different domestic structures that link the main actors in state and society. Both Germany and Japan are characterized by active and consensual policies that seek to enhance international competitiveness. But the mainspring of policy differs for what Kozo Kato describes as Japan's information-rich system of political institutions and Germany's quasi-corporatist polity (Kato 1996: 256–347). Japan's policy networks are geared to a free exchange of information among competing centers of power, Germany's to institutionalized bargaining arrangements.

Differences in domestic structure and in regional settings create different political capacities for change. At the level of industrial sector or for specific technologies, Japanese capacities are larger than German ones. This is illustrated by the fact that Japan's production profile has changed a number of times during the past half century, while Germany's has remained largely unchanged. In Japan, leading industrial sectors have frequently changed during the last half-century, from textiles to steel and shipbuilding, to automobiles and consumer electronics, to computers and semi-conductors. In Germany machinery and machine tools, electrical equipment, chemicals, and automobiles have remained the leading sectors throughout the second half of the twentieth century. Corporate linkages in Japan are primarily group- rather than industry-based as in Germany. And group-based linkages, write Peter Hall and David Soskice:

> provide greater capacities for diffusing new technology across sectors boundaries ... Japanese firms have been better than their German

counterparts at entering new industries, such as semiconductors, and at incorporating the technology developed in one industry into the products of others.

(1999: 28)

At the international level the situation is reverse. Here German capacities exceed Japanese ones as is illustrated by Germany's active participation in a number of European and international technology ventures.

Technology has different political salience in Japan and Germany. In Japan technology is a matter of national security cultivated assiduously. Technology is viewed as an instrument for lowering the country's potential vulnerability to international disruptions in supplies that Japan has little capacity to influence. In so doing it enhances national autonomy. Hence the Japanese government has been very consistent in supporting core technologies, collecting information on the technological advances of foreign competitors, and seeking to advance its political objectives through numerous long-term programs. Japan sees itself as a technological superpower that defines the parameters of social change for others.

In Germany technology is a tool for maintaining economic competitiveness in world markets rather than a way of protecting national security. Because it is viewed to be less central to survival, technology has become one instrument among many through which Germany seeks to advance its goal of a partial pooling of national sovereignty in an emerging European polity, as in a number of high-profile European-centered technology projects. At the national level, on the other hand, German policy-makers and corporate leaders see Germany typically as a "good second" who is very well equipped to diffuse technologies it often does not know how to generate by itself. What from the vantage point of innovation looks like a conservative bias, is in fact very effective in terms of application (Roobeek 1990: 202–4, 212, 218, 220).

In the area of information technology policies, for example, these differences between Japan and Germany are readily apparent (Organisation for Economic Co-operation and Development 1991: 8, 92, 98–9). The "Advanced Information Society" that provides the organizing concept for Japanese policy is an ambiguous term which can be used to motivate a wide variety of economic and social programs promoting the development and application of information technologies in economy and society. Specifically the Japanese government has aimed at supporting technological progress of specific industry segments in the hope of enhancing the international competitiveness of the entire industry. In Germany policy is informed by principles that are more concrete and that seek a rapid and efficient integration of information technologies into the production process in both the manufacturing and service sectors of the economy.

Japan and Germany thus relate differently to the flow of technology. Japanese institutions are especially attuned to technological developments which they follow closely, import freely, improve greatly, and seek to reintroduce into Asia under carefully monitored conditions. Contemporary Germany, by contrast, lacks the domestic institutions to create the innovations with which it could shape regional technological developments on its own terms. It thus chooses to embed itself in broader regional institutions to achieve broader political purposes.

There are also economic reasons for the different reactions of European and Asian polities to the reascendence of Germany and Japan. The degree of imbalance in the two regions differs greatly. Measured at current exchange rates, the spread in the per capita/GDP ratio in post-Cold War Asia is almost four times larger than in Europe (the ratio is 1:28 in Europe compared to 1:110 in Asia; see Lemoine 1997: 21–2, summary). Wage differentials are much larger in Asia than in Europe. The least developed states in Eastern Europe thus are in a better starting position than are the least developed Asian countries. Other statistical indicators also illustrate the contrast between European homogeneity and Asian heterogeneity and the more advantageous position that creates policies of technological catch-up in Europe (Katzenstein 1997a: 23; Katzenstein and Shiraishi 1997b: 365–6).

It is not only the smaller difference in intra-regional imbalances but also the historical experience of other states in dealing with Germany in numerous multilateral European institutions that creates an important difference between Europe and Asia. Diffusing the fear of the re-emergence of Germany's or Japan's regional hegemony and the memory or prospect of bilateral dependence are important political facts in both Asia and Europe. Compared to Japan's reticence to acknowledge, apologize for, and compensate victims of the atrocities it committed in Asia in the 1930s and 1940s, German public discourse and state policy have been more forthcoming in the past three decades, thus alleviating European anxieties about a resurgent Germany. The institutionalization of various international and transnational relations linking Germany in multilateral European arrangements to the smaller states has politically neutralized the fear of economic dependence. Institutionalization has fostered instead the gradual emergence of a collective European identity that Germany has actively and consistently championed. Multilateral institutions are in Europe the proper arena within which bilateral relations should be conducted. This helps the smaller European states to compensate for existing economic and political asymmetries between large and small states. So do the domestic corporatist arrangements that help the losing sectors of society in coping with the change imposed by international economic dependence (Katzenstein 1985). Both international and domestic political institutions have thus counteracted economic and political dependence and thus help neutralize the fear of German hegemony. Technology did not matter.

The differences between Asian and European regionalism thus are very considerable. Yet it would be a mistake to overlook a very important similarity. Besides their regional placement, both Germany and Japan are embedded also in global relations that closely align them with the United States. They are important nodes of a tri-regional international economy and capillaries in an increasingly multicultural world (Lake 1988; Nye 1992). Eschewing autarchy and isolation, both Germany and Japan and European and Asian regionalism are open to the flow in technology, wealth and power that links both regions to a world political economy in which the United States continues to play a central role.

Japan and technology

Since 1945 Japan's indigenization of technology has been inexorable. "What once was purchased," Richard Samuels writes, "soon was licensed for coproduction. What had been coproduced then was codeveloped. Budgets and politics willing, what is now codeveloped will be indigenized" (1994: 187). Japan's national goal is to transform itself into a *gijutsu-rikkoku* which has been translated as both a technology-based or a technonationalist country (ibid.: 48). Since 1945 the number of technology agreements signed with foreign firms has numbered in the tens of thousands. In 1990 alone the government approved 8,000 technology purchases (ibid.: 45). "Japanese firms have licensed for tens of billions of dollars foreign technology developed at a cost of hundreds of billions in a rapidly succeeding effort to achieve autonomy through dependence" (ibid.: 46). In many programmatic trade and industrial policy statements that have accompanied Japan's reconstruction after 1945 and that are now charting its path into the next century, the government has articulated the goal of greater technological autonomy. In so doing, the government extends a tradition dating back to the Meiji restoration. Achieving a position as a technologically pre-eminent power was as pressing a Japanese political goal at the beginning of the twentieth century as it is at the beginning of the twenty-first. In this view Japan does not seek to impose heavy-handedly a military or political order on other states. It offers instead a technological and social model for other states to emulate.

Post-war Japan extricated itself from a position of technological backwardness by instituting a strict government-guided screening system for importing foreign technology, especially from the United States and Western Europe (Odagiri and Goto 1993, 1996). This system was crucial for the government's development strategy in still dynamically growing, mid-tech industries. Japanese producers competed successfully in world markets by improving incrementally both products and production processes (Amsden and Hikino 1991: 2, 7–8, 20, 35; Nafziger 1995: 50). Over the span of the last five decades Japan has built up its competitive advantage in all the major sectors of the Industrial Revolution. The country's dizzying progress and technological advance led from textiles to shipbuilding, to steel, to autos, to consumer electronics, to semi-conductors and computers. Competitive advantage was based on fierce fights for market share at home, scale and learning curve effects in production, well-orchestrated export offensives to establish Japanese producers firmly in world markets, and the move to the next higher-valued added sector or sector segment. Japan's quick ascendance in major, industrial sectors was typically based on the licensing of important foreign technologies, their improvement and adaptation to fit specific Japanese needs, and subsequent production for domestic consumption and export markets at high levels of efficiency (Sato 1978: 1).

Until the mid-1970s much of Japan's R&D expenditures was spent on digesting imported technology needed to make, for example, nylon, transistors and televisions. However, between 1975 and 1985 Japanese producers focused on developing technologies such as integrated circuits, liquid crystal display and carbon fiber which spurred capital investments that fueled growth. Japan's Science and Technology Agency thus has viewed technological progress as increasingly determining economic growth during the post-war years; technological progress accounted for only 20 percent of growth in 1955–60 compared to 65 percent in 1975–80 (Kier 1986: 1).

Compared to other industrial and industrializing states Japan's quest for technological autonomy relies on a broad array of distinctive policies. Like the United States, Britain and France whose policies are aimed at accomplishing specific missions, Japan has deployed a series of government-coordinated policies to advance its technological autonomy. But in sharp contrast to these three countries, since 1945 Japan has stayed clear of relying on military programs to enhance its technological autonomy (Katzenstein 1996). Furthermore, like Germany, Switzerland and Sweden, Japan emphasizes the development of a broad-based capacity to diffuse technologies throughout economy and society. Japan's economic bureaucracy is deeply involved in the formulation of technology policy helped by close relations between business and government. In the implementation of policy decentralization is the rule. Specifically, since the early 1970s Japanese policy has focused on three main aspects: (1) providing a framework and promoting research and economic activities which are at the leading edge compared to the technological capabilities of the core of an industry; (2) investing in the training of engineers and general rather than industry-specific education; and (3) accelerating technological transfer throughout the economy with the aid of about 200 regional laboratories that assist small and medium-sized firms (Ergas 1986: 38–43; Watanabe and Honda 1991).

This strategy is compatible with the fact that national economic growth is influenced more by the speed of imitation than the displacement of the global innovation frontier (Kitschelt 1991: 478; Iizuka 1994). Glenn Fong's (1998) careful empirical work on Japan's high-profile, large-scale national research and development programs in computers and semi-conductors illustrates how Japan quickly became a "follower at the frontier." While US companies enjoyed an enormous lead over their Japanese competitors in the late 1950s, by the mid-1980s that lead had virtually vanished. After the US semi-conductor industry had staged a great comeback, by the mid-1990s the Japanese 40 percent share of the global semi-conductor market was roughly equal to that of the United States (Fong 1995: 9). The elimination of the technology gap has made the task of the government infinitely more difficult. Rather than imitating technologies, it has to make choices with very uncertain pay-offs.

Yet the government continues to commit significant financial resources to technology. The latest Real World Computing Project (1992–2001), for example, is projected to cost 70 billion yen (Fong 1998: 346). (For a convenient set of cross-national data by sector and country see Roobeek 1990: 86–145.) But as Japan has moved to the technological frontier, there have been noticeable changes in policy. In the areas of computers and semi-conductors, for example, the source of government initiatives has shifted (from higher to lower levels); its industrial target has moved (from specific engineering developments to basic and applied research); and its scope has been altered (from a small to a large number of competing technological approaches). The number of corporate participants has increased greatly. Top-heavy government intervention has been replaced by the networking of interlacing technical and industrial circles. Yet despite considerable international diffusion of some aspects of Japan's R&D system, MITI remains a pro-active and involved actor in the development of Japan's technological base even though many Japanese firms are now operating at the technological frontier. The barriers to technology diffusion created by tacit knowledge and the lead-time that policy can create for national producers even when knowledge is diffused have given MITI strong incentives to continue in its traditional quest of strengthening national producers in changing markets (Fransman 1995, 1999).

Japan's policy is formulated and implemented in a cooperative system of consultation in which the government's power to direct corporate behavior through legal or financial instruments is less important than the sharing of information (Fransman 1995, 1999; Doane 1998). Japan's institutional governance and technological development mesh. The government views the economy as a portfolio of industry sectors and segments. It analyzes these according to specific economic criteria, including growth potential, national value added, and international competition. Government policy aims at enhancing the technological position of leading sectors and segments so as to strengthen Japan's overall position.

Distinctive also is the institutionalization of self-reflection. Government officials and top management have a broad vision of where Japan fits in the global system, engage in a systematic scanning of the relevant environment, prepare quantitative and qualitative data, and draw out the implications for corporate, industry, and government policies (McMillan 1996: 78–9). These institutional practices reduce transaction costs and facilitate long-term relations in business and politics. The machinery of governance rests on five components, all of which entail a significant sharing of information: (1) relational contracting; (2) management transfers and lifetime employment for employees; (3) an extensive sharing of information within business groups; (4) cross-over ownership of shares; and (5) selective intervention by major shareholders to force adjustments in business strategies (Kester 1992: 87).

Industrial visions and collective practices do not constitute a plan. They are a political process in which collective learning through public dialogue occurs primarily in a myriad of institutionalized committees of consultation and advice (Weber 1985b: 9). Information sharing is at the core of how the Japanese polity reacts to and affects global technological change. Some branches of the Japanese civil service spend as much as half their time in a variety of advisory councils that are mostly making substantive recommendations which the bureaucracy and political parties subsequently ratify (ibid.: 16). Taylor and Yamamura (1990: 36) thus conclude that "probably the most important contribution policy can make is to continue fostering the national consensus concerning the need to move toward the information age."

Despite many changes in technology and policy, Japanese business has remained remarkably resistant to international diffusion. For example, less than one-fifth of Japan's scientific and technical journals are covered by English-language indexing and abstracting sources (US Congress 1984: 6). This is not to deny that some changes have occurred. Where Japanese technology is lagging and when, for whatever reason, it suits the Japanese bureaucracy, some foreign firms are occasionally accepted in government-sponsored research consortia. For example, in the Real World Computing Program eight of the sixty-four research contractors and associated institutions are non-Japanese (Fong 1998: 360). In biotechnology link-ups with foreign firms and universities are also quite important (Fransman and Tanaka n.d.: 4, 32). But these are relatively isolated instances that do not change the overall picture.

A 1991 study of Japan's National Institute of Science and Technology Policy, for example, found that off-shore Japanese manufacturing producers primarily buy locally from other Japanese firms. "Parts procurement networks are formed by Japanese companies, and there is a wall that prevents technology from being transferred outside this network" (quoted in Normile 1993: 352). Japanese firms are very reluctant to transfer technology that has not yet been fully exploited through commercial applications. In the mid-1990s, Korean semi-conductor producers were dependent on Japanese firms for about three-quarters of their production equipment. Yet Japanese firms, Korean producers complain, transfer only technology that is well established or they transfer only partial technology (Zysman and Borrus 1996: 93). The Japanese government prohibited, until 1995, the transfer of two hundred high technologies to South Korea; only less advanced technology can be transferred freely (Ruigrok and Van Tulder 1995: 297).

The picture is very similar in the relations between Japanese and European corporations. Even though they lead European corporations in most areas of high-technology, in their strategic alliances with European producers Japanese firms have relied on their traditional strategy of trading European market entrance to Japan against technology transfer from Europe. Japanese firms use their European partners largely as screwdriver factories. "International cooperation in such cases," write Rob Van Tulder and Gerd Junne, "does not increase the technological capacities of the receiving firm and in the longer term may even reduce it" (1988: 245).

Other evidence points in the same direction. Japanese corporations retain tight control over their foreign affiliates at the top level of management (Tho 1993: 247–8). Japan remains a net importer of technology. In 1991 it paid $6.5 billion for patents, licenses, know-how and other transfers, mostly to American and European firms; it exported less than $3 billion of its own technology, much of it to Asia (Normile 1993: 352; Hatch 2000: 159, 356). Hemmert and Oberländer (1998: 3–4) report that technology exports exceeded imports for the first time in 1993, and that the export lead has since widened. In 1991 the export/import ratio in technology trade was 0.41, compared to 0.28 a decade earlier (Fransman 1995: 102). Furthermore, between the mid-1970s and mid-1980s the foreign share in national patent applications increased in all industrial economies except in Japan where it declined by 50 percent. That share is five to eight times larger in the USA and Europe than in Japan. In the first half of the 1990s the proportion of Japanese technology exports going to unaffiliated firms declined (Hatch 2000: 356). While Japan has moved rapidly to the technological frontier, it thus remains remarkably insular and resists the global pull that is strongly affecting virtually all other industrial states (Vernon and Kapstein 1991: 12). Among all of the industrial states, Japan ranks first in having virtually all of the patents of its research-intensive large firms issued at home (Reid and Schriesheim 1996: 65). This high degree of insulation may have become a liability as Japan's overall economic position has deteriorated sharply in the 1990s, illustrated by declining total factor productivity, lagging sales growth in key industries, growing unemployment and a rising deficit in intellectual property royalty payments (Hatch 1999). Technological autonomy as a foundation for regional strength looks significantly less secure now than it did a decade or two earlier.

Asian networks

Maintaining control over technology is a key aspect of the process by which Japan and other states in Asia seek to foster the development of their national economies. Host countries welcome the economic growth and improved export performance that foreign investments can bring, particularly when accompanied by technology transfers. But they also remain ambivalent because the new economic linkages tend to be intrafirm and thus are not conducive to technological learning and the growth of autonomous supplier networks. Seeking to escape excessive dependence on Japan, the smaller Newly Industrializing Economies (NIE) thus are seeking to exploit the leverage that international competition between Japanese, USA and European producers may offer (Ernst and O'Connor 1989: 79; Hatch 2000: 355–6).

Japan's neighbors seek to enhance their margin of choice by maneuvering in and out of different production networks (Borrus 1997: 154–6; Doherty et al. 1995: 12–14, 19–27). Japanese networks tend to be closed and are given to cautious and incremental decision. In building regional production networks, Japanese corporations are typically reluctant to share technologies either with other countries or other corporations. The "commonwealth" of overseas Chinese offers an alternative, ethnic capitalism through which production networks spread in Asia. These Chinese networks tend to be commercial rather than technological. Since the mid-1980s, however, some Chinese networks have opened to incorporate US manufacturers. These networks tend to be open, fast and flexible. They are less protective of proprietary technologies and more open to technology transfer to local enterprises. American and European multinational corporations constitute still a third network, less deep than the Chinese one but perhaps better suited to facilitate the flow of technology (Borrus et al. 2000b: 14–31; Linden 2000: 221). By maneuvering in and out of different production networks, Japan's neighbors seek to enhance their margin of choice and to increase their technological capacities and economic growth potential (Borrus 1997: 154–6. Doherty et al. 1995: 12–14, 19–27; Borrus et al. 2000a). Technology thus is transferred through a variety of Asian networks not all of which are controlled by Japanese corporations.

Japanese networks

Since the Meiji restoration Japan has developed a "full-set industrial structure" which blends basic, intermediate and high technology industries (Seki 1994: 29). As Japan succeeded, uniquely among the late industrializers, in moving to the technological frontier, its traditional shopfloor orientation was still reflected in a tight integration between R&D and shopfloor activities (Dertouzos *et al.* 1989). This was true in particular for technology imports. In the case of "turn-key" operations the "know-how" of imported technology must be transformed into the "know-why" of a technological process (Lall 1987). In mastering this transition from know-how to know-why "the shopfloor becomes the strategic battleground" of late industrializers (Amsden and Hikino 1990: 7). Often reverse engineering is insufficient to unlock all the deeper aspects of a technology's structure. For many aspects of technology are implicit and tacit rather than fully specified and completely understood (Nelson 1987). The shopfloor becomes the battleground where borrowed technology is customized to fit conditions specific to particular production processes and targeted markets. By most quantitative and qualitative measures government policies and shopfloor practices succeeded in propelling Japan to the technological frontier in a matter of a few decades (Kitschelt 1991: Table 2, 470; Ergas 1984: Table B, 65; Bylinksy 1986; Taylor and Yamamura 1990: 28).

But in the last two decades regionalization in Asia is leading Japan inexorably into a new historical era (Ernst 2000a). For a variety of reasons, including high labor costs and environmental constraints in Japan, domestic concentrations of small and medium-size firms are eroding in Japan. Foreign suppliers are becoming more important. Arguing the case for increasing regional enmeshment and growing dependence Mitsuhiro Seki writes that:

> Japan's full-set industrial structure, which ensures that all industrial and technological functions are available domestically, is under siege, and the nation is faced with the need to form close relationships with East Asia, especially China, for the survival of the fundamental industrial technologies that drive its high-tech sectors. We are entering the age of an Asian network in technology.
>
> (1994: 86)

In this new era the provision of basic technologies for Japanese corporations is increasingly occurring within "an Asian-network pattern of development" (ibid.: 3). Japan's opening to the world goes beyond the kind of trade and investment liberalization that has been the focus of US political pressures. Opening refers to a growing reliance on the basic technological capacities of Asian producers, tied to Japanese producers in increasingly tight chains. US electronic firms shaped their operations into networks involving contractual relations, including with important Japanese firms. Japanese producers have responded vigorously to local governments' incentives programs, and, in contrast to US firms, rely much more heavily on local and regional markets for procurement and sales (Encarnation 1999: 5). Thus, while the operations of Japanese firms tend to strengthen Asian regionalism, American firms tend to make Asian regionalism more open (Dobson 1997a: 17; Dobson 1997b: 243–5; Yue and Dobson 1997: 254–9; Ernst 2000a; Borrus 2000).

Japanese technology transfer takes on a variety of hybrid forms in different foreign locales. In their detailed empirical studies, Hiroshi Itagaki (1997: 367–72) and his collaborators have demonstrated that the institutional barriers to Japanese technology are lower in East Asia than in Southeast Asia, and they are lowest in the United States. Furthermore, evidence is accumulating that Japanese production networks are becoming more international as they gain more experience and mature (Doherty 1995; Ernst 2000a). This shift requires a fundamental rethinking away from Japan as a self-reliant national economy that seeks to defend its autonomy in a hostile world to Japan as deeply embedded in a system of industrial production systems that tie it intimately to its Asian neighbors. A tripolar structure in Asia is now reorganizing the links between the Tokyo metropolitan area, Japan's prefectural periphery, and the rapidly industrializing economies of East and Southeast Asia (Seki 1994: 44–5).

The regionalization of Japanese production networks has helped in bringing substantial change to Asia. Throughout the postwar period, and in particular after the oil shock, "Japan's national security was premised on the security and stability of Southeast Asia, then a primary source of Japanese imports of petroleum, rubber, tin, and other critical natural resources" (Hatch and Yamamura 1996: 118; see also *ibid.*: 116). Searching for low-cost labor and cheap raw materials in the 1960s and 1970s, Japanese firms were much more willing to form joint ventures and to invest in other forms of interfirm cooperation than were their Western counterparts.

In seeking to penetrate protected domestic markets Japanese subsidiaries built up strong linkages; local content in the products of Japanese affiliates was relatively high and supported some domestic suppliers even at the expense of product quality and cost efficiency (Ernst 1997: 213). In this initial phase Japanese producers were apparently at times willing to diffuse intermediate technologies that were essential to the success of foreign assembly operations (Seki 1994: 99). Asian NIEs thus received some Japanese technology. By 1985 40 percent of OECD imports from the NIEs were in product categories with significant scale economies and extensive product differentiation rather than in resource-intensive or labor-intensive products (Ernst and O'Connor 1989: 30).

This is not to argue that Japanese firms shared their technologies freely (Urata 1999; Sedgwick 1999; Tachiki 1999). In analyzing Japan's foreign investment in Asia up to the mid-1970s, Kunio Yoshihara (1978: 6) sees overseas investment as "an extension of regional factory diversification in Japan." His detailed analysis underlines, among others, the close connections between parent firms and foreign affiliates (ibid.: 36–7) and the importance of political factors and the policies of the Japanese government (ibid.: 11–12, 29, 46) in helping shape the pattern of Japanese foreign investment. In the wake of the sharp appreciation of the Yen after 1985 (*endaka*), an escalation in domestic costs prompted Japanese producers to move important segments of their manufacturing base off-shore. This accelerated a de facto regional integration of some parts of the Asian economies into Japanese corporate structures. By 1992 more than 9,000 Japanese affiliates operated overseas, many of them in Asia (Chen and Drysdale 1995; Dobson and Yue 1997). "An intra-regional, intra-firm division of labor seems to be taking shape in which different countries become production bases for different components and/or final products and intra-firm trade takes place among countries in the region" (Ernst and O'Connor 1989: 42). In this new system Japanese producers achieve economies of scale and profitability through specialization. Between 1983 and 1987 Japanese profits in Asia were three times higher than in the United States and twice as high as in Europe. This difference widened further in the early 1990s. In 1993 Asian profits ran at 4 percent compared to no gains in the United States and losses equivalent to 1 percent in Europe (*The Economist* 1995: 21–2). Profits are defined as recurring profit to sales ratios for overseas subsidiaries of Japanese manufactures.

A further regionalization of Japanese production networks would have required corporate and public policies increasingly facilitating technology transfers. The dynamic technical efficiency that Japanese corporations had achieved through organizing supplier networks inside Japan had to be transferred to producers operating abroad, including to China, an essential provider of basic technologies that other economies are less well equipped to provide (Seki 1994: 3, 30–1, 99, 128, 130–2, 154–6; Murakami 1996). But the Japanese production system faces sharp limitations in the amount of technology transfer that it actually can generate. While, on some occasions, technology transfer to foreign producers has occurred, generally speaking since the mid-1980s large Japanese corporations have been reluctant to share their advanced technologies (Seki 1994: 17, 20–1, 23, 27; see also Dobson 1997b: 246; Yue and Dobson 1997: 258; Ernst 2000a: 86–93; Ernst and Ravenhill 2000: 229–34). Typically, both government and corporations make special efforts to counteract adverse shifts in technology. This is not only done from positions of technological strength that Japanese producers understandably wish to exploit to extract maximum profits. It is done also from positions of anticipated technological weakness. In the early 1990s, for example, seeking to protect "technological national security" MITI announced a plan aimed at strengthening the position of domestic suppliers in the crisis-ridden casting and forging industries. The program was a clear illustration of the sense of urgency "over the hemorrhaging of the nation's fundamental technologies" (Seki 1994: 31).

Concerned with the strength of Japan's technological base, MITI's mission has become inexorably regionalized (Hatch 2000: 236–44). Its 1987 New AID plan was an ambitious scheme that aimed at coordinating Japan's trade and investment policies in Asia. While the plan was shelved due to both domestic and international criticisms, MITI has not abandoned the vision that informed the plan. If it wanted to support the operation of Japanese business abroad, MITI had in fact little choice but to support industrial networks in Asia. In the mid-1990s it developed a new plan to assist in the industrialization drive of transition economies in Cambodia, Laos, and Myanmar that soon came to include all of Southeast Asia. With a headquarter in Bangkok and financed and staffed exclusively by MITI this initiative supports stronger industrial linkages and liberal investment policies in Asia (ibid.: 239). More generally, MITI has had "to include in its mission the recovery and expansion of the Asian regional economy as a whole," for example, by promoting an increase in imports from the region (Kohno 1999: 3). And it is seeking to facilitate tie-ups between Japan's small and medium-sized firms and ASEAN corporations. Specifically, MITI is planning to create a database on important technologies owned by local firms in Southeast Asia which it will distribute to Japanese firms, especially smaller ones, planning to invest in the region (ibid.: 7). Sensing a crisis in Japan rapidly losing control over fundamental technologies in the small and medium-size firm sector, Japan's large corporations are increasingly seeking to develop basic technologies in-house, with the attendant risk of sacrificing increases in efficiency and flexibility that derive from dense and multi-tiered supplier networks (Seki 1994: 134–8).

The protection of technology by Japanese corporations is evident in their foreign operations. In the mid-1990s only one of the forty-six R&D projects that Japanese corporations funded in Asia is supporting a generic technology with substantial potential for productivity enhancements of the host country. In most instances foreign firms intent on setting up operations in East or Southeast Asia must support R&D support services such as software engineering and circuit design before they can actually enter Asia's growing domestic markets (Ernst 1997: 233). The language of the creation of "interdependence" thus is misleadingly liberal.

Institutional practices and business calculations frequently reinforce each other in impeding rather than accelerating technology transfer to foreign producers. Hence asymmetric dependence, not symmetric interdependence, results from the new Japan-centered production networks that are emerging in Asia.

The rapidity of Japan's reorientation after 1985 and the need for controlling cost and quality tightly, help explain why after 1985 Japanese corporations continued to adhere to a centralized model of tightly controlled local subsidiaries and, at best, reluctant technology transfer (Ernst 1997: 215–17; Hatch 2000: 236–44).

> The Japanese tightly controlled their Asian affiliates, leaving them little scope for autonomous decisions; the transfer of technological capabilities remained limited and hardly went beyond on-the-job training and basic manufacturing support services ... As long as the focus was on export platform production, therefore, Japanese electronics firms tried to minimize the transfer of activities in the value chain to East Asia.
>
> (Ernst 1997: 218)

This is the central point of what Zysman and Borrus call a Japan-dominated market hierarchy in which Asian suppliers are subordinate to Japanese firms as final product assemblers for exports who must rely on high value-added Japanese components and equipments (1996: 82–3). In electronics and autos in particular, Asia is becoming an integrated production network for Japanese firms from which they can pursue global corporate strategies. Japan's strategy, Zysman and Borrus argue, has two components.

> One is to spread subsystem assembly throughout Asia, while persuading each government to treat subsystems originating in other Asian countries as being of "domestic origin." The second element is to keep tight control over the underlying component, machinery, and materials technologies by regulating their availability to independent Asian producers and keep advanced production at home.
>
> (Zysman and Borrus 1996: 84)

This is not to deny that individual Asian producers do benefit substantially from entering into tie-ups with Japanese firms that leave them technologically heavily dependent. For they gain access to a network that promises markets and profits if not autonomy. Restrictive strings can also become supportive ties (Hatch 2000: 132–3, 356). Unfavorably restrictive conditions about the use of technology are balanced by favorable access to customers, suppliers, distributors and political allies of the Japanese manufacturer. Japanese technology is part of a larger package of relationships and loses much of its usefulness once it becomes severed from other elements of the network. The advantage was evident in the wake of the Asian financial crisis. Dennis Tachiki (2001: 5–13) shows that Japanese companies used lower labor costs to partially offset higher material input costs, thus delaying layoffs and creating good will among a more loyal workforce. Indeed, rationalization of overhead costs has encouraged employment increases in a number of industries. Yet, on balance, rationalization savings have been insufficient to outweigh costs associated with the underutilization of plant capacities and the strains on cash flow. In the interest of keeping themselves afloat, firms appear to have cannibalized their Asian production networks, moving in the general direction of creating more openness, flexibility and decentralization in these networks.

While the role of technology in this system of control has become more important in recent years, the system has deeper historical roots. In his analysis of Japanese foreign investment in the 1960s and 1970s, Terutomo Ozawa (1979: 25–30, 82) noted the distinctive "immaturity" of Japanese foreign investment, as measured in terms of firm size and technological sophistication; small firms in traditional industries such as textiles were leading Japan's expansion into Asia. Foreign investment became a way by which the ruling political coalition extended the basic institutional arrangements of the Japanese model. In the 1970s,

> Japan's preferential tariff program for manufactured imports from developing countries serves as an integral part of Japan's design to assist her light manufacturing industries to migrate to neighboring countries . . . Yet the fledgling manufacturing industries in these countries are so locked into import dependence on industrial materials from Japan that they cannot easily extricate themselves.
>
> (Ozawa 1979: 76, 199–200)

In the view of Walter Hatch and Kozo Yamamura (1996), technology is not playing the role of helping Japan's neighbors to embark on a path of autonomous development. Instead it helps reinforce a system of domination as Asia is developing in Japan's embrace. Technology is at the center of Asia's regionalization process. Technological disparity helps buttress Japan's economic and political leadership in Asia. Since the mid-1980s Japan has built a region-wide production structure that is extending Japanese-style developmentalism internationally. Hatch and Yamamura (ibid.: 97–111; Hatch 2000: 135–44) provide a wealth of evidence supporting their view that Japanese firms are building regional production networks that control technology transfer closely. Indeed the available evidence suggests that Japan is in the process of increasing its technological lead in Asia (Hatch and Yamamura 1996: 100). Statistical and anecdotal evidence illustrates that Japan is very eager to acquire technology and very reluctant to part with it. Japanese businessmen concede that their tight-fisted approach risks political controversies in the long-term. In the short-term they fear losing control of accumulated know-how.

Typically, that know-how is encased in institutional contexts and practices that make it extremely difficult to transfer technology easily even when host governments insist. Labor practices which discourage employee turnover, that place a large number of Japanese nationals in top management positions, and that emphasize non-transferable on-the-job training, all militate against technology transfer. Hence Asian producers live in the embrace of Japanese producers which brings with it dynamic though dependent growth. Japanese producers make sure that the most important, high-value-added parts of production stay under the control of Japanese-owned enterprises. Seeking to blunt protectionist forces in the US Congress, Japanese corporations are putting their new Asian production alliances in the service of a global strategy. The Japanese government has supported the regionalization of production networks with a host of trade, aid, investment and cultural policies (Hatch and Yamamura 1996: 114–29; Hatch 2000: 241–4). Through regionalization Japan has found a way of extending its increasingly imbalanced trade relations with all of its major trading partners on both sides of the Pacific.

Japan's regional production networks do not rely on state-to-state diplomacy or treaties. They are rather a regional extension of both the strength and the weakness of Japan's domestic structures. The sharp appreciation of the Yen in the mid-1980s reflected the inherent industrial and technological strength of Japanese producers. And it greatly accelerated their move off-shore, among others to neighboring countries in Asia. Walter Hatch (2000) sees in the externalization of Japan's domestic arrangement and in Asian regionalism a defensive move by Japan's coalitional capitalism, an extension in the life cycle of political arrangements that otherwise might already have collapsed under the weight of their numerous internal contradictions. "A nation's business, labor, and government elites may temporarily shore up domestic institutions and ideologies under stress by 'going regional.'" (Hatch 1999: 2)

For better and for worse, Japanese firms are replicating their domestic *keiretsu* structures in Asia and thus are enhancing their regional and global competitiveness. Regional integration has occurred in markets through thousands of vertically organized, quasi-integrated corporate networks. In Japan's dual domestic economy subcontractors cannot defend themselves against the various pressures through which the major corporations squeeze profit margins in hard times. The same is increasingly true throughout Asia. Japan's regional production alliances are both increasing efficiency and remaining exclusive. For both Japan and Asia, the risks

of this strategy may become politically clearer should embraced development turn into captive development (Hatch and Yamamura 1996: 31).

In parts of Northeast and Southeast Asia a technology order thus has
evolved under Japanese leadership that reflects Japan's institutional
norms and practices. It would, however, be a mistake to pose the issue
solely in terms of the deliberate strategizing by the dominant actors in
Japan (ibid.: 22, 115–16). Regionalization is, rather, an extension of the
domestic practices of the institutional model of developmentalism, an
interlocking system of state and corporate policies that is largely taken for
granted and that is being adapted to new conditions in world markets
(ibid.: 176, 193–4. For numerous examples see pp. 115–46). This offers a
plausible explanation for why Japan's Asian policy has been unchanging
in linking international public finance (such as aid, official export credits,
export and investment guarantees) closely to private capital and financial
flows (such as direct foreign investment, trade, bank lending) (Kato 1996:
27, 73–117, 305–14, 349–50). In sum, Japan has regionalized central parts
of its model of capitalism and in so doing it has in significant ways shaped
Asia's technology order.

Chinese networks

There exist in Asia alternatives to Japanese-centered production alliances.
These alternatives, at times bring together Chinese commercial and manufacturing networks with the technology of US corporations. Clustered in
the 1990s around producers based in Taiwan and Singapore the spread of
such networks points to the emergence of non-Japanese alternatives.

With varying degrees of success the Asian NIEs are seeking to escape
from Japan's tight embrace by developing alternatives to the regionalization of Japan's developmental policies. To some extent Japanese corporations themselves provide opportunities for reducing technological
dependence. For example, as Japan's major corporations are forcing their
parts suppliers, more or less gently, to regionalize their operations rather
than building up business ties with local firms, the possible flow of technology from Japan to East and Southeast Asia is further constricted (Hatch
2000: 280). Yet not all Japanese medium-sized and small parts suppliers
are able or willing to regionalize their operations. These firms may enter
into technology tie-ups with local firms to whom they sell their know-how
for a fee. In 1993 Japanese technology exports to Asia exceeded exports to
the USA by about 40 percent (Hatch and Yamamura 1996: 9, 163).
Although the potential importance of this technology trade should not be
overestimated, it is not lost on corporations or governments throughout
Asia (ibid.: 169–70, 177).

Asian governments seek to lessen dependence also through national
policies. Korea, for example, has tried to foster national technology

programs through its large *chaebol* conglomerates, thus hoping to lessen technology dependence on Japan (Enos and Park 1987: 228–30). Yet, in the mid-1980s its consumer goods industry imported most of the parts for its major export products such as video cassette recorders, microwave ovens, facsimiles, personal computers, and printers; in the 1990s the Korean semi-conductor industry also remains heavily dependent on Japanese imports (Smith 1997: 748–9). In contrast, Taiwan, Thailand, and Malaysia tailor their response to local circumstances and to the existence of differently configured and situated economic networks run by overseas Chinese (Zysman and Borrus 1996: 84; Borrus 2000; Ernst 2000b). Thus they hope to sidestep excessive dependence on Japanese producers.

China holds the key to many important aspects of Asia's future. Before the Chinese revolution intellectuals shared in a scientistic view, holding to the belief that scientific methods unlock all secrets of the universe (Kwok 1965). Marxism-Leninism with its utilitarian view of science built on this legacy. It stressed the close relation between theory and practice, science and technology; it made the masses and the party the ultimate arbiter of the utility of science; it saw in science an instrument for the transformation of traditional culture and the reassertion of Chinese nationalism against foreign innovations; and it believed in the planned character of all scientific and technological evolution (Suttmeier 1974, 1986). Before the Cultural Revolution, Soviet-style centralism had prevailed in China's science and technology establishment. Since the 1978 reforms science and technology parks have sprung up and non-governmental high-technology firms have been set up in different parts of China, informed by different policy logics (Segal 1999; Saich 1989). As business and government seek to articulate new partnerships, techno-nationalism retains continuing relevance for contemporary China (Naughton and Segal 2000). In the words of Ding Xinghao of Shanghai's Institute of International Studies "Japan's view is always a flying geese formation with Japan as the head goose. Our memories are long, so we aren't about to fly in Japan's formation" (Hatch 2000: 354).

China is currently in no position to define Asia's emerging technology order. But as its economic and political importance rises, it may well become so in selected market segments in the not too distant future. If it does, China will reinforce rather than challenge how Japan has historically dealt with problems of technology. An autonomous national development in an inherently hierarchical international division of labor is China's preferred goal. And powerful national and prefectural governments with coherent political strategies fostering technological developments are the natural means for enhancing China's military security and economic competitiveness.

What holds for China does not hold for the Overseas Chinese. For Hatch and Yamamura (1996: 96) all the talk about "Greater China" and the idea that an alternative manufacturing and financial network is being built up by and around China is nothing but "idle chatter." In their view, Chinese networks are no more than a series of *ad hoc* deals between sprawling conglomerates lacking synergy. Handicapped in their ability to adopt new technology, even Taiwanese businessmen "have felt compelled to open wide their arms" to Japanese MNCs (ibid.: 96). Chinese networks cultivate rent-seeking, Japanese ones dynamic technological efficiency. In this view, the architecture of Asian regionalism is strictly hierarchical with Japan at the apex. Japan controls the flow of aid and technologies and provides producers in other countries with capital and intermediate inputs. South Korea and Taiwan, though closing the development gap quickly, specialize in somewhat lower technological products and remain dependent on Japanese imports of key technologies and intermediate products. And the NIEs in Southeast Asia provide raw materials, markets and upgrading industrial platforms for assembly and, increasingly, indigenous production (Hui 1995: 207).

Other scholars disagree for good reasons. Hong Kong, for example, is a pivot around which the economy of Southeast Asia revolves, and a vital place also for corporations operating in all of the major markets of the world economy (Yeung 1998, 80–225). Michael Borrus' account of the astonishing turn-around of the US electronics industry "has rested in large part on the growing technical sophistication and competitive strength of Asian-based producers in the China Circle, Singapore, and South Korea" (1997: 141). Confronted by a potentially crippling dependence on their Japanese competitors for memory chips, displays and precision components, and other vital technologies US firms decided to make underlying technologies more open and competitive to firms in Chinese networks. "In conjunction with government policies and local private investors in Asia, US firms gradually turned their Asian production networks into flexible supply-base alternatives to Japanese firms" (ibid.: 145–6). In other words, in contrast to Japanese firms, US producers transferred technology that turned their Asian production networks from simple assembly affiliates to technologically able Asian producers competing effectively with the producers of Japanese technologies. This policy thus exemplifies both a US response to excessive dependence on key components of Japanese suppliers and a move toward an emerging Asian production network of producers greatly strengthened by the decision of US corporations to make advanced technologies available.

The rapidity of that development resulted from the symbiosis of US corporate strategies with both supportive government policies and local Asian investments. The hard disk drive industry is a good illustration (McKendrick *et al.* 2000). It was the globalization of the operations of small and young firms like Seagate that assured their growth and survival and propelled US industry first to Singapore and then throughout

Southeast Asia. More established US firms followed; Japanese firms followed still later, never posing a serious threat to US domination of this industry. The dual structure of the industry is evident, with R&D located in Silicon Valley and production in and around Singapore. Like Korea and Taiwan, Singapore's government is perfecting a strategy to leverage advanced technology which does not merely receive imported technology, but develops an organizational system for managing technology leverage in the interest of quick adaptation, diffusion and improvement through systems of production that link individual firms (Wong 2000). Asian governments have perfected a strategy that leverages advanced technology which, based on an informed assessment of technological trajectories, seeks to diffuse capabilities rather than generating new knowledge in individual firms. Although the specific institutional and organizational mix of factors that has operated in Asia differs from country to country, all governments have relied on a strategy of leveraging technology to accelerate the process of creating competitive advantages in industries where no advantage initially existed (Mathews 1996: 1–5; Mathews and Cho 2000).

Local Asian investments were an important avenue for sidestepping excessive reliance on Japan. Thailand, and Malaysia, among others, tailor their response to local circumstances and to the existence of differently configured overseas Chinese economic networks (Zysman and Borrus 1996, 84).

> Resident ethnic Chinese investors played the principal private entrepreneurial role in the China Circle, Singapore, and later in Malaysia, Indonesia, and Thailand ... The result, by the end of the 1980s, was burgeoning indigenous electronics production throughout the region, with most of it, outside Korea, under the control of overseas-Chinese (OC) capital.
>
> (Borrus 1997: 148; see also Keller and Pauly 2000)

Firms like Taiwan Semiconductor Manufacturing and United Microelectronics act as contractors that make chips based on the designs of their customers. Together they control about two- thirds of the foundry market which in a few years time is estimated to grow to about half of the total output of the semi-conductor industry (Landler 2000, C11). Furthermore, first-tier Taiwanese firms have matured in their control over key technologies and are themselves now riding herd on an extensive indigenous supply base that is spreading technology to "thousands of small and medium-size design, component, parts, sub-assembly, and assembly houses" that have become part of a local production network and supply base (Borrus 1997: 152). Technical specialization thus helped both US firms and indigenous Asian producers in loosening their dependence on Japanese producers. In the coming decades leadership in this industry could easily pass from US and Japanese firms to indigenous Asian producers, and in particular those located in the China Circle which might conceivably end up relying on China's vast demand and considerable technical know-how.

Both government policy and corporate investment thus came together in the astonishing rise of Taiwan's personal computer and chip industries. In a span of less than two decades Taiwan transformed itself from a low-wage economy to the third largest producer of information technologies. It did so neither through a state-led industrial offensive nor through reliance on the unrestricted play of market forces. Instead, the government exploited the economic advantages that could be derived from the international collaboration between producers in Silicon Valley and the Hsinchu-Taipei region. Those connections were made possible first and foremost by the large community of overseas Taiwanese engineers and literally thousands of Taiwanese engineers that have returned especially in the 1990s. Initially, in the 1970s the flow of personnel was overwhelmingly from Taiwan to the USA, later there was a substantial return migration that the Taiwanese government strongly encouraged. Highly skilled, these overseas Chinese were distinguished by both strong ethnic and professional identities which permitted "their deep integration into the technical communities of both technology regions" (Saxenian and Hsu 2000: 7). As the largest group of Silicon Valley's foreign-born engineers, Chinese also were by far the largest group of foreign-born CEOs. Many of these businessmen are often more comfortable than successful entrepreneurs from other Asian countries in setting up branch operations in Silicon Valley (ibid.: 14, 22). This group was a ready target as the Taiwanese government established a burgeoning venture capital market in the early 1980s to help build up its high-tech industry. A one dollar investment in venture capital markets produces three to five times as many patents as a dollar invested in research and development (ibid.: 2). The outcome has been a variety of networks linking Taiwanese firms and engineers as well as US firms operating in Silicon Valley and Hsinchu-Taipei.

The rise of Greater China and its financial and manufacturing networks has affected the strategy of Japanese corporations since the mid-1990s. Since Japanese producers had been reluctant to diffuse their technology to Asian suppliers Michael Borrus is skeptical that there will be a quick turn-around in the corporate strategies of Japanese firms in favor of sourcing from an independent emerging Asian supply base (1997: 149, 153–4). Dieter Ernst, on the other hand, sees Japanese corporations as rapidly opening their production networks in electronics to extend the geographic coverage and the degree of local embeddedness of regional production activities. In his view Japanese corporations have a strong interest in both developing and harnessing Asia's resources and technological capabilities (Ernst 1997: 210–11, 218–36). In contrast to the 1980s, in the 1990s, Ernst writes, "The affiliates of Japanese higher level component suppliers thus increasingly have to rely on domestic Asian subcontractors, mostly through various contractual, nonequity arrangements such as consignment production and contract manufacturing" (ibid.: 223). This development, were it to occur on a large scale, would signal a historic shift from an era "in which, in East Asia, Japan possessed a full-set industrial and technological structure to an age in which technical transfer and mutual interdependence in technology are discussed with the total development of East Asia in mind" (Seki 1994: 32). Change, at best, however, will come slowly. Ernst and Borrus both agree that even in the 1990s, most key components still must be sourced from Japan or from Japanese firms producing in the region (Ernst 1997: 223; Borrus 1997: 153–4).

The competitive networks that are interlacing Asia's political economies create a structural predisposition for openness. Japan's direct foreign investment in Asia is targeted, by sector and country, to harmonize with the structural transformation of Japan's economy. But the dependence of Asian (including Japanese Asian-based affiliates) on the US market in particular is a factor supporting the continued openness of Asian regionalism (Kato 1996: 205–8). Japanese engagement in the rich US and European markets remains unabated. And in terms of both direct foreign investment and exports, Asia's NIE have been leading the way in Asia since the late 1980s, much of it centered in the financial and manufacturing networks of overseas Chinese. Openness to global markets is the likely path for Asian regionalism.

Japanese and Chinese networks and the character of Asian regionalism

The historical source of the Japanese and Chinese networks in Asia differs greatly. Japanese capitalism flowered in an era of state-building, Chinese capitalism in an era of state collapse (Hamilton 1996: 332–3, 336). The number of overseas Japanese is dwarfed by the numbers of overseas Chinese. And Chinese business networks are more extensive and have deeper historical roots than do Japanese networks. Since the mid-nineteenth century Japanese officials built up Japanese networks in full awareness of the severe competition that Japanese firms face in confronting Chinese merchants (Skinner 1979; Curtin 1984: 90–178; Hamashita 1988, 1997). Different historical origins thus have shaped the different character of China's and Japan's economic extension into Asia. In the words of Joel Kotkin, "In contrast to the exceedingly close ties between the Japanese *salarimen* abroad and their home islands, the Chinese global network possess no fixed national point of origin, no central 'brain'" (1993: 167).

This general pattern is evident in specific industrial sectors such as electronics (Katzenstein 1997a: 39–40). Japanese networks of firms rely substantially on known Japanese suppliers with comparable technical capacities. Overseas Chinese firms draw on networks of increasingly high-valued added technical specialization of small and medium-sized firms scattered throughout Asia. Japanese networks are closed, Japan-centered, and long-term. Chinese networks are open, flexible and disposable (Borrus 1994: 3).

Consider the contrast between Japanese and Chinese business networks in the case of Thailand. Based on careful field research Mitchell Sedgwick (1994: 8), concluded that:

> Japanese multinationals in Thailand have reproduced an atomization of labor and strong centralization of decision-making authority – the "Fordism" – that they managed to avoid in post-war Japan ... Beyond internal plant dynamics, however, the strict centralization is also reflected in the position of subsidiaries *vis-à-vis* headquarters. Subsidiaries in Thailand are part of a tightly controlled and rigorously hierarchical organizational structure extending down from Japan.

In contrast, dominated by the Chinese Thailand's business community has adjusted to changing conditions over time. But in the recent era of internationalization of the Thai economy, the most recent generation of Chinese entrepreneurs have run their business along traditional Chinese lines and maintained close contacts with the Chinese business communities in Hong Kong, Singapore, Taiwan and China. Rapid corporate growth resulted from international alliances, typically with the Overseas Chinese who are operating in horizontal and open networks, rather than vertical and closed ones as is true of Japan (Hamilton and Walters 1995: 94, 99–100).

Asian regionalism is built on organizational characteristics of business that differ greatly along different dimensions that set vertical Japanese firm networks apart from horizontal Chinese ones as Gary Hamilton and his colleagues have shown (Hamilton *et al.* 1987: 100; Hamilton and Feenstra 1997: 67–73). In terms of ownership, shareholding of group firms in Japan contrasts with family ownership and partnership for the Overseas Chinese; intra-group networks revolve around cross-shareholding and mutual domination rather than multiple positions held by core personnel; inter-group networks involve cross-shareholding, loans and joint ventures rather than cross-investments by individuals and firms; subcontract relations are structured or semi-formal rather than informal and highly flexible; investment patterns are reflected in vertical and horizontal integration rather than diversification; and growth patterns are marked by bank-financed group activities rather than informal financing and reinvestment (Orrù *et al.* 1997: 183).

The Japanese and Chinese forms of organizing Asian regionalism are both complementary and competitive. The new crop of Chinese tycoons in Southeast Asia has colluded with Japanese business as is true, for example, of the Siam Motor Group in Thailand, the Astra Company and Rodamas Group in Indonesia, the Yuchenco Group in the Philippines, and the Kuik Brothers in Malaysia (Hui 1995: 189; Hamilton-Hart 1998: Chapter 6). But Chinese and Japanese business are also locked in competition with one another. Japanese firms find it very difficult to work without Chinese middle men who dominate the local economy, including both its productive and distributive networks. For instance, in 1974 of 138 joint ventures between Japanese and Indonesian firms, 70 percent of the Indonesian partners were local Chinese (Brick 1992: 3–4; Hui 1995: 189). And Hong Kong elites and the overseas Chinese business elite have benefited from the cultural affinities as well as old familial and business ties to overcome problems of trust and reliability.

Both forms of Asian regionalism are defined in market terms (Katzenstein 1997a: 14). Asian markets, however, do not consist of a series of unconnected and atomized individual transactions. They give expression instead to institutionalized relationships that implicate deeply both business and government. Following the growth of Japanese direct foreign investment, especially after 1985, multinational corporations control an unprecedented share of foreign trade in Asia. Intra-company trade accounts for about 80 percent of total Japanese exports and half of Japanese imports (Encarnation 1994: 2). And foreign investment has spurred the growth of vertical *keiretsu* structures from Japan throughout Asia, as Japanese producers have extended their domestic subcontracting arrangements on a regional scale.

Both, however, and the Asian regionalism they help define, avoid formal institutionalization (Katzenstein 1997a: 40–1). Asian regionalism is marked by the weakness of formal international institutions. It is defined primarily by institutions operating in markets. Japanese *keiretsu* structures and Chinese family firms bring about economic integration without formal, political links. In the 1990s this Asian regionalism is open to developments in the global economy. Its economic form is network-like. Its political shape is multicephalic. And its political definition is contested.

Germany and Europe

Asia's regional technology order differs greatly from Europe's. Because technology is regionally deeply embedded in Europe and less exposed to the international economy, economic security is not a declared objective of German policy. From the perspective of the political and business elites of Europe, including Germany's, dependence on European markets does not constitute a potential security threat. If anything, it creates economic and political opportunities. Germany seeks to defend its traditional position of the "good second" with a broad array of policies. Rather than attempting to create the conditions for technological leap-frogging, German policy aims at diffusing technological advances that it tends to import.

Contemporary Germany thus lacks Japan's sense of geo-strategic vulnerability and strong ideological commitment to the goal of enhanced technological autonomy. Embedded in Europe and not particularly exposed to potential interruptions in the supply of raw materials, German institutions have never regarded their national security as being closely related to economic security and technological autonomy. The concept of interdependence does, however, have a deep public resonance. German policies and politics and most of Germany's institutions are permeated by the notion that the country's only future lies with a deepening and broadening of European integration rather than with enhanced national autonomy. The national unification of Germany in 1990 was predicated on the simultaneous acceleration of European integration. And in its aftermath monetary integration has become the most important political experience for Europe in the 1990s.

In the area of R&D, Germany is also unambiguous in its backing of international corporate alliances, including European corporate alliances, as the natural vehicle for responding to the next wave of high-technology innovations. In semi-conductors the German government supports a special program which ties Siemens to Phillips. In aviation, it supports the Airbus and the Euro-fighter. For advanced nuclear reactors and fuel cycles Germany has entered complex consortia with other European countries. And, seeking to strengthen national technological capabilities since the mid-1980s, Germany has participated actively in the European Community's major technology programs, such as Esprit and Eureka (Cowhey 1990: 127–8). Reflecting both Germany's deep entanglement in Europe and its position of relative technological backwardness, especially in electronics, in their technology forecasts German more than Japanese experts are committed to the necessity of international cooperation (Cuhls and Kuwahara 1994: 62–3, 140–1, 190–2). The partial pooling of Germany's technology policy with European processes in the 1980s thus follows a general pattern that sets Japan and Germany, and Asian and European regionalism apart.

Because of the growing importance of policy initiatives at the European level, in the second half of the 1980s the government reduced by about one half its support of the electronics industry, even though it constitutes in the government's understanding the core of Germany's high-tech sector (Grande and Häusler 1994: 197–8). European integration not national autonomy has increasingly shaped Germany's technology policy. German firms received DM 1.2 billion from the major programs of the EU (ESPRIT I and II and RACE I) (ibid.: 485). And the share of EC expenditures in Germany's total research and development budget increased from 4 percent in 1980 to 12 percent in 1991 (ibid.: 216). While German business sharply reduced funding of basic research, European policy initiatives sought to counter the trend with specific programs supporting basic research with potential for commercial application. The Commission was correct in its assessment of how to complement national programs, but it was overly optimistic in its expectation of how a targeted industrial policy could translate into marketable products (ibid.: 501). Although European policy initiatives were quite substantial in absolute terms, it was dwarfed in comparison to national outlays. Between 1987 and 1991 EC funding amounted to less than 2 percent of the total research funding of the federal government and less than half a percent of Germany's total R&D expenditure (Reger and Kuhlmann 1995: 164). It is thus not surprising that European R&D policy failed in reversing the European and German lags in high-technology products, specifically in electronics (Van Tulder and Junne 1988: 125–55, 209–52; Roobeek 1990: 133–7; Ridinger 1991; Sandholtz 1992; Peterson 1993; Grande and Häusler 1994: 201–315; Reger and Kuhlmann 1995).

The national and European cross-currents affecting Germany's technology policy can be illustrated in the various programs funded in the 1990s. The EU supports with its large ESPRIT program European industry against US and Japanese competitors; the German Federal Ministry of Research, as part of the Joint European Submicron Silicon Initiative (JESSI) program and German-American industrial cooperation, subsidizes the chip development of Siemens and IBM; and individual German states, such as Nordrhein-Westfalen, subsidize the investment plans of Japanese chip producers in Germany (Grande and Häusler 1994: 288–315, 505–6). These contradictions in policy are structural, and with growing Europeanization will increase. Europeanization refers here to the growth of a dense, multidimensional bargaining system which is dominated fully neither by the Council of Ministers in which national governments meet nor by the self-interest of corporate and bureaucratic actors (ibid.: 504).

Economic and technological differences between the European states and regions are so large that it is highly improbable that these will arrive at optimal policy solutions that the homogeneous, German innovation system promises at least in theory. Expenditures for research and development in Germany are 200 times larger than in Greece or Ireland and the big European three (Germany, France and Britain) account for

75 percent of total European expenditures on research and development (ibid.: 507).

Contradictory policies are also encouraged by developments in the corporate sector. In the electronics industry, for example, in the 1960s and 1970s the federal government had to deal only with Siemens and a small number of additional firms. But escalating costs in product development and lagging competitiveness of German producers have led to a multiplication of strategic alliances on a global scale that are leading to a loosening of ties between government and business (ibid.: 1994: 515–16). National programs seeking to enhance the competitiveness of national producers have become "leaky." JESSI's history illustrates the tension between the efforts of national governments to create competition between the three world regions that growing cooperation between Siemens, IBM and Toshiba tends to undercut (ibid.: 511–12).

While the EU is important in structuring a regional complement to national policies, so are regional production networks. More often than not they operate at subnational rather than supranational levels. Charles Sabel, Richard Locke and Gary Herrigel have investigated producer communities in specific industrial districts that are related in dense networks supporting flexible quality production (Piore and Sabel 1984; Locke 1995; Herrigel 1996). These networks often have long histories in which specific technological and institutional capacities are rebuilt over time. Geographically concentrated, small-scale producers built institutions and fashioned identities that provided for collective goods typically in design and production and occasionally in finance and marketing. Success in national and world markets often followed. Compared to Japanese *keiretsu* structures, these European production networks are egalitarian not hierarchical; and they enhance social homogeneity rather than heterogeneity (see also Zysman *et al.* 1996: 29–33).

In brief, what matters politically at the European level during the past half-century are not production networks in which technology is controlled or diffused but an emerging European polity to which both Germany and the states that are dependent on it are drawn. Contemporary European politics revolves around the deepening and broadening of Europe in terms of both membership and issue coverage, not around technology and production. Thus it matters little politically that the proclivity of German corporations for outward processing and participation in the growth of protected domestic rather than exposed European or global markets has not notably enhanced the technological capacities of the southern and central European states. Transfer payments from the European Union (EU) budget to weak regions matter more. Europe has developed its own institutional logic as a multi-level and multi-sectoral governance structure that differs in fundamental ways from the corporate and ethnic structures that knit together Asia.

In sum, on questions of technology Germany is deeply embedded in an European policy networks. Policy is caught between contradictory impulses. In the area of high-technology the German government cannot achieve its objectives by itself; and against the wishes of the German government little can be achieved at the European level (Grande and Häusler 1994: 505). In pre-commercial technologies Europe has become in some areas such a substantial source of funding that the German government has greatly curtailed the scope of national support of technologies deemed to be of critical importance. Such a policy makes sense in Europe. There is no basis for comparable policies in Asia.

Conclusion

Where is Asian regionalism heading on questions of technology? The answer to this question depends in part on our views on the future evolution of Japan's capacity for technological innovation. The rapidity with which Japan has imported, adapted, diffused and reexported technology is, as Herbert Kitschelt has shown, the result of the matching of specific institutional practices of the Japanese polity with specific requirements of technological systems (1991: 480–91). The adaptations of medium-technologies with tightly coupled systems of limited causal complexity to high-technologies require medium–long production runs that lend themselves to improvements through incremental innovations in production processes and product technologies. With relatively low uncertainties and no more than modest interactions between different components of technological systems, efficient governance of technology can draw on devices that characterize the Japanese polity more generally: strong competition between firms, cooperation among firms in pre-commercial research, and ministerial guidance toward specific technological trajectories. Where other conditions prevail, as in aviation or the nuclear industry, the mismatch of institutions has made Japan's experience less successful. Decision-making typically has been too centralized, too consensus-oriented, and has left the private sector with too much risk:

> In a nutshell Japan's institutions have not provided adequate governance structures for global, non-incremental technological change that require a combination of decentralized autonomy in the search for innovative solutions and highly centralized project management in vast technology development programs.
>
> (Kitschelt 1991: 485)

Fumio Kodama argues that the mismatches which Kitschelt and other students of "big" science and technology have detected in Japanese institutions may be decreasing. Japan is developing a new and distinctive high-tech paradigm that favors its specific system of institutional governance in six specific areas: manufacturing, business diversification, R&D competition, product development, innovation pattern and societal diffusion of technology. "A paradigm shift in technology innovation, driven by the rapid evolution of science and engineering, is occurring and favors the Japanese system" (Kodama 1995: 3). Innovation is not a series of dramatic breakthroughs of "single-source" technologies but the "compound" or "fusion" of technologies requiring constant cross-fertilization from different scientific fields, as in optoelectronics, meachtronics and bioelectronics (Makihara 1998: 561). Japan's vaunted ability to make incremental improvements in imported technologies is increasingly matched by a growing ability to foster radical technological advances in specific areas (Taylor and Yamamura 1990: 26–7). Japan thus may be in the process of becoming a polity that is well suited to the techno-economic paradigm of the information industries (Samuels 1994: 15).

But Japan's poor economic performance during the 1990s suggests a less optimistic possibility. Japan is reported to be behind by four to five years in significant information technologies (Ritter 1999: 8). Most companies continue to invest their R&D budget disproportionately in hardware and manufacturing rather than software and services (Yoshida 1999). And Japanese leading researchers themselves believe that Japan is lagging behind the United States and Europe in most areas of basic research (Makihara 1998: 560–1). Recent changes in policy have done little to date to change this situation. In his summary of a substantial number of studies of the performance of Japanese R&D Arthur Alexander (1999) points to substantial weaknesses that have become more evident in the 1990s. With Japan's basic sciences in a much weaker position than its applied research (Coleman 2001), and despite its growing involvement in the private R&D system of the United States (Reid and Schriesheim 1996: 39–139), the country's technological future looks significantly less secure now than it did a decade or two earlier.

The fit between institutions and technology is contingent and can be reinforced, or altered, by significant changes in either sphere. Even during the 1970s and 1980s when Japan's political economy was performing so well, not every technology program that government and business initiated turned out to be a commercial or technological success. And despite the serious economic setbacks that Japan has suffered in the 1990s, many new technologies are being developed successfully and profitably. We lack the empirical information and depth of theoretical knowledge that would permit us to sort out the independent effects of technology and institutions on Japan's economic performance.

In a world in which the R&D system in Japan as in most other countries, is no longer organized along strictly national lines, internationalization is Japan's chosen policy (Fransman 1995). In a longer historical perspective the case for an institutional opening of technology regimes has merits. For centuries the Chinese government, for example, had sought to guard carefully the technological secrets of silk production. Similarly, since the eighteenth century European governments have tried to keep technological innovations within national borders thus seeking to prevent leakage to other countries. Even when these policies proved futile they were considered legitimate (Nelson 1990: 15). In modern times, government attempts to nationalize science have been largely unsuccessful. This is increasingly true of technology as well. The worldwide availability of technologies of best-practice is a relatively recent experience. According to Ernst-Jurgen Horn:

> The entire concept of a country's technology [has] inherent limits in the presence of an open international trade and investment system. A particular technology is first produced in an individual country, but it can then be licensed or sold abroad or applied through foreign affiliates. The know-how involved will become internationally diffused sooner or later.
>
> (1990: 67–8)

Whether Asia will retain its controlled regional technology order or evolve new and, possibly, more open ones will depend substantially on which of the two views of Japan will be closer to the truth: the exhaustion of an old Japanese technology order or the generation of a new one. In either case, it is unlikely that a regional order will come to pass in which, in the words of Seki, "the development of mutual technological interdependencies to form an Asian network will be necessary for the stability and prosperity of the entire region in the twenty-first century" (1994: 100). Should Japanese technology falter, other Asian states, such as China, might take its place. Alternatively, high-technology industries dominated by USA or European producers could further anchor Asia in global hierarchies. In 1995 the USA still provided 71 percent of Japan's technology imports while taking only 29 percent of Japan's technology exports (Makihara 1998: 560). Regional production alliances thus may broaden in geographical scope without necessarily being more supportive of the goal of enhanced national autonomy. Even if Japan were to lose its established position at the apex, deeply entrenched characteristics of Asia's distinctive technology order are likely to endure.

Acknowledgment

I would like to thank the editors and project participants for their criticisms and comments on prior drafts.

References

Alexander, Arthur J. 1999. "Japan's Use of Its Science and Research: Room for Improvement," *JEI Report* No. 14A (April 9).

Amsden, Alice H. and Takashi Hikino. 1991. "Borrowing Technology or Innovating: An Exploration of Two Paths to Industrial Development," Paper No. 31, The Graduate Faculty, Political Economy, New School for Social Research (September).

Baklanoff, Eric N. 1978. *The Economic Transformation of Spain and Portugal.* New York: Praeger.

Black, Stanley. 1997. "Introduction," in Stanley Black (ed.), *Europe's Economy Looks East: Implications for Germany and the European Union.* New York: Cambridge University Press, pp. 1–19.

Borrus, M. 1994. *MNC Production Networks and East Asian Integration: A Research Note.* Berkeley Roundtable on the International Economy, Berkeley, CA: University of California.

Borrus, Michael. 1997. "Left for Dead: Asian Production Networks and the Revival of U.S. Electronics," in Barry Naughton (ed.), *The China Circle: Economics and Electronics in the PRC, Taiwan, and Hong Kong.* Washington, DC: Brookings Institution, pp. 139–63.

Borrus, Michael. 2000. "The Resurgence of US Electronics: Asian Production Networks and the Rise of Wintelism," in Michael Borrus, Dieter Ernst and Stephan Haggard (eds), *International Production Networks in Asia: Rivalry or Riches?* London: Routledge, pp. 57–79.

Borrus, Michael, Dieter Ernst and Stephan Haggard (eds) 2000a. *International Production Networks in Asia: Rivalry or Riches?* London: Routledge.

Borrus, Michael, Dieter Ernst and Stephan Haggard. 2000b. "Introduction: Cross-Border Production Networks and the Industrial Integration of the Asia-Pacific Region," in Michael Borrus, Dieter Ernst and Stephan Haggard (eds), *International Production Networks in Asia: Rivalry or Riches?* London: Routledge, pp. 1–30.

Bowley, Graham. 1997. "Move to the East Pays Off," *The Financial Times* (June 9) (LEXUS-NEXUS).

Bylinsky, Gene. 1986. "The High Tech Race: Who is Ahead?" *Fortune* (October 13): 26–44.

Callan, Bénédicte, Sean S. Costigan and Kenneth H. Keller. 1997. *Exporting U.S. High Tech: Facts and Fiction about the Globalization of Industrial R&D.* New York: Council on Foreign Relations.

Chandler, Alfred D. 1990. *Scale and Scope: The Dynamics of Industrial Capitalism.* Cambridge, MA: Harvard University Press.

Chen, Edward K.Y. and Peter Drysdale (eds) 1995. *Corporate Links and Foreign Direct Investment in Asia and the Pacific.* Pymble, NSW: Harper Educational Publishers.

Coleman, Sam. 2001. "What's Wrong with Japanese Basic Science?" *Japan Policy Research Institute* Working Paper No. 74 (February).

Comisso, Ellen. 1997. "'Implicit' Development Strategies and Cross-National Production Networks," unpublished paper for the workshop "Will there be a Unified European Economy?," Kreisky Forum for International Dialogue, Vienna (June 5–6).

Cowhey, Peter F. 1990. "The Agenda of the Leading Nations for the World

Economy: A Theory of International Economic Regimes," in Günter Heiduk and Kozo Yamamura (eds), *Technological Competition and Interdependence: The Search for Policy in the United States, West Germany, and Japan.* Seattle: University of Washington Press, pp. 107–47.

Cuhls, Kerstin and Terutaka Kuwahara. 1994. *Outlook for Japanese and German Future Technology: Comparing Technology Forecast Surveys.* Heidelberg: Physica.

Curtin, P.D. 1984. *Cross-Cultural Trade in World History.* New York: Cambridge University Press.

Dertouzos, Michael *et al.* 1989. *Made in America: Regaining the Competitive Edge* (Report of the MIT Commission on Industrial Productivity). Cambridge, MA: MIT Press.

Deutsch, Karl W. 1981. "On Nationalism, World Regions, and the Nature of the West," in Per Torsvik (ed.), *Mobilization, Center-Periphery Structures and Nation-Building: A Volume in Commemoration of Stein Rokkan.* Bergen: Universitetsforlaget, pp. 51–93.

Dickman, Steve. 1996. Germany Joins the Biotech Race," *Science* vol. 274, no. 5292 (November 29): 1454. (LEXUS-NEXUS).

Doane, Donna L. 1998. *Cooperation, Technology, and Japanese Development: Indigenous Knowledge, the Power of Networks, and the State.* Boulder, CO: Westview Press.

Dobson, Wendy. 1997a. "East Asian Integration: Synergies between Firm Strategies and Government Policies," in Wendy Dobson and Chia Sio Yue (eds), *Multinationals and East Asian Integration.* Ottawa and Singapore: International Development Centre and Institute of Southeast Asian Studies, pp. 3–27.

Dobson, Wendy. 1997b. "Crossing Borders: Multinationals in East Asia," in Wendy Dobson and Chia Sio Yue (eds), *Multinationals and East Asian Integration.* Ottawa and Singapore: International Development Centre and Institute of Southeast Asian Studies, pp. 223–47.

Dobson, Wendy and Chia Sio Yue (eds) 1997. *Multinationals and East Asian Integration.* Ottawa and Singapore: International Development Centre and Institute of Southeast Asian Studies.

Doherty, Eileen M. (ed.) 1995. *Japanese Investment in Asia: International Production Strategies in a Rapidly Changing World.* San Francisco and Berkeley: The Asia Foundation and the University of California Berkeley Roundtable on the International Economy.

Doherty, Eileen, Andrew Schwartz, and John Zysman. 1995. "Reorganizing the European Economy: Lessons of East Asia for Central/Eastern Europe," paper presented at workshop on Regulatory and Institutional Reform in the Transitional Economies, Warsaw (November).

Donges, Jürgen B. *et al.* 1982. *The Second Enlargement of the European Community: Adjustment Requirements and Challenges for Policy Reform.* Tübingen: J.C.B. Mohr (Paul Siebeck).

Dubos, René. 1968. *So Human an Animal.* New York: Charles Scribner's Sons.

The Economist. 1995. "Japan and Asia: A Question of Balance" (April 22): 21–2.

The Economist. 1997a. "The EU Budget: Just Small Change?" (October 18): 51–2.

The Economist. 1997b. "A Survey of Business in Eastern Europe," (November 22): 1–22.

Eichengreen, Barry. 1997. "Comment," in Stanley Black (ed.), *Europe's Economy Looks East: Implications for Germany and the European Union.* New York: Cambridge University Press, pp. 342–5.

Eichengreen, Barry and Richard Kohl. 1997. "The State and the External Sector in Eastern Europe: Implications for Foreign Investment and Outward-Processing Trade," unpublished paper, delivered at the workshop "Will There be a Unified European Economy?" Kreisky Forum for International Dialogue, Vienna (June 5–6).

Encarnation, D.J. 1994. The Regional Evolution of Japanese Multinationals in East Asia: A Comparative Study. (unpublished paper)

Encarnation, D.J. 1999. "Introduction: Japanese Multinationals in Asia," in D.J. Encarnation (ed.) Japanese Multinationals in Asia: Regional Operations in Comparative Perspective. New York: Oxford University Press, pp. 3–13.

Enos, J.L. and W.-H. Park. 1987. The Adoption and Diffusion of Imported Technology: The Case of Korea. London: Croom Helm.

Ergas, Henry. 1984. Why Do Some Countries Innovate More than Others? CEPS Papers no. 5. Brussels: Centre for European Policy Studies.

Ergas, Henry. 1986. "Does Technology Policy Matter?" Unpublished paper, July 1986.

Ernst, Dieter. 1997. "Partners for the China Circle? The East Asian Production Networks of Japanese Electronic Firms," in Barry Naughton (ed.), The China Circle: Economics and Electronics in the PRC, Taiwan, and Hong Kong. Washington, DC: Brookings Institution, pp. 210–53.

Ernst, Dieter. 2000a. "Evolutionary Aspects: The Asian Production Networks of Japanese Electronics Firms," in Michael Borrus, Dieter Ernst and Stephan Haggard (eds.), International Production Networks in Asia: Rivalry or Riches? London: Routledge, pp. 80–109.

Ernst, Dieter. 2000b. "What Permits David to Grow in the Shadow of Goliath? The Taiwanese Model in the Computer Industry," in Michael Borrus, Dieter Ernst and Stephan Haggard (eds), International Production Networks in Asia: Rivalry or Riches? London: Routledge, pp. 110–40.

Ernst, Dieter and David O'Connor. 1989. Technology and Global Competition: The Challenge for Newly Industrialising Economies. Paris: Organisation for Economic Co-operation and Development.

Ernst, Dieter and John Ravenhill. 2000. "Convergence and Diversity: How Globalization Reshapes Asian Production Networks," in Michael Borrus, Dieter Ernst and Stephan Haggard (eds), International Production Networks in Asia: Rivalry or Riches? London: Routledge, pp. 226–56.

Fawcett, Louise and Andrew Hurrell. 1995. "Introduction," in Louise Fawcett and Andrew Hurrell (eds), Regionalism in World Politics: Regional Organization and International Order. Oxford: Oxford University Press, pp. 1–6.

Fishlow, Albert and Stephan Haggard. 1992. The United States and the Regionalisation of the World Economy. Paris: OECD.

Fong, Glenn. 1998. "Follower at the Frontier: International Competition and Japanese Industrial Policy," International Studies Quarterly 42 (2) (June): 339–66.

Franko, Lawrence. 1976. The European Multinationals: A Renewed Challenge to American and British Big Business. New York: Harper & Row.

Fransman, Martin. 1995. "Is National Technology Policy Obsolete in a Globalised World? The Japanese Response," Cambridge Journal of Economics 19: 95–119.

Fransman, Martin. 1999. Visions of Innovation: The Firm and Japan. Oxford: Oxford University Press.

Fransman, Martin and Shoko Tanaka. 1994. "Government, Globalisation, and Universities in Japanese Biotechnology," *Research Policy* 24 (1): 13–50.

Fransman, Martin and Shoko Tanaka. n.d. *The Strengths and Weaknesses of the Japanese Innovation System in Biotechnology,* JETS Paper No. 3, Edinburgh: University of Edinburgh.

Fröbel, Folker, Jürgen Heinrichs, and Otto Kreye. 1977. *Die neue internationale Arbeitsteilung: Strukturelle Arbeitslosigkeit in den Industrieländern und die Industrialisierung der Entwicklungsländer.* Hamburg: Rowohlt.

Fröbel, Folker, Jürgen Heinrichs, and Otto Kreye. 1986. *Umbruch in der Weltwirtschaft: Die globale Strategie: Verbilligung der Arbeitskraft/Flexbilisierung der Arbeit/Neue Technologien.* Hamburg: Rowohlt.

Grande, Edgar and Jürgen Häusler. 1994. *Industrieforschung und Forschungspolitik: Staatliche Steuerungspotentiale in der Informationstechnik.* Frankfurt: Campus.

Grugel, Jean and Wil Hout. 1999. "Regions, Regionalism, and the South," in Jean Grugel and Wil Hout (eds), *Regionalism across the North-South Divide: State Strategies and Globalization.* London and New York: Routledge, pp. 3–13.

Guerrieri Paolo. 1997. "Trade Patterns, FDI and Industrial Restructuring of Central and Eastern Europe." Working paper for the workshop "Will There be a Unified European Economy?" Kreisky Forum for International Dialogue, Vienna (June 5–6).

Hall, Peter A. and David Soskice. 1999. "Varieties of Capitalism: The Institutional Foundations of Comparative Advantage," unpublished paper (August).

Hamashita, T. 1988. "The Tribute Trade System and Modern Asia," *Memoirs of the Research Department of the Toyo Bunko (the Oriental Library).* Tokyo: The Oriental Library. 46: 1–25.

Hamashita, T. 1997. "The Intra-Regional System in East Asia in Modern Times," in P.J. Katzenstein and T. Shiraishi (eds), *Network Power: Japan and Asia.* Ithaca, NY: Cornell University Press, 113–35.

Hamilton, G.G. 1996. "Overseas Chinese Capitalism," in T. Wei-ming (ed.), *Confucian Traditions in East Asian Modernity: Moral Education and Economic Culture in Japan and the Four Mini-Dragons.* Cambridge, MA: Harvard University Press, pp. 328–42.

Hamilton, G.G., M. Orrú, *et al.* 1987. "Enterprise Groups in East Asia: An Organizational Analysis," *Shoken Keizai* 161: 78–106.

Hamilton, G.G. and R.C. Feenstra. 1997. "Varieties of Hierarchies and Markets: An Introduction," in M. Orrú, N.W. Biggart and G.G. Hamilton (eds), *The Economic Organization of East Asian Capitalism.* Thousand Oaks, CA: Sage, pp. 55–94.

Hamilton, G.G. and T. Walters. 1995. "Chinese Capitalism in Thailand: Embedded Networks and Industrial Structure.," in E.K.Y. Chen and P. Drysdale (eds) *Corporate Links and Foreign Direct Investment in Asia and the Pacific.* New York, Harper Educational in association with the Pacific Trade and Development Conference Secretariat, the Australian National University, Canberra, and the Centre of Asian Studies, Hong Kong: University of Hong Kong, pp. 87–111.

Hamilton-Hart, Natasha. 1998. "States and Capital Mobility: Indonesia, Malaysia, and Singapore" PhD dissertation, Cornell University, New York.

Hannequart, Achille. 1992. *Economic and Social Cohesion in Europe: A New Objective for Integration.* London: Routledge.

Hatch, Walter. 1999. "Rearguard Regionalization: Preserving Core Coalitions in the Japanese Political Economy," PhD dissertation, University of Washington, Seattle.

Hatch, Walter Frank. 2000. "Rearguard Regionalization: Protecting Core Networks in Japan's Political Economy," PhD dissertation, University of Washington.

Hatch, Walter and Kozo Yamamura. 1996. *Asia in Japan's Embrace*. Cambridge: Cambridge University Press.

Hemmert, Martin and Christian Oberländer. 1998. "The Japanese System of Technology and Innovation: Preparing for the Twenty-First Century," in Martin Hemmert and Christian Oberländer (eds), *Technology and Innovation in Japan: Policy and Management for the Twenty-First Century*. London: Routledge, pp. 3–19.

Herrigel, Gary. 1996. *Industrial Constructions: The Sources of German Industrial Power*. Cambridge: Cambridge University Press.

Hirschman, Albert O. 1945 and 1980. *National Power and the Structure of Foreign Trade*. Berkeley, CA: University of California Press.

Hohn, Hans-Willy and Uwew Schimank. 1990. *Konflikte und Gleichgewichte im Forschungssystem: Akteurkonstellationen und Entwicklungspfade in der staatlich finanzierten ausseruniversitären Forschung*. Frankfurt/Main: Campus.

Holman, Otto. 1996. *Integrating Southern Europe: EC Expansion and the Transnationalization of Spain*. London: Routledge.

Horn, Ernst-Jürgen. 1981. "Technology and International Competitiveness: The German Evidence and Some Overall Comments," unpublished paper (DSTI/SPR/81.60). Paris: OECD.

Horn, Ernst-Jürgen. 1990. "West German Technology in the 1980s: Perceptions, Evidence, and Policy Issues," in Günter Heiduk and Kozo Yamamura (eds), *Technological Competition and Interdependence: The Search for Policy in the United States, West Germany, and Japan*. Seattle: Washington University Press, 1990, pp. 64–84.

Howells, Jeremy and Michelle Wood. 1993. *The Globalisation of Production and Technology*. London: Belhaven Press.

Hui, Po-Keung. 1995. "Overseas Chinese Business Networks: East Asian Economic Development in Historical Perspective." Ph.D. Binghamton: State University of New York.

Iizuka, Kozo. 1994. "Innovation and Transfer of Technology-Experience and Problems of Japan," in O.C.C. Lin, C.T. Shih and J.C. Yang (eds), *Development and Transfer of Industrial Technology*. Amsterdam: Elsevier, pp. 83–110.

Itagaki, Hiroshi. 1997. "Conclusions and Prospects," in Hiroshi Itagaki (ed.), *The Japanese Production System: Hybrid Factories in East Asia*. London: Macmillan, pp. 366–79.

Jeremy, David J. (ed.) 1991. *International Technology Transfer: Europe, Japan and the USA, 1700–1914*. Brookfield, VT: Elgar.

Jeremy, David J. (ed.) 1992. *The Transfer of International Technology: Europe, Japan and the USA in the Twentieth Century*. Brookfield, VT: Elgar.

Johnson, Chalmers. 1982. *MITI and the Japanese Miracle: The Growth of Industrial Policy, 1925–1975*. Stanford, CA: Stanford University Press.

Kato, Kozo. 1996. "Helping Others, Helping Oneself: International Positions, Domestic Institutions, and Development Cooperation Policy in Japan and Germany," PhD dissertation, Government Department, Cornell University, New York.

Katzenstein, Peter J. 1985. *Small States in World Markets: Industrial Policy in Europe*. Ithaca, NY: Cornell University Press.

Katzenstein, Peter J. 1996. *Cultural Norms and National Security: Police and Military in Postwar Japan*. Ithaca, NY: Cornell University Press.

Katzenstein, Peter J. 1997a. "Introduction: Asian Regionalism in Comparative Perspective," in Peter J. Katzenstein and Takashi Shiraishi (eds), *Network Power: Japan and Asia*. Ithaca, NY: Cornell University Press, pp. 1–46.

Katzenstein, Peter J. (ed.) 1997b. *Tamed Power: Germany in Europe*. Ithaca, NY: Cornell University Press.

Katzenstein, Peter J. 2000. "Varieties of Asian Regionalisms," in Peter J. Katzenstein, Natasha Hamilton-Hart, Kozo Kato and Ming Yue (eds), *Asian Regionalism*. East Asia Program, Cornell East Asia Series No. 107, Ithaca, NY: Cornell University, Center for International Studies, pp. 1–34.

Katzenstein, Peter J. and Takashi Shiraishi (eds) 1997a. *Network Power: Japan and Asia*. Ithaca, NY: Cornell University Press.

Katzenstein, Peter J. and Takashi Shiraishi. 1997b. "Conclusion: Regions in world Politics, Japan and Asia-Germany in Europe," in Peter J. Katzenstein and Takashi Shiraishi (eds), *Network Power: Japan and Asia*. Ithaca, NY: Cornell University Press, pp. 341–81.

Keller, William W. and Louis W. Pauly. 2000. "Crisis and Adaptation in East Asian Innovation Systems: The Case of the Semiconductor Industry in Taiwan and South Korea," *Business and Politics* 2 (3) (November): 327–52.

Kester, W. Carl. 1992. "Governance, Contracting, and Investment Horizons: A Look at Japan and Germany," *Journal of Applied Corporate Finance* 5 (2) (Summer): 83–98.

Kier, Elizabeth. 1986. "A Comparative Study of the Japanese and West German Research Systems: The Deviant Cases," unpublished paper, Cornell University, New York.

Kitschelt, Herbert. 1990. "Industrial Governance Structures, Innovation Strategies, and the Case of Japan: Sectoral or Cross-national Comparative Analysis?" *International Organization* 45 (4) (Autumn): 453–93.

Kodama, Fumio. 1995. *Emerging Patterns of Innovation: Sources of Japan's Technological Edge*. Boston: Harvard Business School Press.

Kohno Masaru. 1999. "Recent Changes in MITI and Japan–U.S. Relations," unpublished paper, Aoyama Gakuin University, Tokyo.

Kotkin, J. 1993. *Tribes: How Race, Religion and Identity Determine Success in the New Global Economy*. New York: Random House.

Kurz, Constance and Volker Wittke. 1997. "From 'Supply-Base Driven' to 'Market Driven' Integration: Patterns of Integrating Central-East European Economies by Using Their Industrial Capacities," unpublished paper for the workshop "Will there be a Unified European Economy?", Kreisky Forum for International Dialogue, Vienna (June 5–6).

Kwok, Danny. 1965. *Scientism in Chinese Thought, 1900–1950*. New Haven, CT: Yale University Press.

Lake, David. 1988. *Power, Protection, and Free Trade*. Ithaca, NY: Cornell University Press.

Lall, Sanjaya. 1987. *Learning to Industrialize: The Acquisition of Technological Capability by India*. London: Macmillan.

Landler, Mark. 2000. "The Silicon Godfather: The Man behind Taiwan's Rise in the Chip Industry," *The New York Times* (February 1): C1, C11.

Legler, Harald. 1990. "The German Competitive Position in Trade of Technology-Intensive Products," in Günter Heiduk and Kozo Yamamura (eds), *Technological Competition and Interdependence: The Search for Policy in the United States, West Germany, and Japan*. Seattle: University of Washington Press, pp. 163–91.

Lemoine, Françoise. 1997. "Integrating Central and Eastern Europe in the European Trade and Production Network," working paper for the workshop "Will There Be a Unified European Economy? International Production Networks, Foreign Direct Investment, and Trade in Eastern Europe", Kreisky Forum for International Dialogue, Vienna (June 5–6).

Linden, Greg. 2000. "Japan and the United States in the Malaysian Electronics Sector," in Michael Borrus, Dieter Ernst and Stephan Haggard (eds), *International Production Networks in Asia: Rivalry or Riches?* London: Routledge, pp. 198–225.

Locke, Richard. 1995. *Remaking the Italian Economy*. Ithaca, NY: Cornell University Press.

McKendrick, David G., Richard F. Doner and Stephan Haggard. 2000. *From Silicon Valley to Singapore: Location and Competitive Advantage in the Hard Disk Drive Industry*. Stanford, CA: Stanford University Press.

McMillan, Charles J. 1996. *The Japanese Industrial System*, 3rd rev. edn. Berlin: de Gruyter.

Makihara, Minoru. 1998. "The Path Transformed: Redefining Japan's Role in the Information Economy," *Journal of International Affairs* 51 (2) (Spring): 555–64.

Mathews, John. 1996. "High Technology Industrialisation in East Asia," *Journal of Industry Studies* 3 (2) (December): 1–78.

Mathews, John A. and Dong-Sung Cho. 2000. *Tiger Technology: The Creation of a Semiconductor Industry in East Asia*. Cambridge: Cambridge University Press.

Melzer, Arthur M., Jerry Weinberger, and M. Richard Zinman (eds) 1993. *Technology in the Western Political Tradition*. Ithaca, NY: Cornell University Press.

Miller, Karen Lowry and John Templeman. 1997. "Germany's New East Bloc," *Business Week* (February 3) (LEXUS-NEXUS).

Muñoz, Juan, Santiago Roldán, and Angel Serrano. 1979. "The Growing Dependence of Spanish Industrialization on Foreign Investment," in Dudley Seers, Bernard Schaffner and Marja-Liisa Kiljunen (eds), *Underdeveloped Europe: Studies in Core–Periphery Relations*. Atlantic Highlands, NJ: Humanities Press, pp. 161–77.

Murakami, Yasusuke. 1996. *An Anti-Classical Political-Economic Analysis*. Stanford, CA: Stanford University Press.

Nafziger, E. Wayne. 1995. *Learning from the Japanese: Japan's Pre-War Development and the Third World*. Armonk, NY: M.E. Sharpe.

Naughton, Barry and Adam Segal. 2000. "Technology Development in the New Millennium: China in Search of a Workable Model," paper presented to the second meeting of Innovation and Crisis: Asian Technology after the Millennium, Cambridge, MA (September 15–16).

Nelson, Richard R. 1987. "Innovation and Economic Development: Theoretical Retrospect and Prospect," in Jorge M. Katz (ed.), *Technology Generation in Latin American Manufacturing Industries*. New York: St. Martin's Press, pp. 78–93.

Nelson, Richard R. 1990. "What Has Happened to U.S. Technological Leadership?" in Günter Heiduk and Kozo Yamamura (eds), *Technological Competition and Interdependence: The Search for Policy in the United States, West Germany, and Japan*. Seattle: University of Washington Press, pp. 3–24.

Normile, Dennis. 1993. "Japan Holds on Tight to Cutting-Edge Technology," *Science* 262 (15 October): 352.

Nye, Joseph S., Jr. 1992. "What New World Order?" *Foreign Affairs* 71 (2) (Spring): 83–96.

Odagiri, Hiroyuki and Akira Goto. 1993. "The Japanese System of Innovation: Past, Present, and Future," in Richard Nelson (ed.), *National Innovation Systems: A Comparative Analysis*. Oxford: Oxford University Press, pp. 76–114.

Odagiri, Hiroyuki and Akira Goto. 1996. *Technology and Industrial Development in Japan: Building Capabilities by Learning, Innovation, and Public Policy*. Oxford: Clarendon Press.

Organisation for Economic Co-operation and Development, Secretary General. 1991. *Change in Focus in Information Technology Policies during the 1980s: A Comparison of Changing Public Policies in: Austria, Germany and Japan*. General Distribution OCDE/GD (1991)62. Paris: OECD.

Orrú, M., G.G. Hamilton, *et al.* 1997. "Patterns of Interfirm Control in Japanese Business," in M. Orrú, N.W. Biggart and G.G. Hamilton (eds), *The Economic Organization of East Asian Capitalism*. Thousand Oaks, CA: Sage, pp. 188–214.

Ozawa, Terutomo. 1979. *Multinationalism Japanese Style: The Political Economy of Outward Dependency*. Princeton, NJ: Princeton University Press.

Pauly, Louis W. and Simon Reich. 1997. "National Structures and Multinational Corporate Behavior: Enduring Differences in a Globalizing World," *International Organisation* 51 (1) (Winter): 1–30.

Pellegrin, Julie. 1997. "Outward Processing Trade between the EU and the CEECs," working paper for the workshop "Will There Be a Unified European Economy? International Production Networks, Foreign Direct Investment, and Trade in Eastern Europe," Kreisky Forum for International Dialogue, Vienna (June 5–6).

Peterson, John. 1993. *High Technology and the Competition State: An Analysis of the Eureka Initiative*. London: Routledge.

Piore, Michael J. and Charles F. Sabel. 1984. *The Second Industrial Divide: Possibilities for Prosperity*. New York: Basic Books.

Reger, Guido and Stefan Kuhlmann. 1995. *European Technology Policy in Germany: The Impact of European Community Policies upon Science and Technology in Germany*. Heidelberg: Physica.

Reid, Proctor P. and Alan Schriesheim (eds) 1996. *Foreign Participation in U.S. Research and Development: Asset or Liability?* Washington, DC: National Academy Press.

Ridinger, Rudolf. 1991. *Technologiekooperation in Westeuropa: Die Suche nach grenzüberschreitenden Antworten auf technologiepolitische Herausforderungen*. Hamburg: Dr. R. Krämer.

Ringer, Fritz K. 1969. *The Decline of the German Mandarins: The German Academic Community 1890–1933*. Cambridge, MA: Harvard University Press.

Ritter, Eric. 1999. "Asia's Time Lag," *The International Economy*, 13 (6) (November/ December): 8–11, 58.

Roobeek, Annemieke J.M. 1990. *Beyond the Technology Race: An Analysis of Technology Policy in Seven Industrial Countries*. Amsterdam: Elsevier.

Ruigrok, Winfried and Rob Van Tulder. 1995. *The Logic of International Restructuring*. London: Routledge.

Saich, Tony. 1989. *China's Science Policy in the 1980s*. Atlantic Highlands, NJ: Humanities Press.

Salmon, Keith. 1995. "Spain in the World Economy," in Richard Gillespie, Fernando Rodrigo and Joanathan Story (eds), *Democratic Spain: Reshaping External Relations in a Changing World*. London: Routledge, pp. 67–87.

Samuels, Richard. 1994. *"Rich Nation, Strong Army": National Security and the Technological Transformation of Japan*. Ithaca, NY: Cornell University Press.

Sandholtz, Wayne. 1992. *High-Tech Europe: The Politics of International Cooperation*. Berkeley, CA: University of California Press.

Sar Desai, D.R. 1997. *Southeast Asia: Past and Present*, 4th edn. Boulder, CO: Westview Press.

Sato, Hideo, 1978. "The Politics of Technology Importation in Japan: Case of Atomic Power Reactors," unpublished paper.

Saxenian, AnnaLee and Jinn-Yuh Hsu. 2000. "The Silicon Valley–Hsinchu Connection: Technical Communities and Industrial Upgrading," unpublished paper, Berkeley, CA (August).

Saxenian, AnnaLee and Chuen-Yueh Li. 2000. "Bay-to-Bay Strategic Alliances: The Network Linkages between Taiwan and the U.S. Venture Capital Industries," unpublished paper, Berkeley, CA.

Schmidt, Klaus-Dieter and Petra Naujoks. 1993. *Western Enterprises on Eastern Markets: The German Perspective*. Kiel Working Paper No. 607 (December) Institut für Weltwirtschaftsforschung.

Sedgwick, M.W. 1994. *Does the Japanese Management Miracle Travel in Asia? Managerial Technology Transfer at Japanese Multinationals in Thailand*. Workshop on Multinationals and East Asian Integration, MIT Japan Program, Cambridge, MA: MIT Japan Program.

Sedgwick, Mitchell W. 1999. "Do Japanese Business Practices Travel Well? Managerial Technology Transfer to Thailand," in Dennis J. Encarnation (ed.), *Japanese Multinationals in Asia: Regional Operations in Comparative Perspective*. New York: Oxford, pp. 163–82.

Segal, Adam. 1999. "High Technology Firms in China (tentative title)," PhD dissertation, Government Department, Cornell University, New York.

Seki, Mitsuhiro. 1994. *Beyond the Full-Set Industrial Structure: Japanese Industry in the New Age of East Asia*. Tokyo: LTCB International Library Foundation.

Skinner, G.W. (ed.) 1979. *The Study of Chinese Society: Essays by Maurice Freedman*. Stanford, CA: Stanford University Press.

Smith, David A. 1997. "Technology, Commodity Chains and Global Inequality: South Korea in the 1990s," *Review of International Political Economy* 4 (4) (Winter): 734–62.

Spaulding, Robert Mark. 1997. *Osthandel and Ostpolitik: German Foreign Trade Policies in Eastern Europe from Bismarck to Adenauer*. Providence, RI: Berghahn Books.

Sperling, James. 1997. "Third Bite at the Apple? A Reconsideration of German Hegemony in Postwar Europe," unpublished paper, Department of Political Science, University of Akron, Akron, Ohio.

Suttmeier, Richard. 1974. *Research and Revolution: Science Policy and Societal Change in China*. Lexington, MA: D.C. Heath.

Suttmeier, Richard. 1986. "New Directions in Chinese Science and Technology," in John Major (ed.), *China Briefing*. Boulder, CO: Westview Press, pp. 91–102.

Tachiki, Dennis S. 1999. "The Business Strategies of Japanese Production Networks in Asia," in Dennis J. Encarnation (ed.), *Japanese Multinationals in Asia: Regional Operations in Comparative Perspective*. New York: Oxford, pp. 183–212.

Tachiki, Dennis S. 2001. "Japanese FDI After the Asian Crisis: The Role of Production Networks in Regional Integration," paper prepared for delivery at the 53rd Annual Meeting of the Association of Asian Studies, Chicago, March 23.

Taylor, Sully and Kozo Yamamura. 1990. "Japan's Technological Capabilities and Its Future: Overview and Assessment," in Günter Heiduk and Kozo Yamamura (eds), *Technological Competition and Interdependence: The Search for Policy in the United States, West Germany, and Japan*. Seattle: University of Washington Press, pp. 25–63.

Tho, Tran Van. 1993. "Technology Transfer in the Asian Pacific Region: Implications of Trends since the Mid-1980s," in Takatoshi Ito and Anne O. Krueger (eds), *Trade and Protectionism*. Chicago: The University of Chicago Press, pp. 243–72.

Tulder, Rob Van and Gerd Junne. 1988. *European Multinationals in Core Technologies*. New York: John Wiley & Sons.

Tulder, Rob Van and Winfried Ruigrok. 1997. "European Cross-National Production Networks in the Auto Industry: How Eastern Europe is Becoming the Low End of European Car Complexes," unpublished paper for the workshop "Will there be a Unified European Economy?," Kreisky Forum for International Dialogue, Vienna (June 5–6).

Urata, Shujiro. 1999. "Intrafirm Technology Transfer by Japanese Multinationals in Asia," in Dennis J. Encarnation (ed.), *Japanese Multinationals in Asia: Regional Operations in Comparative Perspective*. New York: Oxford, pp. 143–62.

US Congress, House of Representatives. 1984. "The Availability of Japanese Scientific and Technical Information in the United States," report prepared by the Congressional Research Service, Library of Congress, for the Subcommittee on Science, Research and Technology, Washington, DC. (November).

Värynen, Raimo. 1996. "Post-Hegemonic and Post-Socialist Regionalism: A Comparison of Central Europe and East Asia," paper prepared for the ISA-JAIR Joint Convention in Makuhari, Japan (September 20–22).

Vernon, Raymond and Ethan B. Kapstein. 1991. "National Needs, Global Resources," *Daedalus* 120 (4) (Fall): 1–22.

Wade, Robert. 1996. "Globalization and its Limits: Reports of the Death of the National Economy are Greatly Exaggerated," in Suzanne Berger and Ronald Dore (eds), *National Diversity and Global Capitalism*, Ithaca, NY: Cornell University Press, pp. 60–88.

Watanabe, Chihiro and Yukio Honda. 1991. "Inducing Power of Japanese Technological Innovation – Mechanism of Japan's Industrial Science and Technology Policy," *Japan and the World Economy* 3: 361–90.

Webber, Douglas, Jeremy Moon, and J.J. Richardson. 1984. "State Promotion of Technological Innovation in France, Britain and West Germany: Preliminary Findings from Comparative Research," paper presented at European Consortium for Political Research, Joint Session, Salzburg, April.

Weber, Hajo. 1985a. "Technokorporatismus – Zur Steuerung des technologischen Wandels durch Staat, Wirtschaftsverbände und Gewerkschaften," unpublished paper, University of Bielefeld (March).

Weber, Hajo. 1985b. "Zwischen Markt und Staat – Aspekte japanischer und deutscher Technologiepolitik," unpublished paper, University of Bielefeld (November).

White, David. 1997. "Spain Prepares to Fight for EU Grants," *Financial Times* (November 18): 4.

Winner, Langdon. 1977. *Autonomous Technology: Technics-out-of-Control as a Theme in Political Thought.* Cambridge, MA: The MIT Press.

Wong, Poh-Kam. 2000. "Riding the Waves: Technological Change, Competing US-Japan Production Networks, and the Growth of Singapore's Electronics Industry," in Michael Borrus, Dieter Ernst and Stephan Haggard (eds), *International Production Networks in Asia: Rivalry or Riches?* London: Routledge, pp. 176–97.

Yakushiji, Taizo. 1985. "The Dynamics of Techno-Industrial Emulation," Berkeley Roundtable on the International Economy (BRIE) Working Paper 22 (Summer), Berkeley, CA.

Yakushiji, Taizo. 1986. "Techno-Emulous Countries: Japan's Initial Conditions in Euro-American Contexts," paper presented at the 2nd International Symposium on Technological Innovation, Saitama University, Urawa, Japan (September 17–19).

Yakushiji, Taizo. 1992. "Schaffe, Schaffe, Häusle Baue: A Report on Germany," unpublished paper, Keio University (July).

Yakushiji, Taizo. 1994. "Technology and the Setting for Japan's Agenda," in Yoichi Funabashi (ed.), *Japan's International Agenda.* New York: New York University Press, pp. 57–80.

Yamamura, Kozo. 1995. "Efficient but Exclusionary: Japan's Developmentalist Capitalism of Cooperation," unpublished paper (October).

Yeung, Henry Wai-chung. 1998. *Transnational Corporations and Business Networks: Hong Kong Firms in the ASEAN Region.* London: Routledge.

Yoshida, Phyllis Genther. 1999. ". . . While Japan Boosts its S&T Commitment," *Research Technology Management* 42, 5 (September/October): 3–4.

Yoshihara, Kunio. 1978. *Japanese Investment in Southeast Asia.* Honolulu: The University Press of Hawaii.

Yue, Chia Siow and Wendy Dobson. 1997. "Harnessing Diversity," in Wendy Dobson and Chia Sio Yue (eds), *Multinationals and East Asian Integration.* Ottawa and Singapore: International Development Centre and Institute of Southeast Asian Studies, pp. 249–65.

Zysman, John. 1993. "Regional Blocs, Corporate Strategies and Government Policies: The End of Free Trade?" in Marc Humbert (ed.), *The Impact of Globalisation on Europe's Firms and Industries.* New York: St. Martin's Press, pp. 105–13.

Zysman John and Michael Borrus. 1996. "Lines of Fracture, Webs of Cohesion: Economic Interconnection and Security Politics in Asia," in Susan Shirk and Christopher P. Twomey (eds), *Power and Prosperity: Economics and Security Linkages in Asia-Pacific.* New Brunswick, NJ: Transaction Books, pp. 77–99.

Zysman, John, Ellen Doherty, and Andrew Schwartz. 1996. "Tales from the 'Global' Economy: Cross-National Production Networks and the Re-organization of the European Economy," Berkeley Roundtable on the International Economy (BRIE), University of California, Berkeley, Working Paper No. 83 (June).

Chapter 7

Historical capitalism, East and West

Giovanni Arrighi, Po-keung Hui, Ho-fung Hung and Mark Selden

East–West relations over the past 500 years present two main puzzles. The first concerns the extraordinary geographical expansion of the European system of states. By 1850 or shortly thereafter, that system had come to encompass the entire globe, thereby reducing the China-centered tribute-trade system to a regional subsystem of a now European-centered global economy. What is most puzzling about this tendency – which is what we shall understand by "the rise of the West" – are its modest origins. On the eve of its first major expansion across the Atlantic and around the Cape in the late fifteenth century, the European system of states was a peripheral and chaotic component of a global economy that had long been centered on Asia. In spite of this first expansion, two centuries later no European or American state had managed to create within its domains a national economy that could match the size, complexity and prosperity of the Chinese economy. And yet, within the short span of another century, tiny "Great" Britain was poised to incorporate within its domains the entire Indian subcontinent, and then, in cooperation and competition with other Western powers, to turn China from the center into a peripheral component of the global economy. How can we explain this turnaround?

The second puzzle concerns the extraordinary vitality of the East Asian region in the 150 years since its subordinate incorporation in the European- and later North American-centered global economy. By 1970 or shortly thereafter, this vitality translated into a crisis of Western hegemony that has yet to be resolved. Integral to this crisis has been an acceleration of economic growth in the East Asian region that has made a re-centering of the global economy on East Asia a distinct historical possibility, recent setbacks notwithstanding. This tendency – which is what we shall understand by "the rise of East Asia" – is no less puzzling than the first. The peripherality and chaos that had been emblematic of Europe on the eve of its overseas expansion came to characterize East Asia throughout the last half of the nineteenth and first half of the twentieth century. The results were devastating. By 1950, China had become one of the world's poorest countries; Japan had been reduced to a vassal state of the United

States; and the Cold War was creating a seemingly unbridgeable gulf between maritime East Asia and Mainland China. And yet, less than half a century later the gulf was bridged by a dense web of commercial exchanges; Japan and other lesser "islands" of East Asia's "capitalist archipelago" had replaced the United States as the world's leading creditor nations; and Mainland China's weight in the global economy was increasing far more rapidly than that of any other entity of comparable demographic size. Whether this turnaround is the preamble to a re-centering of the global economy on East Asia is too early to tell. But whether it will or not, explaining the dynamic of the turnaround and how the turnaround relates, if at all, to the legacy of the China-centered tribute-trade system and the East Asian regional economy constitutes a major challenge for the historical social sciences.

In seeking at least partial solutions to these puzzles, we shall begin by recasting the contentions of previous chapters in an analytical framework that focuses on the dynamic of systems of states. Next, we use this framework to seek a solution to the first puzzle through a comparative analysis of the still distinct but related dynamics of the East Asian and European inter-state systems in early modern times. Then, we analyze the dynamic and contradictions of the single global system that emerged out of the nineteenth-century globalization of the European system of states. Finally, we seek a solution to the second puzzle by investigating the relationship between the economic vitality of East Asia under US hegemony and the historical legacy of the China-centered tribute-trade system.

Concepts for analysis

In their contributions to this volume, Sugihara, Pomeranz, and Hamilton and Chang present new evidence and arguments in support of the view that economic development in East Asia through the eighteenth century was in most respects at least as advanced as in Europe. Indeed, as R. Bin Wong (1997), André Gunder Frank (1998) and Pomeranz himself (1999; 2000) had previously argued, in the late eighteenth century the Chinese national market far surpassed in size and density any Western national market. This greater size and density of the Chinese national market were not just due to China's much greater population. It was due also to levels of commercialization, agricultural productivity, sophistication of manufactures and per capita incomes as high as, or higher than those of Europe's wealthiest countries. Implicitly or explicitly, the proponents of this view argue further that the nineteenth-century "great divergence" between the economic and political fortunes of Europe and East Asia *cannot* be traced to a prior technical and organizational edge of European institutions *vis-à-vis* their East Asian counterparts.

The strongest claim in this respects is Hamilton and Chang's contention that the buyer-driven organization of textile production and distribution that emerged in late imperial China constituted a highly efficient alternative to the producer-driven, "Fordist" type of organization that emerged in the early twentieth century in the United States. More generally, as Sugihara argues in his chapter, the eclipsing of the East Asian industrious revolution by the European industrial revolution in the course of the nineteenth century was not due to a lesser economic efficiency of the East Asian developmental path. Rather, it was due to a bifurcation of the two paths and a gradual exhaustion of the potential for efficient growth along the industrious revolution path.[1]

Most of these accounts limit themselves to describing rather than explaining the divergence in question. Pomeranz (2000) does provide an explanation by tracing the divergence to differences in resource endowments and in core–periphery relationships – to the fact, that is, that the Americas provided core regions of Northwest Europe with a far more abundant supply of primary products and demand for manufactures than East Asian core regions could obtain from their own peripheries. As he puts it in his contribution to this volume, this difference

> allowed European technology and investment to develop in labor-saving, land and energy-gobbling directions at the very moment when the intensification of resource pressures previously shared by all core regions were forcing East Asian development along ever more resource-saving, labor absorbing paths.

This explanation of the divergence of the European and East Asian developmental paths is compelling in so far as it goes but begs a number of questions that bear directly on the two puzzles that we set out to solve in this chapter. For one thing, it does not tell us why starting in the fifteenth century European states showed a much stronger disposition than East Asian states to expand territorially overseas and to create the kind of core–periphery relations with their overseas domains that eventually enabled Britain to open up the path of the industrial revolution. What forces drove European states to build overseas empires and to establish the kind of core–periphery relations with their overseas domains that enabled European economies to develop in land-and-energy-intensive and labor-saving directions? To this we should add that the great nineteenth-century divergence between the East Asian industrious-revolution path and the European industrial-revolution path was premised on a greater European command not just over natural and energy resources but over financial resources as well. Where did that greater command come from bearing in mind that, as Frank (1998: 283, 356–7) has convincingly argued, China remained through the eighteenth century the "ultimate sink" of the world's money?

Another set of questions arise from the fact that the onset of the "first" industrial revolution in Britain was associated with a sharp contraction of European empires in the Americas and a quickening of the pace of British territorial expansion in Asia. What was the connection between this geographical shift of European colonialism and the subsequent diffusion of the industrial revolution from textiles to railways, steamships and an increasing number and variety of capital goods? And how did this diffusion affect political and economic relationships between Europe and the rest of the world in general and East Asia in particular? Finally, what forces promoted the eventual *fusion* of the industrious and industrial revolution paths that Sugihara sees emerging first in Japan and then in the East Asian region at large? Why did the fusion start in Japan when it did, and what are the chances that it will decrease income inequalities worldwide, as Sugihara envisages?

Our contention in this chapter is that, in order to answer these questions, we must focus on two related aspects of the comparative and relational dynamic of the European and East Asian regions. One concerns the role of inter-state relations within and between the two world regions and the other the role of capitalism in shaping regional and global processes.

On the first aspect little needs to be added to what has already been said in the Introduction. The comparison of particular institutions or developmental processes as they operate or unfold *within* different world-regional systems is essential to an understanding of the macro-dynamic of those systems. There are nonetheless aspects of that dynamic that emerge out of the *combination* and *interaction* of the systems' units and, therefore, can only be grasped by comparing the combinations and interactions themselves rather than the units that combine and interact. An especially important instance of such systemic aspects of regional macro-dynamics is a feature of early modern European states that is widely recognized to distinguish them from East Asian states in general and China in particular. This distinguishing feature is the intense competition that set European states against one another and recurrently led to the displacement of one state by another in the role of regional leader. As we shall see, although East Asian states also competed with one another, the nature of their mutual competition was very different from the European, as witnessed among other things by the fact that through the eighteenth and into the early nineteenth century China occupied a far more stable hegemonic position in the East Asian inter-state system than any state did in the European system. As Takeshi Hamashita has shown, during often protracted periods of stability, the China-centered tributary-trade system frequently provided a basis for mediating inter-state relations and articulating hierarchies with minimal recourse to war, certainly by comparison with Europe.

Be that as it may, the scope and intensity of inter-state competition are typical systemic properties that can only be grasped by paying due attention to other systemic properties, such as the number and variety of states that interact in a given setting, the distribution of power and resources among the interacting states, the existence and nature of complementarities among the interacting states, the rules and norms that inform the interaction, and so on. As our analysis will show, the identification of systemic properties must pay special attention to the strategies and structures of specific states. The states that are singled out for analysis here are chosen not because of their significance as representative examples of a region's states but because of their significance in shaping systemic structures and processes.[2]

Turning now to the role of capitalism in regional and global developmental processes, we concur with Frank (1998: 330–2) in not finding at all useful the notion of capitalism understood as a mode of production. Unlike him, however, we find an alternative notion of capitalism essential to answering several of the questions we raised earlier, and especially the question of why money capital accumulated more rapidly and massively in European than in East Asian core regions even when China was the ultimate sink of world money. This alternative notion of capitalism is based on Braudel's characterization of the world of trade as a three-layered structure. In this structure, "capitalism" occupies the top layer and consists of those participants in trade who systematically appropriate the largest profits, regardless of the particular nature of the activities (financial, commercial, industrial or agricultural) in which they are involved. This layer presupposes the existence of a lower (intermediate) layer – the "market economy" – consisting of regular participants in buying and selling activities whose rewards are more or less proportionate to the costs and risks involved in these activities. Finally, at the bottom of the hierarchy there lies the "non-market economy" of barter and self-sufficiency, consisting of individuals and organizations that participate only intermittently (or not at all) in buying and selling but whose activities are directly or indirectly an important source of vitality for the upper layers (Braudel 1981: 23–5; 1982: 21–2, 229–30; see also 1977: 39–78).

The usefulness of this definition has not escaped Wong who uses it to distinguish "between a Braudelian commercial capitalism and the operation of a Smithian dynamics of economic expansion." In his view, China had gone farther than any European state in the creation of a *market economy* (that is, in promoting and experiencing a Smithian dynamics of economic expansion) but "did not have some of the organizational forms and financial institutions of early modern Europe that promoted the creation of [Braudelian] commercial capitalism" (1997: 50–1). More specifically:

Much European commercial wealth was tapped by needy governments anxious to expand their revenue bases to meet ever-escalating expenses of war ... Amidst the mercantilist competition among European merchants and their governments for wealth and power, maritime expansion played a role of particular importance. Both European merchants and their governments benefited from their complex relationship, the former gaining fabulous profits, the latter securing much-needed revenues. The late imperial Chinese state did not develop the same kind of mutual dependence on rich merchants. Lacking the scale of financial difficulties encountered in Europe between the sixteenth and eighteenth centuries, Chinese officials had less reasons to imagine new forms of finance, huge merchant loans, and the concept of public as well as private debt. Not only did they depend little on mercantile wealth to support the state, they also feared the potentially disruptive consequences of both concentrated wealth and the *pursuit* of such wealth.

(Wong 1997: 146; emphasis in the original)

As we shall see, there is a close correspondence between this and our own assessment of the comparative East Asian and European dynamics in early modern times. Nevertheless, our distinction between a (Smithian) market dynamic and a (Braudelian) capitalist dynamic does not confine the latter to commercial activities, as Wong does. Braudel himself underscored how the essential feature of historical capitalism over its *longue durée*, that is, over its entire lifetime, has been "its unlimited flexibility, its capacity for change and *adaptation*," rather than the concrete forms (commerce included) it assumed at different places and at different times (Braudel 1982: 433; emphasis in the original). This conceptualization explicitly includes "industry" as one of the "specializations" that came to characterize historical capitalism at a certain stage of its development. This specialization led many "to regard industry as the final flowering which gave capitalism its 'true' identity." But this is a short-term view.

[After] the initial boom of mechanization, the most advanced kind of capitalism reverted to eclecticism, to an indivisibility of interests so to speak, as if the characteristic advantage of standing at the commanding heights of the economy ... consisted precisely of *not* having to confine oneself to a single choice, of being eminently adaptable, hence non-specialized.

(Braudel 1982: 381; emphasis in the original; translation amended as indicated in Wallerstein 1991: 213)

As these passages show, the distinguishing feature of a Braudelian capitalist dynamic is not the undertaking of commercial rather than industrial or agricultural activities. It is instead the continual switching of resources from one kind of activity to another in an "endless" pursuit of monetary profit. As in Karl Marx's "general formula of capital" (M–C–M'), the investment of money (M) in a particular combination of commodities (C), be it purely commercial or commercial-industrial or whatever, is strictly instrumental to an increase in the monetary value of the investor's assets from M to M' (1959: 146–55). Indeed, in a strictly capitalist dynamic the transformation of money into commodities may be skipped altogether (as in Marx's "abridged formula of capital," M–M'), whenever systemic circumstances allow the capitalist stratum to reap greater profits in the credit system than in the trade and production of commodities. This has been recurrently the case in all the leading centers of capitalist accumulation, from early fifteenth-century Genoa, Florence and Venice to late twentieth-century United States, Western Europe, Japan, Singapore and Hong Kong (Arrighi 1994).

If the Braudelian capitalist dynamic is best symbolized by a mixture/alternation of Marx's general and abridged formulas of capital (M–C–M' and M–M', respectively), the Smithian market dynamic is best symbolized by Marx's formula of commodity exchange, C–M–C', in which money (M) is mere means in the transformation of a set of commodities C into another set C' of greater use value. Ideo-typically, the main difference between the two dynamics is that, other things being equal, the first tends to generate surpluses of means of payment (the accumulation of such surpluses being pursued as an end in itself), whereas the second does not (money being just a means of transforming one set of commodities into another of greater use value). This difference, as we shall see, helps in explaining why in the seventeenth and eighteenth centuries the leading capitalist states of Europe came to be affected by a surplus of capital, in comparison with China's shortage, in spite of the latter's persistent balance of payment surplus *vis-à-vis* Europe.

In the analysis that follows we shall show how the intense political-military competition that from the start set European states against one another was an essential ingredient in the enlarged reproduction of the (Braudelian) capitalist dynamic that recurrently engendered an ever growing surplus of capital within the European regional system. This ever growing surplus of capital, in turn, provided both the means and incentives of new rounds of political-military competition on an ever expanding geographical scale. Directly and indirectly, this self-reinforcing cycle of capital accumulation and territorial expansion was the main driving force of those technological and organizational innovations ("industrial revolutions" included) that eventually moved the European system to dominion globally.

Our analysis will nonetheless also show that this self-reinforcing cycle attained its limits once it resulted in the incorporation of the East Asian regional system within the structures of the globalizing European system. In the short-to-medium run, the impact of the incorporation proved highly disruptive for the East Asian system. Over time, however, the incorporation created regional and world-systemic circumstances favorable to the fusion of the industrial and industrious revolutions paths that constitutes the mainspring of the recent East Asian economic renaissance.

The European and East Asian dynamics compared

In comparing the structures and dynamics of the European and East Asian regional systems, we may begin by noticing the almost exact correspondence between the period of European history that Braudel has called the "extended" sixteenth century (1350–1640) and the Ming period in East Asian history (1368–1643). In the course of these three centuries the two regional dynamics came to influence one another to an unprecedented degree and, at the same time, the seeds for the subsequent divergence began to germinate. The divergence materialized only in the two centuries following the Peace of Westphalia in the West and the demise of the Ming in the East. But its origins can be traced to the different responses of the two regions' leading governmental organizations to the fourteenth-century collapse of the Mongol empire and the consequent disintegration of the thirteenth-century Afro-Eurasian world trading system reconstructed by Janet Abu-Lughod (1989). Let us look at each of these two regional responses in turn.

The European dynamic

The European response was characterized by long wars that went far toward launching a Braudelian capitalist dynamic in inter-state and intrastate relations. One such war pitted the main intermediaries and beneficiaries of European trade with the East, the Italian city-states, against one another in what Braudel has called the "Italian" Hundred Years War (1976, I: 331, 388). The outcome of this secular struggle influenced the subsequent transformation of the European world system in three main ways. First, the Peace of Lodi that at the end of the war in 1454 institutionalized the northern Italian balance of power, provided a model for the institutionalization of the European balance of power by the Westphalia treaties two centuries later (Mattingly 1988: 178). Second, the state that emerged victorious from the confrontation (Venice) became the prototype of the strong capitalist state in the double sense of "perfect example" and "model for future instances" of such a state – a model that was still advocated by leading members of the British business community at the end of the Napoleonic Wars (Ingham 1984: 9). Finally, least recognized but most important, the great loser of the war (Genoa or more precisely the expatriate Genoese business diaspora) became the main capitalist driving force behind the subsequent overseas expansion of the Iberian states (Arrighi 1994: 109–22).

Equally significant were the better known Anglo-French Hundred Years War (1337–1453) and the subsequent Castilian-Aragonese expulsion of the Moors from the Iberian peninsula. These wars jointly consolidated the formation in the European subcontinent of competing national states of approximately equal capabilities in a condition of permanent struggle for power in peace and war. Integral to this condition was the intense inter-state competition for mobile capital that, as Max Weber noted (1961: 249), created unique opportunities for the take-off of a capitalist dynamic in Europe.

These unique opportunities were created in two complementary ways. On the one hand, intense inter-state competition for mobile capital inflated the profits as well as the "invisible" but nonetheless substantial power of the transnational ethnic business communities that had come to control the most prolific sources of mobile capital in Europe – that is, the Florentine, the Genoese and the German, and to a lesser extent the Lucchese and the English (Boyer-Xambeu *et al.* 1994). On the other hand, it created extraordinary incentives for the rulers of the territorial states of Europe to tap directly the main sources of mobile capital through an "internalization" of capitalism within their domains, that is, by themselves undertaking, or by encouraging their own merchant classes to undertake, the lucrative business of long-distance trade with the East.

For most of the sixteenth century the first tendency was predominant. The history of the European overseas expansion of this period has largely been written in terms of Iberian leadership, both in the rounding of the Cape and in the conquest of the Americas. That the Portuguese and the Spaniards were themselves following in the footsteps of Venice in their attempts to appropriate the largest share possible of European trade with Asia is a widely acknowledged fact. What remains to be acknowledged is what we may call – to paraphrase Alan Rix (1993) – the leadership "from behind" that the Genoese capitalist diaspora exercised *vis-à-vis* the Iberian states. This leadership was largely invisible because of the particular relationship of political exchange through which it operated. In this relationship, the Iberian rulers specialized in the highly visible pursuit of power and organization of overseas expansion, while the Genoese capitalist diaspora specialized in the less visible pursuit of profits and transformation of the products of overseas expansion into money and credit (Arrighi 1994: 109–26).

Thanks to this relationship, in the seventy years that Braudel calls the "Age of the Genoese" (1557–1627), Genoese merchant-bankers came to exercise a rule over European finances comparable to that exercised in the twentieth century by the Bank of International Settlements at Basel –

"a rule that was so discreet and sophisticated that historians for a long time failed to notice it" (Braudel 1984: 157, 164). For most of this period, according to Richard Ehrenberg, "it was not the Potosi silver mines, but the Genoese fairs of exchange which made it possible for Philip II to conduct his world power policy decade after decade" (quoted in Kriedte 1983: 47). By 1617, Genoese capitalists had squeezed so much out of their Iberian connection as to turn Spain and Portugal, in Suárez de Figueroa's words, into "the Indies of the Genoese" (quoted in Elliott 1970: 96).

Increasingly, however, the tendency for the ruling groups of Europe's emerging national or proto-national states to tap directly the main sources of mobile capital became predominant. The chief instrument in this endeavor was the launching of joint-stock chartered companies. Although England was the first to launch several of these companies, throughout the seventeenth century by far the most successful (and the model that all others sought to replicate) was the Dutch *Verenigde Oost-Indische Compagnie* (VOC). The VOC inaugurated a new era, not just in business history, as Nils Steensgard (1974, 1981, 1982) has maintained, but also in European and world history. Without the large and steady cash flow generated by the activities of the VOC in Southeast Asia, Amsterdam may have never become the site of the first stock exchange in permanent session with a volume and a density of transactions that outshone all previous stock markets (Braudel 1982: 100–6; 1984: 224–7; Israel 1989: 75–6; 256–8). Once established, and until it was displaced by London in the late eighteenth century, the Amsterdam stock exchange became the central clearing house of European high finance. This function of central financial entrepôt put in the hands of the Dutch capitalist oligarchy a power *vis-à-vis* the larger territorial states of Europe that bore no relationship to the limited (and shrinking) political-military capabilities of the Dutch state (Arrighi and Silver *et al.* 1999: Chapters 1, 2).

The success of the VOC in Southeast Asia, and the lesser success of the *West-Indische Compagnie* (WIC) in the Atlantic, initiated a race among European states to form exclusive overseas commercial empires. This race gained momentum after the European balance of power was institutionalized by the Treaties of Westphalia (1648) – an institutionalization largely due to Dutch leadership "from behind." The Atlantic soon became and remained throughout the eighteenth century the main arena of the competitive struggles engendered by this race. But Asia remained the unwitting arbiter of the European struggle. As Charles Davenant observed in the late seventeenth century, whoever controlled the Asian trade was in a position to "give law to all the commercial world" (quoted in Wolf 1982: 125).

The East Asian dynamic

The European and East Asian regional systems in early modern times were sufficiently similar to make their comparison analytically meaningful. Both consisted of a multiplicity of political jurisdictions that appealed to a common cultural (i.e., civilizational) heritage and traded extensively within their region. Although cross-border trade was more publicly regulated in East Asia than in Europe, since Song times (960–1276), private overseas trade had flourished and transformed the nature of tribute trade itself. As Takeshi Hamashita notes of the tributary-trade system:

> Although the categories and quantities of goods to be traded were also officially prescribed, the volume of private trade gradually increased over time. As a result, the main purpose of the tribute trade came to be the pursuit of profits through the unofficial trade that was ancillary to the official system.
>
> (1993: 75–6)

Equally important for our purposes was the flourishing of trade networks linking central and southern coastal China and Southeast Asia that were entirely independent of the tributary system, and often directly flouted imperial edicts.

We can even detect analogies in the inter-state competition that characterized the two regional systems. The separate domains that were held together by the tribute-trade system centered on China were "close enough to influence one another, but ... too far apart to assimilate and be assimilated." The tribute-trade system provided them with a symbolic framework of mutual political–economic interaction that nonetheless was loose enough to endow its peripheral components with considerable autonomy *vis-à-vis* the Chinese center. Thus, Japan and Vietnam were peripheral members of the system but also competitors with China in the exercise of the Imperial title awarding function, Japan establishing a tributary type relationship with the Ryukyu kingdom, and Vietnam with Laos (Hamashita 1994: 92; 1997: 114–24).[3] Sugihara goes even further in maintaining that the diffusion of the best technology and organizational know-how within East Asia makes it "possible to think of the presence of an East Asian multi-centered political system, at least with regard to China and Japan, with many features analogous to the inter-state system in Europe" (1996: 38).

Moreover, the Chinese center itself recurrently came under pressures analogous to those that fueled inter-state competition for mobile capital in Europe. Pressures of this kind contributed to the great expansion of Chinese private sea trade during the Southern Song period (1127–1276). The heavy military expenditures and reparations involved in the wars with

Mongol and Tungusic peoples on China's northern frontiers induced the Song court to encourage private sea trade as a source of revenue – a source that became all the more essential with the loss of control of the North and the silk route, and the weakening state capacity to sustain such profitable government monopolies as salt, iron and wine production (Tian 1987: 143; Zhuang 1989: 19; Lin and Zhang 1991: 13). Particularly significant was the Southern Song administration's encouragement of Chinese navigation technology through the provision of financial and technical support to shipbuilders. Chinese junks then became the most advanced vessels in the world. Their sharp-head, flat-rear and sharp-base design allowed them to navigate with high speed in turbulent seas and Chinese pioneered the use of the compass in navigation (Lo 1969: 77–91; Chen 1989).

Finally, military pressure and territorial losses in the north provoked a major increase in north–south migrations toward the regions south of the Yangzi River. These warmer regions were the most suitable for high-yielding wet-rice cultivation (Bray 1986: 119). As the population of these regions increased rapidly, achieving densities far higher than those in Europe, so did the mastery of the techniques of wet-rice agriculture leading to what Mark Elvin (1973: Chapter 9) has called the "revolution in farming." The efficiency of wet-rice cultivation in guaranteeing sufficient food supplies enabled farmers to increase the quantity and variety of products that they cultivated and marketed and to engage in non-agricultural activities. As Ravi Palat observes:

> Since the productivity of fields could be achieved through additional inputs of labor, areas under wet-rice cultivation could support increasingly greater densities of population. The demographic growth made possible by intensive farming both facilitated an expansion in non-agricultural occupations and exerted a downward pressure on labor costs.
>
> (1995: 59)

Under the impact of state encouragement and the development of wet-rice cultivation, the maritime trade and the market economy of the coastal regions entered a long upswing characterized by advances in navigation technology, the consolidation of the "sea silk route," and the flourishing of Guangzhou, Quanzhou, and smaller port cities on the Southeastern coast as centers of tributary trade. At the same time, private sea trade, linking China's coastal regions and the South China Sea, spurred by the formation of Chinese communities throughout insular Southeast Asia, soon surpassed official or tributary trade to become the dominant mode of economic exchange between China and maritime Asia (Lo 1969: 57–8; Quan 1991a: 405–8; Hui 1995: 29–30). This "commercial revolution" outlasted the fall of the Song in 1276. Under the Yuan (1277–1368), continuing support for private sea trade and Chinese migration to southeast Asia led to the formation of overseas Chinese trading networks across the Southern Seas and the Indian Ocean as extensive as any of the contemporary European networks (Shiba 1983: 106–7; Yang 1985: 32–4, 40–4; Chen 1989: 36–40; Zhuang 1989: 8–12, 21; Guan 1994: 57–60).

The main tendencies that characterized the capitalist transformation of the European system can thus be detected also in the East Asian system – tendencies that were especially strong in Song and Yuan times (see, for example, Yang 1952; and Elvin 1973: Chapter 14). This lends credibility to Christopher Chase-Dunn and Thomas Hall's contention that capitalism "nearly occurred first" in Song China (1997: 47). Under the Ming (1368–1644), however, the tendencies in question did not become stronger as they did in Europe, where they subjected even the most powerful states to a capitalist logic thereby propelling inter-state competition toward the formation of overseas commercial and territorial empires. On the contrary, they were brought under control through governmental policies that prioritized security and the strengthening of domestic trade and at times banned or proscribed foreign trade.

This reorientation of Chinese policies originated in the serious deterioration of economic conditions and financial crisis that characterized the transition from Yuan to Ming rule. Once the Ming regime consolidated, the capital was shifted from Nanjing to Beijing in order to protect more effectively the northern part of the empire from the threat of Mongolian invasions. The shift led to the further extension to the north of the circuits of market exchanges that had formed in the south under the Song with a consequent consolidation of the national economy (Dannoue 1995). The Ming repaired and extended the canal system connecting the prosperous rice growing southern regions to the northern political center, in order to guarantee the supply of food to the capital and the surrounding region. The further growth of the market economy and "canal cities" like Hangzhou in the lower Yangzi region was thereby facilitated (Xu and Wu 1985: 83–6, 269–72; Wei 1988: 51–2; Dannoue 1995; Hung 2001a: 491–7). Also important in this respect was the early Ming's promotion of cotton growing in the north. The ensuing specialization of the north in the production of raw cotton and of the lower Yangzi in the manufacturing of cotton textiles fostered north–south trade along the grand canal, promoting further the expansion of the national market (Wu 1965: 230–3).

While promoting the formation and expansion of a national market, the Ming government imposed administrative restrictions on sea trade and on Chinese migration to Southeast Asia in an attempt to maintain central control over revenues and contain the power of Overseas Chinese and Japanese merchants. Between 1405 and 1433 it further sought to extend the reach of the Chinese state by sponsoring Admiral Zheng He's seven great voyages to Southeast Asia and across the Indian Ocean. With ships that probably displaced 1,500 tons, compared to the 300-ton flagship of Vasco Da Gama, China's seaborne capacity at this time had no peer (McNeill 1982: 44). While strengthening political and commercial relations, manifesting China's military and seafaring power throughout a large region, thereby extending the borders of the East Asian regional system, the Zheng expeditions asserted Chinese suzerainty, extended tributary-trade relations, and sanctioned and encouraged Chinese migration and trade throughout maritime East Asia and as far as the East coast of Africa. These expeditions, however, turned out to be exceedingly expensive. They were therefore discontinued, and the Ming regime turned inward, restricting the number of tributary missions, circumscribing private maritime commerce and even banning the building of seagoing ships. The Ming became more preoccupied with immediate military threats, notably but not exclusively those on its northern frontiers. Suspicious of unofficial external trade, it strengthened internal trade and cracked down on unauthorized external trade with maritime Asia (McNeill 1982: 47; Zhang 1991: 49–51; Hui 1995: 34–8, 53; Wang 1998: 316–23).

The eventual lifting of trade restrictions in the 1560s occurred in the midst of a serious political, economic and social crisis. By the early sixteenth century, the capacity of the Ming regime to rule effectively was seriously undermined internally by widespread corruption and increasing budget deficits. Internal degradation was accompanied by mounting external pressure, in the north from the expansion of the Jurchens and along the southeastern coast from the expansion of illegal trade which bypassed Ming tax collectors. Carried out by armed Chinese and Japanese traders (*wo-kou*, or "Japanese pirates," in the Chinese government's characterization), the illegal trade was actively encouraged by local Japanese warlords who sought to use the profitable trade in Chinese products to finance their mutual struggles (Huang 1969: 105–23; Wills 1979: 210–11; Wakeman 1985: Chapter 1; Lin 1987: 85–111; Tong 1991: 115–29; He 1996: 45–7; Hung 2001c: 12–18). But with the financially strapped Ming cutting back on the costly tributary trade, and unable to exercise effective military control over southern coastal areas, private trade became once again the main form of economic exchange in the region (Zhang 1991: 48–50).

These various tendencies reinforced one another resulting in the explosive growth of social disturbances in the mid-sixteenth century (Tong 1991). Faced with the growing ungovernability of the empire, the Ming rulers sought to solve the crisis by easing peasants' grievances through tax reforms and the exploitation of the flourishing private trade. Corvée labor, one of the primary causes of peasant hardship and unrest, together with taxation in crop form, were largely replaced by the "Single-Whip Tax" payable in silver. The crippled paper currency was abandoned in favor of a silver standard, and in order to expand the silver influx from overseas, restrictions on sea trade with Southeast Asia were relaxed and licensed seafaring merchants were taxed (Wills 1979: 211; Atwell 1986; Elisonas 1991: 261–2; Chao 1993; Flynn and Giraldez 1995; Quan 1996; 1987; Hung 2001a: 498–500).

This important shift in fiscal, monetary and trade policies was made possible and encouraged by the massive silver influx from overseas trade, principally initially the trade with Japan, the major silver supplier in the region, and subsequently with Europe and the Americas (Atwell 1998: 403–16). At the same time, restrictions on sea trade to Southeast Asia were relaxed and the Ming began to tax licensed seafaring merchants (Wills 1979: 211; Chao 1993; Flynn and Giraldez 1995; Quan 1996, 1987). It is no historical accident that the shift coincided with the Spanish conquest of the Philippines in the late 1560s and the opening of the Potosi silver mines (in present-day Bolivia) in the 1570s (Brook 1998: 205). Spanish shipments of much of their South American silver to their base in Manila to pay for Chinese exports helped ease the Ming fiscal crisis and growing pressure on the peasantry. At the same time they established a new firm trade link between the European and the East Asian regions. From the sixteenth until well into the eighteenth century, fully three-quarters of new world silver found its way to China, a product both of China's highly competitive exports of silk, porcelain and tea, and a Chinese thirst for silver that drove silver prices to levels twice those prevailing in other parts of the world (Flynn *et al.* 1999: 23–4).

The expansion of intra- and inter-regional trade under the late Ming boosted the fortunes not just of China's coastal areas and maritime East Asia but of the Overseas Chinese as well. During the first two hundred years of Ming rule the trade networks of the overseas Chinese had continued to expand, despite restrictions on private overseas trading and on Chinese migrations to Southeast Asia. Trade and the associated migration became the principal means of livelihood for significant parts of the population of the southeast coastal regions of China, the source of extraordinary profits for merchants, and the primary source of revenue for local governments (Hui 1995: 35–6). "Chinese merchants, craftsmen and sailors," in John Wills' words, "became extremely vigorous participants in building a new world of trade and settlement around the South China Sea" (1998: 333). From the fifteenth century forward, despite Ming restrictions, periodic reverses and challenges from Muslims and others, Chinese were the dominant traders throughout the East Asian region, some establishing business, commercial, and financial networks extending to the village level across Southeast Asia. They linked China with a wide array of partners embracing a kaleidoscope of peoples and cultures across East

Asia, and provided a steady flow of remittances back to the southeastern coastal villages that spawned the migration and which in turn became among the wealthiest, most productive, and commercially expansive regions of East Asia (Wang 1991: 85–6; 1998: 320–3; Hui 1995).

The power of the Overseas Chinese was consolidated by the arrival of the Europeans, who, far from curbing the activities of Chinese traders, boosted trade throughout the region and beyond by supplementing the Japanese supply of silver and linking regional trade to global networks. Unlike local rulers, moreover, they had little restraint in challenging the authority of the Chinese imperial court. They thus provided political and military support for Chinese traders who circumvented the restrictions imposed by the Chinese government. This resulted in an increasing involvement of Chinese merchants in highly profitable smuggling activities with active European encouragement (Chang 1991: 16; Flynn and Giraldez 1994: 71, 74–5, 79–83; Hui 1995: 67–8; see also Chang 1969: 69–85).

Europeans also destroyed many indigenous trading classes and networks in an effort to consolidate their control over local resources and populations. They thereby strengthened the capacity of the overseas Chinese, who escaped the onslaught, to monopolize the role of commercial intermediaries between the Europeans and the region's polities and societies (Alatas 1977: 184–7, 191–5; Curtin 1984: 147, 162–8; Reid 1990: 652–4; Blusse 1991: 334). And the more valuable and exclusive Chinese trading networks became in their intermediary role, the more Europeans were induced to compete with one another in securing the cooperation of the overseas Chinese. The formation of a large merchant community in seventeenth-century Batavia, for example,

> was the result of the deliberate Dutch policy, which sought to gain a total monopoly of eastern and southeastern Asian trade through making use of the Chinese trading networks already established throughout the Malay archipelago, the Indo-China coasts and Japan ... They welcomed Chinese cooperation and tried to woo them wherever possible away from the Portuguese and the Spanish. In that way, a Dutch supported chain of Chinese communities grew up between Batavia and areas like the Moluccas to the east, Siam to the north and China and Japan to the northeast.
>
> (Wang 1991: 88)

The wealth and power of Chinese merchants attained new heights in the course of the seventeenth-century transition from Ming to Qing rule. Despite the injection of trade revenues and taxes in the form of silver, Ming financial difficulties skyrocketed with the costly Chinese military campaign to oust Hideyoshi's Japanese forces from Korea in the 1590s, the outbreak of full-fledged warfare with the Manchus in the 1610s, and mounting corruption at court and throughout the administration. Japanese trade restrictive policies imposed in the 1630s, combined with the sharp decline in European silver supplies in the 1630s and 1640s, interrupted silver inflow into China and increased peasant burdens by driving up the price of silver. The result was a resurgence of empire-wide turbulence culminating in the collapse of the Ming in 1644 (Atwell 1986 and 1998: 407–15).

It was at this time that the Zheng merchant family created a maritime empire in some respects comparable to the contemporary Dutch empire in Southeast Asia. By the 1620s, their military and commercial power, centered in Fujian and Guangdong on the South China coast and extending to Taiwan, was such that it eliminated whatever maritime supremacy the Portuguese had managed to establish in the region. In the 1630s, Zheng Zhilong, styling himself "the King of South China," had seized control of the extensive trade networks that linked coastal China and lucrative Southeast Asian markets. Utilizing resources and contacts he had gained when working for the Dutch VOC and trading with the Portuguese and Spanish, Zheng deployed European-style warships and firearms to dominate maritime trade, defy Ming tax collectors and naval forces, and defend his kingdom. At its zenith, the Zhengs monopolized the silk and ceramics trade and built a sphere of influence that stretched from Guangdong and Fujian to Japan, Taiwan, and Southeast Asia. By 1650, the Zhengs had created a rebel state on the southeast coast. But, failing to defeat the Manchus, in 1662 they retreated to Taiwan, expelled the Dutch and founded the kingdom of Taiwan. A former Dutch governor of colonial Taiwan in 1675 compared the rise of the Zhengs as a seaborne power to the rise of the Dutch in Europe a century earlier (Coyett 1903 [1675]; Wills 1979, 1998; Struve 1988; Wong 1983; Hung 2001c). After observing that in marketing Japanese wares abroad the VOC was following in the footsteps of the Zhengs, Chumei Ho (1994: 44) has claimed with some reason that

> The Zheng networks of commercial and political intelligence must have been at least as effective as those of either of its main enemies, the Manchus and the Dutch ... Arguably, the Zheng organization had some of the same traits as the VOC.

Equally important, the Zheng maritime empire was from the start a key player in the ongoing dynastic struggle in mainland China. A respected ally of the Ming in the early stages of the struggle – when many members of the Zheng family became officers and generals of the Ming army – Zheng Zhilong attempted to switch sides after the Qing army entered Fujian in 1647. The attempt failed, as the Qing responded to Zheng

Zhilong's overtures by jailing and eventually executing him. But under Zheng Chenggong, the power of the Zhengs reached new heights until their downfall in 1683.[4]

The divergence of the European and East Asian dynamics

The expatriate business networks that constituted the pre-eminent capitalist organizations of sixteenth-century Europe invite comparison with the Chinese and other ethnic networks that constituted the pre-eminent capitalist organizations of sixteenth-century East Asia. As Braudel pointed out:

> Everywhere, from Egypt to Japan, we shall find genuine capitalists, wholesalers, the rentiers of trade, and their thousands of auxiliaries – the commission agents, brokers, money-changers and bankers. As for the techniques, possibilities or guarantees of exchange, any of these groups of merchants would stand comparison with its western equivalents. Both inside and outside India, Tamil, Bengali and Gujerati merchants formed close-knit partnerships with business and contracts passing in turn from one group to another, just as they might in Europe from the Florentine to the Lucchese, the Genoese, the South Germans or the English.
>
> (1984: 486)

Although in this passage Braudel does not refer explicitly to Chinese business networks, elsewhere he draws a parallel between the merchants and bankers of Shanxi province and the overseas Chinese originating from Fujian and other southern coastal provinces, on the one hand, and Florentine, Genoese, and Lucchese merchants on the other (1982: 153). Moreover, as we have just underscored, the seventeenth-century Zheng empire had some traits in common with the VOC, the half-governmental and half-business organization that in the seventeenth century displaced expatriate business networks as the leading organization of European capitalism. There can be little doubt, therefore, that capitalist organizations comparable to the European could and did emerge in East Asia as well. As William Rowe has noted, "whatever the reason, the divergences between Chinese and Western social histories since 1500 are not due to the fact that the progressive West discovered capitalism and the modern state and China did not" (1990: 262).

The presence of comparable capitalist organizations, however, did not make the development of the two regional systems equally capitalist in orientation. For capitalism to become dominant at the level of the system, an additional ingredient was required. While acknowledging the presence in China and in the surrounding region of business networks as capitalist as those of the Genoese and the Florentine, Braudel himself underscores how "the Chinese example most opportunely supports my insistence on separating the *market economy* and *capitalism*" (1982: 588; emphasis in the original; cf. Wong 1997: part 2; Hung 2001a: 497–505):

> For contrary [to the] argument – no capitalism, no market economy – China did have a solidly-established market economy … with its chains of local markets, its swarming population of small artisans and itinerant merchants, its busy shopping streets and urban centers. So at ground level, trade was brisk and well-provided for, encouraged by a government primarily concerned with agricultural production; but *at upper levels*, the state … expressed unmistakable hostility to any individual making himself "abnormally" rich … So there could be no capitalism, except within certain clearly-defined groups, backed by the state, supervised by the state and always more or less at its mercy.
>
> (Braudel 1982: 589; emphasis in the original)

In Braudel's scheme of things, this situation contrasts sharply with that obtaining in the European states in which capitalism did triumph.

> Capitalism only triumphs when it becomes identified with the state, *when it is the state*. In its first great phase, that of the Italian city-states of Venice, Genoa, and Florence, power lay in the hands of the moneyed elite. In seventeenth-century Holland the aristocracy of the Regents governed for the benefit and even according to the directives of the businessmen, merchants, and money-lenders. Likewise, in England the Glorious Revolution of 1688 marked the accession of business similar to that in Holland.
>
> (Braudel 1977: 64–5; emphasis added)

The contrast is undoubtedly exaggerated. Nevertheless, Braudel's hyperbole does point to an aspect of the capitalist transformation of the European regional system from the fifteenth through the eighteenth centuries that has no parallel in the dynamic of the East Asian regional system. This is the *sequence* of states with which capitalism became identified – the Italian city-states, the Dutch proto-nation-state, and eventually a state, the English, that was in the process of becoming not just a nation-state but the center of a world-encircling maritime and territorial empire. In this sequence, each state is larger and more complex than its predecessor, and it is this sequence, more than anything else, that evinces the capitalist transformation of the European regional system. And conversely, the absence of anything comparable to such a sequence can be taken as the clearest sign that, in spite of the existence of capitalist organizations analogous to the European varieties and of greater advances than in

Europe in the formation of market economies, the East Asian regional system itself was not at this time in the process of becoming capitalist.

In pinning down the difference between a regional system that was and one that was not becoming capitalist, it may be helpful to conceive of the transformation as an epidemic, or more precisely, "a rash of epidemics" (Jameson 1998: 139–40). In the European system the capitalist virus spread rapidly from its original focus in tiny city-states and expatriate business networks to larger and ever more powerful territorial states. These more powerful states "internalized" capitalism by following in the footsteps of the city-states in seeking to promote and reap the profits of long-distance trade, and by encouraging their own nationals to undertake the activities previously monopolized by foreigners organized in transnational business networks. As a result, capitalism as mode of accumulation and rule turned from an interstitial into a dominant property of the system.

In the East Asian system, in contrast, capitalism did not become identified with the system's more powerful states. For all we know the capitalist virus might very well have been as widespread as (or even more widespread than) in Europe. But if so the "immune" system in East Asia was stronger, so that no rash of epidemics ensued. Under the Ming and especially the Qing, capitalism became even more an interstitial formation than it had been under the Song or the Yuan. It became embodied ever more exclusively in the Overseas Chinese diaspora and was marginalized in Southern Chinese coastal areas, with the result that its influence on the region's main seats of power remained insignificant, despite its importance in linking the Chinese coast to Southeast Asia. *At the level of the system,* that is, capitalism was "externalized" in the sense that it developed most fully on the outer rims rather than at the center of the region's most powerful states.

There were three partial and temporary exceptions to this tendency. One was insular Southeast Asia after the Ming's disengagement from the area.[5] Although many Southeast Asian states continued to recognize Chinese suzerainty formally and symbolically, their political and economic dependence on the Ming court decreased while their connections with private traders strengthened. Many of these states were autonomous port-states, commercial nodes that thrived on the profits of trade. Their number increased considerably during the commercial boom of the sixteenth century. When the Portuguese arrived in 1509, Southeast Asian trade was concentrated on Melaka. Within half a century of the Portuguese conquest of Melaka in 1511, trade had dispersed among the rising centers of Patani, Johor, Pahang, Aceh and Benten, and in the course of the next century, as Anthony Reid (1993: 208–14) observes, at least fifty-five such political and commercial centers emerged including Manila, Hue, Champa and Palembang.

This formation of autonomous port-states presents many similarities with contemporary and earlier formations of port- and city-states in the Mediterranean, North and Baltic Seas. In Braudel's sense, at least some of the Southeast Asian states were as capitalist as their European counterparts. Nevertheless, individually and collectively they never became "models" for the larger East Asian states, as the Italian city-states did for the larger European states. On the contrary, in some cases they were absorbed by the region's larger states (as in the case of Champa's absorption by Vietnam). In a few other cases they themselves became subregional powers within the China-centered tribute-trade system as in the case of Siam. For the most part, however, they were incorporated within the domains of European colonial empires, thereby contributing to the further spread of the capitalist virus within the expanding European system and to its containment in the contracting East Asian system.

The second exception was Japan in the Ashikaga period (1368–1573). In that period, Japan lacked a centralized authority and was in a chronic state of war among warlords. Cities and long-distance trading communities thrived not only because there was no central authority capable of containing capitalism as in Ming China. They thrived also because the competing warlords sought the assistance of cities and merchants in their attempts to secure revenue (Braudel 1982: 589–94). As Perry Anderson (1974: 440) has noted, this fragmentation of polities and growth of towns made the Japanese scenario comparable to the European. Nevertheless, the subsequent unification of Japan by Toyotomi Hideyoshi and the latter's defeat in the war with China on Korean soil from 1592 to 1598 prevented the Japanese variety of the capitalist virus from spreading to the entire region.

The third exception to the tendency toward the externalization of capitalism in East Asia was the growing power of the Zheng commercial empire in the transition from the Ming to the Qing. As we have seen, not only was this commercial empire comparable to that of the Dutch. For a while at least, it also wielded non-negligible influence on the dynastic struggles that were being waged on mainland China. Nevertheless, the very comparability of the Zheng and the Dutch commercial empires makes their opposite fates particularly instructive. In the European context, the Dutch became the leaders of the institutionalization of the balance of power among Europe's territorial states, the empowerment of capitalist strata within these same states, and the intensification of their mutual competition in building overseas commercial and territorial empires. In the East Asian context, in contrast, the downfall of the Zheng cleared the way for the demilitarization of the Chinese merchants, the consolidation of national economy-making both in Qing China and Tokugawa Japan, and the precipitous decline of the power and influence of the Overseas Chinese *vis-à-vis* the region's territorial states and the consolidating European colonial outposts. As Pomeranz (2000: 204) notes, the Zheng empire "stands as an illuminating example of a kind of activity that successfully paralleled European armed trading and colonization but was not a normal part of the Chinese state system."

Braudel does not answer, indeed, does not even raise the question of why in early modern times capitalism spread like an epidemic in the European world but did not catch on in East Asia. All he says, more implicitly than explicitly, is that the difference cannot be traced to a prior greater development of a market economy, because a market economy was more developed in many parts of Asia, East Asia included, than in Europe. But if, as we also think, the prior development of a market economy does not explain the difference, what does?

It seems to us that the most plausible and economical explanation is both structural and relational. The structural explanation has to do primarily with the more balanced and decentralized structure of power in the European than in the East Asian inter-state system. Without such a power structure, it would have been difficult, if not impossible, for capitalist organizations that were either territorially insignificant or without a territorial foundation at all to wield the kind of power and influence that the Italian city-states did in the fourteenth and fifteenth centuries, the Genoese diaspora in the sixteenth century, and the Dutch Republic in the seventeenth and early eighteenth centuries. Nor would inter-state competition for mobile capital among the larger territorial organizations of the European system have been as intense as it was throughout these centuries. And in the absence of these conditions, it is hard to imagine how the capitalist epidemic would have spread in the European system as fast as it did (cf. Arrighi 1994: 27–47).

Counterfactual evidence in support of this contention comes precisely from East Asia, where the huge territorial and demographic size of China, combined with the power it exercised through the tributary-trade system, created a fundamental underlying imbalance and centralization of power in the region. As this imbalance and centralization of power were consolidated first under the Ming, and after an interlude under the Qing, the possibility that capitalist city-states would become models of state-and-war-making for the larger territorial states (as was the case in fifteenth-century Europe) became in East Asia even more remote than it already was. The same imbalance and centralization did not prevent expatriate ethnic networks of merchant-bankers comparable to the European from forming in East Asia. But they did prevent these networks from gaining the upper hand in relationships of political exchange with the rulers of the region's most powerful territorial state, as the Genoese network did with Imperial Spain in the sixteenth century. And finally, for all its similarities with the Dutch maritime empire, the Zheng empire really never had a chance to lead "from behind" the larger territorial organizations of East Asia to institutionalize the balance of power as the principle regulating their mutual relations (as the Dutch Republic did with the European states at Westphalia), for the simple reason that in East Asia there was no such balance of power to institutionalize (Hung 2001a: 501–3; Hung 2001c).

This (comparative) structural explanation of the divergence of the European and East Asian developmental paths in early modern times can be seriously misleading unless it is combined with a relational explanation, namely with the fundamental asymmetry of East–West trade as a source of wealth and power in the two regional systems. For throughout early modern times, East–West trade was an incomparably more important source of commercial wealth and power for the governmental and business organizations of the West than of the East, most notably in the case of China. It was this fundamental asymmetry that made the fortunes of Venice and induced the Iberian states, instigated and assisted by Venice's Genoese rivals, to seek a direct link with the markets of the East. And it was this same asymmetry that underlaid the low returns, relative to costs, of Zheng He's fifteenth-century expeditions in the Indian Ocean. Were it not for this asymmetry, Zheng He might very well, in Paul Kennedy's words, have sailed "around Africa and 'discover[ed]' Portugal several decades before Henry the Navigator's expeditions began earnestly to push south of Ceuta" (1987: 7).

Columbus' accidental "discovery" of the Americas while seeking a shorter route to the wealth of Asia changed the terms of the asymmetry by providing European governments and businesses with new means to seek entry in Asian markets, as well as with a new source of commercial wealth and power in the Atlantic. But almost two centuries after the discovery, the Dutch were still in a position – to paraphrase Davenant – to lay down the law to the commercializing European world by monopolizing one of the most profitable of the Asian trades. In the East Asian system, in contrast, the primary source of inter-state power and legitimation continued to be situated at the very center of the system's largest territorial state, China. Once the overambitious attempt of Zheng's Taiwan regime to fight back on the mainland imploded, the Qing succeeded in establishing itself firmly as the region's pre-eminent power.

The re-centering of the global economy on Europe

With the consolidation of Qing rule in China, the trend toward national economy-making initiated by the Ming resumed with greater vigor. Its ultimate result was the remarkable peace, prosperity, and demographic growth that China experienced for much of the eighteenth century – what Sugihara (this volume) aptly calls the "Chinese miracle." By world-historical standards this was a remarkable achievement and a source of inspiration for leading figures of the European Enlightenment. Leibniz,

Voltaire, and Quesnay, among others, "looked to China for moral instruction, guidance in institutional development, and supporting evidence for their advocacy of causes as varied as benevolent absolutism, meritocracy, and an agriculturally based national economy" (Adas 1989: 79; Hung 2000: 5–10; Hung 2001b: 3–7). The most striking contrast with European states was the Chinese empire's size and population. In François Quesnay's characterization, the Chinese empire was "what all Europe would be if the latter were united under a single sovereign" – a characterization which was echoed in Adam Smith's remark that China's "home market" was as big as that of "all different countries of Europe put together" (Quesnay 1969: 115; Fairbank 1983: 170).

Equally impressive was the peace and tranquillity of these huge and populous domains which European visitors and residents of China, Jesuit missionaries in particular, contrasted with Europe's social strife and incessant warfare (Adas 1989: 80–1; Hung 2000: 12–17). To be sure, in the early eighteenth century Qing China expanded its borders dramatically into Inner Asia through various military campaigns, and in 1788–9 it was at war also in the south with Vietnam. In comparison with contemporary Europe, and indeed with East Asia itself in the sixteenth and early seventeenth centuries, inter-state relations in eighteenth-century East Asia were nonetheless remarkably peaceful. Even the most convinced proponents of China as a model for Europe qualified their enthusiasm by acknowledging the stagnation of scientific learning in China relative to European advances in the preceding century or two. Nevertheless, neither Leibniz and Voltaire, nor the Jesuit writers whose accounts inspired them, saw any contradiction between relative stagnation in the sciences and excellence in the art of government and in moral philosophy. After all, European advances in the sciences had occurred in the context of generalized warfare, state breakdowns and social strife, and had done little to produce stable government and tranquil lives (Adas 1989: 81–9).

The contrast between peace and stable government, on the one hand, and war and scientific progress, on the other, was symptomatic of an ongoing fundamental divergence between the trajectories of the East Asian and European regional systems. For the same inter-state competition that propelled the capitalist transformation of the European system was relentlessly prompting its globalization as well. As William McNeill sums up with specific reference to the period 1600–1750:

> Within the cockpit of western Europe, one improved modern-style army shouldered hard against its rivals. This led to only local and temporary disturbances of the balance of power, which diplomacy proved able to contain. Toward the margins of the European radius of action, however, the result was systematic expansion – whether in India, Siberia or the Americas. Frontier expansion in turn sustained an

expanding trade network, enhanced taxable wealth in Europe, and made support of the armed establishment less onerous than would otherwise have been the case. Europe, in short, launched itself on a self-reinforcing cycle in which its military organization sustained, and was sustained by, economic and political expansion at the expense of other peoples and polities of the earth.

(1982: 143)

No self-reinforcing cycle of this kind could be observed in East Asia. Qing China did expand its frontiers north and west, but the economic benefits of expansion fell far short of what would have been required to sustain the costs of an armament race, European-style. As Wong points out, the logic of political economy emphasizing competition with foreign states had little in common with China's emphasis on the mutual benefits of domestic exchange:

> Rather than extract resources from peripheries, the Chinese state was more likely to invest in them. Political expansion to incorporate new frontiers committed the government to a shift of resources to the peripheries, not extraction from them. Late imperial Chinese political economy obeyed a set of principles very much at odds with those of [European] mercantilism.
>
> (1997: 148)

The same principle that Wong notes for China's domestic peripheries to a large extent applied also to peripheral regions of the tributary-trade system.

As previously noted, the separate political jurisdictions of the East Asian inter-state system did in a sense compete with one another. Sugihara (1996: 37–8), for example, detects a competitive relation in two complementary tendencies typical of Tokugawa Japan: its attempt to create a tribute-trade system centered on Japan instead of China, and its extensive absorption of technological and organizational knowledge in agriculture, mining and manufacturing from Korea and China. In other words, as Heita Kawakatsu (1994: 6–7) put it, "Japan was trying to become a mini-China both ideologically and materially." In this endeavor Japan was eventually highly successful, matching and eventually overtaking Qing China's industrious revolution (see Sugihara, Chapter 3, this volume). Nevertheless, this kind of competition drove the East Asian developmental path not closer but further apart from the European: toward a deepening of the division of labor within households and micro-regions rather than between metropolitan core regions and overseas peripheral regions; toward short-distance (intra-regional) rather than long-distance (inter-regional) trade; toward state-making rather than war-making.

The extent of this divergence can be gauged by the opposite trends of foreign trade in the two systems in the eighteenth and early nineteenth centuries. In this period, a growing number and variety of European states and business organizations built overseas commercial empires of growing scale, scope and sophistication. As a result of these activities, European trade not only expanded far more rapidly than in the seventeenth century, but it expanded so as to promote a division of labor with the Americas that enabled European core regions to specialize in labor-saving and land- and energy-intensive directions. East Asian states, in contrast, showed no tendency whatsoever to build overseas commercial empires. Even trade contacts among Asian countries, as Sugihara acknowledges, "shrank sharply from the early-18th century and did not recover until the West forced China and Japan to open their ports to foreign trade in the middle of the 19th century" (1996: 38–9). As a result, the very success of the industrious revolution both in China and Japan intensified the shortage of natural resources, forcing development in both countries along ever more resource-saving, labor-intensive paths.

Under these circumstances, capitalism in the East Asian region continued to expand but remained an interstitial formation. As William Skinner notes, the scorched earth policy through which the Qing denied mainland resources to Zheng's Taiwan regime destroyed the prosperity of China's southeast coast:

> for periods of varying lengths between 1661 and 1683, the population of the coastal strip from Zhejiang to Guangdong was forcibly removed inland, and most settlements – villages, market towns, and cities – were burned to the ground. In 1717 Chinese were forbidden once again to go privately overseas, and in 1757 the fate of the whole Southeast Coast region was sealed for nearly a century by the designation of Guangzhou as the sole legal port for foreign trade.

The economic decline and then stagnation of the southeast coast over the next 150 years, in turn, provoked dramatic centrifugal effects:

> Millions emigrated permanently and tens of thousands left the region to spend their productive years elsewhere ... By 1800 Hakkas from the Han Basin subregion were settled in permanent enclaves in Sichuan, Taiwan, West Borneo, and Bangka, and merchants from Zhangquan subregion were firmly established in great commercial centers throughout Southeast Asia and in every other macroregion of China.
>
> (Skinner 1985: 278–9)

These migrations further expanded the scale and scope of Chinese trading networks on the outer boundaries and interstices of the East Asian tribute trade system. The main beneficiaries of this expansion, however, were neither East Asian states nor the overseas Chinese. The inward-looking developmental policies of Qing China and Tokugawa Japan left a political void in the maritime regions of East and Southeast Asia that the demilitarized Chinese merchants were ill-equipped to fill.[6] Gradually, the void was filled by European states, companies and merchants whose capacity to subordinate to their own ends the Overseas Chinese increased rapidly at the turn of the eighteenth and nineteenth centuries. Critical in this respect was the continuing decline of Chinese shipbuilding industries and navigation technologies at a time of rapid European advances in both (Tian 1974: 281; Cushman 1993: 136; Hui 1995: 79–80).

Rapid improvements in shipbuilding industries and navigation technologies were but one aspect of the great leap forward of European capabilities that ensued from the so-called first industrial revolution. This was not the outcome of greater European advances along the industrious revolution path and the formation of market economies, since in both respects the East Asian region was equally if not more advanced, as Sugihara, Pomeranz and Hamilton and Chang (this volume) argue from different perspectives. Rather, it was the culmination of three-to-four centuries of operation of McNeill's "self-reinforcing cycle" of escalating intra-European military competition sustaining, and in turn being sustained by economic and political expansion at the expense of other peoples and polities of the earth. This self-reinforcing cycle did not just create the kind of core–periphery relations between Europe and the Americas that according to Pomeranz enabled Britain to open up the land- and energy-intensive industrial-revolution path. It played also a decisive role in creating the conditions for the "take-off" of the revolution in the capital goods industries. As McNeill underscores:

> both the absolute volume of production and the mix of products that came from British factories and forges, 1793–1815, was profoundly affected by government expenditures for war purposes. In particular, government demand created a precocious iron industry, in excess of peacetime needs, as the postwar depression 1816–20 showed. But it also created the condition for future growth by giving British ironmasters extraordinary incentives for finding new uses for the cheaper products their new, large-scale furnaces were able to turn out. Military demands on the British economy thus went far to shape the subsequent phases of the industrial revolution, allowing the improvement of steam engines and making such critical innovations as the iron railway and iron ships possible at a time and under conditions which simply would not have existed without the wartime impetus to iron production.
>
> (1982: 211–12)

This wartime impetus to production in Britain's capital goods industries was associated with a massive expansion of British public expenditure from £22 million in 1792 to £123 million in 1815. Such an expansion was out of all proportions to Britain's tax revenue, resulting in a three-fold increase in the sum needed annually to service the British public debt from £9 million in 1783 to £30 million in 1815 (Jenks 1938: 17; Dickson 1967: 9; Ingham 1984: 106). It is hard to imagine how this massive expansion of British public expenditure and debt could have occurred (let alone boosted British wealth and power, instead of undermining them), were it not for the fact that prior to the start of the Napoleonic Wars Britain had bought back the national debt from the Dutch, and London had displaced Amsterdam as the main financial entrepôt of Europe and the Americas (Arrighi 1994: 108–12; Arrighi and Silver *et al.* 1999: 51–6).

It is in this connection that the contemporaneous shift of British territorial expansion from North America to South Asia acquires its full world historical significance. It has been authoritatively stated that the plunder perpetrated by the East India Company following its military victory at Plassey "did not start the Industrial Revolution, but it did help Britain to buy back the National Debt from the Dutch" (Cain and Hopkins 1980: 471). More important, Plassey plunder initiated the process of conquest of a territorial empire in India that, as we shall see in the next section, was an essential ingredient of the nineteenth-century globalization of the UK-centered system of rule and accumulation. This globalization radically changed the relationship between the European and East Asian regional systems. The two systems' interacting but separate dynamics of previous centuries began to merge into a single dynamic – the dynamic, that is, of the subordinate incorporation of the East Asian regional system within the structures of the globalizing European system. To this new dynamic we now turn.

East Asia in the UK-centered global capitalist system

In analyzing the subordinate incorporation of East Asia within the structures of the globalizing European system, we shall begin by underscoring the Asian foundations of British global supremacy in the nineteenth and early twentieth centuries. Our argument will be that tribute extracted from India, rather than any special competitive advantage in commodity markets was central to Britain's ability to occupy and retain for more than a century the position of political and economic center of the globalizing European system. We shall further argue that the need to facilitate the transfer of Indian tribute to the British center was the primary motivation of the British-led onslaught on the China-centered tribute-trade system. The onslaught transformed but did not destroy the legacy of that system.

At first, the resulting dynamic had disastrous consequences for the power, wealth and welfare of the region's states and peoples. Over time, however, it created conditions conducive to the East Asian economic renaissance of the late twentieth century.

The Asian foundations of the UK-centered global capitalist system

Contrary to widespread opinion, Britain's nineteenth-century global supremacy was not based on any kind of superiority in the way in which its business enterprises were organized. In Britain no less than in China, family enterprise was the rule in most branches of manufacturing, commerce and finance:

> The popularity of family-oriented enterprise in eighteenth- and nineteenth-century Britain was a product of a complex array of legal, economic and cultural forces. With the spectre of bankruptcy ever present, a combination of the common law partnership and unlimited liability meant that many businessmen preferred to be associated with their family connections than outsiders ... Once established ... a peculiarly British type of familial capitalism persisted and evolved through the nineteenth century and into the twentieth.
>
> (Rose 1994: 63–4)

To this we should add that in the West "familial capitalism" became even more dominant in the nineteenth century than it had been in the preceding two centuries. By the end of the eighteenth century joint-stock chartered companies had become an endangered species, with its remaining specimen – the English East India Company – leading an increasingly precarious existence until the abolition of the Company's China trade monopoly in 1833 sounded its death knell. As this early form of Western corporate capitalism withered away, first in the Atlantic and later in Asia, "the more flexible system of competitive enterprise emerged triumphant" (Davies 1957: 46; see also Arrighi 1994: 244–50; Arrighi et al. 1999: 104–6, 114–16).

This more flexible system of competitive enterprise consisted of networks of family businesses. It is often stated that Chinese capitalism did not experience the kind of vertical integration that gave rise to the multidivisional, multi-national corporation typical of twentieth-century US capitalism (see, for example, Faure 1996: 26 and Wong 1997: 57–8). What is just as often forgotten is that throughout the entire period of British hegemony British capitalism also failed to experience vertical integration. Indeed, if anything, British business seems to have been more vertically integrated at the beginning than at the end of the nineteenth century.

Thus, in the early stages of the industrial revolution, leading London and provincial textile manufacturers had ventured into the direct procurement of raw cotton in the United States and the West Indies. After the end of the Napoleonic Wars, however, they found it more profitable to specialize in production at home, leaving the purchase of inputs and sale of outputs in the hands of specialized firms that promoted and financed the formation of truly global networks of commission agents and small general merchants (Chapman 1984: 9–15; 1992: 116; see also Farnie 1979: 83). In manufacturing itself, an early tendency toward the vertical integration of spinning and weaving was reversed after 1850. As a result, at the turn of the nineteenth and twentieth centuries, the British system of business enterprise was more than ever an ensemble of highly specialized family firms held together by a complex web of commercial transactions – a web that was centered on Britain but spanned the entire world (Copeland 1966: 371; Tyson 1968: 119; Hobsbawm 1968: 47–8; Gattrell 1977: 118–20; Crouzet 1982: 204–5, 212; Arrighi et al. 1999: 126–8).

The global competitiveness of British business was due not to any peculiarity of its units but to the world-encompassing nature of British commercial networks. As Melvin Copeland has underscored with special reference to the cotton industry, the fragmented structure of British business involved very high transaction costs. Nevertheless, these high transaction costs were more than compensated for by the advantages of being located at the center of dense networks of specialists connected to the markets of the entire world by a highly flexible commercial network (1966: 327–9; 371).

As foreign competitors developed techniques of production, procurement and distribution more efficient than the British, either through vertical integration (most notably in the United States) or horizontal combinations (most notably in Germany), British business could meet the challenge by specializing more fully in the high-value-added activities associated with Britain's role as the central entrepôt of world commerce and finance. It was precisely at the time of waning industrial supremacy that

> [Britain's] finance triumphed, her services as shipper, trader, insurance broker, and intermediary in the world's system of payments, became more indispensable. Indeed, if London ever was the real economic hub of the world, the pound sterling its foundation, it was between 1870 and 1913.
>
> (Hobsbawm 1968: 125)

As Halford Mackinder told a group of London bankers at the turn of the century, the industrialization of other countries enhanced the importance of a single clearing house. And the world's clearing house "will always be where there is the greatest ownership of capital." The British "are essentially the people who have capital, and those who have capital always share in the activity of brains and muscles of other countries" (quoted in Hugill 1993: 305). This was certainly the case on the eve of the First World War, when nearly one-half of Britain's assets were overseas and about 10 percent of its national income consisted of interest on foreign investment (Cairncross 1953: 3, 23).

As Peter Mathias (1969: 329) noted, British foreign investment "was not just 'blind capital' but the 'blind capital' of *rentiers* organized by financiers and businessmen very much with a view to the trade that would be flowing when the enterprise was under way." British railway building in the United States, and *a fortiori* in countries like Australia, Canada, South Africa and Argentina "was instrumental in opening up these vast land masses and developing export sectors in primary produce ... for Britain" (see also Chapman, 1992: 233ff.). Capital lending was no less "blind" in creating outlets for Britain's own exports:

> The complex of activities into which capital lending fitted can be most clearly seen in such a case as China where the British firm Jardine Matheson was in the lead. They organized the raising of loans to Chinese provincial governments (on which they took the margin). They supplied the railways at a profit, sometimes shipped the equipment on their own shipping lines, which brought in freight charges, and supplied equipment and arms to the contestants in the wars whose strategy was being shaped by the railways.
>
> (Mathias 1969: 328)

The abundant liquidity that accumulated in, or passed through, British hands was a powerful instrument in the competitive struggle not just in commodity markets but in the armament race as well. From the mid-1840s through the 1860s most technological breakthroughs in the design of warships were pioneered by France. And yet, each French breakthrough called forth naval appropriations in Britain that the French could not match, so that it was "relatively easy for the Royal Navy to catch up technically and surpass numerically each time the French changed the basis of the competition" (McNeill 1982: 227–8).

Britain's role as the central entrepôt of world commerce and finance that underlaid the competitiveness of British business was the outcome of a long drawn-out process. It originated in Britain's growing supremacy in European colonial and overseas trade in the eighteenth and early nineteenth centuries but became truly global in scope only when Britain liberalized its trade *unilaterally*. In the twenty years following the repeal of the Corn Laws in 1848 and of the Navigation Acts in 1849, close to one-third of the exports of the rest of the world went to Britain. Massive and rapidly expanding imports cheapened the costs of vital supplies in Britain, while providing the means of payment for the rest of the world to buy British manufactures. A large and growing number of states and territories were thus "caged" in a world-scale division of labor that strengthened each one's interest in participating in the British-centered global market, the more so as that market became virtually the sole source of critical inputs and sole outlet for remuneratively disposing of outputs.

But if unilateral free trade enabled Britain to consolidate and expand its role as the central commercial and financial entrepôt of the world, it was its overseas empire that provided Britain with the flexibility and resources needed to keep expanding the sway of the British-centered global market and to practice free trade unilaterally in spite of persistent deficits in its balance of trade (see, among others, Frank 1978). Critical in both respects was Britain's Indian empire. India's huge demographic resources buttressed Britain's global power both militarily and financially. Militarily, in Lord Salisbury's words, "India was an English barrack in the Oriental Seas from which we may draw any number of troops without paying for them" (Tomlinson 1975: 341). Paid for entirely by the Indian tax-payer, these troops were organized in a European-style colonial army and used regularly in the endless series of wars (by one count, seventy-two separate campaigns between 1837 and 1900) through which Britain opened up Asia and Africa to Western trade, investment and influence. They were "the iron fist in the velvet glove of Victorian expansionism ... the major coercive force behind the internationalization of industrial capitalism" (Washbrook 1990: 481).

Military manpower was not the only kind of tribute that Britain extracted from India. Equally important, the infamous Home Charges and the Bank of England's control over India's foreign exchange reserves, jointly turned India into the "pivot" of Britain's global financial and commercial supremacy. India's balance of payments deficit with Britain and surplus with the rest of the world enabled Britain to settle its deficit on current account with the rest of the world. Without India's forcible contribution to the balance of payments of Imperial Britain, it would have been impossible for the latter "to use the income from her overseas investment for further investment abroad, and to give back to the international monetary system the liquidity she absorbed as investment income." Moreover, Indian monetary reserves "provided a large *masse de manœuvre* which British monetary authorities could use to supplement their own reserves and to keep London the centre of the international monetary system" (de Cecco, 1984: 62–3).

In sum, the nineteenth-century UK-centered global capitalist system rested from beginning to end on tribute from India. It was tribute from India that made possible the sixfold increase in British public expenditure that in 1792–1815 laid the foundations of British supremacy in the capital goods industries over the next half century. And it was tribute from India that consolidated Britain's centrality in world-scale processes of capital accumulation when its industrial supremacy began to wane. Tribute and trade were thus as closely interwoven in the UK-centered global system as they were in the China-centered regional system. The difference is that the tribute that India paid to Britain – at first as sheer plunder and then, increasingly, in the form of military manpower and means of payments – was a form of coercively imposed taxation that had no counterpart in the East Asian system. Substantively, it corresponded more closely to the original meaning of the Chinese term for "tribute" (chao-gong) than did relations in the China-centered tribute-trade system. In this term, chao means the act of submission through which vassal states sought recognition from the central state, while gong means the valuable offerings of the vassal states to the central state – a coercively imposed tax. Ever since the establishment of a unified taxation system under the Qin and Han dynasties more than two thousand years ago, however, tributary relations between the Chinese imperial court and its vassal states no longer included the collection of a tax. On the contrary, especially after the Tang dynasty, and with the sole exception of the Yuan dynasty, vassal states offered the imperial court only symbolic gifts and received in return much more valuable gifts. What was nominally "tribute," was in fact a two-way transaction motivated by the symbolic or material interests of the vassal and central states – a two-way transaction in which the vassals often benefited economically far more than the central state (Gao 1993: 1–78).

The human and material resources that Britain extracted from India, in contrast, were and remained a coercively imposed tax. Moreover, they were essential to Britain's capacity to hold the center of the global capitalist system. The mobilization and deployment of Indian tribute on the scale required to reproduce and consolidate this capacity, however, presented difficult problems. It was precisely this challenge that drove Britain to clash with China in the two mid-nineteenth century Opium Wars.

Throughout the first half of the nineteenth century, opium was, in Joseph Esherick's words, "the West's only feasible entree into the China market" (1972: 10). More precisely, it was the only commodity that could contain the hemorrhage of silver from the West to China. From a British perspective, the main significance of British sales of Indian opium to China lay in the role that such sales played in facilitating the transfer of Indian tribute to the metropolis. As the head of the statistical department at the East India House put it in explaining the triangular relationship: "India, by exporting opium, assists in supplying England with tea. China by consuming opium, facilitates the revenue operations between India and England. England by consuming tea contributes to increase the demand for the opium of India" (Thornton 1835: 89).

The need to expand the India–China trade in order to facilitate the revenue operations between India and England had been from the start the main stimulus behind the expansion of the opium trade. As early as 1786, Lord Cornwallis, then Governor General of India, saw the expansion of the India–China trade as essential to paying at least in part for Chinese exports of tea and silk to Britain and other European countries and, above all, as the only way in which the vast tribute of Bengal could be transferred to England *without heavy losses through exchange depreciation* (Bagchi 1982: 96; Greenberg 1951: Chapter 2). When the abrogation of the India trade monopoly induced the East India Company to redouble its efforts in promoting opium smuggling into China, shipments expanded rapidly (more than threefold between 1803–13 and 1823–33) and the soundness of Cornwallis' advice was fully vindicated. In the words of a contemporary account, from the opium trade:

> The Honourable Company has derived for years an immense revenue and through them the British Government and nation have also reaped an incalculable amount of political and financial advantage. The turn of the balance of trade between Great Britain and China in favour of the former has enabled India to increase tenfold her consumption of British manufacture; contributed directly to support the vast fabric of British dominion in the East, to defray the expenses of His Majesty's establishment in India, and by the operation of exchanges and remittances in teas, to pour an abundant revenue into the British Exchequer and benefit the nation to an extent of £6 million yearly.
>
> (Quoted in Greenberg 1951: 106–7)

The "Honourable Company" was squeezed out of this lucrative branch of British commerce by the abrogation of its China monopoly in 1833. But the abrogation further emboldened the forces of free trade, which went on to agitate for "the strong arm of England" to bring down the restrictions that the Chinese government imposed on their freedom of action. The Chinese government for its part, far from yielding to British pressures, moved swiftly to suppress a trade that was as baneful for China as it was beneficial for Britain. Beyond the deleterious impact on the fabric of Chinese society of a growing number of addicts, the opium trade had highly disruptive political and economic effects on the Chinese state.

The proceeds of opium smuggling trickled down to Chinese officials whose corruption seriously impaired the execution of official policy in all spheres and directly and indirectly fed social unrest. At the same time, the trade caused a massive and growing drain of silver from China to India: 1.6 million taels a year in 1814–24; 2.1 million taels a year in 1824–37; and 5.6 million taels a year in the two years preceding the first Opium War (Yen *et al.* 1957: 34). Taking the period 1815–50 as a whole, 150 million Mexican Silver Dollars flowed out of China (Lin 1991: 11). As the imperial edict of 1838 emphasized in announcing the decision to destroy the trade, the effects of the drain on the financial and fiscal integrity of the Chinese state (and, by implication, on its capacity to hold the center of the East Asian regional system) were devastating. "If steps not be taken for our defence," declared the edict, "the useful wealth of China will be poured into the fathomless abyss of transmarine regions" (quoted in Greenberg 1951: 143) – a "pouring," we may add, which is precisely what the British were after.

In putting the vigorous and incorruptible Lin Zexu in charge of the suppression of opium smuggling, the Chinese government had no intention of thwarting commercial opportunities in other branches of China's foreign trade, such as silk, tea and cotton goods, which it continued to encourage. Lin himself was careful in drawing a distinction between the illegal opium trade – which he was determined to suppress with or without the cooperation of the British government – and other, legal forms of trade, which he invited the British government to encourage as a substitute for the illegal traffic (Waley 1958: 18, 28–31, 46, 123; Hao 1986: 113–15). But having failed to persuade the British government to cooperate in the suppression of the traffic in the name of international law and common morality, he proceeded to confiscate and destroy smuggled opium and to incarcerate some smugglers. This police operation was denounced in the British Parliament as "a grievous sin – a wicked offence – an atrocious violation of justice, for which England had the right, a strict and undeniable right," by "the law of God and man," "to demand reparation by force if refused peaceable applications" (quoted in Semmel 1970: 153; see also Owen 1934).

Evidently, two quite different views of international law and common morality held sway in Britain and China. But while the Chinese view claimed a right to lay down and enforce the law only at home, the British view claimed a right to lay down and enforce the law not just at home but in China as well. To paraphrase Karl Marx (1959: 235), between equal rights force decides, and Britain had all the firepower it needed to make its view of right and wrong prevail over the Chinese. China had no answer to the steam-powered warship that in a single day in February 1841 destroyed nine war junks, five forts, two military stations, and one shore battery (Parker 1989: 96). After a disastrous war, an explosion of major rebellions, and a second, equally disastrous war with Britain (now joined by France), China virtually ceased to be the center of a "world in itself" (the East Asian system) to become a subordinate member of the UK-centered global capitalist system.

East Asian dynamics under Western dominance

Marx and Engels famously claimed that cheap commodities were the "heavy artillery" with which the European bourgeoisie "batter[ed] down all Chinese Walls" (1967: 84). Contrary to this claim, even after British gunboats had battered down the wall of governmental regulations that enclosed the Chinese domestic economy, the British variant of family capitalism had a hard time in out-competing the Chinese variant both in China and throughout the East Asian region. From the 1830s imports of British cotton textiles did devastate some sectors and regions of the Chinese economy, most notably Jiangsu which had long been a base of nankeen production, re-processing, and exports. With the newly invented power loom enabling British manufacturers to quadruple output and halve price, and with world cotton prices falling as a result of widespread introduction of the cotton gin, the textile industries of the Lower Yangzi had a hard time surviving the competition of foreign-made cotton yarn (Johnson 1993: 171–4). Yet British cotton cloth was never able to compete in rural markets with stronger Chinese cloth. As late as 1894, indigenous handicraft industry still supplied 86 percent of the Chinese market for cotton cloth. By then, foreign imports were rapidly displacing handicraft spinning of cotton yarn, which suffered an estimated 50 percent contraction between 1871–80 and 1901–10. But the use of cheaper, machine-produced foreign yarn gave new impetus to the domestic weaving industry, which managed to hold its own and even expand (Feuerwerker 1970: 371–5; Wu 1987: 148; Xu *et al.* 1992: 155–7; see also Sugihara, Chapter 3, this volume, and Hamilton and Chang, Chapter 5, this volume).

The competitiveness of Western firms that set up production facilities within China was even less impressive. They could never penetrate effectively the vast interior of the country and had to rely on the indigenous Chinese traders for the supply of the raw materials and the marketing of their products (Kasaba 1993). In the case of silk and tea, as with opium, Chinese merchants made huge profits by cooperating with the Europeans, while others established their own businesses, gaining the upper hand in competing with foreign businesses (Chen 1984: 58–61; Xu *et al.* 1989: 75–81). In the silk industry, for example, foreign ventures incurred major losses, while local business prospered – the number of workers employed and exports of modern, Chinese-owned filatures increasing by a factor of 10 between the 1880s and the 1890s. "Foreigners" – lamented a British consul in Canton – "had little left to them other than the export trade" (So 1986: 103–16; So and Chiu 1995: 47). Western products and businesses did triumph in a few industries. But outside of railways and mines, the triumph was limited to such products as cigarettes, which did not compete with any indigenous product, and kerosene, which replaced local vegetable oil. Generally speaking, it is hard to dispute Andrew Nathan's observation that "the China market spelled frustration for foreign merchants. Foreign goods made but a superficial mark in Chinese markets" (1972: 5).

Opium, of course, was the great exception, leaving as it did a deep and long-lasting mark. But while the predominance of opium among Chinese imports throughout the nineteenth century may be taken as a measure of the continuing lack of competitiveness of most other foreign goods in the Chinese market, in the final analysis even the opium trade spelled frustration for foreign merchants. Access to the final consumers of the drug could be gained only through Chinese intermediaries organized in groups and networks on the basis of language, residence, kinship and political patronage. The "squeeze" that these intermediaries exercised on foreign merchants was the subject of recurrent complaints. Even when formally employed by foreign merchants, Chinese middlemen, in all trades, often made more money than their Western principals; they were quick to learn what there was to be learned of Western business techniques; and in competing with foreign firms they had the great advantage of much lower overheads and of not being "squeezed" by a middleman (Hao 1970: 110–11; Murphey 1977: 192–3; Hui 1995: 91, 96–8). By the end of the nineteenth century, these advantages had enabled Chinese traders to develop their own domestic supplies of opium, cutting imports sharply and destroying Britain's grip on the opium trade. Between 1870 and 1900 opium fell from 43 percent to 15 percent of Chinese imports (Feuerwerker 1980: 9, 489).

Far from destroying indigenous forms of family capitalism, the subordinate incorporation of China within the structures of the UK-centered global capitalist system led to a renewed expansion of the Chinese merchant networks and communities that over the previous millennium had developed in the coastal regions of China and in the interstices of the China-centered tribute-trade system. As the capacity of the Qing government to control channels between the Chinese domestic economy and the outer world declined in the wake of the Opium Wars and intervening domestic rebellions, profitable opportunities for Chinese merchants operating within these networks and communities proliferated. Many of these merchants made their "first tank of gold" in the opium trade. But the greatest expansion of the Overseas Chinese capitalist stratum was based on the "coolie trade," the procurement and transshipment of indentured labor for service overseas and bank profits on their remittances home. The transformation of much of the "periphery" of the China-centered system into a major source of raw materials for European countries created a sudden expansion in the demand for cheap labor in the region. At the same time, the ongoing disintegration of the political economy of the Qing inflated the surplus population in China and undermined the capacity of the regime to interfere with the resettlement of the surplus overseas. As a result, between 1851 and 1900, more than two million "contract laborers" were shipped off from China, two-thirds of them to Southeast Asia (Hui 1995: 108–9, 115, 138–41; Northup 1995). From another perspective, we can locate this resettlement as the latest phase in the long-term expansion of Chinese laborers and merchants into Southeast Asia, the basis for the deepening economic bonds linking the region.

The boom in the coolie trade boosted the expansion of the Overseas Chinese trading diaspora in several related ways. Although transportation was in the hands of European shipping companies, most other branches of the trade were controlled by Chinese secret societies in the major ports of China and Southeast Asia. Profits were high and became the foundation of many new fortunes among Chinese merchants. Besides making the fortunes of individual merchants, the coolie trade also made the fortunes of the port-cities of Singapore, Hong Kong, Penang and Macao, all of which to varying degrees became major seats and "containers" of the wealth and power of the Chinese business diaspora, and all of which became home to large overseas Chinese populations even as these localities became key nodes of European colonialism in the region. Equally important, the coolie trade, like earlier migrations, left a legacy of Chinese settlement throughout Southeast Asia that strengthened the capacity of the Overseas Chinese to profit from one form or another of commercial and financial intermediation within and across jurisdictions in the East Asian region (Peng 1981: 196–200; Headrick 1988: 259–303; Lin and Zhang 1991: 173; Hui 1995: 127–38, 142–5, 149–53; 1997: 118).

As in earlier periods of strengthening of their position, the capitalist stratum of the Overseas Chinese benefited from the fiscal and financial pressures faced by the late Qing as a result of wars, rebellions, worsening trade conditions, and natural disasters. These pressures forced the Qing court not only to relax controls on their activities but to turn to the Overseas Chinese for financial assistance. The fact that anti-Qing forces, from the Taiping to various organizations associated with Sun Zhongshan, were very active in Overseas Chinese centers was a further reason for seeking closer ties with Overseas Chinese business networks. In exchange for assisting the Qing court, the Overseas Chinese obtained offices, titles, protection for their properties and connections in China, and access to the highly profitable arms trade and government loan business (Huang 1974: 251–2; Lin and Zhang 1991: 180–90; Tsai 1993: 63). These closer ties were not an unmixed blessing for the Overseas Chinese. From the start, they were the cause of tension with the governments in which they resided or did business (Tate 1979: 22; Tsai 1993: 82, 90). Nevertheless, up to the final collapse of the Qing in 1911 the Overseas Chinese capitalist stratum managed to profit from the intensifying competition among the region's governments, both indigenous and colonial (Hui 1995: Chapter 3).

The revitalization of Chinese family capitalism in China and overseas was not the only result of the intensification of inter-state competition that ensued from the subordinate incorporation of East Asia within the structures of the UK-centered global system. Its most important result for at least one century was the launching of major industrialization drives both in China and Japan. Kawakatsu has maintained that the strongest motivation for Japanese industrialization "was not so much a process of catching up with the West, but more a result of centuries-long competition within Asia" (1994: 6–7). Similarly, Hamashita has argued that Japanese industrialization was a response to Japanese difficulties in successfully competing with Chinese rather than Western business networks:

> The main reason why Japan chose the direction of industrialization was its defeat in attempts to expand commercial relations with China. Japanese merchants faced the well-established power of overseas Chinese merchants built through the Dejima trade in Nagasaki during the Edo period. Chinese merchants monopolized the export business for sea-foods and native commodities and Japanese merchants simply could not break their hold.
>
> (1988: 20)

Japanese industrialization, and the territorial and commercial expansion of Japan that went with it (including the imposition of unequal treaties on China and Japan's colonial acquisition of a range of territories in East Asia) were indeed a continuation by new means and in a new systemic context of the centuries-long Japanese attempt to re-center upon itself the East Asian tribute trade system. And as we have ourselves just argued, in most consumer goods industries Chinese business networks were hard to out-compete not just by Japanese but by Western business networks as well. Nevertheless, the change in systemic context transformed radically the nature of the inter-state competition that had characterized the East Asian system since the consolidation of the Tokugawa and Qing regimes and made competition in the capital goods industries far more important politically and economically than competition in the consumer industries. In the new context, inter-state competition within East Asia was inseparable from attempts to catch up with Western proficiency in the capital goods industries, whose modernization (in East Asia no less than in Europe) was intimately associated with the enhancement of military capabilities.

The Opium Wars revealed brutally the full implications of Western military superiority, and thereby awoke the ruling groups of China and Japan to the imperatives of accelerated military modernization. The awakening led the scholar-official Wei Yuan to develop the old idea of using the barbarians to control the barbarians into the new idea of using barbarian *armaments* (and the means to produce them) to control the barbarians (Tsiang 1967: 144). In China the idea became central to the Self-Strengthening Movement that took off after the second Opium War (cf. Fairbank 1983: 197–8; So and Chiu 1995: 49–50). A few years later the Meiji Restoration also embraced the idea and propelled Japan along the same path of rapid modernization. The armament race that had long been a feature of the European inter-state system was thus "internalized" by the East Asian system.

For about twenty-five years after they were launched, industrialization efforts yielded similar economic results in China and Japan. On the eve of the Sino-Japanese War of 1894, in Albert Feuerwerker's assessment, "the disparity between the degree of modern economic development in the two countries was not yet flagrant" (1958: 53). Nevertheless, Japan's victory in the war was symptomatic of a fundamental difference in the impact of the industrialization drive on the social and political fabric of the two countries. In China, the main agency of the drive was provincial authorities, whose power *vis-à-vis* the central government had increased considerably in the course of the repression of the rebellions of the 1850s, and who used industrialization to consolidate their autonomy in competition with one another. In Japan, in contrast, the industrialization drive was an integral aspect of the Meiji Restoration that centralized power in the hands of the central government and disempowered provincial authorities (So and Chiu 1995: 53, 68–72).

The outcome of the Sino-Japanese war, in turn, deepened the underlying divergence in the trajectories of Japanese and Chinese industrialization. On the one hand, China's defeat weakened national cohesion, initiating half a century of political chaos marked by further restrictions on sovereignty, crushing war indemnities, the final collapse of the Qing regime and the growing autonomy of semi-sovereign warlords, followed by Japanese invasion, and recurrent civil wars between the forces of Nationalism and Communism. On the other hand, victory over China in 1894, followed by victory over Russia in the war of 1904–5, established Japan – to paraphrase Akira Iriye (1970: 552) – as "a respectable participant in the game of imperialist politics," a position perhaps best substantiated by the Anglo-Japanese alliance from 1902. The acquisition of Chinese territory, most notably, Taiwan in 1895, followed by the Liaodong peninsula and the securing of all Russian rights and privileges in South Manchuria in 1905, and culminating in China's recognition of Japanese suzerainty over Korea (annexed as a colony in 1910), provided Japan with valuable outposts from which to launch future attacks on China, as well as with secure overseas supplies of cheap food, raw materials and markets (Peattie 1984: 16–18).[7] At the same time, Chinese indemnities amounting to more than one-third of Japan's GNP helped Japan to finance the expansion of heavy industry and to put its currency on the gold standard. This, in turn, improved Japan's credit rating in London and its capacity to tap additional funds for industrial expansion at home and imperialist expansion overseas (Feis 1965: 422–3; Duus 1984: 143, 161–2).

This bifurcation of the Japanese and Chinese developmental paths culminated in the 1930s in the eclipsing of Britain by Japan as the dominant power in the region. With the Japanese seizure of Manchuria in 1931, followed by the occupation of North China in 1935, full-scale invasion in an undeclared war on China from 1937 and the subsequent conquest of parts of Inner Asia and much of Southeast Asia, ousting European powers originally occupying these areas, Japan seemed to be finally succeeding in re-centering upon itself the East Asian region. The Japanese bid for regional supremacy, however, could not be sustained, not only because of the failure in the course of a fifteen-year war to subjugate China, but also because Japan, following the Pearl Harbor attack, simultaneously fought the United States and its allies. Both fronts would exact heavy burdens on an overburdened Japan, leading to a rollback of its advances in Southeast Asia and the Pacific as early as 1942. As the massive destruction inflicted on Japan by the US strategic bombing campaign in the final months of the war demonstrated even before Hiroshima and Nagasaki, Japanese advances in Western military technology could not keep up with the most powerful military-industrial complex of the era, the USA. But the Japanese bid collapsed also because it called forth in China countervailing forces as firmly opposed to Japanese as to Western domination. Once the Japanese had been defeated, the formation of the People's Republic of China would contest Western hegemonic drives in a struggle for centrality in East Asia that has shaped trends and events in the region ever since.

US hegemony and the East Asian economic renaissance

The establishment of US hegemony at the end of the Second World War thoroughly transformed inter-state relations within the East Asian region and the world at large. The transformation involved a foreign military presence in East Asia that had no precedent even at the height of late nineteenth- and early twentieth-century imperialism. At the same time, however, it involved the emergence of hybrid forms of inter-state relations that combined features of the historic European and East Asian regional systems. It was in this context that the East Asian region began to experience an economic renaissance that recent setbacks have slowed down but not reversed. In this section, we shall first sketch the change in the regional political economic context that ensued from the establishment of US hegemony and the trajectory of the subsequent regional economic expansion. We shall then show how this expansion has deep roots in the multiple historical legacies of the region.

The context and trajectory of the East Asian economic renaissance

The US military occupation of Japan in 1945 and the division of the region in the aftermath of the Korean War into two antagonistic blocs created, in Bruce Cumings' words, a US "vertical regime solidified through bilateral defense treaties (with Japan, South Korea, Taiwan and the Philippines) and conducted by a State Department that towered over the foreign ministries of these four countries."

> All became semisovereign states, deeply penetrated by U.S. military structures (operational control of the South Korean armed forces, Seventh Fleet patrolling of the Taiwan Straits, defense dependencies for all four countries, military bases on their territories) and incapable of independent foreign policy or defense initiatives ... There were minor demarches through the military curtain beginning in the mid-1950s, such as low levels of trade between Japan and China, or Japan and North Korea. But the dominant tendency until the 1970s was a unilateral U.S. regime heavily biased toward military forms of communication.
>
> (Cumings 1997: 155)

The militaristic nature of this unilateral US regime, strengthened by its rigid ideological commitments, had no precedent in the East Asian region, with the partial exception of the Yuan regime in the late thirteenth and early fourteenth centuries and the aborted Japanese regime in the early twentieth century. And yet, the interpenetration of tribute and trade relations between an imperial center whose economic might was incomparably greater than that of its vassal states invites comparison between the US regime and the old China-centered tribute-trade system. The contrast with the nineteenth-century UK-centered global capitalist system is clear. As we have seen, three closely related features characterized the latter: the global commercial and financial entrepôt functions exercised by Britain; Britain's unilateral free trade regime, which widened and deepened those functions; and massive tribute from India, which made Britain's unilateral free trade possible. In all three respects, the US-centered global capitalist system instituted after the end of the Second World War differed radically from its UK-centered predecessor. At the height of its hegemony, from the late 1940s through the 1960s, the United States exercised no entrepôt functions of global significance; nor did it practice free trade *unilaterally*; nor did it have an empire from which to extract coercively military manpower and means of payments. It was instead the "container" of a self-centered, largely self-sufficient, continent-sized economy. This giant state did promote the liberalization of trade but not through the unilateral opening up of its domestic market to the exports of the whole world, as Britain had done. Rather, it did so through a combination of bilateral and multilateral agreements with and among states that for all practical purposes were its vassals in the politico-military confrontation with the USSR (cf. Arrighi 1994: 67–72, 274–95).

At the same time, this US-centered system presented two important similarities with the early modern East Asian system centered on China. One was the disproportionately greater size of the central state's domestic market relative to all other domestic markets. And the other was the relationship of political and military vassalage *vis-à-vis* the central state that other states had to accept in order both to receive regime legitimation and to gain access to its domestic market. In this respect, we may well say that US supremacy in East Asia after the Second World War was realized through the transformation of the periphery of the former China-centered tribute-trade system into the periphery of a US-centered tribute-trade system, a transformation that was predicated on breaking their trade and other bonds with China. The US-centered system, however, was far more militaristic in structure and orientation than its China-centered predecessor. Not only was it based on a military-industrial apparatus of incomparably greater size, technological sophistication and destructive power, rather than on a culturally shared notion of a hierarchical world order. More important, the US-centered system also fostered a functional specialization between the imperial and the vassal states that had no precedent in the old China-centered system. As in the Iberian-Genoese relationship of political exchange of sixteenth-century Europe mentioned earlier, the United States specialized in the provision of protection and the pursuit of political power regionally and globally, while its East Asian vassal states specialized in trade and the pursuit of profit.[8]

This relationship of political exchange between the United States and Japan played a decisive role in launching the first and most spectacular of the late twentieth-century East Asian economic "miracles." As Franz Schurmann (1974: 143) wrote at a time when the "miracle" was still in the making, "freed from the burden of defense spending, Japanese governments have funneled all their resources and energies into an economic expansionism that has brought affluence to Japan and taken its business to the farthest reaches of the globe." Japan's economic expansion, in turn, generated a "snowballing" process of concatenated, labor-seeking rounds of investment that promoted and sustained a region-wide economic expansion (Ozawa 1993: 30–1; Arrighi 1996: 14–16).

The process is described in Figure 7.1 by means of successive descending flows of labor-seeking investment from higher- to lower-income jurisdictions and ascending counter-flows of labor-intensive exports. In this regional space-of-flows, labor-seeking investments mobilize the cheaper or more abundant labor supplies of lower-income locales to contain costs of

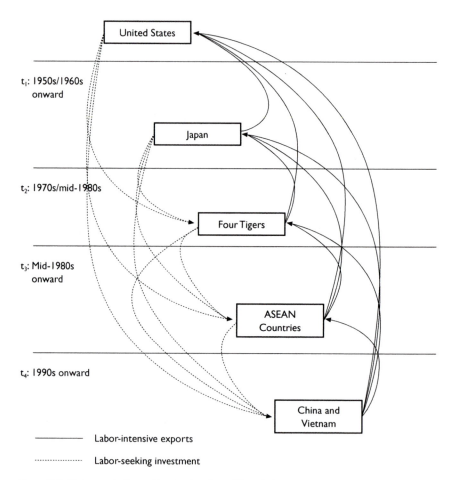

Figure 7.1 The snowballing effect in the rise of East Asia

Source: Adapted from Ozawa (1993: 143).

production and consumption in higher-income locales, while labor-intensive exports tap the wealthier or larger markets of higher-income locales to boost the prices fetched by the productive combinations of lower-income locales. Analogous spaces-of-flows have of course been in operation in other regional economies and in the global economy as a whole. We nonetheless concur with Terutomo Ozawa's contention that in East Asia the density and intensity of such a space have been greater than elsewhere and provide a good part of the explanation of the region's exceptionally good economic performance over the last half century.

This exceptional performance is perceived most clearly in the region's ascent in the global hierarchy of wealth and in the rapid increase in its share of the global market. The Gross National Product (GNP) of a particular state or group of states converted in US$ at market exchange rates measures the income or value added that accrues to the residents of that state or group of states. Expressed as a percentage of world GNP, it constitutes the best available measure of the share of the world market (or effective world demand) controlled by the residents of that state or group of states. Table 7.1 shows this percentage for different regions of the world from 1960 to the latest year for which data are available.[9]

The most striking feature of the table is the doubling of the East Asian share of world GNP between 1960 and 1999, in sharp contrast with the stagnant or declining share of most other regions. The only other regions whose share experienced a significant increase are the Middle East and

Table 7.1 Regional shares of world GNP (and population)

Region	1960	1970	1980	1990	1999
East Asia	13.0	19.5	21.8	25.9	25.9
	(38.2)	(38.3)	(38.0)	(37.1)	(35.9)
Australia and New Zealand	1.7	1.6	1.5	1.5	1.6
	(0.5)	(0.5)	(0.5)	(0.5)	(0.5)
North America	35.1	30.6	29.2	29.2	29.8
	(7.9)	(7.4)	(6.8)	(6.2)	(6.1)
South and Central America	5.8	5.7	7.0	5.6	5.8
	(8.2)	(8.8)	(9.3)	(9.5)	(9.7)
Western Europe	40.5	38.7	36.4	33.5	32.3
	(12.4)	(10.9)	(9.5)	(8.1)	(7.7)
Sub-Saharan Africa	1.3	1.3	1.2	1.0	1.0
	(6.8)	(7.2)	(7.8)	(8.8)	(9.4)
Middle East and North Africa	1.2	1.3	1.7	1.7	1.7
	(4.0)	(4.2)	(4.5)	(4.9)	(5.1)
South Asia	1.3	1.3	1.2	1.5	1.9
	(22.0)	(22.7)	(23.8)	(24.8)	(25.7)
Total	100.0	100.0	100.0	100.0	100.0
	(100.0)	(100.0)	(100.0)	(100.0)	(100.0)

Source: Our calculations based on World Bank (1984, 2001).

Notes
Countries included: East Asia: China, Hong Kong, Indonesia, Japan, South Korea, Malaysia, Philippines, Singapore, Taiwan, Thailand. North America: Canada, United States. South and Central America: Argentina, Bolivia, Brazil, Chile, Colombia, Costa Rica, Dominican Republic, Ecuador, El Salvador, Guatemala, Haiti, Honduras, Jamaica, Mexico, Nicaragua, Panama, Paraguay, Peru, Trinidad and Tobago, Uruguay, Venezuela. Western Europe: Austria, Belgium, Denmark, Finland, France, Germany, Luxembourg, Netherlands, Norway, Sweden, Switzerland, United Kingdom, Greece, Ireland, Israel, Italy, Portugal, Spain. Sub-Saharan Africa: Benin, Botswana, Burkina Faso, Burundi, Cameroon, Central African Republic, Chad, Rep. of Congo, Congo Dem. Rep., Cote d'Ivoire, Gabon, Ghana, Kenya, Lesotho, Madagascar, Malawi, Mauritania, Mauritius, Niger, Nigeria, Rwanda, Senegal, South Africa, Tanzania, Togo, Uganda, Zambia, Zimbabwe. Middle East and North Africa: Algeria, Arab Rep. of Egypt, Morocco, Saudi Arabia, Sudan, Syrian Arab Rep., Tunisia, Turkey. South Asia: Bangladesh, India, Nepal, Pakistan, Sri Lanka.

North Africa, broadly corresponding to the lands of the former Ottoman Empire (with an increase of 39.5 percent) and South Asia (with an increase of 47.7 percent). In both instances, however, the increase was less than half the increase in the East Asian share. More important, the share of both regions, unlike the East Asian share, was and remained rather insignificant, still accounting for less than 2 percent of world GNP at the end of the period. In the 1990s, the increase in the East Asian share tapered off. It is nonetheless noteworthy that the combination of the East Asian crisis and the North American resurgence contained rather than reversed the earlier trend toward a rise in the East Asian share and a decline in the North American share.

The nature and extent of the East Asian expansion can be brought into sharper relief by examining other indicators. An increase (decrease) in a region's or country's share of world GNP (or share of the world market) in itself does not tell us anything about that region's or country's rise or fall in the global value-added pecking order, because it may be due primarily or even exclusively to an increase (decrease) in that region's or country's share of world population. In order to gauge such a rise or fall, we must examine changes in relative GNP per capita (GNPPC). Thus, Table 7.2 shows the GNPPC of different regions as a percentage of "world" GNPPC and Table 7.3 shows the GNPPC of the different jurisdictions of the East Asian region also as a percentage of "world" GNPPC.

Table 7.2 highlights even more clearly than Table 7.1 the exceptionally strong economic performance of the East Asian region. Over the four decades recorded here, the region's ascent in the global value-added ranking surpassed by a wide margin that of any other region, its GNPPC rising more than twice as fast as the world average. The next best performing regions by this criterion (Western Europe and South Asia) improved their position relative to the world average by less than one-fourth the East

Table 7.2 Regional GNPPC as percentage of "world" GNPPC

Region	1960	1970	1980	1990	1999
East Asia	34.2	51.0	57.4	69.8	72.1
Australia and New Zealand	339.4	330.5	321.0	317.1	356.9
North America	442.9	415.7	432.8	468.9	489.4
South and Central America	70.7	65.0	75.7	58.9	59.9
Western Europe	327.6	353.4	384.2	411.4	417.4
Sub-Saharan Africa	18.8	17.4	15.5	11.8	10.5
Middle East and North Africa	31.2	31.1	37.5	35.5	33.9
South Asia	5.8	5.6	5.0	6.1	7.4
Weighted Average	100.0	100.0	100.0	100.0	100.0

Source: See Table 7.1.

Note
Countries included: see Table 7.1.

Table 7.3 Breakdown of East Asian GNPPC as percentage of "world" GNPPC

Jurisdiction	1960	1970	1980	1990	1999
China	3.3	2.7	3.5	6.4	12.4
Hong Kong	103.8	148.5	236.2	346.5	372.9
Taiwan	20.9	31.3	70.6	159.3	211.3
Singapore	105.9	152.0	236.3	369.6	461.7
Japan	281.9	500.3	577.8	715.2	703.8
South Korea	45.4	54.2	77.1	146.6	196.7
Malaysia	32.7	33.9	47.4	56.1	70.8
Thailand	15.5	19.0	23.3	36.4	43.7
Indonesia	8.6	7.5	10.1	13.7	14.9
Philippines	24.1	20.7	24.3	19.5	19.8
Weighted Average	34.2	51.0	57.4	69.8	72.1

Source: See Table 7.1.

Asian improvement.[10] Thanks to this exceptionally strong performance, East Asia was the only lower-income region that improved significantly its position relative to all three higher-income regions (North America, Western Europe and Australasia).

Despite its sustained character, the East Asian ascent has been a highly uneven process. As Table 7.3 shows, not only did the degree of overall advancement (or decline) in the course of the four decades vary considerably from jurisdiction to jurisdiction. In addition, the speed of the advance (or decline) varied from period to period. Taking the period as a whole, the best performers were Taiwan, Singapore, South Korea, China and Hong Kong, in that order – all but South Korea primary sites of residence of the Overseas Chinese. Table 7.3 also shows that the general advance of the region's jurisdictions (except for the Philippines, which lost ground relative to the world average) had only a minor impact on the huge income gaps that separate the wealthier from the poorer countries within the region. Thus, in spite of their advances, the two most populous countries in the region (China and Indonesia) remain low-income countries by world standards, while Japan has surpassed by a good margin the average GNPPC of the world's wealthiest regions. As a result, income inequalities among countries within the region not only continue to mirror income inequalities in the world at large, but are larger than in any other region of the world.[11]

A further dimension of the East Asian economic renaissance is the comparative success of the region's industrialization. The success can be gauged from Table 7.4, which shows regional shares of world value added in manufacturing for 1960, 1980 and 1998 (the latest year for which a minimally complete set of this kind of data is available). As Table 7.4 shows, East Asia was not the only region that increased its share of world

Table 7.4 Regional shares of "world" value added in manufacturing

Region	1960	1970	1980	1990	1998
East Asia	16.4	27.8	28.8	35.6	35.2
Australia and New Zealand	1.4	1.4	1.4	1.1	1.2
North America	42.2	33.4	29.6	26.9	29.9
South and Central America	6.0	6.0	8.7	6.9	6.6
Western Europe	32.4	29.3	29.0	25.9	23.4
Sub-Saharan Africa	0.7	0.8	0.9	1.0	0.8
Middle East and North Africa	0.5	0.6	0.8	1.3	1.3
South Asia	0.4	0.7	0.9	1.3	1.6
TOTAL	100.0	100.0	100.0	100.0	100.0

Source: Our calculations based on World Bank (1984, 2001).

Notes
Countries included: East Asia: China, Hong Kong, Indonesia, Japan, South Korea, Malaysia, Philippines, Singapore, South Korea, Thailand. Australia and New Zealand: [No New Zealand in 1960 and 1970]. North America: Canada, United States. South and Central America: Argentina, Brazil, Chile, Colombia, Costa Rica, Dominican Republic, Ecuador, El Salvador, Guatemala, Honduras, Jamaica, Mexico, Nicaragua, Panama, Paraguay, Peru, Uruguay. Western Europe: Austria, Belgium, Denmark, Finland, France, Luxembourg, Netherlands, Norway, Sweden, United Kingdom, Greece, Italy, Portugal, Spain [No Netherlands in 1970]. Sub-Saharan Africa: Botswana, Burkina Faso, Cameroon, Central African Republic, Chad, Congo Dem. Rep., Congo Rep., Cote d'Ivoire, Gabon, Ghana, Kenya, Lesotho, Malawi, Mali, Mauritania, Mauritius, Niger, Nigeria, Rwanda, Senegal, South Africa, Togo, Zambia, Zimbabwe. Middle East and North Africa: Algeria, Egypt Arab Rep., Morocco, Oman, Saudi Arabia, Tunisia, Turkey. South Asia: Bangladesh, India, Pakistan, Sri Lanka.

value added in manufacturing. Indeed, taking the period as a whole, all low-income regions did, while the share of all high-income regions declined. There are nonetheless two important differences between the increase of the East Asian share and that of all other low-income regions. First, the share of all other low-income regions remained very small, their *combined* share at the end of the period being only 37.5 percent of the Western European share and 29.4 percent of the North American share. The East Asian share, in contrast, by 1990 had surpassed both the Western European and the North American share by a good margin. Second and most important, East Asia was the only region for which the increased share in industrial output was associated with a major upgrading in the global value-added pecking order measured by relative GNPPC. The upgrading of South Asia and the Middle East and North Africa was far less significant, while South and Central America and Sub-Saharan Africa experienced a downgrading (see Table 7.3).

It follows that rapid industrialization in East Asia was not just (or even primarily) a product of the relocation of low-value-added manufacturing activities to low-income regions. There was, of course, plenty of relocation of low-value-added manufacturing activities to East Asia, indeed, far more than anywhere else. Nevertheless, the fact that East Asia improved its position in the global value-added ranking *vis-à-vis* the high-income regions so significantly is indicative of the fact that its rapid industrialization was the expression of competitiveness not just at the lower end of the value-added chain but also at the middle and higher ends. This has been true not only in such obvious cases as Japan, Taiwan, Singapore and South Korea, but also for China and to a lesser extent Thailand and Malaysia. In view of this more balanced competitiveness, it is no exaggeration to say that by the 1990s East Asia was well on its way to regaining the industrial supremacy it had held for so long in early modern times.

Last but by no means least, is the financial dimension of the East Asian economic renaissance. The "financialization" of the global economy in general, and of the economies of high-income countries in particular, is a widely acknowledged phenomenon of the 1980s and 1990s. Indeed, the explosive growth of world financial markets in the course of these two decades is the strongest piece of evidence in the armory of advocates of the thesis that we have entered a new phase of deepening "globalization" (cf. among others, Harvey 1995; Cohen 1996; Sassen 1996; Arrighi and Silver *et al.* 1999; Held *et al.* 1999; Rowley and Benson 2000). Most accounts of this tendency focus on the centrality of the US government and business in promoting and benefiting from the financial expansion of the 1980s and 1990s. Just as important, however, is the underlying tendency toward the demise of the United States and the rise of Japan and "Greater China" as the world's leading creditor nations. Tables 7.5 and 7.6 starkly illustrate this change of guard with the period since 1980 displaying the turnabout.[12]

Focusing exclusively on US–Japanese relations, Eamonn Fingleton (2001: 6; cf. Fingleton 1995) has recently noted that Japan's continuing advance in manufacturing activities relative to the United States in the 1990s had a major impact on their respective balances of payments, for the simple reason that manufacturing generates eleven times more exports per unit of output than service businesses. Large and persistent

Table 7.5 Current account surplus (+) or deficit (−) (million US$, annual average)

Jurisdiction	1960–1	1970–1	1980–1	1990–1	1998–9
United States	+3,320	+440	+3,495	−37,515	−279,740
United Kingdom	−367	+2,352	+10,495	−24,415	−10,870
Germany	+925	+895	−8,410	+15,315	−12,730
China	n.a.	n.a.	n.a.	+12,635	+23,570
Hong Kong	n.a.	n.a.	n.a.	n.a.	+6,091
Singapore	n.a.	−684	−1,516	+4,001	+21,139
Japan	−420	+3,895	−2,990	+56,140	+138,755

Source: Our calculations based on International Monetary Fund (1990 and 2000).

Table 7.6 Regional shares of the ten largest official foreign exchange reserves

Region	1980	1990	1999
East Asia	9.72	32.30	78.12
North America	10.31	14.72	7.13
Western Europe	65.62	52.98	14.75
Others	14.35	0.00	0.00
Total	100.00	100.00	100.00

Source: Our calculations based on *Japan Almanac* (1993: 89) and (2002: 112).

surpluses in the Japanese balance of trade and deficits in the US balance, in turn, have deepened the reversal of positions between the two countries in the international credit system:

> Japan is now exporting more capital in real terms than any nation since America's days of global economic dominance in the 1950s ... [As a result,] in the first nine years of the 1990s Japan's net external assets jumped from $294 billion to $1,153 billion. Meanwhile, U.S. net external liabilities rocketed from $49 billion to $1,537 billion. In the long run this changing balance of financial power will be about the only thing that historians will remember about U.S.–Japanese economic rivalry in the last decade. Yet it was the one thing that Western observers generally overlooked.

If we broaden the picture to take into account the rapidly growing capital outflows from the "China Circle" (as shown only in part in Table 7.5, because of the lack of data for Taiwan) – combined with the large and growing East Asian share in world value added in manufacturing (as shown in Table 7.4) and the continuing upgrading of the region in the global value-added ranking (as shown in Table 7.3) – Fingleton's warning about a fundamental Western misreading of the 1990s begins to ring true (cf. Yeung and Olds 2000). As we have seen, by some indicators the East Asian rise does appear to have slowed down in the 1990s, especially in Japan. But persistent recession in Japan has been accompanied by unabated expansion elsewhere in the region, most notably in the PRC, raising the possibility that we may indeed be – as Gills and Frank (1994: 6–7) put it – "at the beginning of a return [to a global economy] in which parts of Asia play again a leading role ... as they did in the not so distant past." Be that as it may, the question that concerns us here and to which we must now turn is whether we can detect any connection between the region's ongoing economic renaissance and its multiple historical heritages.

Lineages of the East Asian economic renaissance

The importance of East Asia's multiple historical heritages in shaping and sustaining the region's economic integration and expansion is best perceived by focusing on the succession of agencies that have played a leading role in the process of labor-seeking investments depicted in Figure 7.1. This succession can be likened to "a three-stage rocket" – a process, that is, in which the leading agencies of each stage created the conditions for the emergence of the leading agencies of the next. In the first stage, the main agency of expansion was the US government, whose strategies of power propelled the upgrading of the Japanese economy and created the political conditions of the subsequent transborder expansion of the Japanese multilayered subcontracting system. In the second stage, Japanese business itself became the main agency of expansion. As the catchment area of its investment and subcontracting networks came to encompass the entire East Asian region, Overseas Chinese business networks were revitalized. In the new climate provided after 1970 by the US–China opening, the fortunes of these networks became linked with the double pursuit by the Chinese government of economic advancement and national unification, creating the basis of a grand Chinese economic circle. In the incipient third stage, it is precisely the Chinese government acting at times in concert with the Chinese capitalist diaspora in Taiwan, in Hong Kong, throughout Southeast Asia and in North America that seems to be emerging as a leading agency in the expansion of the Chinese and East Asian economies, at a time when Japan's economy has experienced a decade of stagnation (cf. Arrighi 1996: 36–7).

From the perspective adopted in this chapter, these three stages of the East Asian economic renaissance can be interpreted also as stages of a process of revival of key features of the East Asian tribute-trade system in a radically transformed global context. The initial stage was one of seemingly absolute Western supremacy. The Cold War had split the region into two antagonistic camps and reduced most East Asian states to the status of "vassals" of one or the other contending "imperial" center – the United States and the USSR. As the Korean War demonstrated, however, even at this stage Western supremacy was more precarious than it seemed. It was indeed this precariousness that induced the United States to revive unwittingly a typical feature of the seemingly defunct East Asian tribute-trade system – that is, a regime of "gifts" and trade between the imperial and the vassal states that was very favorable economically to the vassal states. This was "the 'magnanimous' ... early postwar ... trade [and aid] regime of Pax Americana" to which Ozawa (1993: 130) traces the origins of the process of regional economic integration and expansion reproduced in Figure 7.1.

In spite of US "magnanimity," the fault-lines between the US and Soviet spheres of influence in the region started breaking down soon after they were established – first by the Chinese rebellion against Soviet domination in the late 1950s, and then by the US failure to split the Vietnamese nation along the Cold War divide. The breakdown can ultimately be traced to the lack of legitimacy of US and Soviet pretensions to remake the political geography of East Asia in almost complete disregard of the region's historical heritage of state formation and civilizational integration. Attempts to enforce coercively this anti-historical strategic geography backfired, both politically and economically. Politically, US defeat in Vietnam demonstrated that, for all its effectiveness in reproducing a balance of terror with the USSR, the high-tech and capital intensive US military apparatus was ineffectual in enforcing US commands against the determined resistance of the Vietnamese people backed by Chinese and Soviet support. Economically, massive US spending at home and abroad to sustain the war effort in Southeast Asia precipitated a major fiscal crisis of the US warfare–welfare state and contributed decisively to the collapse of the US-centered, Bretton Woods world monetary system. As a result, US global power fell precipitously, reaching its nadir at the end of the 1970s with the Iranian Revolution, the Soviet invasion of Afghanistan, and a new crisis of confidence in the US dollar (Brodine and Selden 1972; Arrighi 1994: 321–3).

In the midst of this crisis, the militaristic US regime in East Asia began to unravel as the Vietnam War destroyed what the Korean War had created. The Korean War had instituted the US-centric East Asian regime by excluding Mainland China from normal commercial and diplomatic intercourse with the non-communist part of the region, through blockade and war threats backed by "an archipelago of American military installations" (Cumings 1997: 154–5). Defeat in the Vietnam War, in contrast, forced the United States to readmit China to normal commercial and diplomatic intercourse with the rest of East Asia. The scope of the region's economic integration and expansion was thereby broadened considerably but the capacity of the United States to control its dynamic politically was reduced correspondingly (Arrighi 1996; Selden 1997).

It was in this context that the Asian economic renaissance entered its second stage – the stage of Japanese-driven regional economic expansion and integration. As previously noted, Japanese leadership in regional economic expansion and integration was based on a division of labor between the US pursuit of power and the Japanese pursuit of profit that had no precedent in the indigenous East Asian tribute-trade system. Nevertheless, the gradual substitution of Japanese business for the US government as the leading agency of regional economic expansion marked the re-emergence of a pattern of inter-state relations in the region and beyond that resembled more closely the indigenous (East Asian) than the transplanted (Western) pattern of inter-state relations.

In the historic East Asian pattern, centrality in the inter-state system was determined primarily by the relative size and sophistication of the system's national economies. In the transplanted Western pattern, in contrast, centrality had come to be determined primarily by the relative strength of the system's military-industrial complexes. One of the most consequential (and disastrous) effects of the mid-nineteenth-century incorporation of East Asia within the structures of the Western system was the "internalization" of industrial militarism in the struggle for centrality. In the 1930s and 1940s Japan's attempt to center upon itself the East Asian regional system by industrial military means had been a failure. But its unintended result was the establishment of a US-centered regime in maritime East Asia that marked the apogee of industrial militarism in the region.

The limits of industrial militarism as a source of power were laid bare by the defeat of the United States in Vietnam. But it was the prodigious upgrading of the Japanese national economy from the 1950s through the 1980s, and the expansion of Japanese business networks in the region and beyond in the 1970s and 1980s, that jointly demonstrated the increasing effectiveness of economic relative to military means as a source of world power. Japan's growing influence in world politics in the 1980s was based primarily on the role that the Japanese government and Japanese business played in supplying the credit and cheap commodities that enabled the United States to reverse the precipitous decline of its power. Without this credit and commodities, the Reagan Administration's combination of a drastic reduction in domestic taxation and a major escalation of the armament race with the USSR, if at all possible, would have resulted in an increase instead of a decrease in inflationary pressures at home, and in a further weakening instead of a strengthening of the US dollar in world financial markets. This tendency transformed the previous relationship of Japanese political and economic vassalage vis-à-vis the United States into a relationship of mutual dependence. Japan remained in the grip of US military power. But the reproduction of the US protection-producing apparatus came to depend ever more critically on Japanese finance and industry.

Japan's growing economic power in the 1980s was not based on any major technological breakthrough. Rather, it was due primarily to a reversal of a secular trend in business organization that Japan was particularly well positioned to turn to its own advantage. For the very expansion of the US system of multinational corporations created conditions favorable to the revitalization of nineteenth-century forms of business organization (Arrighi *et al.* 1999). In the words of Manuel Castells and Alejandro Portes:

> The large corporation, with its national vertical structure and the separation of its functions between staff and line, does not appear any more as the last stage of a necessary evolution toward rationalized

industrial management. Networks of economic activities, networks of firms, and coordinated clusters of workers appear to comprise an emergent model of successful production and distribution.

(1989: 29–30)

The main feature of this emergent model is its "informality," in sharp contrast with the "formality" of the previously dominant model of corporate capitalism based on the regulatory powers of big business, organized labor and big government (Castells and Portes 1989: 27–9; for similar claims, see Piore and Sable 1984: 4–5, 15, 19–20). "The trend of a century is being reversed" – *The Economist* editorialized in 1989 – "as now it is the big firms that are shrinking and small ones that are on the rise" (quoted in Harrison 1994).

As Bennett Harrison has pointed out, there is much exaggeration in these claims. But as he himself acknowledges (ibid.: 244–5), it is nonetheless true that the worldwide intensification of competition among corporations that ensued from the proliferation in their number and variety has forced them to subcontract to small businesses activities previously carried out within their own organizations. The tendency toward the bureaucratization of business through vertical integration that had made the fortunes of US corporate business since the 1870s, thus began to be superseded one hundred years later by a tendency toward informal networking and the subordinate revitalization of small business (Arrighi *et al.* 1999).

The strategy of big business, operating transnationally, to turn the advantages of small business into an instrument of the consolidation and expansion of its own power has been in evidence everywhere. But nowhere has it been pursued more consistently and successfully than in East Asia. Without the assistance of multiple layers of formally independent subcontractors – notes JETRO (Japan's External Trade Organization) – "Japanese big business would flounder and sink" (Okimoto and Rohlen 1988: 83–8). Close relationships of cooperation between large and small firms are buttressed by informal arrangements among the parent companies themselves in the form of semi-permanent trade agreements and inter-group shareholding that enable management to concentrate on long-term rather than short-term performance (Eccleston 1989: 31–4). Starting in the early 1970s, the scale and scope of this multilayered subcontracting system increased rapidly through a spillover into a growing number and variety of East Asian states (Arrighi *et al.* 1993: 55ff.).

The spillover was an integral aspect of the snowballing process of regional economic integration and expansion that strengthened the competitiveness of Japanese big business regionally and globally. Japanese business was the leading agency of the spillover. But the spillover could occur as rapidly and extensively as it did only by relying heavily on the business networks of the Overseas Chinese. Overseas Chinese were from the start the main intermediaries between Japanese and local business in Singapore, Hong Kong and Taiwan – where ethnic Chinese constituted the majority of the population – and, later on, in most ASEAN countries, where the ethnic Chinese minority occupied a commanding position in local business networks. The region-wide expansion of the Japanese multi-layered subcontracting system was thus supported, not just by US political patronage "from above," but also by Chinese commercial and financial patronage "from below" (cf. Hui 1995; Irwan 1995).

Over time, however, patronage from above and below began to constrain rather than support the capacity of Japanese business to lead the regional economic expansion. For the incorporation in the snowballing process of politically and militarily autonomous states like China changed radically the nature of the process. "For the first time in a very long time" – notes Jonathan Friedland – "there [was] open discussion of Japan's growing economic vulnerability to political forces beyond its control and just what to do about it." As a representative of Japanese big business explained: "We don't have military power. There is no way for Japanese businessmen to influence policy decisions of other countries ... This is a difference with American business and it is something Japanese business-men have to think about" (Friedland 1994: 42). This difference between US and Japanese business did not just mean that Japanese business could not match the capacity of a US government–business nexus to influence the policy decisions of third countries. Equally important, it meant that Japan's own policy decisions were far more susceptible to being shaped by US interests than US policies were of being influenced by Japanese inter-ests. The very specialization in the pursuit of profit that had propelled the Japanese ascent, in other words, also limited the extent to which the ascent could go on eclipsing the United States as the center of the regional political economy.

Equally important is the fact that US business began restructuring itself to compete more effectively with Japanese business in the exploitation of East Asia's rich endowment of labor and entrepreneurial resources. This development is portrayed in Figure 7.1 by the three flows of labor-seeking investment that connect the United States to the Four Tigers, the ASEAN countries, and China and Vietnam. In Ozawa's original model these flows were missing, presumably to emphasize the fact that the main role played by the United States in the process of East Asian economic expansion has been as a destination of labor-intensive exports. While this is undoubtedly true, in the 1980s and 1990s a growing number of US corporations have been involved in tapping the region's labor supplies, not just through direct investment, but also and especially through all kinds of subcontract-ing arrangements. Indeed, in the 1990s East Asia emerged as one of the most favored destinations of US-centered "buyer-driven commodity chains" (cf. Gereffi 1994).

As Hamilton and Chang (Chapter 5, this volume) underscore, vertically disintegrated or loosely integrated, buyer-driven commodity chains were a distinctive feature of business organization in late imperial China and still are in contemporary Taiwan and Hong Kong. We may therefore interpret the formation and expansion in East Asia of US-centered chains of this kind as another instance of Western convergence toward East Asian patterns. This convergence of US business practices toward the Chinese model of buyer-driven commodity chains is an aspect of the reversal of the secular trend toward the formation of centralized, formally regulated and rigidly specialized business structures noted earlier. But the fact that the convergence has been particularly strong in the East Asian context is due primarily to the presence in the region of the extensive and strategically positioned business networks of the Overseas Chinese – that is, to the same condition that facilitated the transborder expansion of Japanese business.

By mobilizing these networks, US business could and did recoup some of its competitiveness both regionally and globally. In so doing, however, it was following in the footsteps of Japanese business rather than replacing Japanese business in the role of leading agency of the regional economic expansion. If the process of snowballing labor-seeking investments not only continued but gained momentum in the 1990s in spite of a weakening of Japanese leadership, it was because the process had entered a third stage – the stage of Chinese-driven integration and expansion. For the reincorporation of mainland China in regional and global markets in the late 1970s and in the 1980s brought back into play a state whose demographic size, abundance of entrepreneurial and labor resources, and growth potential surpassed by a good margin that of all other states operating in the region, the United States included. Within less than twenty years after Richard Nixon's mission to Beijing, and less than fifteen after the formal re-establishment of diplomatic relations between the United States and the PRC, this giant "container" of human resources already seemed poised to become again the powerful magnet of means of payments it had been in early modern times.

If the main attraction of the PRC for foreign capital has been its huge and highly competitive reserves of labor from the perspective of cost, quality and control – along with the actual and potential markets created by the mobilization of these reserves – the "matchmaker" that has facilitated the encounter of foreign capital and Chinese labor is the Overseas Chinese capitalist diaspora (Lardy 1992: 37–82; Fukasuku and Wall 1994: 26–42).

> Drawn by China's capable pool of low-cost labor and its growing potential as a market that contains one-fifth of the world's population, foreign investors continue to pour money into the PRC. Some 80% of

that capital comes from the Overseas Chinese, refugees from poverty, disorder, and communism, who in one of the era's most piquant ironies are now Beijing's favorite financiers and models for modernization. Even the Japanese often rely on the Overseas Chinese to grease their way into China.

(Kraar 1993: 40)

In fact, Beijing's reliance on the Overseas Chinese to ease Mainland China's re-incorporation in regional and world markets is not the true irony of the situation. The true irony of the situation is that one of the most conspicuous legacies of nineteenth-century Western encroachments on Chinese sovereignty emerged in the 1980s as a powerful instrument of Chinese and East Asian emancipation from Western dominance. As we have seen, the Overseas Chinese diaspora had for centuries been the primary locus of the seeds of capitalism that sprouted in the interstices of the China-centered tribute-trade system. But the greatest opportunities for the growth of this interstitial capitalist formation came with the subordinate incorporation of East Asia within the structures of the UK-centered global system in the wake of the Opium Wars. In the early twentieth century, significant parts of the capitalist stratum of the diaspora attempted to transform its growing economic power into political influence over mainland China by supporting the 1911 revolution and the GMD in the warlord era. But in the face of escalating political chaos associated with warlordism and civil war, the takeover of China's coastal regions by Japan, and the eventual defeat of the GMD by the CCP, the diaspora was marginalized.

The Communist victory replenished the entrepreneurial ranks of the diaspora by generating a new spurt of Chinese migration to Southeast Asia and especially Hong Kong and Taiwan as well as the United States (cf. Wong 1988). Shortly afterwards, the price boom associated with the Korean War revived the flow of interregional trade and created new business opportunities for the Overseas Chinese. And so did the withdrawal of the European and US colonial-era large-scale enterprises and the arrival soon after of new multinational corporations seeking capable joint-venture partners (Mackie 1998: 142). Nevertheless, under the US unilateral regime that emerged out of the Korean War the Overseas Chinese role as commercial intermediaries between Mainland China and the surrounding maritime regions, was stifled as much by the US embargo on trade with the PRC as by the PRC's restrictions on domestic and foreign trade – restrictions that became particularly crippling during the Cultural Revolution of the 1960s (cf. Baker 1981: 344–5).

Moreover, through the 1950s and 1960s the expansion of Overseas Chinese capitalism was held in check (both directly and indirectly) by the spread of nationalism and national development ideologies and practices in Southeast Asia. It was held in check indirectly by the privileging of economic links and connections within rather than across national boundaries. And it was held in check directly by anti-Chinese campaigns that restricted the freedom of action of the Overseas Chinese politically, economically and culturally (Suryadinata 1989: 122).

In spite of this unfavorable environment, Overseas Chinese business networks managed to hold their own and develop further. By the mid-1970s, a rough estimate of Chinese assets in Southeast Asia was US$10–16 billion – an amount that in real terms was equal to two or three times the 1937 figure and placed the Overseas Chinese at the commanding heights of most Southeast Asian economies (Wu and Wu 1980: 30–4; Mackie 1992: 165; Hui 1995: 184–5). The Overseas Chinese were thus eminently well positioned to seize the highly profitable business opportunities that were opened up by the transborder expansion of the Japanese subcontracting system, the growing demand by US corporation for business partners in the region and, above all, the reintegration of the PRC in regional and global markets. As soon as these opportunities arose, they quickly seized them to become one of the most powerful capitalist networks in the region, in many ways overshadowing the networks of US and Japanese multinationals, and the leading force in foreign investment in China and regional economic and financial integration. Suffice it to mention that by the mid-1990s their assets were estimated to be in the order of US$1.5–2.0 trillion (Lin 1996: 236).

This extraordinary expansion was not due solely to the entrepreneurship of the Overseas Chinese. It was just as much due to the determination with which the PRC under Deng sought their assistance in the upgrading of the Chinese economy and in seeking national unification in accordance with the "One Nation, Two Systems" model whose twin goals were China's economic expansion and the reunification of China including the recovery of Hong Kong, Macau and, eventually, Taiwan. A close political alliance was established between the Chinese Communist Party and Overseas Chinese business, one that would be strengthened following the 1997 reversion of Hong Kong and the further integration of Hong Kong and other overseas Chinese business interests through their role in governing Hong Kong and their participation in China's National People's Congress.

As Chinese entrepreneurs began moving from Hong Kong into Guangdong almost as fast as (and far more massively than) they had moved from Shanghai to Hong Kong forty years earlier, the Chinese government redoubled its efforts to win the confidence and assistance of the Overseas Chinese. In 1988, many of the privileges previously granted to Hong Kong's residents were extended to Taiwan's residents as well (So and Chiu 1995: Chapter 11). The response of Taiwan's capitalists was as enthusiastic as that of Hong Kong's. Taiwanese investments in mainland China shot up from US$100 million in 1987 to US$1 billion in 1989, and to US$2 billion in 1990, doubling again over the next two years (*Far Eastern Economic Review*, September 19, 1992: 12; see also Selden 1997: 324–32). By 1990, the combined investments of US$12 billion from Hong Kong and Taiwan accounted for 75 percent of the total of all foreign investment, almost 35 times more than Japan (calculated from So and Chiu 1994 and *Far Eastern Economic Review* September 19, 1992: 12, and June 9, 1994: 44).

An unknown but by all accounts significant portion of the investment from Hong Kong and to a lesser extent Taiwan was in fact Japanese capital invested through the intermediation of Chinese businesses. It is nonetheless unlikely that any correction of the figures to take this fact into account would change substantially the overall picture of an expansion of foreign investment in China increasingly driven by the activities (including activities of intermediation) of the Overseas Chinese operating in close alliance with the PRC's ruling elites. These activities were also instrumental in promoting the rapid growth of the foreign trade of the countries out of which the Overseas Chinese operated. Suffice it to mention that in 1993 the $613 billion combined exports and imports of China, Hong Kong and Taiwan already surpassed Japan's total trade of $569 billion, and by 1998 they accounted for $900 billion compared with Japan's total of $668 billion (Japan External Trade Organization 1999: 7).

As we have underscored throughout the chapter, the fortunes of the Overseas Chinese in the indigenous East Asian regional system went through considerable ups and downs over the centuries. The present upturn in their fortunes is one of the clearest signs that the transformations of the global system in recent decades have reorganized and restructured rather than destroyed the pre-existing regional system. While some features of the pre-existing system did not survive the restructuring, others have been revitalized. It was only to be expected that so fertile a seed-bed of capitalism as the Overseas Chinese would be revived by the incorporation of East Asia in a global system that provided a far more favorable environment than the indigenous system for the unfettered development of capitalism. So far, this revival has been associated with a widening and deepening of the regional economic expansion. But how far this synergy can go, and whether it can go far enough to bring East Asia back to the center of the global economy, remain for now entirely open questions.

Conclusion

Our analysis started out with two puzzles – one concerning the rise of the West in early modern times and the other the rise of East Asia in our own times. The solution we have proposed to the first puzzle is that the extraordinary geographical expansion of the European system of states from the late fifteenth through the nineteenth century can be traced to two major features of that system: a balance of power that continually reproduced inter-state competition within the system on the one side, and the critical role that profits from trade with the non-European world (Asia in particular) played in determining the outcome of that competition on the other. Taken jointly, these two systemic circumstances created an environment conducive to the combined development of capitalism and militarism – a development that sustained and was in turn itself sustained by economic and political expansion at the expense of other peoples and polities.

In the East Asian system, in contrast, the unbalanced structure of inter-state power and the insignificance of profits from trade with the non-East Asian world in determining the outcome of inter-state competition created an unfavorable environment for the combined development of capitalism and militarism along the European path. At certain times – as under the Southern Song and the Yuan – the environment was more favorable than at other times. But the further development of national markets under the Ming and the Qing in China and in Tokugawa Japan tended to externalize rather than internalize capitalism. Capitalism did thrive in the East Asian world system, but primarily as an interstitial formation embedded in the business networks of the Overseas Chinese.

In the short-to-medium run – bearing in mind that in these matters, to paraphrase Joseph Schumpeter (1954: 163), a century is a "short run" – this bifurcation of the European and East Asian developmental paths resulted in the further expansion of the market economy in China and Japan and in a condition of peace and stable government in the East Asian system that contrasted sharply with the situation of generalized warfare and state breakdowns typical of the European system. In the longer run, however, the bifurcation resulted in a strengthening of the capacity and disposition of Western states to pursue the subordinate incorporation of East Asian states within the structures of their own system on the one side, and in a decreasing capacity of East Asian states to prevent such an incorporation on the other. But once the incorporation actually occurred, as it did in the wake of the Opium Wars, the historical heritage of the East Asian system did not vanish in a generalized convergence toward Western practices and patterns of political and economic interaction. There was convergence but through a process of hybridization that preserved and eventually revived important features of the East Asian system. In our view it is precisely in this process of hybridization that we can find a good part of the solution to our second puzzle – the puzzle, that is, of the extraordinary vitality of the East Asian region after its subordinate incorporation in the globalizing Western system.

More specifically, our argument has been that the East Asian dynamic under Western dominance has gone through two distinct stages, one broadly corresponding to the transition from British to US world hegemony and the other to the period of US hegemony. In the first stage, convergence was predominantly toward Western practices, as both China and Japan engaged in major industrialization drives aimed at strengthening themselves militarily in competition with one another and with the Western powers in the context of escalating inter-imperialist rivalries. Inter-state competition in East Asia thus converged toward the European pattern with most disastrous results for China and Korea but eventually, in the Second World War for Japan as well.

In the second stage, in contrast, a hybrid pattern of political and economic interaction combining features of the Western and East Asian systems began to emerge. Politically, the United States could exercise its hegemonic functions in the region only by adopting a trade regime that on close inspection had more in common with the China-centered tribute-trade system than with the nineteenth-century UK-centered system. Economically, rapid regional integration and expansion could occur only through the mobilization and revival of forms of business organization that resembled more closely the informally integrated networks of Chinese enterprises than the vertically integrated and bureaucratically managed structures of US enterprises.

As the data presented earlier show, the benefits of the regional economic renaissance that ensued from this process of hybridization have been distributed very unevenly among the region's jurisdictions. Moreover, in most countries but especially in China (where almost two-thirds of the region's population is concentrated) the economic upgrading of the national economy has been accompanied by a sharp increase in income inequalities and the specter of large-scale unemployment. The renaissance has thus been an extremely uneven process that has magnified inequalities among and within the region's political jurisdictions and brought palpable benefits to no more (and probably less) than one-fifth of the region's population, while sharply raising expectations of the benefits of prosperity for all.

These tendencies constitute a departure from the pattern of more even development characteristic of the historic East Asian system during the era of Chinese preponderance in favor of the Western pattern of uneven development. They constitute also a major limit to further expansion. For growing inequalities do not just engender social and political tensions and resistance (Perry and Selden 2000). They also restrain the growth of the regional market thereby reproducing the dependence of the expansion on the willingness and capacity of the United States and other Western countries to absorb ever increasing labor-intensive imports from East Asia. This willingness and capacity cannot be taken for granted in view of the growing foreign indebtedness of the United States and the near economic stagnation of the EU. Ultimately, the fate of the East Asian economic renaissance depends on whether East Asians can find effective ways and means of moderating its uneveness nationally and internationally. If such ways and means are found, East Asia may well become once again the center of the global economy.

Notes

1 This exhaustion is what Mark Elvin (1973: 314) calls a (Smithian) high-level equilibrium trap. We would like to emphasize, as Sugihara (this volume) also suggests, that this "trap" should not be confused with traps of the Malthusian, low-level equilibrium type. A Smithian, high-level equilibrium trap refers to a situation in which the potential for efficient growth of an economy with a particular endowment of resources has been fully exploited. Although in such a situation production, trade and income cannot grow further, they are at historically high levels. A Malthusian, low-level equilibrium trap, in contrast, refers to a situation in which an increase in incomes calls forth an increase in population that depresses returns to labor and brings income back to historically low levels.

2 This methodology introduces two kinds of asymmetry in our comparative analysis, one concerning early modern times and the other the nineteenth and twentieth centuries. In comparing the interacting but still distinct European and East Asian dynamics of early modern times, a greater number and variety of states will enter our story of the European dynamic than our story of the East Asian dynamic, the latter being focused primarily on China and only secondarily on Japan. This asymmetry is due to the fact noted above that in early modern times China's hegemonic position in the East Asian region was far more stable than that of the several states that became hegemonic in the European region. This situation changed in the nineteenth century, as the European regional system became global and the East Asian system became a regional sub-system of the globalized European system. From then on, the distinct stories of the two regional systems merge into a single story. In this single story non-East Asian states (most notably, the United Kingdom in the nineteenth century and the United States in the twentieth century) join East Asian states as protagonists in the structuring and re-structuring of the East Asian region.

3 Japan doubly challenged China's position as the unique tributary center in the region, first by not sending tribute missions to China beginning in 1549, and continuing throughout the entire 268-year Tokugawa reign (Lee 1999: 8; Wills 1979; Flynn and Giraldez 1995), and second by exacting tribute from the Ryukyus through the Satsuma domain, even as the Ryukyuans preserved their tributary relationship with China (Hamashita 1988: 14–15). Vietnam, for its part, in the Qing era required tribute missions from Laos and Cambodia although, in contrast to Japan, it continued to send tributary missions to China (Reid 1993: 234–40).

4 In the 1660s and 1670s, their regime in Taiwan remained a de facto independent kingdom exacting tribute and conducting trade with the Spanish Philippines, the Ryukyus, and various kingdoms of Southeast Asia. While Zheng Chenggong aspired to oust the Manchus and restore the Ming, his successor Zheng Jing repeatedly rejected Qing offers of a semi-autonomous status in negotiations in the 1660s and 1670s, and proposed recognition as a tribute vassal of the Qing based on Korean and Ryukyu precedents. The Kangxi

Emperor, however, insisted that "the thieves in Taiwan are Fujianese, Taiwan is not comparable to Korea and Ryukyu" (Hung 2001c: 33–7).

5 The number of Southeast Asian tributary missions to China peaked at 52 from seven states in the 1420s. In the 1450s there were only ten missions from four states, and by the first decade of the sixteenth century, only Siam, Champa and Melaka sent a total of five missions (Reid 1993: 15–16).

6 Though the Qing regime lifted the sea ban in 1683, it imposed strict regulations on the shipbuilding industry, restricting the size and weight of all trading junks, and outlawed bringing firearms on board (Tian 1987: 12–16). A new era was thus inaugurated in which "trade was legal, but maritime China had lost its fragile political autonomy" (Wills 1979).

7 Japan's territorial expansion in the 1890s and 1900s was a continuation on a much enlarged scale of its previous incorporation of the semi-autonomous Ainu homeland of Hokkaido in 1869, and Okinawa in 1879 (Howell 1997: 612–13; Rabson 1997: 640–1; Elisonas 1991: 299–300).

8 The United States did nonetheless require of its vassals subordinate military and paramilitary functions. These included Japanese supplies of material in the Korean and Vietnamese wars; a large Korean troop contingent in Vietnam and the support for the US military effort of various Laotian tribes and Tibetan exiles.

9 We use GNP instead of GDP data because they include the incomes that the residents of the state or group of states derive from transfers from abroad (such as repatriated profits or worker remittances) and exclude the incomes transferred abroad. We do not adjust data for differences in costs of living not just because prior to the 1980s "purchasing power parity" (PPP) data for many countries either do not exist or are extremely unreliable. We do not make such an adjustment also because here we are interested mainly in the relative command of the residents of different countries/regions on one another's resources in the world market, rather than in their comparative command over resources in their respective national markets. While PPP-based GNP data are better indicators of the second kind of command, GNP data converted into US$ at market exchange rates (FX-based data) are better indicators of the first kind of command (cf. Korzeniewicz and Moran 2000 and Firebaugh 2000). We have excluded from the calculations of world GNP and regional shares thereof the former USSR and Eastern Europe, along with some African, Asian and Latin American countries, because of lack of comparable data for one or more of the years shown in the table. Nevertheless, in 1999 the states included in the calculation accounted for about 96.7 percent of world GNP. The percentages of Table 7.1 thus constitute very close approximations to the actual shares of the world market controlled by the residents of the different regions. To this we should add that in 1990, when comparable data first became available, the former USSR and Eastern Europe accounted for 4.6 percent of world GNP. By 1999 their share had dropped to 2.6 percent. That was the worst performance of all regions, including Sub-Saharan Africa. It follows that the inclusion of the former USSR and Eastern Europe in our data set would improve proportionately the performance of all the regions, East Asia included (all the above figures have been calculated from World Bank 2001).

10 More specifically, over the four decades 1960–99 the GNPPC of both Western Europe relative to the world average increased by 27 percent, while that of East Asia increased by 111 percent.

11 Income inequality in East Asia is larger than in any other region of the world because, unlike any other region, East Asia includes both a country (Japan) with one of the highest per capita incomes in the world and countries (like

Vietnam) with some of the lowest per capita incomes. China's actual position in the ranking of countries by GNPPC has been a highly controversial issue. The controversy is partly due to a major discrepancy between China's PPP-based and FX-based GNPPC (see note 9 for the difference between the two kinds of measurement). Since this discrepancy had been instrumental in denying China "developing nation" status in the negotiations over its entry into the WTO, it is hard to tell whether the discrepancy reflects an extraordinary capacity of the Chinese social system to squeeze high levels of material consumption out of a low income, or a politically motivated statistical exaggeration of that capacity by the officials of the World Bank and other international institutions. The issue is further complicated by the rapid growth of income inequality within China – an inequality that is estimated to have become among the largest in the world (Riskin *et al.* 2001). If this is indeed the case, and the evidence is compelling, the upward mobility of the PRC in the global value-added hierarchy would in fact reflect a far greater upward mobility of a limited number of (predominantly coastal) areas on the one side, and a lesser upward mobility (or even downward mobility) of much of the rest of the country. As we underscore in the chapter's concluding section, this domestic unevenness of China's economic expansion has important social and political implications. Nevertheless, it has no bearing on our present concern with the comparative performance of different countries and regions in generating national wealth.

12 Leaving aside "errors and omissions," the current account surpluses shown in Table 7.5 are indicative of net outflows of capital and deficits of net inflows.

References

Abu-Lughod, Janet. 1989. *Before European Hegemony: The World System A.D. 1250–1350*. New York: Oxford University Press.

Adas, Michael. 1989. *Machines as Measure of Men: Science, Technology and Ideologies of Western Dominance*. Ithaca, NY: Cornell University Press.

Alatas, Syed Husein. 1977. *The Myth of the Lazy Native: A Study of the Image of the Malays, Filipinos and Javanese from the 16th to the 20th Centuries and Its Function in the Ideology of Colonial Capitalism*. London: Frank Cass.

Anderson, Perry. 1974. *Lineages of the Absolutist State*. London: New Left Books.

Arrighi, Giovanni. 1994. *The Long Twentieth Century: Money, Power, and the Origins of Our Time*. London: Verso.

Arrighi, Giovanni. 1996. "The Rise of East Asia: World Systemic and Regional Aspects," *International Journal of Sociology and Social Policy*, XVI (7): 6–44.

Arrighi, Giovanni, Kenneth Barr and Shuji Hisaeda. 1999. "The Transformation of Business Enterprise," in G. Arrighi and B.J. Silver *et al.* (eds), *Chaos and Governance in the Modern World System*. Minneapolis: Minnesota University Press.

Arrighi, Giovanni, Satoshi Ikeda and Alex Irwan. 1993. "The Rise of East Asia: One Miracle or Many?" in R.A. Palat (ed.), *Pacific Asia and the Future of the World-Economy*. Westport, CT: Greenwood Press, pp. 42–65.

Arrighi, Giovanni and Beverly J. Silver *et al.* 1999. *Chaos and Governance in the Modern World System*. Minneapolis: Minnesota University Press.

Atwell, William S. 1986. "Some Observations on the 'Seventeenth-Century Crisis' in China and Japan." *Journal of Asian Studies* XLV: 223–44.

Atwell, William S. 1998. "Ming China and the Emerging World Economy. C. 1470–1650," in D. Twitchett and F. Mote (eds), *The Cambridge History of China Vol. 8 (2), The Ming Dynasty*. Cambridge: Cambridge University Press, pp. 376–416.

Bagchi, Amiya Kumar. 1982. *The Political Economy of Underdevelopment*. Cambridge: Cambridge University Press.

Baker, Christopher. 1981. "Economic Reorganization and the Slump in Southeast Asia." *Comparative Studies in Society and History* XXIII, 3: 325–49.

Blusse, Leonard. 1991. "In Praise of Commodities: An Essay on the Cross-cultural Trade in Edible Bird's Nests," in R. Ptak and R. Dietmar (eds), *Emporia, Commodities and Entrepreneurs in Asian Maritime Trade, c.1400–1750*. Stuttgart: Franz Steiner Verlag, pp. 317–38.

Boyer-Xambeu, Marie-Therese, Ghislain Deleplace and Gillard Lucien. 1994. *Private Money and Public Currencies: The Sixteenth Century Challenge*. Armonk, NY: M.E. Sharpe.

Braudel, Fernand. 1976. *The Mediterranean and the Mediterranean World in the Age of Philip II*. 2 Vols. New York: Harper & Row.

Braudel, Fernand. 1977. *Afterthoughts on Material Civilization and Capitalism*. Baltimore, MD: Johns Hopkins University Press.

Braudel, Fernand. 1981. *Civilization and Capitalism, 15th–18th Century*, vol. I: *The Structures of Everyday Life*. New York: Harper & Row.

Braudel, Fernand. 1982. *Civilization and Capitalism, 15th–18th Century*, vol. II: *The Wheels of Commerce*. New York: Harper & Row.

Braudel, Fernand. 1984. *Civilization and Capitalism, 15th–18th Century*, vol. III: *The Perspective of the World*. New York: Harper & Row.

Bray, Francesca. 1986. *The Rice Economies: Technology and Development in Asian Societies*. Berkeley, CA: University of California Press.

Brodine, Virginia and Mark Selden (eds). 1972. *Open Secret: The Kissinger–Nixon Doctrine in Asia*. New York: Harper & Row.

Brook, Timothy. 1998. *The Confusions of Pleasure: Commerce and Culture in Ming China*. Berkeley, CA: University of California Press.

Cain, P.J. and A.G. Hopkins. 1980. "The Political Economy of British Expansion Overseas, 1750–1914," *The Economic History Review*, 2nd ser. XXXIII (4): 463–90.

Cairncross, A.K. 1953. *Home and Foreign Investment, 1870–1913*. Cambridge: Cambridge University Press.

Castells, Manuel and Alejandro Portes. 1989. "World Underneath: The Origins, Dynamics, and Effects of the Informal Economy," in A. Portes, M. Castells, and L.A. Benton (eds), *The Informal Economy. Studies in Advanced and Less Developed Countries*. Baltimore, MD: Johns Hopkins University Press, pp. 11–39.

Chang, Pin-tsun. 1991. "The First Chinese Diaspora in Southeast Asia in the Fifteenth Century," in R. Ptak and D. Rothermund (eds), *Emporia, Commodities and Entrepreneurs in Asian Maritime Trade, c.1400–1750*. Stuttgart: Franz Steiner Verlag, pp. 13–28.

Chang, Tien-tse. 1969. *Sino-Portuguese Trade from 1514 to 1644*. Leiden: E.J. Brill.

Chao Zhongchen. 1993. "Wanming baiyin dliang liuru ji qi yingxiang." (Massive inflow of silver in Late Ming and its Influences) *shixue yuekan*. 93 (1): 33–9.

Chapman, Stanley D. 1972. *The Cotton Industry in the Industrial Revolution*. London: Macmillan.

Chapman, Stanley D. 1984. *The Rise of Merchant Banking*. London: Unwin Hyman.

Chapman, Stanley D. 1992. *Merchant Enterprise in Britain: from the Industrial Revolution to World War I.* New York, Cambridge University Press.

Chase-Dunn, Christopher and Thomas Hall. 1997. *Rise and Demise: Comparing World-Systems.* Boulder, CO: Westview Press.

Chen Bisheng. 1989. *Shijie huaqiao shi* (History of Overseas Chinese in Southeast Asia). Nanchang: Jiangxi renmin chubanshe.

Chen Ciyu. 1984. "Yi Zhongyinyang sanjiao maoyi wei jichu tantao shiji shijii Zhongguode duiwai maoyi." (On the foreign trade of China in the 19th Century and the China–India–Britain Triangular Trade) in *Zhongguo haiyang fazhanshi lunwenji bianji weiyuanhui ed. (Essays in Chinese Maritime History).* Taipei: Sun Yat-sen Institute for Social Sciences and Philosophy, Academia Sinica, pp. 131–73.

Cohen, Benjamin. 1996. "Phoenix Risen: The Resurrection of Global Finance," *World Politics,* 48: 268–96.

Copeland, Melvin T. 1966. *The Cotton Manufacturing Industry of the United States.* 2nd impression. New York: Augustus M. Kelley.

Coyett, Frederick. [1675] 1903. 'Verwaerloosde Formosa' in William Campbell (ed.), *Formosa Under the Dutch: Described From Contemporary Records.* London: Kegan Paul, Trench, Trubner, pp. 383–538.

Crouzet, François. 1982. *The Victorian Economy.* New York: Columbia University Press.

Cumings, Bruce. 1997. "Japan and Northeast Asia into the Twenty-first Century," in P.J. Katzenstein and T. Shiraishi (eds) *Network Power: Japan and Asia.* Ithaca, NY: Cornell University Press, pp. 136–68.

Curtin, Philip D. 1984. *Cross-cultural Trade in World History.* Cambridge: Cambridge University Press.

Cushman, Jennifer Wayne. 1993. *Fields from the Sea: Chinese Junk Trade with Siam during the Late Eighteenth and Early Nineteenth Centuries.* Studies on Southeast Asia, Southeast Asia Program, Ithaca, NY: Cornell University Press.

Dannoue Hiroshi. 1995. "Ming chao chengli de guiiji – Hongwu chao de qingxi ji shoudu wenti" (The Trajectory of the Founding of the Ming Dynasty – the Purges in the Hongwu Reign and the Capital Question) in Liu Zhenwen (ed.), *Riben Qingnian Xuezhe Lun Zhongguo Shi* (Japanese Scholars on Chinese History). Shanghai: Guji chubanshe pp. 329–68.

Davies, Kenneth G. 1957. *The Royal African Company.* London: Longmans.

de Cecco, Marcello. 1984. *The International Gold Standard: Money and Empire.* 2nd edn. New York: St. Martin's Press.

Dickson, P.G.M. 1967. *The Financial Revolution in England: A Study in the Development of Public Credit.* London: Macmillan.

Duus, Peter. 1984. "Economic Dimensions of Meiji Imperialism: The Case of Korea, 1895–1910," in R.H. Myers and M.R. Peattie (eds), *The Japanese Colonial Empire, 1895–1945.* Princeton, NJ: Princeton University Press, pp. 128–71.

Eccleston, Bernard. 1989. *State and Society in Post-War Japan.* Cambridge: Polity Press.

Elisonas, Jurgis. 1991. "The Inseparable Trinity: Japan's Relations With China and Korea," in John Hall (ed.), *The Cambridge History of Japan, Vol. 4, Early Modern Japan.* Cambridge: Cambridge University Press, pp. 235–300.

Elliott, J.H. 1970. *The Old World and the New 1492–1650.* Cambridge: Cambridge University Press.

Elvin, Mark. 1973. *The Pattern of the Chinese Past.* Stanford, CA: Stanford University Press.

Esherick, Joseph. 1972. "Harvard on China: The Apologetics of Imperialism," *Bulletin of Concerned Asian Scholars* IV (4): 9–16.

Fairbank, John K. 1983. *The United States and China.* Cambridge, MA: Harvard University Press.

Farnie, D.A. 1979. *The English Cotton Industry and the World Market, 1815–1896.* Oxford: Clarendon Press.

Faure, David. 1996. "Capitalism and the History of Chinese Business," paper presented at the Chinese Business History Conference: The Rise of Business Corporations in China from Ming to Present, Center of Asian Studies, The University of Hong Kong, July 12–13.

Feis, Herbert. 1965. *Europe: The World's Banker, 1870–1914.* New York: Norton.

Feuerwerker, Albert. 1958. *China's Early Industrialization: Sheng Hsuan-Huai 1844–1916 and Mandarin Enterprise.* Cambridge, MA: Harvard University Press.

Feuerwerker, Albert. 1970. "Handicraft and Manufactured Cotton Textiles in China, 1871–1910," *Journal of Economic History* XXX (2): 338–78.

Feuerwerker, Albert. 1980. "Economic Trends in the Late Ch'ing Empire, 1870–1911," in John Fairbank and Kwang-ching Liu (eds), *Late Ch'ing, 1800–1911,* Part 2: 1–69 in Denis Twitchett and John Fairbank (eds), *The Cambridge History of China.* Cambridge: Cambridge University Press.

Fingleton, Eamonn. 1995. *Blindside: Why Japan Is Still on Track to Overtake the U.S. by the Year 2000.* Boston: Houghton Mifflin.

Fingleton, Eamonn. 2001. "Quibble All You Like, Japan Still Looks Like a Strong Winner," *International Herald Tribune,* January 2, p. 6.

Firebaugh, Glen. 2000. "Observed Trends in Between-Nation Income Inequality and Two Conjectures," *American Journal of Sociology* 106 (1): 215–21.

Flynn, Dennis O., Lionel Frost and A.J.H. Latham (eds). 1999. *Pacific Centuries: Pacific and Pacific Rim History Since the Sixteenth Century.* London: Routledge.

Flynn, Dennis O. and Arturo Giraldez. 1994. "China and the Manila Galleons," in A.J.H. Latham and H. Kawakatsu (eds), *Japanese Industrialization and the Asian Economy.* London: Routledge, pp. 71–90.

Flynn, Dennis O. and Arturo Giraldez. 1995. "Born with 'Silver Spoon': The Origin of World Trade in 1571," *Journal of World History* VI (2): 201–11.

Frank, André Gunder. 1978. "Multilateral Merchandise Trade Imbalances and Uneven Economic Development," *Journal of European Economic History* V (2): 407–38.

Frank, André Gunder. 1998. *ReOrient: Global Economy in the Asian Age.* Berkeley, CA: University of California Press.

Friedland, Jonathan. 1994. "The Regional Challenge," *Far Eastern Economic Review,* June 9, 40–2.

Fukasaku, Kiichiro and David Wall. 1994. *China's Long March to an Open Economy.* Paris: OECD.

Gao Weinong. 1993. *Zou xiang jinshi de Zhongguo yu "chaogong" guo guanxi* (The Relation between China and its Tributary States in Modern Times). Guangdong: Guangdong gaodeng jiaoyu chubanshe.

Gattrell, V.A.C. 1977. "Labour, Power, and the Size of Firms in Lancashire Cotton in the Second Quarter of the Nineteenth Century," *Economic History Review* 2nd ser., XXX (1): 95–139.

Gereffi, Gary. 1994. "The International Economy and Economic Development," in

N.J. Smelser and R. Swedberg (eds), *The Handbook of Economic Sociology*. Princeton, NJ: Princeton University Press.

Gills, Barry and André G. Frank. (1994). "The Modern World System under Asian Hegemony. The Silver Standard World Economy 1450–1750," unpublished paper.

Guan Luquan. 1994. *Songdai Guangzhou de haiwai maoyi* (The Guangzhou Sea Trade in the Song Dynasty). Guangzhou: Guangdong renmin chubanshe.

Greenberg, Michael. 1951. *British Trade and the Opening of China 1800–1842*. Cambridge: Cambridge University Press.

Hale, David H. 1995. "Is It a Yen or a Dollar Crisis in the Currency Market?," *Washington Quarterly* XVIII 4: 145–71.

Hamashita, Takeshi. 1988. "The Tribute Trade System of Modern Asia," *The Memoirs of the Toyo Bunko* XLVI: 7–25.

Hamashita, Takeshi. 1993. "Tribute and Emigration: Japan and the Chinese Administration of Foreign Affairs," *Senri Ethnological Studies* XXV: 69–86.

Hamashita, Takeshi. 1994. "The Tribute Trade System and Modern Asia," in A.J.H. Latham and H. Kawakatsu (eds), *Japanese Industrialization and the Asian Economy*. London and New York: Routledge, pp. 91–107.

Hamashita, Takeshi. 1997. "The Intra-Regional System in East Asia in Modern Times," in Peter. J Katzenstein and T. Shiraishi (eds), *Network Power. Japan and Asia*. Ithaca, NY: Cornell University Press, pp. 113–35.

Hao, Yen-p'ing. 1970. *The Comprador in Nineteenth-Century China: Bridge between East and West*. Cambridge, MA: Harvard University Press

Hao, Yen-p'ing. 1986. *The Commercial Revolution in Nineteenth-Century China*. Berkeley, CA: California University Press.

Harrison, Bennett. 1994. *Lean and Mean: The Changing Landscape of Corporate Power in the Age of Flexibility*. New York: Basic Books.

Harvey, David. 1995. "Globalization in Question," *Rethinking Marxism* 8 (4): 1–17.

He Fengquan. 1996. *Aomen yu Putaoya da fanquan: Putaoyu yu zaoqi Jindai Taipingyang maoyi wangluo de xingcheng.* (Macao and the Portuguese Galleon: Portugal and the Formation of the Early Modern Pacific Trade Network). Beijing: Beijing Daxue chubanshe.

Headrick, Daniel R. 1988. *The Tentacles of Progress: Technology Transfer in the Age of Imperialism, 1850–1940*. London: Oxford University Press.

Held, David, Anthony McGrew, David Goldblatt and Jonathan Perraton. 1999. *Global Transformations. Politics, Economics and Culture*. Stanford, CA: Stanford University Press.

Ho, Chumei. 1994. "The Ceramic Trade in Asia, 1602–82," in A.J.H. Latham and H. Kawakatsu (eds), *Japanese Industrialization and the Asian Economy*. London and New York: Routledge.

Ho, S.P.S. 1984. "Colonialism and Development: Korea, Taiwan and Kwangtung," in R. Myers and M. Peattie (eds), *The Japanese Colonial Empire*. Princeton, NJ: Princeton University Press, pp. 348–98.

Hobsbawm, Eric J. 1968. *Industry and Empire: An Economic History of Britain since 1750*. London: Weidenfeld & Nicolson.

Howell, David. 1997. "The Meiji State and the Logic of Ainu 'Protection,'" in Helen Hardacre (ed.), *New Directions in the Study of Meiji Japan*. Leiden: E.J. Brill, pp. 612–34.

Huang, Ray. 1969. "Fiscal Administration During the Ming Dynasty," in Charles O. Hucker (ed.), *Chinese Government in Ming Times*. New York: Columbia University Press, pp. 73–128

Huang Yifeng. 1974. "Diguozhuyi qinlue Zhongguo de yige zhongyao zhizhu – maiban jieji" (The Comprador Class – Important Support for the Imperialist Invasion of China), in Cui Xueshe (ed.), *Zhongguo jin san bai nian shehui jingji shi lun ji*, Vol. 4, 249–268. Hong Kong: Chongwen shudian.

Hugill, Peter J. 1993. *World Trade Since 1431: Geography, Technology and Capitalism*. Baltimore, MD: Johns Hopkins University Press.

Hui, Po-keung. 1995. "Overseas Chinese Business Networks: East Asian Economic Development in Historical Perspective," PhD diss., Department of Sociology, State University of New York at Binghamton.

Hung, Ho-fung. 2000. "Orientalism in the Modern World-System: the Western Conception of China, 1500–1968," paper presented at the American Sociological Association Annual Conference, PEWS paper session. August, Washington, DC.

Hung, Ho-fung. 2001a. "Imperial China and Capitalist Europe in the Eighteenth-Century Global Economy," in *Review* (Fernand Braudel Center) XXIV (4): 473–513.

Hung, Ho-fung. 2001b. "Orientalism and the Two Cultures: Sinology as a Discipline," in Immanuel Wallerstein (ed.), *The Two Cultures in Question*. Unpublished book manuscript. Fernand Braudel Center, State University of New York at Binghamton.

Hung, Ho-fung. 2001c. "Maritime Capitalism in Seventeenth-Century China: The Rise and Fall of Koxinga in Comparative Perspective," unpublished manuscript. Department of Sociology, Johns Hopkins University, MD.

Ingham, Geoffrey. 1984. *Capitalism Divided? The City and Industry in British Social Development*. London: Macmillan.

International Monetary Fund (various years). *International Financial Statistics Yearbook*. Washington, DC: International Monetary Fund.

Iriye, Akira. 1970. "Imperialism in East Asia," in J. Crowley (ed.), *Modern East Asia*. New York: Harcourt, pp. 122–50.

Irwan, Alex. 1995. "Japanese and Ethnic Chinese Business Networks in Indonesia and Malaysia," PhD diss., Department of Sociology, State University of New York at Binghamton.

Israel, Jonathan I. 1989. *Dutch Primacy in World Trade, 1585–1740*. Oxford: Clarendon Press.

Jameson, Frederic. 1998. *The Cultural Turn: Selected Writings on the Postmodern, 1983–1998*. London: Verso.

Japan Almanac (various years). Tokyo: Asahi Shimbun Publishing Co.

Japan External Trade Organization (JETRO). 1999. *White Paper on International Trade*. Tokyo: JETRO (http://www.jetro.go.jp/it/e/pub/whitepaper/trade1999/index.html).

Jenks, Leland H. 1938. *The Migration of British Capital to 1875*. New York and London: Knopf.

Johnson, Linda Cooke. 1993. "Shanghai: An Emerging Jiangnan Port, 1638–1840," in Linda Cooke Johnson (ed.), *Cities of Jiangnan in Late Imperial China*. Albany, NY: State University of New York Press, pp. 151–82.

Kasaba, Resat. 1993. "Treaties and Friendships: British Imperialism, the Ottoman Empire, and China in the Nineteenth Century," *Journal of World History* IV (2): 213–41.

Kawakatsu, Heita. 1994. "Historical Background," in A.J.H. Latham and H. Kawakatsu (eds), *Japanese Industrialization and the Asian Economy*. London and New York: Routledge, pp. 4–8.

Kennedy, Paul. 1987. *The Rise and Fall of the Great Powers: Economic Change and Military Conflict from 1500 to 2000*. New York: Random House.

Korzeniewicz, Roberto Patricio and Timothy Patrick Moran. 2000. "Measuring World Income Inequalities," *American Journal of Sociology*, 106 (1): 209–14.

Kraar, Louis. 1993. "The New Power in Asia," *Fortune*, October 31: 38–44.

Kriedte, Peter. 1983. *Peasants, Landlords, amd Merchant Capitalists: Europe and the World Economy, 1500–1800*. Cambridge: Cambridge University Press.

Lardy, Nicholas R. 1992. *Foreign Trade and Economic Reform in China, 1978–1990*. Cambridge: Cambridge University Press.

Lee, John. 1999. "Trade and Economy in Preindustrial East Asia, *c.*1500–*c.*1800: East Asia in the Age of Global Integration," *The Journal of Asian Studies* 58: 2–26.

Lin, Manhong. 1991. "Zhongguode baiyin wailiu yu shijie jinyin jianchan (1814–1850)." (The Silver Drain of China and the Reduction in World Silver and Gold Production (1814–1850)), in Wu Jianxiong (ed.), *Zhongguo haiyang fazhanshi lunwenji bianji weiyuanhui ed. (Essays in Chinese Maritime History IV)*. Taipei: Sun Yat-sen Institute for Social Sciences and Philosophy, Academia Sinica, 1–44.

Lin Qitan. 1996. "Huaren jingji he Yatai jingji hezuo" (Overseas Chinese Economy and Asian Pacific Economic Integration), in Xia Yulong *et al.* (eds), *Yatai diqu jingji hezuo yu Zhongguo Yatai jingji zhanlue* (Asia Pacific Economic Integration and China's Asia Pacific Economic Strategy). Shanghai: Shanghai renmin chubanshe.

Lin Renchuan. 1987. *Ming muo Qing qu de hai shang siren maoyi* (Private Sea Trade in Late Ming and Early Qin). Shanghai: Huadong Shifan Daxue.

Lin Yuanhui and Zhang Yinglong. 1991. *Xinjiapo Malaixiya Huaqiaoshi* (History of Overseas Chinese in Singapore and Malaysia). Guangdong: Gaodeng jiaoyu chubanshe.

Lo, Jung-pang. 1969. "Maritime Commerce and its Relation to the Sung Navy," *Journal of the Economic and Social History of the Orient* XII: 57–101.

Mackie, Jamie. 1992. "Changing Patterns of Chinese Big Business," in R. McVey (ed.), *Southeast Asian Capitalists*. Southeast Asian Program, Ithaca, NY: Cornell University.

Mackie, Jamie. 1998. "Business Success Among Southeast Asian Chinese – The Role of Culture, Values, and Social Structures," in Robert W. Hefner (ed.), *Market Cultures: Society and Morality in the New Asian Capitalism*. Boulder, CO: Westview Press.

McNeill, William. 1982. *The Pursuit of Power: Technology, Armed Force, and Society since A.D. 1000*. Chicago: Chicago University Press.

Marx, Karl. 1959. *Capital.* Vol. 1. Moscow: Foreign Languages Publishing House.

Marx, Karl, and Frederick Engels. 1967. *The Communist Manifesto*. Harmondsworth: Penguin.

Mathias, Peter. 1969. *The First Industrial Nation: An Economic History of Britain 1700–1914*. London: Methuen.

Mattingly, Garrett. 1988. *Renaissance Diplomacy*. New York: Dover.

Murphey, R. 1977. *The Outsiders: The Western Experience in India and China.* Ann Arbor, MI: University of Michigan Press.

Nakao, Shigeo. 1995. *The Political Economy of Japanese Money.* Tokyo: University of Tokyo Press.

Nathan, Andrew J. 1972. "Imperialism's Effects on China." *Bulletin of Concerned Asian Scholars* IV, 4: 3–8.

Northrup, David. 1995. *Indentured Labour in the Age of Imperialism, 1834–1922.* Cambridge: Cambridge University Press.

Okimoto, Daniel I. and Thomas P. Rohlen. 1988. *Inside the Japanese System: Readings on Contemporary Society and Political Economy.* Stanford, CA: Stanford University Press.

Owen, D.E. 1934. *British Opium Policy in China and India.* New Haven, CT: Yale University Press.

Ozawa, Terutomo. 1993. "Foreign Direct Investment and Structural Transformation: Japan as a Recycler of Market and Industry," *Business and the Contemporary World* V (2): 129–50.

Palat, Ravi A. 1995. "Historical Transformations in Agrarian Systems Based on Wet-Rice Cultivation: Toward an Alternative Model of Social Change," in P. McMichael (ed.), *Food and Agrarian Orders in the World-Economy.* Westport, CT: Praeger, pp. 55–77.

Parker, Geoffrey. 1989. "Taking Up the Gun," *MHQ: The Quarterly Journal of Military History* I, 4: 88–101.

Peattie, Mark. 1984. "Introduction," in Ramon Myers and Mark Peattie, *The Japanese Colonial Empire, 1895–1945.* Princeton, NJ: Princeton University Press, pp. 3–26.

Peng Jiali. 1981. "Shijiu shiqi xifang qinluezhe dui Zhongguo lugong de lulue" (The Seizure of Chinese Labor by Western Invaders in the 19th Century), in Chen Hansheng (ed.), *Huagong Chuguo Shi Ziliao Huibian* Vol. 4. Zhonghua shuju.

Perry, Elizabeth and Mark Selden (eds). 2000. *Chinese Society: Change, Conflict, and Resistance.* London: Routledge.

Piore, Michael J. and Charles F. Sabel. 1984. *The Second Industrial Divide: Possibilities for Prosperity.* New York: Basic Books.

Pomeranz, Kenneth. 1999. "Two Worlds of Trade, Two Worlds of Empire: European State-making and Industrialization in a Chinese Mirror," in D.A. Smith, D.J. Solinger and S. Topik (eds), *States and Sovereignty in a Global Economy.* London: Routledge.

Pomeranz, Kenneth. 2000. *The Great Divergence: Europe, China, and the Making of the Modern World Economy.* Princeton, NJ: Princeton University Press.

Portes, Alejandro. 1994. "The Informal Economy and its Paradoxes," in N.J. Smelser and R. Swedberg (eds), *Handbook of Economic Sociology.* Princeton, NJ: Princeton University Press, pp. 426–49.

Quan Hansheng. 1987. *Ming Qing jingjishi yanjiu* (Studies in the Economic History of Ming and Qing). Taipei: Lianjin chubanshe.

Quan Hansheng. 1991a. "Songdai guanyuan jingyingde shiren jingji." (The Private Business Run By Officials in the Song), in Quan Hansheng, *Zhongguo jingjishi yanjiu* (Study of Chinese Economic History). Hedao chubanshe, pp 393–466.

Quan Hansheng. 1991b. "Songdai Guangzhou de guonei he haiwai maoyi" (Internal and External Trade in Guangzhou in the Song), in Quan Hansheng, *Study of Chinese Economic History.* Hedao chubanshe, pp. 477–550.

Quan Hansheng. 1996. *Lun Zhongguo jingjishi* (Essays on Chinese Economic History). Taipei: Hedao chubanshe.

Quesnay, François. 1969. "From *Despotism in China,*" in F. Schurmann and O. Schell (eds), *Imperial China*. New York: Vintage, pp. 115–20.

Rabson, Steve. 1997. "Meiji Assimilation Policy in Okinawa: Promotion, Resistance, and Reconstruction," in Helen Hardacre (ed.), *New Directions in the Study of Meiji Japan*. Leiden: Brill, pp. 635–55.

Reid, Anthony. 1990. "The Seventeenth Century Crisis in South-East Asia," *Modern Asian Studies* XXIV: 639–59.

Reid, Anthony. 1993. *Southeast Asia in the Age of Commerce 1450–1680*. Vol. II *Expansion and Crisis*. New Haven, CT: Yale University Press.

Riskin, Carl, Zhao Renwei and Li Shih (eds). 2001. *Retreat from Equality. Essays on the Changing Distribution of Income in China, 1988 to 1995*. Armonk, NY: M.E. Sharpe.

Rix, Alan. 1993. "Japan and the Region: Leading from Behind," in Richard Higgott, Richard Leaver, and John Ravenhill (eds), *Pacific Economic Relationships*. Boulder, CO: Lynne Rienner, pp. 62–82.

Rose, Mary B. 1994. "The Family Firm in British Business, 1780–1914," in Maurice W. Kirby and Mary B. Rose (eds), *Business Enterprise in Modern Britain – From the Eighteenth to the Twentieth Century*. London and New York: Routledge.

Rowe, William. 1990. "Modern Chinese Social History in Comparative Perspective," in P.S. Ropp (ed.), *Heritage of China: Contemporary Perspectives on Chinese Civilization*. Berkeley, CA: University of California Press.

Rowley, Chris and John Benson (eds). 2000. *Globalization and Labour in the Asia Pacific*. London: Frank Cass.

Sanger, David E. 1997. "Paper Tiger: 'Asian Money,' American Fears." *The New York Times*, January 5, IV: 1, 4.

Sassen, Saskia. (1996). *Losing Control? Sovereignty in an Age of Globalization*. New York: Columbia University Press.

Schumpeter, Joseph. 1954. *Capitalism, Socialism and Democracy*. London: Allen & Unwin.

Schurmann, Franz. 1974. *The Logic of World Power: An Inquiry into the Origins, Currents and Contradictions of World Politics*. New York: Pantheon.

Selden, Mark. 1997. "China, Japan and the Regional Political Economy of East Asia, 1945–1995," in Peter Katzenstein and Takashi Shiraishi (eds), *Network Power. Japan and Asia*. Ithaca, NY: Cornell University Press, pp. 306–40.

Semmel, Bernard. 1970. *The Rise of Free Trade Imperialism*. Cambridge: Cambridge University Press.

Shiba, Yoshinobu. 1983. "Sung Foreign Trade: Its Scope and Organization," in Morris Rossabi (ed.), *China among Equals: The Middle Kingdom and its Neighbors, 10th–14th Centuries*. Berkeley, CA: University of California Press, pp. 89–115.

Skinner, W.G. 1985. "The Structure of Chinese History," *Journal of Asian Studies* 44 (2): 271–92.

So, Alvin Y. 1986. *The South China Silk District*. Albany, NY: State University of New York Press.

So, Alvin Y. and Stephen W.K. Chiu. 1995. *East Asia and the World-Economy*. Newbury Park, CA: Sage.

Steensgard, Niels. 1974. *The Asian Trade Revolution of the Seventeenth Century: The*

East India Companies and the Decline of the Caravan Trade. Chicago: University of Chicago Press.

Steensgard, Niels. 1981. "The Companies as a Specific Institution in the History of European Expansion," in L. Blussé and F. Gaastra (eds), *Companies and Trade.* Leiden: Leiden University Press, pp. 235–57.

Steensgard, Niels. 1982. "The Dutch East India Company as an Institutional Innovation," in M. Aymard (ed.), *Dutch Capitalism and World Capitalism.* Cambridge: Cambridge University Press, pp. 235–57.

Sugihara, Kaoru. 1996. "The European Miracle and the East Asian Miracle: Towards a New Global Economic History," *Sangyo to keizai* XI (12): 27–48.

Suryadinata, Leo. 1989. "National Integration and the Chinese in Southeast Asia," *Solidarity* (Manila) 123.

Tate, D.J.M. 1979. *The Making of Modern South-East Asia.* Kuala Lumpur: Oxford University Press.

Thornton, Edward. 1835. *India, its State and Prospects.* London: Parbury, Allen & Co.

Tian Rukang. 1974. "Zai lun shiqi shiji zhi shijiu shiji zhongye Zhongguo fanchuanye de fazhan," in Cui Xueshe (ed.), *Zhongguo jin sanbainian shehui jingjishi lun (Di San Ji).* Chongwen shudian, pp. 289–99.

Tian Rukang. 1987. *Zhongguo fanchuan maoyi he dui wai guanxi shi lunji* (Chinese Junk Trade and History of China Foreign Relations. A Collection). Zhejiang renmin chubanshe.

Tomlinson, B.R. 1975. "India and the British Empire, 1880–1935," *The Indian Economic and Social History Review* XII (4): 337–80.

Tong, W. James. 1991. *Disorder Under Heaven: Collective Violence in the Ming Dynasty.* Stanford, CA: Stanford University Press.

Tsai, Jung-Fang. 1993. *Hong Kong in Chinese History: Community and Social Unrest in the British Colony, 1842–1913.* New York: Columbia University Press.

Tsiang, Ting-fu. 1967. "The English and the Opium Trade," in F. Schurmann and O. Schell (eds), *Imperial China.* New York: Vintage, pp. 132–45.

Tyson, R.L. 1968. "The Cotton Industry" in D.H. Aldcroft (ed.), *The Development of British Industry and Foreign Competition 1875–1914: Studies in Industrial Enterprise.* London: George Allen & Unwin, pp. 100–27.

Wakeman, Frederic. 1985. *The Great Enterprise: The Manchu Reconstruction of Imperial Order in Seventeenth-Century China.* Berkeley, CA: University of California Press.

Waley, Arthur. 1958. *The Opium War through Chinese Eyes.* London: Allen & Unwin.

Wallerstein, Immanuel. 1991. *Unthinking Social Science: The Limits of Nineteenth Century Paradigms.* Cambridge: Polity Press.

Wang, Gungwu. 1991. *China and the Chinese Overseas.* Singapore: Times Academic Press.

Wang, Gungwu. 1998. "Ming Foreign Relations: Southeast Asia," in D.C. Twitchett and F.W. Mote (eds), *The Cambridge History of China* Vol. 8 (2), *The Ming Dynasty,* Cambridge: Cambridge University Press, pp. 301–32.

Wang Shaoguang and Hu Angang. 1994. (*A Report on the State Capacity of China*). Zhongguo guojia nengli baogao. Hong Kong: Oxford University Press.

Washbrook, David. 1990. "South Asia, the World System, and World Capitalism," *The Journal of Asian Studies* XLIX (3): 479–508.

Weber, Max. 1961. *General Economic History*. New York: Collier.

Wei Anning. 1988. "1600–1850 nianjian Zhong Yi liang guo de guan shang" (The Official Merchants of China and Japan in the 1600–1850 Period), *Riben Yanjiu*, 4: 51–7.

Wei Yongli. 1987. "Youguan jindai zhongguo youfou xingcheng tongyi quanguo shichangde wenti" (On the Question of Whether or not Modern China has Formed a Unified National Market), in Shen Jian (ed.), *Zhongguo jingjishi lunwenji* (Collection of Articles on Chinese Economic History). Zhongguo Renmin Daxue chubanshe.

Wills, John E. Jr. 1979. "Maritime China From Wang Chih to Shih Lang: Themes in Peripheral History" in Jonathan D. Spence and John E. Wills, Jr. (eds), *Conquest, Region, and Continuity in Seventeenth Century China*. New Haven and London: Yale University Press, pp. 203–38.

Wills, John E. Jr. 1998. "Relations With Maritime Europeans," in Denis Twitchett and Frederick Mote (eds), *The Cambridge History of China* Vol. 8 (2), *The Ming Dynasty*. Cambridge: Cambridge University Press, pp. 333–75.

Wolf, Eric. 1982. *Europe and the People without History*. Berkeley, CA: University of California Press.

Wong, R. Bin. 1997. *China Transformed: Historical Change and the Limits of European Experience*. Ithaca, NY: Cornell University Press.

Wong, Siu-lun. 1988. *Emigrant Entrepreneurs*. Hong Kong: Oxford University Press.

Wong, Young-tsu. 1983. "Security and Warfare on the China Coast: The Taiwan Question in the Seventeenth Century," *Monumenta Serica* XXXV: 111–96.

World Bank. 1984. *World Tables* Vols 1 and 2. Washington, DC: World Bank.

World Bank. 2001. *World Development Indicators*. CD-ROM. Washington, DC: World Bank.

Wu Chengming. 1987. *Zhongguo zibenzhuyi yu guonei shichang* (Chinese Capitalism and the Domestic Market). Taipei: Gufeng chubanshe.

Wu Han. 1965. *Zhu Yuanzheng zhuan* (A Biography of Zhu Yuanzheng). Beijing: Renmin Daxue chubanshe.

Wu, Yuan-li and Chun-hsi Wu. 1980. *Economic Development in Southeast Asia: The Chinese Dimension*. Stanford, CA: Hoover Institution Press.

Xu Dixin and Wu Chengming (eds). 1985. *Zhongguo zibenzhuyi de mengya* (Sprouts of Chinese Capitalism). Beijing: Zhongguo Renmin Daxue chubanshe.

Xu Xinwu *et al.* (eds). 1989. *Zhongguo saosi gongye shi* (A History of the Silk Industry in Modern China). Shanghai: Shanghai renmin chubanshe.

Xu Xinwu *et al.* (eds). 1992. *Jiangnan tubu shi* (A History of Jiangnan Indigenous Cloth). Shanghai: Shanghai Academy of Social Sciences.

Yang Jiancheng. 1985. *Huaqiao Shi* (History of Overseas Chinese). Taibei: Zhonghua Xueshuyuan Nanyang Yanjiusuo.

Yang, Lien-sheng. 1952. *Money and Credit in China: A Short History*. Cambridge, MA: Harvard University Press.

Yen Zhongping *et al.* 1957. *Zhongguo jindai jingjishi tongji* (Collections of Statistical Data of Modern Chinese Economic History). Beijing: Scientific Publishers.

Yeung, Henry Wai-chung and Kris Olds (eds) (2000). *Globalization of Chinese Business Firms*. New York: St. Martin's Press.

Zhang Binchuan. 1991. "Mingqing haishang maoyi zhengce: biguanzishou?" (The

Sea Trade Policy of Ming and Qing: Closed Door and Conservative) *Selected Essays in Chinese Maritime History* IV: 45–59. Taipei: Academia Sinica.

Zhuang Guotu. 1989. *Zhongguo fengjian zhengfu de Huaqiao zhengce* (The Chinese Feudal Government's Policies Toward the Overseas Chinese). Xiamen Daxue chubanshe.

Index

Note: page numbers in italics refer to figures separated from their textual reference.